SINGING

the Mechanism

and the Technic

by William Vennard, A.B., B.Mus., M.Mus.

Chairman, Voice Department, School of Music

The University of Southern California

Past President, National Association of Teachers of Singing

Illustrations by the Author

Revised Edition, Greatly Enlarged

Sole selling agents for the world

Carl Fischer, Inc.

62 Cooper Square

New York, N.Y. 10003

1967

First Edition, Copyright 1949
Second Edition, Copyright 1950
Third Edition, Copyright 1964
Fourth Edition, Copyright 1967
William Vennard

Lithographed in U.S.A. by
EDWARDS BROTHERS, INC.
Ann Arbor, Michigan

PREFACE

As the title indicates, this book is frankly mechanistic. It is an attempt to compile under one cover objective findings from various reliable sources and to relate them to the art of singing. There are those teachers who feel that applying science to an art is quackery, but I believe that our only safeguard against the charlatan is general knowledge of the most accurate information available.

If you are one who has always preferred the empirical approach, perhaps you should read my last chapter first. You may then agree that the knowledge of literal fact is the only justifiable basis for the use of imagery and other indirect methods. Whether you are a singer or a teacher of singing, I hope you will find here truths which you may profitably add to your philosophy, or at least a rationale for harmonizing some of the apparent conflicts in our profession.

The paragraphs above were written for the 1949 edition. Some time thereafter I had the good fortune to read "Keep Your Voice Healthy," by Friedrich S. Brodnitz. I was so impressed that I sought out the author, who introduced me to the whole world of current voice research. His valued friendship through the years led to my collaborating with several important men of science. Directly or indirectly through Dr. Brodnitz I met first Raoul Husson, then Janwillem van den Berg (in whose laboratory I spent the academic year, 1959-60), Aatto A. Sonninen, Knud Faaborg-Andersen, Paul Moore, Hans von Leden, Nobuhiko Isshiki, and Henry J. Rubin.

The stimulus of these men and others represented in scientific journals which had not previously been a part of my primarily musical world has resulted in this greatly enlarged edition. There are happily not many statements made in 1949 which require correction, but much more exact information can now be added.

W. V.

Los Angeles, January, 1967

iii

To

Leona

who helped in many ways

from encouragement and wise criticism

to much patient work

TABLE OF CONTENTS

Chapter 1

ACOUSTICS

1   There are certain fundamentals of the science of acoustics that all voice teachers should know. Too many have a superficial acquaintance with the vocabulary and dress up their pedagogy with terms that sound impressive but lead to confusion when the student, in the course of learning physics, finds out what the words really mean. Scientists laugh at the imagery with which the voice teacher tries to express himself, and they have even more justification when the imaginings are clothed in words like "resonance," "fundamental and overtone," "soundingboard," etc., which have specific denotations in the laboratory.

2   Some teachers take the position that, since much of singing is still unexplained scientifically, and since it lies below the level of direct conscious control anyhow, it is better for us to avoid these discussions, to admit that we are unscientific, and let it go at that. They feel that knowledge of the anatomy of the vocal instrument only makes the student self-conscious, that any knowledge of the physics of its operation tends to make him mechanistic when he should be artistic. It is true that singing can be taught entirely by abstract, more or less emotional appeals to the entire personality of the student, but I cannot escape the conviction that many times more direct methods bring quicker and better results. There is also the fact that this is the age of science, and many students are going to ask questions which deserve answers. The teacher is like the parent who is questioned by a child about the "facts of life." The day of saying, "You are too young to know," is past.

3   Regardless of how much he thinks best to tell the student, I believe the more the teacher knows, the better. He should read several of the excellent books available on acoustics. The following discussion is a bare minimum which I hope will serve two purposes: it should provide enough information to make intelligible the things I shall have to say about the voice, and it should pique the curiosity to go more deeply into this rewarding subject.

The Nature of Sound

4   The air about us is made up of submicroscopic units of matter, called *molecules*. They move about independently, but tend to stay a certain distance apart, other conditions remaining the same. If they are forced closer together they fly apart again, and if they are forced apart, they fly back together again. This property of matter is called *elasticity*.

5   If we disturb the balance of the molecules in the air, *compressing* them, they fly apart. This little explosion causes the molecules surrounding it on all sides to be compressed. When they fly apart they create compression in the molecules surrounding them, etc., so that the compression expands like a balloon, in a series of spheres with their center at the source of the disturbance. The elasticity of the air is such that at normal temperature on earth, this balloon, which is called a *compression wave*, will have a radius of 1100 feet in one second and it will continue to grow at the same speed. The energy in the compression naturally is being dissipated in proportion to the increasing area of the sphere, until it becomes negligible. That is to say, *sound travels at 1100 feet per second and its intensity is in inverse proportion to the square of the distance*. The *intensity* is interpreted by the ear in terms of *loudness*, though the relationship between the two is somewhat complicated.

1

6   Probably no sound is so simple as to consist of only one compression wave. The source is usually such that it not only compresses the air but immediately thereafter it moves in the opposite direction and creates a partial vacuum. The air molecules rush in to restore the normal density, and the partial vacuum is then a small sphere surrounding the source. Molecules rush in from outside to fill *this* partial void, and so the *rarefaction wave*, as it is called, follows the compression wave, like another balloon being blown up inside it. This process continues as long as power is being supplied.

7   The waves, alternately compression and rarefaction, reach the ear drum of the listener, causing it to move in a manner corresponding to the source of the sound, and this movement is analyzed mechanically in the inner ear, and the results transmitted to the brain. The intricate manner in which this is accomplished is a fascinating story to any musician. It has been well told so many times that I shall not give space to it here, since it makes no difference to our discussion.

Musical Tone

8   If the series of sound waves is *irregular*, we call it *noise*. If it forms a pattern that repeats itself regularly, it is *musical tone*. The distinction is of interest to singers, because we learn to produce tones first, and then we interrupt the tone with various noises. The tones are called vowels, and the *noises, consonants*. They may be combined in socially accepted patterns that have meaning, in addition to whatever beauty there may be in the tones. This makes singing an art combining music and literature. Other instruments make noises also, but they have no symbolical meaning, and only detract from the beauty of the sound.

9   The simplest musical tone has a pattern consisting of compression-rarefaction-compression-rarefaction-etc., at a constant frequency. Such a vibration is said to be *pendular*, because it repeats itself like the swing of a pendulum. You can easily perform the experiment of hanging up a weight on a string and counting the number of times it will swing back and forth in a given period of time. You will demonstrate for yourself the law of the pendulum, which is that if the conditions remain unchanged, *the frequency remains the same regardless of the width of the arc through which the pendulum swings*. If you change the length of the string, you will change the frequency, but otherwise, it will take just as long for the weight to swing an inch, when it is almost "run down," as to swing two feet when you start it.

10   The simplest musical instrument, the *tuning fork,* is really a pair of pendulums upside down. In this case, the elasticity of the metal and not gravity operates it, but the law of the pendulum still applies. The arms of the fork alternately compress and rarefy the air in a simple, back and forth pattern, at a constant frequency. We find an example of an equally elementary *wind* instrument in an ordinary bottle. A body of air has properties of elasticity that make it a pendular vibrator, like a tuning fork. If you will blow across the mouth of a bottle, any bottle, you will start its molecules to compressing and rarefying. That is, it will give forth a tone. Another instrument produces a regular series of compression waves by making a succession of little puffs of air. The power is some kind of a blower that compresses air, and the vibrator is a revolving disc that has a series of holes in it and allows the air to escape in puffs. This machine is called a *siren.* We have all heard samples on ambulances, police cars, etc. The motion of the vehicle creates the air pressure, and the revolving of the motor turns the mechanism that breaks it up into puffs. There is no pendulum, but since the pattern produced conforms to the law, the vibration is still "pendular."

11   These instruments are too simple to be of interest musically, but they have been used for scientific research in sound laboratories. It has been discovered that musical tone has five essential properties: *pitch, duration, intensity, timbre,* and *sonance*. These can all be studied scientifically because they are all measurable.

Pitch

12   The most discussed property of sound, I suppose, is pitch. The *frequency* of the impulses
from the source is also the frequency with which the waves beat upon the ear, and this is
interpreted by the brain in terms of pitch. For example, when any instrument is tuned to
International Concert Pitch, A on the treble staff will be 440 vibrations per second. The fork
which is used to test this pitch is so made that its arms swing back and forth exactly 440 times
times in a second. All the instruments in the orchestra, different as they are in structure and
operation, must agree at the start by producing 440 vibrations a second, and the ear, while
recognizing that the sounds are different in other respects, hears them all at the same pitch.

13   Long ago, Pythagoras, the famous mathematician, discovered that if one doubles the number of vibrations per second, the pitch is raised by the interval which we call an *octave*. He
sounded a taut string, and then divided it in two, which raised the pitch an octave because it
multiplied the frequency by two. Pythagoras used a string to demonstrate the principle, but,
since the voice is a wind instrument, I should like to put it in terms of the siren. Anyone can
construct a simple siren by attaching a cardboard wheel to a motor and blowing air at it through
a rubber tube. Make a series of ten holes at a given radius, and a series of only five in a
smaller circle. When you blow through the five-series you will hear one pitch, and when you
blow through the other you will hear a tone an octave higher, or with twice the frequency.

14   The slowest vibration one can hear as a tone is fifteen or sixteen cycles per second. Less
frequent impulses are heard individually. Incidentally, this gives us one of the parallels between sight and hearing, because when one operates a movie projector at less than fifteen
frames per second, the images flickers, that is, the eye sees individual pictures instead of
continuous motion. The ear can report frequencies up to 20,000 or so. Beyond this point pitches
are still audible to some animals and insects, but eventually we reach the level of *ultrasonics*
which cannot be heard at all, and instead produce bizarre effects which science is just beginning
to explore.

Duration and Intensity

15   The property of sound which is taken for granted is *duration*. The meaning of the word is
obvious. It is important to musicianship because without a discriminating sense of duration,
correct rhythm is impossible. However, we are now concerned with learning to produce tone,
and musicianship is a long way off.

16   *Intensity* refers to the extent to which equilibrium is disturbed by the sound. How much were
the molecules compressed? How far was the ear drum indented? How loud was the tone? The
first two questions are answered directly in terms of intensity, or *amplitude,* which is a synonym. In the case of *loudness,* subjective factors enter. Increase the intensity and you will increase the loudness, but the ear adjusts itself so that doubling intensity will not double loudness.
Having twice as many people in your chorus will make it louder, and perhaps better, but not
twice as loud, and probably not twice as good. It is also interesting to note that a high tone
sounds louder than a low one of the same intensity; the ear is more sensitive to high pitches.
Generally speaking, intensity, and also loudness, vary with the power that is used to generate
the tone, but in complex musical instruments it is often true that in producing soft tone, the
efficiency of the instrument is so reduced that, to get desirable quality, greater skill and even
greater power is necessary. This is true of the voice.

17   We must, of course, differentiate between the energy used by the singer and the energy
that actually emerges as part of the tone. One sometimes speaks of a tone's being more intense without being louder. The tone that lacks intensity is usually breathy, that is, breath is
being expelled from the instrument without being efficiently used. To make a loud breathy tone

would require tremendous respiratory effort. Suggesting "intensity" to such a singer sometimes causes him to close his glottis more efficiently, so that he gets a louder sound (that is, more energy in the tone) but actually uses no more respiratory energy. Hence he does not think he is singing more loudly. He is working less and merely "thinking intensity."

18   The listener may also evaluate this tone as "no louder, but more intense," because he empathizes with the singer. Also the loudness of such a tone does not intrude upon the listener because its timbre (Par. 21) is such that the energy in the tone is interpreted psychologically as "carrying power." It is true that some tones actually lose loudness less than others in travelling to the back of a hall, even though they are at the same volume level in front where they are produced. This is due to differences in timbre, and gives some physical basis to the idea of differentiating between intensity and loudness. But probably the chief basis for speaking of vocal tone as "no louder, but more intense" is psychological.

19   In some instruments duration and intensity are related mathematically. The greater the initial amplitude, the longer the duration will be, and the intensity at any given moment will be in inverse proportion to the length of time the tone has been sounding. That is, the greater the push or the pull with which you start a pendulum, the harder you strike a tuning fork, the more you disturb a string when you pluck it, the longer will it sound before the intensity has faded to zero.

20   However, if you attach a motor of some sort to your pendulum, as in the case of a clock, the amplitude and duration will depend upon how much power you have and how efficiently you apply it. A plucked or a struck string fades in loudness, but a bowed string can increase or decrease the volume of tone at the will of the performer. The duration depends upon the length of the bow. In the case of all wind instruments, including the voice, the power is in the lungs and the duration of the tone depends upon the vital capacity (only a certain percentage of which can be used) and the control of the muscles that maintain breath pressure. Intensity is related to this factor, and also to a peculiarity by which the voice differs from other instruments—the ability to vary the flexibility of the vibrator. This unique characteristic also enters into the control of pitch and timbre. (See Chapter 4)

Timbre

21   *Timbre* is perhaps the most difficult property of tone to explain. Synonyms are *quality*, and *tone-color*, or *klang-farbe*, as Helmholtz called it. I mentioned above that all the instruments of the orchestra can sound the same pitch, but the ear will still recognize them as being different. The differences are in *timbre*, and also in *sonance*, to be discussed later (Par. 38).

22   So far we have considered elementary tone producers, like the tuning fork, that produce simple, or "pure" tone. There are instruments for recording vibration so that it becomes visible, and these instruments help us to *see* what is *heard* by the ear as quality or timbre. Attach a pencil to a pendulum and move a strip of paper under it at constant speed. You will get the result shown in Figure 1, in which distance from left to right will represent time, and the distance up and down will show amplitude or intensity. Frequency can be computed by counting peaks in units of length known to correspond to units of time.

23   Exactly the same thing has been done with tuning forks. Helmholtz was the first in this as in many of the fundamentals in the science of acoustics. He put a stylus on the end of a tuning fork and let it write on a moving strip of paper while the fork was sounding. He got the same result as with a pendulum, only smaller, of course. (Helmholtz, p. 20.)

24   Since that time much more elaborate and efficient instruments have been developed to graph sound. After all, if a groove can be scratched in a phonograph record to correspond to a sound,

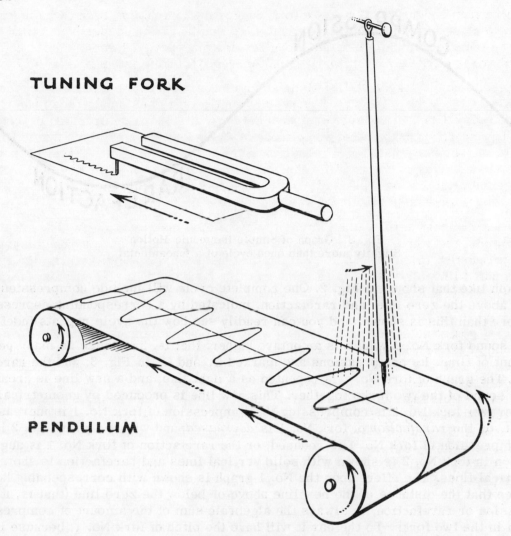

Fig. 1. Tuning Fork and Pendulum Compared

why can't a line be drawn on paper? The lines made by simple instruments, like forks, are all alike, differing only in frequency and amplitude, but the lines made by instruments that have interesting color are different. They have quavers in them. The pattern of quavers keeps repeating, like a wall paper border, and you can measure frequency or pitch by counting the number of repetitions. It is hard to see the relationship between a quavery graph like this and the graph of a pendulum, but the pendulum has been such a help to us in understanding sound up to this point, that the scientists are reluctant to let go of this concept. As long ago as 1822, Fourier enunciated the theorem that any curve that repeats itself without doubling back or making loops (and sound waves never do such tricks-the motion of the strip of paper makes doubling back impossible) can be demonstrated to be the sum of a number of simple, pendular undulations. In other words the graph of a musical instrument is like a graph made by several pendulums or tuning forks all vibrating at once. Fourier was primarily interested in heat, but light and sound obey the same laws.

25   The problem has been solved several ways, all with the same results. Helmholtz proved it synthetically by sounding several tuning forks at a time and reproducing complex timbres. Suppose, for example, we start with a fork with a good strong tone at a low frequency. It will

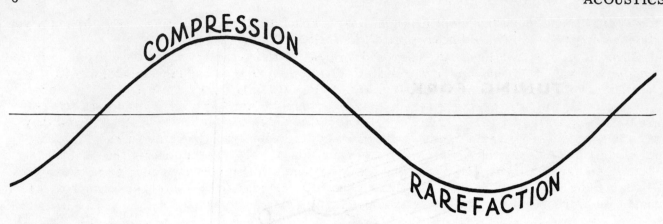

Fig. 2. Graph of Simple Harmonic Motion
Slightly more than once cycle of a fundamental

make a graph like that shown in Fig. 2. One complete cycle will include compression, indicated by an arch above the zero line, and rarefaction, indicated by a corresponding depression below. Slightly more than this is shown, and you can readily see how the cycle repeats indefinitely.

26   Now we sound fork No. 2, which is an octave higher, that is, has twice as many peaks in the same amount of time. Its compressions are marked C_1 and C_2 in Fig. 3, and the rarefactions, R_1 and R_2. The graph of fork No. 1 is repeated as a light line, and a new line is created representing the sound of the two forks together. This new line is produced by geometrical addition; that is, wherever fork No. 2 is compressing the compression of fork No. 1 is increased by a like amount, or the *rarefaction* of fork No. 1 is *decreased;* and wherever fork No. 2 is rarefying, the compression of fork No. 1 is reduced, or the rarefaction of fork No. 1 is augmented. Compression in fork No. 2 is shown with solid vertical lines and rarefaction is shown with broken vertical lines. The effect upon the No. 1 graph is shown with corresponding horizontal lines. Notice that the distance of the new line above or below the zero line (that is, its amount of compression or rarefaction) is always the algebraic sum of the amount of compression or rarefaction in the two forks. To the ear it will have the pitch of fork No. 1, because it will repeat at the same frequency, but it will be a somewhat "richer" sound. If you listen carefully, of course, you will be able to distinguish the second fork from the first. Incidentally, a flute

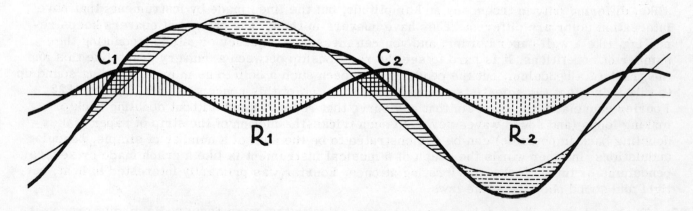

Fig. 3. Geometrical Addition of Two Simple Curves
Curves represent first two partials (fundamental and overtone)

tone would sound much like this; it might make a graph like the "new" line in Fig. 3; and if you listened carefully, you would hear a pitch like fork No. 2 sounding in it.

27   Fork No. 1 is called the *first partial* and fork No. 2, the *second partial*. They are also called *fundamental* and *first overtone*, respectively. Flute tone has a strong fundamental and first overtone, and the other overtones, if any, are so faint that they are almost negligible. More often than not, the first overtone is much stronger than the fundamental. By the way, choir-masters frequently test for purity of vocal tone by listening for the first overtone. When they get a section singing a certain note exactly in tune, they can hear the octave above it singing out clearly and sweetly. In massed choirs of hundreds of voices, experimental conductors sometimes have a dozen altos double the bass part and a dozen sopranos double the tenor part. Of course the women's voices are an octave above the men's, and the effect is to improve the quality and strength of the lower parts by reinforcing the overtone.

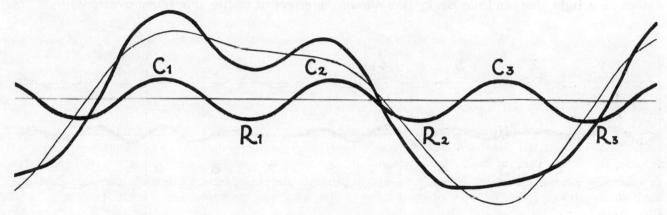

Fig. 4. Addition of Third Partial

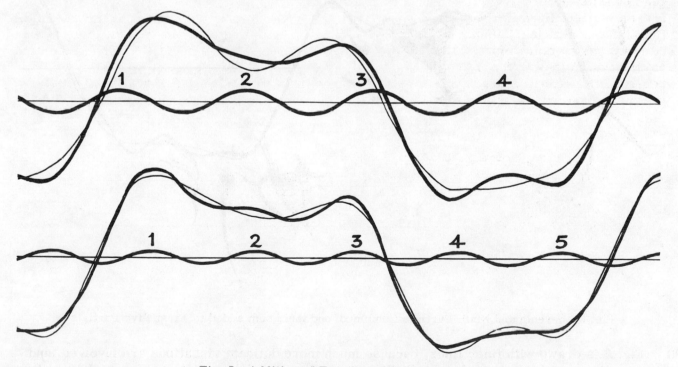

Fig. 5. Addition of Fourth and Fifth Partials

28   The human voice has other overtones, as do most musical instruments, so we must continue our experiment by adding more forks. In Fig. 4 we have the graph of the third partial. It has three compressions in the same period of time, marked C_1, C_2, and C_3, alternating with rare-factions. The line representing the sum of the first two partials appears again, lighter this time, and the sum of all three partials shows as a heavy line. The same geometrical addition can be traced, though it is not indicated with vertical shading. Notice that the three partials do not begin their cycles at the same time; that is, the graphs do not cross the zero line at the same place. This is expressed by saying that they are not *in phase*. It is a relationship that is of interest to the mathematician, but has little significance for the musician, since the sound is the same regardless of phase.

29   In Fig. 5 we add the fourth and fifth partials. To avoid cluttering the increasingly compli-cated drawings, only the compressions are numbered. In each case, the preceding sum is shown as a light line, and the heavy line shows the effect of adding one more overtone.

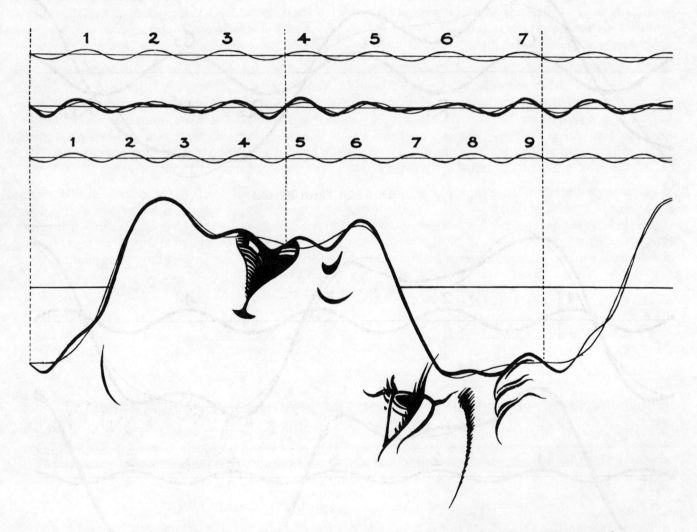

Fig. 6. Seventh and Ninth Partials Combined, and their sum added to First Five Partials

30   Fig. 6 is drawn with finer lines, because much more delicate vibrations are involved, and heavier lines would destroy the detail. We assume that the sixth partial was so weak as to be

negligible; indeed in the tone of most musical instruments, certain partials hardly sound—this is what makes the difference in their tone qualities. The top graph shows the seventh partial, and the third graph is the ninth partial. The eighth, like the sixth, is assumed to have dropped out. In the second graph, the seventh partial appears as a light line, and the sum of the seventh and ninth is drawn upon it, as a heavier line.

31   Notice that the two partials are in phase twice in each fundamental cycle, as indicated by the vertical broken lines. When the vibrations are in phase they augment each other; when out of phase, they nullify each other. The result is that when they are added to the sum of the first five partials (shown as a fine line) they merely produce a few ripples at the moments they are in phase.

32   Just for a joke I have made the sum of the seven partials (1,2,3,4,5,7, and 9) turn out to be a girl's profile, and to make it more obvious I have added an eye and a few other realistic details. If you don't think she is good enough looking, my excuse is that to improve the outline one must add many more high partials. Believe me, the profiles of most musical tones have even less appeal. In case you are curious as to what kind of a sound is graphed in Fig. 6, I must admit that I have not actually heard it, but we shall see that horn tone has partials in roughly the same proportions.

33   The process can be reversed. That is, the graph of any tone can be put in a calculating machine called a *harmonic analyzer,* and instead of its computing compound interest at so much per annum, it will tell you what overtones must be present and what their intensity must be. Let us suppose that we began with the girl's profile, and analyzed it harmonically, according to Fourier's theorem. We should have arrived at the simple curves shown in the preceding figures. The relative intensities of these partials could then be shown in one graph, which would be called the *spectrum* of the tone, a term borrowed from the science of light.

34   Suppose we assume that our fundamental (Fig. 2) was middle C. It really makes no difference, but I have shown it as such in Fig. 7. Above this note in our chart we draw a heavy vertical line representing the intensity of our fundamental. The Pythagorean experiment of dividing a string in two tells us that the second partial will be an octave higher, and over this note we draw a line one third as high, because the second partial has one third the intensity of the fundamental.

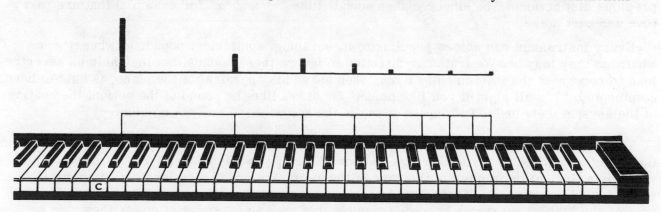

Fig. 7. Spectrum of Profile in Fig. 6
Fundamental arbitrarily assumed to be Middle C.

Intensity is gauged by measuring the greatest vertical distance between the curve and the zero line, which will be the same for compression as for rarefaction. We divide our string by three and get the pitch a fifth above the second partial. Here we make a line representing the third partial, and continue, completing the spectrum as shown.

35   In Fig. 8 the *harmonic series* is extended. For convenience, the fundamental is placed on a lower pitch. Any tone could have been taken—the intervals would remain the same. The *harmonic partials* form a *Chord of Nature* over every fundamental that is played or sung; indeed, the whole history of harmony as we know it is implied in a single tone with its overtones. The exact frequencies are shown, and also the nearest frequency that can be played on a piano. The story of the *tempered scale* is interesting, but it does not concern this discussion.

36   It is the nature of most vibrating bodies used for music that every overtone will have a frequency that is an exact multiple of that of the fundamental. However, some of the more complex vibrators produce *inharmonic* partials, overtones that are *not* exact multiples. This creates a dissonance, which may or may not be pleasing. In bells, for instance, we like it, even though they sound "out of tune" to unsophisticated ears. More often inharmonic partials are unsatisfactory. Singers usually must learn to eliminate them, though the "ring of the voice" may be due to their presence.

37   Spectra for the harmonic partials of all the common orchestral instruments have been derived, and a few of them are included for your interest in Fig. 9. These are based on the findings of Miller, and it is assumed in the chart that all are sounding A above Middle C. You will notice that the spectrum for the French horn is the one most like Fig. 7, our pretty girl profile. All these are *average* tones; the harmonic components of musical sounds change somewhat under different conditions. This is especially true of the voice, which will be discussed at length in Chapter 6. Vocal spectra are shown there.

Sonance

38   There remains one more property of tone. Some theorists do not count it, but there are ideas involved in the concept of *sonance* which are important. At any given instant, sonance is not present, but when we listen to tone over a period of time we hear fluctuations of intensity, timbre, even pitch, and these changes form a pattern to which the term *sonance* is applied. In other words, if a tone has duration, it will have sonance. This is a borderline concept, because it involves various noises that are mixed with tone. Theoretically a noise is not a tone, and therefore sonance is not strictly a property of tone, but we practical people cannot afford such precious distinctions. The singer makes sounds (like "v" and "z" for example) that are part tone and part noise.

39   Every instrument has noises peculiar to it, scraping, sputtering, pounding, wheezing, or whatever they may be. We train our attention to ignore these sounds, but they help us nevertheless to recognize the instruments. Bach, when asked his appraisal of the piano, is said to have commented, "It's all right if you like noise." He didn't like the sound of the action, the beating of the keys in their beds. To him the twang of the harpsichord was not a noise.

40   There are differences in intensity patterns. I have already mentioned the difference between the sound of plucked or struck strings and bowed strings in this respect. There is the *vibrato* which is a fluctuation in pitch in the case of the violin, but which also involves intensity in the case of wind instruments. There is furthermore a wavering of the color, since with a drop in volume the highest overtones become inaudible, but with a new surge of power they ring out again. Helmholtz remarked that in a well trained voice the high partials sound like the ringing of tiny silver bells, (Par. 702).

41   If two individuals sing a phrase, it is much easier to distinguish them than if they sing a single tone with a minimum of vibrato. This is because of the elements of sonance. If they speak, it is still more easy to recognize individual differences, because the musical element is reduced and there are more elaborate patterns of sonance, such as inflection, consonant formation, etc. Thus we see that "color" or "quality" is as much sonance as it is timbre.

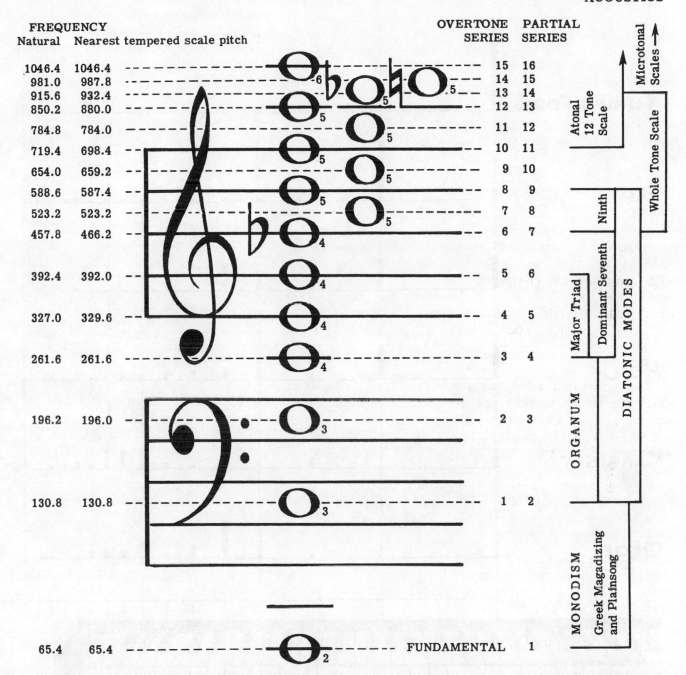

Fig. 8. Chord of Nature

Fundamental assumed to be C below bass staff. Other frequencies are multiples of this, paralleled by their nearest equivalents on tempered keyboard, A-440. In Partial Series, from 1 to 2 is an octave; 2 to 3, a 5th; 3 to 4, a 4th; 4 to 5, a major 3rd; 5 to 6, a minor 3rd; 6 to 7, a minor 3rd, but smaller than 5 to 6; next six intervals are whole steps, progressively smaller, and next three half steps, progressively smaller, going on through quarter and even eighth steps. Partials 2, 4, 8, 16, etc., are octaves above fundamental. Chart at right illustrates how history of music theory parallels harmonic series. Notes in this figure are numbered in accordance with system used for all pitch references in this text. The lowest C on the piano is C_1 and the notes up to the next C are D_1, E_1, etc. Middle C is C_4. Convenient mnemonic device: A_4 is 440 cps.

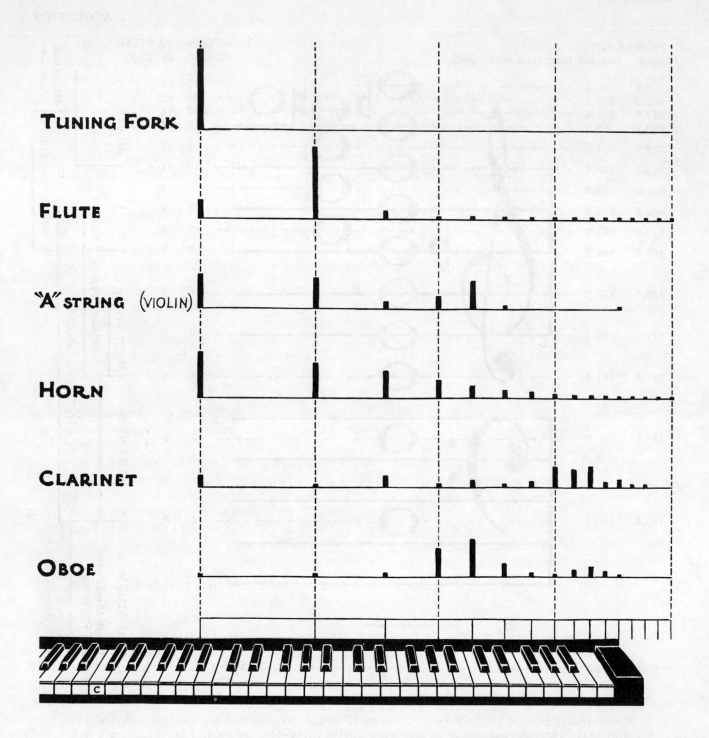

Fig. 9. Spectra of Common Orchestral Timbres
Average tones, all assumed to be sounding Concert A
Based on spectra by Dayton C. Miller, *The Science of Musical Sounds,* Copyright 1916 by The
Macmillan Company and used with their permission, pp. 171, 198, 201.

Resonance

42   We come now to a term that, like the word "democracy," has been used so much that it means something different almost every time it is used. Singers have been more guilty than any other group in the careless use of the word *resonance*. It is most commonly misused as a synonym for desirable qualities of *timbre*. If we like a certain voice, we say, "It is a rich, resonant baritone," meaning, "it has a rich baritone timbre." We speak of "adding resonance" when we mean "improving the quality." It is usually associated with "ring," or "brilliance," but the same speaker may also use it in connection with "warmth," or "depth," which are the opposite. I have made the resolution not to use the word *resonance* at all, except in accord with its scientific definition. I recommend the same to you, and believe that such practice would eliminate much confusion.

43   To the physicist, *resonance is a relationship that exists between two vibrating bodies of the same pitch*. When one vibrator causes another to vibrate in tune with it, the phenomenon is called *resonance*. There are two kinds, *sympathetic* and *forced*. Resonance in the vocal instrument is of the former variety, so it is of greater interest to us, and I shall describe it first.

44   Once more we draw upon our analogy with the pendulum. You can start a pendulum with one mighty push, or, as is known by any child who has ever pushed a swing, you can make it swing just as violently as the result of a series of gentle impulses. The important thing is that you synchronize the impulses with the frequency of the pendulum. If you push at the wrong moment, you slow down the pendulum, but if you push exactly at the beginning of each swing, it will go a little farther each time, faster and faster, farther and farther, but always at the same frequency.

45   Suppose we have a string tuned to 440 cycles per second, and suppose we operate a siren so as to make 440 puffs of air per second. The puffs of air will stimulate our ears so that we get the sensation of A on the treble staff, but they will also do something else. They will beat against the string. The effect of one puff is imperceptible but the cumulative effect of thousands of puffs is to set the string to vibrating, and after a few seconds we can stop the siren and listen to the string until it dies down. You can do the same thing by singing A on the treble staff. Your piano will provide the means for this experiment, so just open the damper on the A string by silently depressing the key, sing the note and then listen to the string continue to sound it. This is called *sympathetic resonance*, or *free resonance*, because the string is free to vibrate with the tone with which it is in sympathy and with no other tone.

46   Sympathetic resonance provides an easy and interesting demonstration of the principle of fundamental and overtones. Hold open the damper for C below the bass clef and then strike C above it (the first overtone) sharply several times. The low C string will vibrate in sympathy, at the pitch of the upper string, after the upper string has ceased. This proves that this tone is actually in the low C. Reverse the experiment and make the upper C sound (at its own frequency) as a result of striking the lower C. The sympathetic tone will always be the upper pitch. In other words, it is not the low C that set the upper in vibration, but the first overtone of the low C string, which is in tune with the upper C string. The same can be done with low C and G, top space of the bass clef. After you have done it both ways a few times, try sounding just the low C by itself and listen closely. See if you do not hear the G sounding in it.

47   The same sort of thing can be done with the other overtones, but will be less satisfactory because they are fainter, and more important, the strings to which they correspond are not exactly in tune with them. We use a piano with a *tempered scale*, in which only the octaves are in tune. The fifths are fairly true, but the others are only compromises. However, the following experiment works quite well, and will sensitize one's ear to overtones, if one has not listened for them before. Hold open the low C and strike the chord, C E G, treble staff, a few times

staccato. The low C will still sound the major triad and the three tones can be heard and differentiated. Later strike the low C and listen for the triad sounding in it.

48   So far we have talked about strings, and the voice is a wind instrument. Resonance properties are similar, but harder to explain, and I am going to leave most of this for you to read about in more scientific writings. I shall stay in our improvised laboratory and ask you to blow lightly across the mouth of a bottle. The tone you get is the *natural frequency* of the air in the cavity. It is determined by the dimensions of the bottle, and will not change unless you change the dimensions, as you can, for instance, by pouring in water. The more water, the smaller the cavity, and the higher the pitch, other things being equal. It is also true that a cavity with a smaller mouth will have a lower tone.

49   Air cavities are used to amplify the tone of weak vibrators. For instance, a tuning fork cannot be heard unless you hold it close to your ear, or unless you *resonate* it by attaching it to a box whose natural frequency is the same. The prongs do not disturb enough air to affect the ear at any distance, but by *free resonance*, the air in the box is set into *sympathetic vibration*, making enough sound to be heard. The same box will resonate other forks, provided they are in its overtone series.

50   Helmholtz did an experiment similar to the one described in Paragraph 46, only with cavities of air instead of sympathetic strings. He made a series of brass *resonators* in the shape of turnips, each having two openings. The small end, with the small opening in it, he put in his ear. For a sound to go through, it had to be of the same frequency as the resonator. He would play a note on the piano, and try all his resonators in succession. The ones that were in tune with overtones sang them out loudly, the others just muffled the sound. Singers should know about the Helmholtz resonators, because the resonance system of the voice resembles those more than the resonators of any other musical instrument. (See Chapter 5) (Helmholtz, pp. 43-45, 372-374.)

51   *Forced resonance* is quite another matter. Take a dinner fork, and make it sound by tweaking the tines. The sound will be faint, but will continue several seconds. Touch a plate with the vibrating fork, and its sound will be amplified loudly. There is no sympathy between the two objects-the plate has simply been forced to vibrate at the same frequency. It takes energy out of the fork faster, so that the tone will not last as long, but it will be louder because the plate is big enough to disturb more air than the tines of the fork.

The Elements of a Musical Instrument

52   A musical instrument, of course, is a machine designed to produce musical tone. It must offer a range of controlled frequencies, must be able to sustain them the necessary length of time at various intensities, must have interesting timbre, and its sonance must not detract too much from its musicality. Some instruments do not perform perfectly on all counts, but make themselves useful because of compensations. Such a machine must have three elements: actuator, vibrator(s), resonator(s).

53   The actuator is the source of power. In the case of strings, it is the bow operated by the arm of the player. In the case of percussions, it is the hammer (more or less elaborate, culminating in the action of the piano) plus the arms and hands of the players. In the case of winds it is either a mechanical contrivance for controlling the air pressure, as in the bagpipes (even that most intricate of bagpipes, the organ) or it is simply the respiratory system of the player.

54   The vibrator turns the energy of the actuator into a series of compression and rarefaction waves. In the violin family, it is the strings. With the percussions, it is the member that is struck. The winds fall into two classes again, the organ combining both. The clarinet and oboe

group has a reed or reeds with a pendular motion; the trumpet and trombone group depends upon the lips of the player. The lips hold back the breath until its pressure becomes greater than their tension. Then a minute puff of air escapes, reducing the pressure to the point where the lip tension can stop the flow of breath again. This process, which is cyclical, or pendular, repeats itself hundreds of times a second as long as the breath pressure can be maintained. This is called the "buzz" principle of *embouchure*. Many fine brass players prefer a different concept, which I believe is based on the Bernoulli Effect. This is a kind of suction which is created when air is in motion, and which is a factor in drawing the lips together again after they have separated. The "buzz" principle emphasizes lip tension, but if one emphasizes the aerodynamic effect which Bernoulli described it results in a more delicate adjustment of the embouchure, and consequently a more subtle tone with no loss of power and other requisites. The vocal vibrator may aptly be compared to the lips of a trumpeter, and I shall have occasion to explain the Bernoulli Effect more fully in Chapter 3.

55   The resonator takes the product of the vibrator and increases its intensity, or improves its timbre, or both. Sometimes the line between these two elements of an instrument is hard to draw. This will not worry you if you remember that the resonator is really a secondary vibrator. One vibrator must dominate the other. If they are equally strong, as in the case of two tuning forks, they may resonate, but more often than not they cancel each other out. One "zigs" while the other "zags" as it were, and they work against each other, stopping the vibration. A physicist would say they are "out of phase 180°." It is likely that such a thing happens in the voice at one of the most important register transitions. I shall refer to this again, (Par. 316).

56   Strings use forced resonance of the kind I described with the fork and the dinner plate. A string alone does not disturb enough air, but by means of a bridge the vibration is communicated to a sounding board, which vibrates enough air to be heard. Sympathetic resonance should not enter the picture. That is, the resonator must be carefully made so that it responds equally well to all the tones that the strings will produce. Sometimes, in a poor violin, the sound box is in tune with certain pitches and produces *wolf tones*, as they are called. At these frequencies the resonator refuses to be the slave of the vibrator and produces the kind of interference I described in the paragraph above.

57   In the case of reeds the pipe determines the pitch and forces the reed to conform, or rather the player knows that the reed must conform to the pitch of the pipe and he bites his reed accordingly. As in the case of the flute, or of the bottle, the column of air has its own natural frequency, and the vibrator merely causes it to sound. We may speak of the resonator as vibrating freely. There is a little compromise between the two, but we may ignore it. The pitch is altered by opening a hole in the tube. The tone goes out the hole instead of the bell and it is as if the tube had been shortened.

58   Here we come to another interesting fact about air cavities. After you have sounded the natural frequencies of your instrument, which are the *fundamental tones* (on the clarinet they are called the *chalumeau*), if you blow harder, or in a different manner, you cause an *overtone* to sound, and you get a whole new series of tones in this higher register by using all the holes in the tube again. What happens is hard to understand, but it is something like this: Compression waves bump into one another, as it were, at places called *nodes*. Molecules at these places do not move, but bounce the waves in both directions instead of passing them on down the entire length of the pipe. If there is *one* node, in the middle, any given wave travels through only half of the tube and the pitch rises an octave. If *two* nodes should form, waves travel through only a third the length, and the third partial sounds. It is like the Pythagorean experiment of dividing strings. It is possible, theoretically at least, to produce the whole harmonic series above any fundamental by this process of *overblowing*. Without discussing it in detail, I mention this because in discussions of vocal registration, of producing the falsetto

voice, for example, one sometimes hears the phenomenon explained on the basis of overblowing. We shall consider this idea later, but I will say here simply that I do not believe it is possible to overblow the voice.

59   With the brasses, the resonance is largely free. A poor player may not get the proper tension in his lips for the desired pitch, and the instrument will still sound, but the intonation and the quality will be better if vibrator and resonator are exactly in tune. A good trumpeter can play a tune for you on his lips with no horn at all. Overblowing is still more important than with the reeds, in fact, the bugle affords a good illustration of playing entirely upon the overtones. If you are able to utilize the tones higher in the series, you can play more nearly diatonic passages (with smaller intervals) as did the *clarini* players of the seventeenth century. The longer the tube, the lower the fundamental, and the smaller the diameter, the easier the overblowing. Indeed, with some of the brasses, it is almost impossible to sound the fundamental at all. Most of the contemporary instruments of this family fill out the scale tones between those in the harmonic series by increasing the distance from mouthpiece to bell, using valves that open up extra lengths of tube. The trombone uses the slide for the same purpose.

The Voice as an Instrument

60   The voice is not a stringed instrument, although certain parallels can be drawn. For instance, the vocal "cords" change their pitch by changing their tension, and in this manner resemble strings. But strings do not alter their tension while they are being played. The vocal "cords" function much more like the lips of a trumpet player, and are frequently called *bands*, or *lips*. The way in which their tension is modified is much more complicated than either the strings of a piano or the lips of a wind player.

61   Another simile between the voice and a stringed instrument is even less justified, namely references to the hard palate and other bony surfaces as "sounding boards." This concept has been discredited, since it implies forced resonance. The voice has no strings, or if one considers the vocal cords as such, there is no bridge to any part of the body that might be called a sounding board. Furthermore, the palate is too small to act as a sounding board, and it is muffled in a soft, fleshy covering, as is also the chest.

62   The voice is a wind instrument. The actuator, naturally, is the wind supply in the lungs of the singer. It is no coincidence that the *bellows* of the bagpipes and the *belly* of the wind player are both called by derivatives of the Old English word, *belg*, meaning "bag."

63   The vibrator is in the *larynx*, or *voice-box*. It has been neglected by teachers until recently because it lies below the level of consciousness. Since it could not be directly controlled, it was not trained, except by imagery and suggestion. Lately, more attention has been given to this element of the vocal mechanism, and indeed some teachers have been inclined to regard it as paramount and have neglected the older branches of pedagogy. They have even branded any reference to resonance as sheer quackery.

64   However, the third element is also important. For the most part, the resonance system does not so much increase the volume as it improves the quality, though there is still room for debate on this point. If the throat and mouth are shaped correctly, they encourage those partials in the tone which are most desirable, by sympathetic resonance, working somewhat like the Helmholtz resonators, (Par. 50).

65   In the "Golden Age of Song" teachers knew little of the physics of music. The *bel canto* that they taught was based on the experienced sensations of the singers. Breathing, which is consciously controlled, they understood well and taught directly. The words of the pedagogs of that day have come down to us largely in the writings of Caccini, Mancini, and Tosi, and in

maxims. "Sing on the breath." "Support the tone." "Let the tone float on the breath." These are typical precepts. Legato, so that the tones were like "pearls on a string," was central in their ideals.

66   However, they also spoke of "opening the throat," "loosening the neck," and "singing the tone forward, at the lips." Such concepts relate to the shaping of the resonators. They foreshadow the "scientific school." With the great physicist, Helmholtz, in the latter nineteenth century, knowledge of acoustics changed the theoretical approach to voice production. Garcia was the first great scientific teacher. Others, inspired by his example and equipped with a smattering of Helmholtz, taught strange and wonderful ideas. In reading their books, one must continually discriminate between what they really knew, as great singers and teachers, and what they thought they knew about science. One should not discount them entirely, as the scoffers like to do, because these were sincere people who did their best to impart knowledge about an art in which they were well qualified. One must interpret their writings with tolerance and understanding based on current information.

67   The late nineteenth and early twentieth century theoreticians were preoccupied with resonance. They had much to say about the shape of the mouth, the position of the tongue, soft palate, etc. They also counted all the sinuses and actually convinced themselves that these cavities were important resonators. It is true that these small chambers of air do respond to high frequencies, and sensations in the sinuses may be proof of the presence of desirable overtones in the voice, but scientists today agree that the sinuses do not add anything to the tone that is heard by anyone other than the singer himself.

68   As an outgrowth of the fallacy that the voice at various pitches is augmented by resonance from various cavities, there developed an unfortunate theory of *registers*. There was a "head register" and a "chest register," and when these categories seemed inadequate, "palatal register," was added. In spite of the fact that Garcia[2] said, "These names are incorrect" (p. 7), and associated the whole matter with laryngeal function, the idea gained currency that some tones are sung straight out the top of the head, and others reflected off the "sounding board" of the chest. The effect of this ideology was that students sang their upper tones in one "voice" and their lower tones in another, and in the middle there was a regrettable problem of "blending the registers." In revulsion from this vocal schizophrenia, some contemporary teachers discredit the whole idea of "registers," and are almost afraid to use the word.

69   However, different qualities of voice all in the same throat are an undeniable fact of human experience. Some teachers may have had unfortunate results from talking about "registers," but shutting the mind to the facts will not alter them. As far back as Caccini, who taught *voce piena* (full voice) and *voce finta* (feigned or false voice), the question was openly considered. The greatest mistake in the theory of registers was in assuming that resonance chambers determined the basic quality of the voice.

70   Russell explored the matter of resonance chambers by the use of the X-ray. He found that no one particular shape of the oral cavity is the *sine qua non* of a particular vowel or quality. He concluded that while the *shape* of the resonator undoubtedly conditions the tone for better or for worse, the *texture* of the resonator (the muscular tension) is also important; and that the function of the laryngeal muscles is really the primary determiner of the sound.

71   The study of breathing goes back to the eighteenth centruy, or earlier; the study of the resonators came in the nineteenth; and in the twentieth, attention centers on the vibrating mechanism. Which of the three is more important could make for useless debate. Charlatans have made good livings by building up one or another of the phases to the exclusion of the others. As a matter of fact, all three elements of the vocal instrument are interdependent. The teacher should be prepared to concentrate on whichever the pupil needs the most to develop.

Chapter 2

BREATHING

72   There are those teachers who consider breathing the most important factor in tone production. They believe that everything else will take care of itself if the breath is properly controlled, that conversely poor singing is directly the result of poor breathing, that consequently there is just one thing to teach in the studio—correct inhalation and exhalation.

73   It seems wasteful to spend more than one or two lessons on breathing by itself. It is primary in importance, but it is easy to understand and can be practiced without the aid of a teacher. Lesson time is usually expensive. The one thing that the teacher *must* supervise is actual phonation, coordinating the actuator with the vibrator. The pupil can easily practice singing poor tone without knowing it. He will never practice wrong breathing by himself if he pays attention to what he is doing. The ideal situation would be for the beginner to have fifteen minutes a day vocalizing with his teacher, and no private vocalization until the teacher is sure that he knows what he is after.

74   The teacher should discuss habits of breathing with all beginners in an early lesson, and he should be watching advanced students continually to notice cases where he should review the subject. Indeed, advanced singers may come to him who have never really learned breathing technic properly. It is a mistake to blame previous teachers for this; the subject is dull and few singers enjoy such drills. For this reason I have reached a policy of never teaching breath management in the first lesson. The student has come to learn to sing, and so we begin immediately making tone. By the end of the first lesson, if the student's breath control is inadequate, I call attention to it, and promise to give him specific help in the *next* lesson. By then he will have what the progressive educator calls "readiness."

75   Breathing should be explained in detail, and its importance should be stressed. Then the teacher should point out that the pupil can form the correct habits by practice outside the studio. All the muscles involved in respiration can be consciously controlled. The only involuntary reaction is the necessity of taking a new breath when the oxygen content of the lungs runs low. If the student will spend five minutes (by the clock) at the beginning of each practice period practicing breathing exercises conscientiously, he will make rapid progress. He can also get in moments at odd times during the day, if he wants to, and master the correct habits even more quickly.

76   After the first lesson or two, in which breathing has been taught, the teacher should go on to other matters, but should keep watching to see whether the pupil is really learning. If after a month or so the student still inhales with a great heave of the chest, he probably is not practicing. If the pupil will not practice outside, then lesson time must be given to it. Some few people actually will have trouble coordinating phonation with proper exhalation without the patient help of the instructor.

77   Finally, it must be admitted that quite a few singers are successful in spite of theoretically poor habits of breathing. Lilli Lehmann is a good example, (Par. 101). After all, everyone does breathe; and some can inhale enough for the required phrase and exhale with enough steadiness to avoid tremolo, even though they do it inefficiently. But still it may be said that no matter how well a person sings, if his breathing can be improved his singing can also.

Correct Posture

78   It is easy to overemphasize posture. A teacher may like to teach it because he can feel sure he is correct in his instructions, but it soon becomes dull to the student and takes the fun out of singing. Furthermore, opera singers demonstrate continually that there is no one posture that is the *sine qua non* of good singing. However, the beginner must be reminded that opera stars probably learned orthodox posture at one time, and the positions they assume on stage, apparently spontaneously, are all such that they do not violate good technic, and they involve compensations to make up for their unorthodoxy.

79   Before trying to play any instrument one should learn how to hold it. Vocally this means posture. The head, chest, and pelvis should be supported by the spine in such a way that they align themselves one under the other—head erect, chest high, pelvis tipped so that the "tail is tucked in." The position of the head should allow the jaw to be free, not pulled back into the throat. This liberates the organs in the neck. The high chest implies that the shoulders go back, but they should relax and be comfortable. There should be no straining like a soldier on parade. A certain amount of tonicity of the abdominal muscles will be needed to keep the pelvis upright, but there must not be so much that deep breathing is impossible. This aspect of posture should be ignored if it prevents abdominal breathing.

80   Some teachers emphasize that the basis of good posture is the position of the pelvis, tail tucked in, which can be achieved by tensing the buttocks and pressing them together. It may well be that a few students will profit by this instruction. It is certainly true that in moments of strenuous voice production—as in singing a loud high tone—if one will direct his attention to it, he will realize that the *gluteal* muscles are very tense. I am rather inclined to believe that this emphasis makes singers over-tense and muscle-bound more often than it helps them.

81   The muscles of posture will work by themselves (as will all the others) if we know what they should be accomplishing and concentrate on that. For example, if I put my weight on my left foot my left buttock will automatically be firm and my right will be relaxed. If I shift my weight to the right foot, the tension will move from one buttock to the other. I do this by thinking of the posture instead of the muscles. *This is an important point to remember about all the musculature that I shall be discussing throughout this book.* A teacher should know what he is talking about, but that does not mean that he gives a voice lesson as if he were teaching anatomy. All muscles are controlled indirectly, in terms of their effects beyond themselves.

82   It helps to imagine that you are a marionette, hanging from strings, one attached to the top of your head and one attached to the top of your breast bone. This keeps the head erect and lifts the chest, allowing the pelvis just to "hang" in position. Imagine that the strings pull you a little toward the audience. The famous statue, the Winged Victory of Samothrace, is considered an inspiration for singers. A good exercise consists of swinging the arms circularly as if they were wings, rising on toes with each swing to add to the psychological effect. This relaxes the shoulders and expands the thorax. Other relaxing exercises, like the "rag doll" exercise of letting the torso hang limp, are beneficial.

83   The forward stride of the Winged Victory is exaggerated, of course, but it is good to have one foot a little in front of the other. An aggressive stance commands the attention of the audience. Avoid spreading the legs too far from side to side, creating a vulgar impression; and above all don't put your weight on your heels. Stand well supported, leaning perhaps a little forward. If your legs weary after considerable singing it is a good sign. The hands should be inconspicuous, hanging at the sides or lightly clasped, but not behind the singer. A student should practice before a mirror and keep asking himself, "Would I pay money to look at that?"

84   There are many variations upon the basic principles, but these have to do more with platform appearance, interpretation, artistry, which do not concern us this early. The main thing is to achieve that happy combination of muscular poise in which the parts which are to do the work are free and alert and the rest of the body is relaxed. There must also be an expansion of the ribs to provide leverage for the muscles of breathing, (Par. 113).

85   Respiration is a complex physiological process of which phonation is only a secondary function. For purposes of study it may be analyzed into three types of breathing: chest, rib, and diaphragmatic or abdominal. The first should be deemphasized; the most efficient breathing for singing is a combination of the latter two.

86   One should have at least a nodding acquaintance with *all* the muscles involved. Only this way can the essentials fall into the proper perspective. It is all very well to say, "You don't have to take your watch apart in order to tell time," but if your watch is not keeping *good* time you go to someone who *can* take it apart. When a singer comes to a teacher in the hope of improving his technic, he has a right to expect the teacher to know as much as possible about the subject.

The Framework of the Respiratory System

87   In order to understand the muscular activity we must have a clear picture of the underlying *bone* structure. It is really a system of levers which are actuated by pulleys (the muscles). The levers (bones) are held together by *ligaments* and moved by *muscles*. Muscles attach to the bones by means of *tendons*, which are of much the same tough tissue as ligaments, and will stretch very little. The muscles, on the other hand, are stretched when they relax and they shorten when they contract. They are long and thin when they are not working, and short and thick when they are pulling.

88   The backbone, or *spine*, is composed of twenty-four *vertebrae*. Each vertebra has a body which rests upon the body of the one below (with a cushion of connective tissue between) and which provides a resting place for the one above. Behind the body of each vertebra is a bony loop through which the spinal cord passes, a large cable of nerve fibres descending from the brain and branching to serve all parts of the body. Extending from the bony ring I have mentioned are various bony *processes*. One projects downward from the middle of the back of the vertebra, and it is called the *spinous process* or just *spine*. Two project horizontally, one from each side, and they are called *transverse processes*. There are also two *articular processes* above and two below. The two above articulate (join) with the two lower ones of the vertebra above.

89   The vertebrae are graduated in size from the smallest in the neck to the largest in the small of the back. There are seven bones in the neck, called *cervical* vertebrae, twelve in the chest (*thorax*) called *thoracic* vertebrae, and five more below, called *lumbar* vertebrae. (Don't you think it is convenient to remember seven plus five equals twelve?) Below the lumbar bones is the spade-shaped *sacrum*, which is actually five vertebrae fused into one. Still lower is the tiny *coccyx*, like four or five little tail bones fused. We humans keep this humiliating detail (pun intended) hidden. Fused with the sacrum on either side are the large, irregular-shaped hip bones, with which we must associate three names. The parts we sit on form the *ischium*. The parts which meet at the front at the very bottom of the trunk form the *pubis*. The big, semicircular ridges we feel when we "place hands on hips" are the *ilii* (one *ilium* on each side). All these parts I have just mentioned, beginning with the sacrum, are fused into one complex, somewhat basket-shaped structure called the *pelvis*.

90   Joined to the top of each thoracic vertebra are two *ribs*, one on each side. The ribs, or *costae*, are roughly semicircular and the upper seven of them connect with the *breastbone* in front, forming a rough circle. Actually the shape is more like the outline of an apple when you cut through the core. The backbone fits into a depression in the "circle" at the point where the

stem of the apple would be. In fact, the spinous process could be the stem. The cross section of the *sternum* (breastbone) would be at the opposite end of the core. (See Fig. 10).

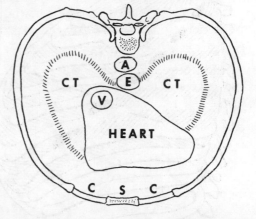

Fig. 10. Shape of Diaphragm Seen From Above
Upper surface of diaphragm is central tendon (CT). From this, muscle fibres radiate, extending downward and attaching to lower ribs, sternum (S), and backbone (represented by typical thoracic vertebra at top). Shape is essentially that of two ribs.
A, aorta; C, cartilaginous part of rib; E, esophagus; S, cross section of sternum; V, vena cava.

91   Now this apple-shape is almost horizontal in the case of the first (top) ribs, and it is also small. With each successively lower pair of ribs the shape is larger and less horizontal, that is, the ribs curve downward so that numbers seven to ten are at about a 45° angle when the body is erect. From seven to ten also the ribs become progressively smaller. The whole thing is an egg-shaped *cage*. Each rib is composed of bone for the most part, but has a short section of cartilage to join it with the sternum. The cartilages from ribs eight, nine, and ten, do not reach directly to the breastbone, but merge each with the cartilage above. They have been called *false ribs*, and also *abdominal ribs*. The eleventh and twelfth ribs are short and have very little cartilage. Because they do not reach the breastbone at all they are called *floating ribs*.

The Muscles of the Ribs

92   The most important rib muscles are the *intercostals*, so called because they are between the ribs. There are two sets, external and internal. The outer set, the *external intercostals* have fibres which run diagonally downward away from the backbone. Since the backbone is relatively fixed and the ribs are movable, the contraction of the external intercostal fibres pulls the ribs upward, toward the backbone. This is easy to see if we look at those fibres which are near the spine (Fig. 11, back view) and if we continue our logic we realize that no matter what muscle fibre we choose, the attachment to the upper rib is always more fixed and the attachment to the lower is always more mobile, so the pull will still be an upward pull. The external intercostal muscles are therefore *inspiratory*, because pulling the ribs upward will increase both diameters of the thorax. The slope of the ribs is such that pulling them up moves the sternum forward, and also expands the cage sideward.

93   There is an inner layer of muscles whose fibres run at right angles to the ones we have just considered. These fibres make the opposite diagonal, running from the backbone *upward* and outward. Hence, after the externals have pulled the ribs up, the *internal intercostals* pull them down again, producing *exhalation*.

94   If you are following this carefully, and (as I should hope) looking at fine drawings in some anatomy book (which you really should own) you may notice that the cartilaginous part of the ribs at the front near the breastbone make a right angle with the osseous part. This means that the diagonals of the intercostals pull in the opposite manner, and reverse their effectiveness for inspiration and expiration. Since this is such a small part of the rib-cage, we may ignore the problems it raises. The external intercostals are inspiratory and the internals are expiratory. The two sets are capable of a bellows action, expanding and contracting the cage, drawing air in and expelling it.

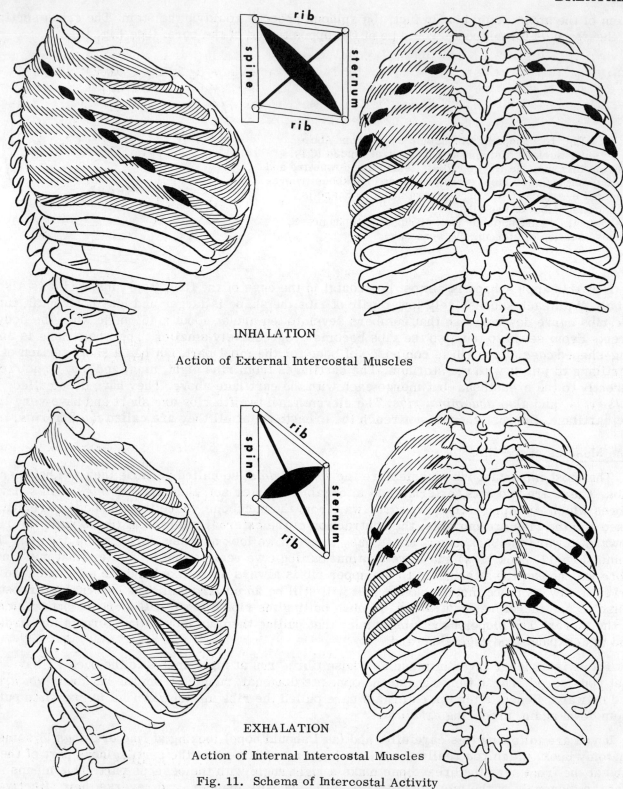

INHALATION

Action of External Intercostal Muscles

EXHALATION

Action of Internal Intercostal Muscles

Fig. 11. Schema of Intercostal Activity
Left: Side view. Right: Back view.
Intercostal muscles are shown semi-realistically by lines running in direction of respective
fibres. Muscle-fibres are indicated only between upper nine or ten ribs, and external fibres are
shown only between upper ribs so that internal fibres may appear between lower ribs. Small
muscles shown in back view extending from transverse processes to ribs: Levatores costarum.
Any intercostal muscle-fibre may be considered a link in a chain connecting ribs with spine.
Chains of contracting fibres are shown schematically as thickened black lozenges. Chains of
relaxing fibres are shown as thin black lines. Compare length of contracted chains with corresponding drawings of them when relaxed. Principle is oversimplified in two small diagrams
between drawings of ribs.

95   Other, less important muscles should be mentioned. Skip to Par. 100, if you like. First, additional inspiratory muscles: Deep in the neck, attaching to the transverse processes of the cervical vertebrae is a three-fold muscle on each side that attaches to the two uppermost ribs, pulling them up. These are called *scaleni* because they form a scalene triangle. They are the top link in a chain formed by the external intercostals to pull up the whole rib-cage. Deep in the back of the neck is a pair of muscles that attach to the spinous processes of the two lowest cervical and two uppermost thoracic vertebrae, and run downward and outward to the four uppermost ribs, pulling them up. The four rib attachments look like saw teeth and so the muscle is called *serratus* (meaning saw-toothed). The complete name is *serratus posterior superior* (saw-toothed muscle in back at the top). Finally, please note a set of twelve little muscles on either side of the spine (See Fig. 11). Each comes from the transverse process of a thoracic vertebra and runs down and out to the rib below, occasionally the second rib below. Notice that this means their fibres parallel those of the external intercostals, and so they work the same way, pulling the ribs up, even though their leverage is small. These are called *levatores costarum* (lifters of ribs).

96   Please bear with me. There are also several less important *expiratory* muscles. Some of these go with the internal intercostals and are inside the rib-cage. Next to the intercostals are nerves and blood vessels that run between the ribs. These are covered with a thin layer of muscles called *intercostales intimi*. They might be considered part of intercostales interni. The levatores costarum have their counterparts in a set of little muscles near the backbone on the inside. These run from one rib near the spine, outward and upward skipping one or two ribs and attaching to one above. They pull downward, of course, running parallel to the fibres of the internal intercostals. They are called *subcostales*. At the front, attaching to the inside of the sternum at the bottom are six pairs of muscles that fasten to the ribs at the point where the cartilage meets the bone. These also pull down. They are called *transversus thoracis*.

97   A few more muscles which may be considered expiratory are found in the back, outside the ribs. The back muscles are primarily postural, that is, they enable us to stand. As such, naturally, they make respiration possible by providing a foundation for the action of the breathing muscles. Just how much they participate in respiration is debatable, and sometimes we may think of them as expiratory and in one or two cases perhaps inspiratory. When a muscle simply holds, providing a base for the pulling of other muscles, this is called *synergy*. "They also serve who only stand and wait." The muscles I am about to mention *may* be actively expiratory, but are at least synergistic with the respiratory system.

98   The backbone is held together with many ligaments, and between almost any two processes on different vertebrae a muscle may be found. The deepest of these are the shortest and run from one vertebrae to the next. Working in various combinations these little muscles twist or bend the spine, or simply hold it in any given position. Longer muscles, that skip one or more vertebrae, overlie the little deep ones. Overlying these, in a mid-layer, is a family of muscles extending from tail to head and called *sacrospinalis* or *erector spinae*. There are many bundles of muscle in this group, attaching to all the vertebrae and all the ribs, and having many names, but we need only remember two: *longissimus dorsi* and *iliocostalis*.

99   The first of these (the longest of the back) is a group in the middle of sacrospinalis, attaching to the transverse processes and also to the ribs a little way from the backbone. The outer portions of sacrospinalis, running parallel with longissimus, are called iliocostalis because the bundles extend from the upper edge of the hip bone (ilium) to the ribs. These muscles undoubtedly are expiratory because they exert considerable leverage on the ribs to pull them down. One is sometimes surprised to see a singer who seems at the end of his breath eke out a few more spoonfuls by leaning backward. This is poor technic, of course, but it illustrates the action of these muscles. Lying just over sacrospinalis and attaching to the ribs

still further outward from the spine is *serratus posterior inferior* (saw-toothed muscle in back at the bottom). It arises from the spinous processes of the two uppermost lumbar and the two lowest thoracic vertebrae, and pulls downward on the four lowest ribs in the same manner that serratus posterior superior pulls upward on the four uppermost ribs. Neither of the serratus posterior muscles is too important to us, because they consist largely of the tendonous sheet which attaches them to the spine. This sheet overlies sacrospinalis and serves to bind it in place. Near the attachment to the ribs there is a relatively small amount of muscle fibre. So we return to our original statement that these muscles are primarily postural.

The Muscles of the Belly

100   The most important of all inspiratory muscles is the *diaphragm*, which may be considered the floor of the ribcage or the ceiling of the belly. It is described as a large dome-shaped muscle which divides the trunk into two parts, with the lungs and heart above and the rest of the viscera below. Actually it is almost a double dome, with the stomach and spleen under the left dome and the liver under the right. The heart is in the middle above, and the two domes are separated by the backbone (remember that apple-shape? Fig. 10). The upper portion of the diaphragm is the *central tendon,* and running down from it are muscular walls which attach to the lowest ribs, the sternum, and the backbone. Normally it is arched rather high in its relaxed position, and when it tightens it tends to flatten. (You can illustrate this by forming a dome with your hands, fingers interlaced, and showing how flattening the dome creates more space above it.) When the diaphragm exerts itself, the capacity of the air chamber is increased because its floor is dropped. Naturally this flattening of the dome will be coordinated with the expanding of the ribs, to which it is attached at its circumference.

101   At one time it was thought that the action of the diaphragm pulled the ribs up. It was supposed that the abdomen should draw in tightly, holding its contents high against the central tendon so that it could not descend. The central tendon would then become a "fulcrum" for the lifting of the ribs. Lilli Lehmann used this technic for twenty-five years before learning to relax the abdomen for inhalation (pp. 20-24). This was called "pancostal breathing" and the concept went well with the tight corsets that were worn in those days--sometimes even by men. It is true that a tight garment around the middle helps some singers with "breath control," and preventing the diaphragm from descending normally may be a factor. Browne and Behnke crusaded against this idea, and against corsets, and today few accept it. The fluoroscope now makes it very clear that the diaphragm always descends for inhalation, and in really deep breathing it descends radically (Fig. 12). After all, the ribs can be actuated by muscles enumerated above. It is better to list the diaphragm under belly breathing.

102   Indeed, serratus posterior inferior (Par. 99) is sometimes listed as inspiratory, with the idea that it *holds down* the lowest ribs, providing anchorage for the diaphragm. Another such muscle is *quadratus lumborum* (quadrangular muscle in the lumbar region) which extends from the ilium near the spine and attaches to the lowest rib, and also joins the transverse processes of the lumbar vertebrae. The primary function of this muscle is to flex the body sidewards, but it also serves to anchor the lower ribs for the diaphragm. The muscles mentioned in this paragraph are postural muscles which may synergize with inhalation, or which may be counted as expiratory. Their secondary function is ambiguous, in other words.

103   The expiratory muscles of the belly are four in number (each a pair, of course). The *rectus abdominis* runs straight up and down (that is the meaning of *rectus)* the middle of the abdomen, from the pubic bone to the cartilages of the fifth, sixth, and seventh ribs. It has four "bellies" of its own; that is, each rectus abdominis is really four flat muscles joined by tendon to each other and the top part attaches to the ribs and the bottom to the pubis. The muscles are enclosed in a tendonous double sheath, which has a separation in the midline called the *linea alba.* This double envelope provides attachment for more abdominal muscles which run from

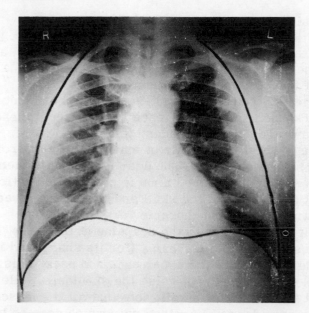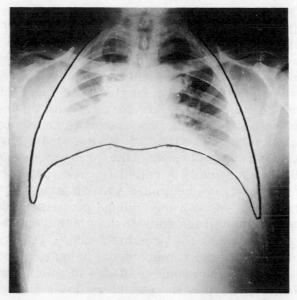

Fig. 12. X-Rays of Thorax in Breathing
Left: Deep inhalation. Right: Deep exhalation.
X-ray study of a prominent operatic singer. From Friedrich S. Brodnitz, *Vocal Rehabilitation*.
Similar studies can be found in various places. See James Terry Lawson, *Full-Throated Ease*,
p. 13.

the pelvis to the lower ribs, at the sides of the belly. The outer layer of these muscles is called
obliquus abdominis externus and its fibres run in the same direction as those of intercostales
externus. The layer below, *obliquus abdominis internus*, has its fibres in the opposite diagonal,
like intercostales internus. Still deeper is a third layer, *transversus abdominis*, whose fibres
run horizontally. It may be thought of as continuous with transversus thoracis, whose lowest
fibres are almost horizontal, but whose upper fibres, running from the bottom of the sternum
upward to the ribs, form deeper and deeper V's.

104   For the sake of thoroughness it should be mentioned that the muscles of the pelvic outlet
(including the gluteal muscles already mentioned in Par. 80) must tighten in order that the
pressure created by the abdominal muscles be directed upward for exhalation. The same pres-
sures are used for defecation, when the laryngeal outlet is closed and the pelvic outlet is
relaxed. Needless to say, the action of these muscles is instinctive, as is the case with most of
the respiratory musculature. Training these muscles consists of conditioning these reflexes
into patterns which are more efficient for singing, and this only modifies the overall behavior
somewhat, as will be discussed later, beginning in Par. 113.

The Muscles of the Shoulders

105   Shoulder movements can be used for breathing, because muscles connect the shoulders and
the ribs. Ordinarily these muscles move the shoulders, the ribs remaining still, but if the
need is great enough the shoulders can be fixed and the muscles will move the ribs instead.
In cases of paralysis of the normal respiratory system, as an emergency measure while the
iron lung is being readied the patient may grasp the head of his bed to hold up his shoulders
and use his shoulder muscles to create bellows action of the ribs. Exhausted athletes heave
their shoulders and upper chests (and incidentally their phonation is uncontrolled under such
conditions).

106   There are two groups of these muscles. First let us enumerate those that connect the shoulders to the spine. The bony framework of the shoulders is called the *shoulder girdle*. It consists of two *clavicles* (collarbones) which attach by ligaments to the top of the sternum and to two *scapulae* (shoulder blades). Just below the juncture of clavicle and scapula there is a socket in the latter into which the round head of the *humerus* (upper arm bone) fits. The scapulae are two right triangles. The upper edges are horizontal and each has a prominent ridge. The inner edges are parallel with the backbone. A muscle on each side connects these edges with the spinous processes. Its action draws the shoulder blades together and raises them slightly. It is called *rhomboideus*, because of its shape. A pair of muscles running from the transverse processes of the three upper neck bones down to the shoulder blades pulls them up directly; hence it is called *levator scapulae*. A diamond-shaped muscle has for its vertical axis the backbone, beginning with an attachment to the base of the skull and connecting directly or indirectly with all the spinous processes down to the lowest thoracic vertebra. Its outer corners attach to the ends of the clavicles and it also attaches to the scapulae at the outer corners and along the prominent ridge. This muscle is called *trapezius* (for its shape) and it covers most of the rhomboideus, being just under the skin of the upper back and neck. This muscle draws the shoulder blades together, and upper fibres of it raise the shoulders while the lower part pulls the shoulders down. Except for this latter detail, note that all the muscles I have mentioned so far in this category pull the shoulders *up*. Another pair which does so to some extent is the *sternocleidomastoid*, named for the parts it connects. These muscles form a prominent V in the neck, with the larynx between them. They arise from the sternum and the clavicles together and go to the *mastoid process* behind each ear. I mention them in this paragraph because they attach to the shoulder girdle, but they do not raise the shoulders much. Perhaps they should be listed with the scalene muscles as raising the ribs (by way of the breastbone). Actually they are postural muscles, holding the head erect or turning it, but singers who breathe in the upper chest, and who often raise the shoulders in doing so, also show activity in the sternocleidomastoids as they inhale.

107   There is one more muscle connecting the shoulders to the spine. It is called *latissimus dorsi* (broadest of the back). There is a big sheet of tendon (such a sheet is called an *aponeurosis*) covering much of sacrospinalis and running up to the top thoracic vertebrae (under trapezius). Extending triangularly from this aponeurosis on each side are muscle fibres which run to a point under the arms and attach to the humerus at the armpits. We might say this muscle pulls the shoulders down toward the spine, but it is ambiguous because on its under surface there are attachments to the three lowest *ribs*. With minor exceptions, then, *all the muscles which attach to the spine pull the shoulders upward*.

108   The muscles which pull them *downward* attach to the *ribs*. These form two-link chains with the ones we have just noted, pulling the ribs upward, providing we pull the shoulders upward as a prerequisite. For example the rhomboids pull upward on the inner edges of the scapulae. Attaching to the same edges and running underneath the scapulae to pull on the first eight or nine ribs is another muscle called *serratus* (because those eight or nine rib insertions make a saw-tooth pattern) and further called *serratus magnus* (because it is bigger than the serratus posterior muscles) or *serratus anterior* (also to distinguish it from the posterior ones). Now this muscle normally moves the shoulders, but in coordination with rhomboideus it would expand the ribcage.

109   Similarly we find that *pectoralis minor* (small breast muscle) attaches to a process of the scapula that projects to the front of the shoulder, and this muscle also attaches to ribs three, four, and five, in front. Let trapezius and levator scapulae pull the shoulder up and pectoralis minor will raise the upper ribs. Or consider *pectoralis major* which covers *p. minor*, arising from the edge of the breastbone, part of the collarbone, and six upper ribs, and inserted into the upper arm at the shoulder. Or consider *subclavius*, the little muscle under the clavicle

connecting with the first rib and its cartilage. All these muscles are to move the shoulders normally, but if we pull the shoulders up they will raise the ribs. This is even true of latissimus dorsi when you think of its attachments to the lower ribs.

110   *So the shoulder muscles are practically all inspiratory!* We can't make a clear case for any of them as expiratory. They are used for desperate gulps of air, leaving expiration uncontrolled, depending upon gravity or some of the muscles we have assigned to other categories. Since phonation is expiratory, and singing especially demands fine control, we see here the prime reason why this kind of breathing is inefficient for singers. Of course, no one breathes exclusively in one way—shoulder, rib, or belly—but there are pedagogical reasons for analyzing the subject this way. Singers often show one type predominantly.

Clavicular, Chest, or Shoulder Breathing

111   This is the kind of breathing used by the exhausted athlete, the person who is "out of breath." It is "last resort," desperate breathing. Witherspoon calls this *clavicular* breathing, "the breath of exhaustion." (The clavicles are the collar bones.) The heaving chest is the symptom of of inability to get enough oxygen otherwise. Used in combination with other methods it has a part in the most complete change of the air in the lungs that is possible. Thus it may be justified occasionally, to prevent an accumulation of carbon dioxide in the top of the lungs, but such breathing is better between numbers rather than during a song.

112   Generally movement in the upper part of the thorax should be avoided. First, it is inefficient. It is inspiratory and provides no control over exhalation. It is better not to resort to it unless it becomes absolutely necessary. A good singer is seldom so in need of breath that he must do this. Second, it looks bad. When a singer collapses his chest, his shoulders droop, his posture becomes poor. When he inhales he hauls himself erect again. This movement up and down, up and down, can detract from the impression he makes upon the audience. Third, chest breathing can easily lead to muscular tension in the throat. The muscles that raise the breast bone have attachment at the top of the neck. The same is true of the musculature of the shoulders, and elevation of the shoulders, while they are really independent of the thorax, regularly accompanies this type of breathing. The *sternocleidomastoids* (the muscles extending from behind the ears, down to the *sternum,* or breast bone) of a chest-breather stand out noticeably with each inhalation, and so do the *trapezius* muscles at the back. These muscles are not directly involved in singing, or should not be, but they are so near the ones that are, that sympathetically they are likely to have a bad effect if they become tense. Fourth, abdominal breathing, which is the best, cannot take place correctly when the ribs are heaving.

113   One should form the habit of raising the chest comfortably, not excessively, relaxing the shoulders and letting the arms hang loosely. This should be the position maintained all through the song, while the breathing is a matter of expansion and contraction at the bottom of the lungs, that is at the diaphragm. This position of the ribs provides leverage for the action of the belly muscles. If the ribs collapse, the abdominal muscles cannot pull as effectively.

114   For some students this is difficult. For most it is not "natural" in the sense that the habit is already formed. It will require conscious practice, but attention and perseverance are all that are necessary. Women generally find it more difficult than men, though they have no monopoly, by any means. Most nurses will testify that women are "chest-breathers" and men are "belly-breathers." They discover this when taking pulse and respiration counts in hospitals. The women's chests go up and down, while men breathe abdominally. A biological explanation for this is that nature has prepared the child-bearing sex for the time when deep breathing will be difficult or impossible. However accurate this theory may be, it is at least interesting.

115   Correct breathing may be summarized with the three adverbs, "in, down, and out." The air is taken "in" through the nose or mouth, preferably the latter. In most cases it cannot be taken fast enough through the nose without dilating the nostrils noticeably, and furthermore, inhaling

through the mouth tends by reflex action to adjust the resonators correctly. For vegetative purposes, nature has designed the nose as a filter for incoming air, but for singing—a superimposed function—the mouth is better. The breath goes "down" into the lungs, causing the walls of the thorax to expand, "out." Without this last outward movement, it will be shallow breathing.

116   The singer should imagine that a friend has placed a tape measure not under the armpits, where chest expansion is frequently measured, but about at the latitude of the *solar plexus*, around the lower ribs. With each breath the tape measure should register an increase of as many inches as possible, for breathing exercise, and as many inches as necessary, for singing, depending on the phrase to be sung.

Costal, or Rib Breathing

117   The sideward expansion of the ribs characterizes the second type of respiration: *costal* or rib breathing. The student can check to see how well he is doing it by placing the heels of his hands against the lower ribs, at the sides. He should place them so that when he has exhaled the fingertips are just touching in front. Then, when he inhales, his objective will be to push them as far apart as he can. Of course, he may be able to make the exercise look good by shifting his hands apart, but there is no point in fooling anyone. The ribs should push the hands apart.

118   The same maneuver with the fingers meeting in back will show a certain amount of expansion there also. Some teachers emphasize this back expanding as if it were the secret of an additional reservoir of breath. Of course the ribs cannot move as far in this area because they are attached to the spine. I shall discuss this concept more fully in Par. 137.

119   Many great teachers of singing have agreed with S. Marchesi (p. 17) who did not believe in costal breathing any more than in clavicular. They felt that the rib muscles should only be used to expand the ribs and keep them in this position making possible the most efficient operation of lower muscles, the true motors of breathing. This may be extreme, but we may be sure that the normal expansion of the ribs is primarily *sideward,* partly *forward* and very little *upward* so that it coordinates with belly breathing rather than shoulder breathing. Probably breath control depends upon resisting the tendency to collapse the ribs as long as possible.

Diaphragmatic-abdominal, or Belly Breathing

120   The third type of breathing has received the most publicity. It is *diaphragmatic*. The diaphragm is one of the most powerful muscles in the body, and certainly a most important one. It is not only a partition between the ribcage and the belly, but it is related to both types of breathing and thus implies that they should be coordinated. The believers in "pancostal breathing" (Par. 101) actually thought of it as the power that raised the ribs. This idea is discredited, but we know that when the diaphragm contracts it flattens, lowering the floor of the chest and drawing in the breath. Probably more breath can be inhaled in this manner than by the sideward expansion of the ribs, though the point is academic since both movements occur at once.

121   One sometimes hears the instruction, "Place your hand on your diaphragm." This is a little confusing, because the diaphragm is inside the body, and to touch it one would have to take out his lungs and put his hand down his throat. What is meant is to place the hand on the abdominal muscles, near the top, at the place where the ribs arch in front, just below the breast-bone. This region is called the *epigastrium,* and it is a handy spot to feel the action of the diaphragm. When it flattens, this area will push forward. Plunket Greene called it "the breathing muscle." (p. 291). Place one hand on the ribs at the side and the other hand "on the diaphragm" in front, so that you can check on both costal and *abdominal* expansion at the same time.

122   The word "abdominal" is used advisedly, for diaphragmatic action is bound to involve the abdomen. When the diaphragm drops, it presses down upon the stomach and other organs and there must be some place for them to go. They cannot be compressed. This is why it is impossible for one to sing well after too heavy a meal. The body simply cannot be full of food and full of air at the same time, and if the stomach has been crammed, it will interfere with deep breathing. But in any case, the diaphragm forces down the organs of the belly and the abdominal wall must relax enough to allow these displaced organs to move forward a little.

123   This leads to a second explanation of why chest breathing is so common, perhaps more convincing than the biological explanation outlined in paragraph 114. Almost everyone has a preconceived idea of good posture that associates raising the chest with drawing in the abdomen. Many a rookie has been told by his sergeant what he must suck in when he assumes the position of a soldier. Most uninstructed singers, when asked to take a deep breath, raise the chest, which is good, but at the same time they pull in the abdomen so that it cannot move. This forces the organs of the belly up against the diaphragm and makes a really deep breath impossible. So when the singer exhales, there is nothing for him to do but drop his chest. When he inhales again, he once more hauls up his chest and shoulders. What he should be doing is the exact opposite. The shoulders and chest should remain motionless, and the diaphragm and abdomen should move. It is true that a sagging abdominal wall is poor posture, but while it need not relax at the *bottom*, the *top* of the abdomen must make way for the motion of the diaphragm.

Belly Breathing Exercises

124   One simple exercise for developing the right coordination is performed while lying flat on the back on some rigid surface, like the floor or a table. A weight, such as a few large books, is placed on the abdomen near the ribs. When the person inhales, he should raise the weight, and when he exhales, the weight should go down. It is good psychology to imagine that the pressure of of the weight expels the breath, and that the only muscular action is for inhalation. In singing, one takes breath voluntarily, between phrases, with a quick action; but one does not usually force the breath out. The normal elasticity of the walls of the thorax is enough to accomplish most breath support. It is as if one took in the air, and "let" it out. More about this later.

125   Another exercise, similar to the one just described, but much more strenuous, requires the use of a small object about the size and shape of a pint milk bottle. Hold the object against the "breathing muscle," between the ribs, and lean so that the other end of the object presses against a wall. Stand on tiptoe, with feet far enough back so that a good deal of weight is converted into pressure on the epigastrium. Release the breath, but do not exhale abdominally; rather, let the bottle, or whatever is being used, expel the air by pushing in below the ribs. Inhale, pushing the weight of the body away from the wall. This is too rugged an exercise to practice for long periods of time. Instead it should be considered a kind of test. Beginners may find it very difficult, but as they develop the "breathing muscle" they will be able to exert a greater thrust. The teacher may care to demonstrate the development of his diaphragm by having the pupil extend a fist and pushing against it in the manner just explained.

Muscular Antagonism

126   At this point it is necessary to refer to the principle of *muscular antagonism*. The same factor will be important in discussing the function of the larynx. No muscle works alone; it is opposed, and steadied, in its action by one or more other muscles. Sometimes it is a simple pulley arrangement as in the case of the biceps and triceps of the arm. Often it is much more complex, as in the larynx. In the case of the intercostals the internals are the antagonists of the externals. However, the abdominals are also the antagonists of the external intercostals, because they pull the ribs downward. Recognition of this fact leads to an understanding of the coordination

of rib and belly breathing, which is the best technic. The relationship is emphasized by the
fact that the lower ribs are called "abdominal ribs" (Par. 91).

127   The contraction of the diaphragm causes it to lower and partly flatten, increasing the
capacity of the thorax. It is the muscle of *inhalation*. The contraction of the abdominal muscles
decreases the capacity of the entire trunk, including the thorax except in certain functions. They
are the muscles of *exhalation*. They are resisted and steadied in their contraction by the
diaphragm, but it only causes confusion to think of this muscle as being the active factor. The
diaphragm does *not* "support the tone." I know that my argument will not be enough to scotch
this fallacious bit of folklore; I catch even myself using the expression, so common is it;
nevertheless I repeat: The diaphragm *steadies* the tone, but it does not *support* it.

128   W. S. Drew[2] says, "Anyone who said that the biceps muscle bends the arm when it contracts
and extends the arm when it relaxes would be contradicted at once; but innumerable people state
that the diaphragm draws air in when it contracts and pushes 'the voice' out when it relaxes—a
curious privilege, accorded no doubt to a foreign-sounding name—always potent in matters of
art," (p. 130). I agree gleefully, having long thought that "diaphragmatic breathing" has received
so much publicity largely because of the *ph* and the *gm*; you must take at least one lesson just
to learn how to pronounce it!

The Bouncing Epigastrium

129   This brings us back to the bulging epigastrium described in paragraph 121, regarded as
proof of good "diaphragmatic development." When both sets of muscles (diaphragm and abdominals) tense, the epigastrium pushes forward, and the better the muscular development the
more startling the thrust. This is represented by a dot and dash outline in Fig. 13. In fact, the
demonstration with the pint milk bottle can be done with no reference to respiration at all. The
breath can be retained and the body bounced merely by alternate contraction and relaxation of
the "breathing muscle." We still have the principle of antagonism, though in this case it is
gravity and not some counter-muscle that provides the opposition. However, this ceases to be a
breathing exercise and allows confusion as to the function of the respective muscles. I recommend that all exercise of the muscles of breathing include actual respiration.

130   Frequently students are taught that when there is a sudden expulsion of breath, as in a
staccato attack, the epigastrium should bounce. You can feel this by placing your hand there
and then coughing. Thus, in some pedagogies, contraction of the abdomen is associated with a
thrust of the epigastrium. I don't mind this so much as long as it does not create the illusion
that the attack is initiated by a contraction of the *diaphragm*. I am even willing to admit that
often at the inception of a long sustained phrase there will be a filling out and stiffening of the
top part of the *rectus abdominis*. Indeed, the whole abdominal wall should stiffen. The diaphragm
will also tighten, just enough to resist but not to inhibit the action of the abdominals. It is really
the contraction of both muscles that causes the outward motion of the epigastrium, and this
happens at the *beginning* of the phrase. At the end of the phrase the abdominals will be completely contracted, the diaphragm will have been pushed back to its top, arched position, and
the epigastrium will have lost its convexity.

131   Thus, while there may be an illusion of expansion about the equator at the start of the tone,
the total motion is one of contraction. You cannot produce a usable tone while inhaling. In general the motion of inhaling is "in, down, and *out*," and this outward movement of the "stomach"
must not be thought of as part of exhaling. The tightening of the muscles, causing the bulging
epigastrium, is not so much for expiration as for its control. To say that the diaphragm "controls the breath" is quite true, and not the same as to say that it "supports the tone."

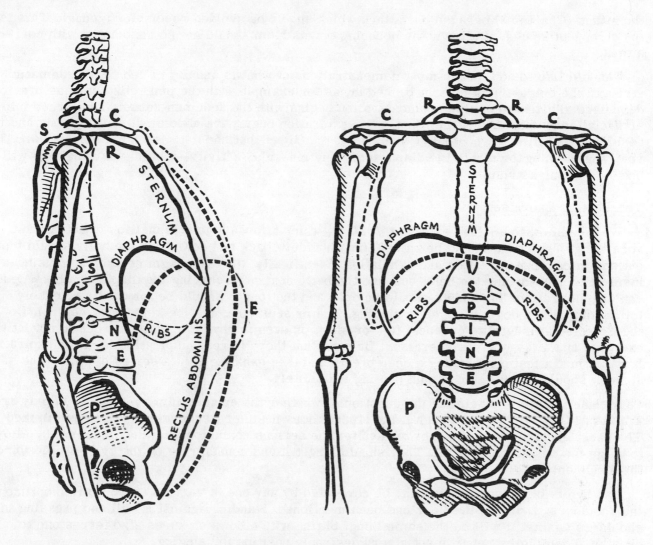

Fig. 13. Coordination of Rib and Belly Breathing
C, clavicle; E, epigastrium; P, pelvis; R, first rib; S, scapula. Solid lines represent position
of organs at completion of forced exhalation; broken lines, forced inhalation. Movement is
exaggerated in side view, but not in front view. Diaphragm is lower on left side because of
position of heart. Dot-and-dash line shows how simultaneous contraction of both diaphragm and
lower abdominals produces bulge of epigastrium. Some singers make a fetish of this muscular
development.

132   Coughing is often cited as proof that "Nature intends" that a tone should be initiated with a
"diaphragmatic attack." Such verbalization confuses the issue. A cough is indeed a reflex,
"Nature's way" of doing something important, expelling foreign particles from the larynx. This
is done with a rush of air created by a violent contraction of the *abdomen*. This great force
could well damage the larynx, so the diaphragm instinctively contracts at the same instant to
control the force. Some of it causes the epigastrium to bounce outward and some of it causes
the diaphragm to bounce upward. It is the latter that expels the foreign substance from the
throat. Imagine that you have (inside you) a beach ball, of which the diaphragm is the upper
surface. If you strike the beach ball from below the top of it will bounce upward, but the sides
will also bounce outward. Most throat authorities insist that coughing, even with its built-in
control, is hard on the vocal cords and should be avoided. Remember this when we consider

the attack (Chapter 3) because one attack which should be avoided resembles a cough. This is the strongest reason of all why the bouncing epigastrium should not be associated with correct attack.

133   I should like to add that in most demonstrations of what is usually called "diaphragmatic" strength the epigastrium is first pushed in, as for example with the pint milk bottle as previously described. That is to say, the demonstration begins with the abdomen relaxed and forced into an artificial concavity. Of course, then, when expiration begins the abdominal wall tightens and in assuming its tense flat contour it thrusts out the object that had depressed the epigastrium. This really has nothing to do with the diaphragm! Any muscular activity—inhaling or exhaling—will bounce the epigastrium.

The Panting Exercise

134   We come now to another exercise, *panting*, which affords a good transition to actual vocalizing. The chest should be raised, the shoulders back and down, and the belly should move out and in causing inhalation and exhalation. Specifically, the diaphragm contracts, causing inspiration and forcing the belly out; and the belly contracts, forcing the diaphragm back up and causing expiration. The mouth should be open and the tongue should be forward, preferably lolling out, like a dog's when he is panting. The musculature must be kept under control. Do the exercise at a definite cadence, fast or slow, or even in rhythmic patterns, but do not let the exercise run away with the exerciser. Be sure that there is real inspiration for each expiration. It is not just a matter of taking a deep breath and then exhaling it in a series of puffs. The student should be able to continue panting indefinitely.

135   In practicing this discipline the question of whether the epigastrium goes out or in may arise. This is not too important, though if the student does it simply, "bouncing" will be minimized. The chest breathers are the ones who suffer the serious confusion, and they must not be allowed to bulge the epigastrium at all. They should forget it and concentrate on the over-all motion of the abdomen.

136   Bad habits of chest collapse may be corrected by any one of various tricks to immobilize the shoulders. Lying on the floor has been mentioned. Standing against a wall and pressing the shoulders against it will do the same thing. Sitting with elbows on knees also forces one to breathe abdominally, but it is not a very desirable position for singing.

Back Breathing

137   Another cause for confusion, similar to the bouncing epigastrium and perhaps related to it, is the possibility of back breathing. Enlarging the ribcage is obviously necessary, and "expanding the diaphragm" is recognized by most teachers, but the real "secret of breath control" (supposedly) is "breathing in the back." This is a frequent assertion by singers and teachers, but I have been able to find only two places in the literature where authors have seriously attempted to explain it. These are Proschowsky and Shakespeare.

138   Proschowsky, on pp. 39 and 43, shows profile outlines of the trunk with the lumbar region marked "*a*," and on p. 43 he identifies this as the "point of relaxation in small of back from where breathing starts." This book is an interesting mixture of the scientific and the psychological, and I am inclined to think that the statement just quoted is a pseudo-scientific instruction whose effect is chiefly psychological. I can produce a bulge in the lumbar region, but not by relaxing. It is done in the same way that the epigastrium can be made to bulge: by maximum antagonism between the diaphragm and the abdominals.

139   Shakespeare (not the famous playwright, but a fine tenor and teacher who lived and wrote in England at the turn of our century) quotes Huxley, a top contemporary authority on

physiology, and goes on to give his own views as a singer. These views are excellent, practically speaking, but the scientific references to diagrams which are supplied sound like the report of an intelligent singer who has conferred with a competent physiologist, caught the general idea, missed many details and partially confused those he still remembers. On p. 12 we find a "front view of the chest" in which the muscles are identified only by letters to which he refers in his discussion. No muscles are named, but we gather that he approves of the use of serratus magnus and not pectoralis minor. Pectoralis major is not shown, but there is a curious in-nominatum, to look at it in the drawing, which would have to include subscapularis, teres major, and latissimus dorsi. A front view is not the best to show any of these muscles, but nowhere else are they shown. Subscapularis and teres may be dismissed as having nothing to do with breathing. We have serratus magnus and latissimus dorsi remaining, both *shoulder* muscles! (See Par. 107, 108).

140   On p. 16 Shakespeare gives practical breathing instructions, beginning with relaxation of the shoulders so that shoulder muscles will *not* be used.

> Now extend both arms forwards and outwards, keeping the elbows in, the palms of the hands upwards, and the thumbs in a line with the fingers, as though in the act of imploring. This position slightly twists the muscles under the shoulder blades, and shows us, while drawing in the breath, whether we are using the important back rib-raising muscles. . . . (It is generally recognized that the artist on the stage can sing better when acting or on the concert platform when holding the book well forward.)

All this can only refer to the use of latissimus dorsi. Our only conclusion can be that at this point Shakespeare deceived himself. He used shoulder muscles for inhalation and considered this all right as long as the shoulders were only pulled forward and not raised.

141   The use of this device to assist in the "holding" whereby expiratory muscles are opposed as long and as steadily as possible may be good. The big fault of the shoulder breather is that he pulls his shoulders up to inhale and simply collapses as soon as he begins to sing. I shall have more to say about this under the heading of "Breath Control." Incidentally, a man looks more broad-shouldered in front view when his shoulders are somewhat forward than when they are drawn back in the "position of a soldier."

Breath Control

142   Before considering the function of the larynx, a little special attention should be directed to the ideas implied by the expression, "breath control." Users of this phrase seem to think of the thorax not simply as the source of pressure for producing a good, full tone, but more specifically as a reservoir of raw material for sustaining tone for a long period of time without pause. They point to various passages in vocal literature where for either musical or literary reasons it seems desirable to include an unusual number of beats in one phrase. Singers who cannot manage this feat are said to lack "breath control." Those who can connect ordinary phrases without stopping for breath are admired. For example, there is the shameless trick of singing *"Die Rose, die Lillie,"* from *"Dichterliebe"* by Schumann, all on one breath.

143   It is true that overlong phrasing becomes a stunt and detracts from the artistic merit of the performance, but this should not be made an excuse for lack of control. First, there is the matter of getting enough breath with the inhalation. The principles of correct inspiration become all the more vital: the chest *must* be high at the outset, there *must* be sideward costal expansion, the abdomen *must* relax to allow the full descent of the diaphragm. This will not look to the audience like poor posture if the ribs are sufficiently expanded. A distended abdomen is a crime only when the chest is flat.

144   Second, there must be no waste of the breath. Short-winded singers often take in air with obvious effort toward maximum chest expansion, but with the first word the thorax collapses.

Some breath was thus lost on the first consonant, but the real catastrophe was that with the lowering of the ribs the abdomen and the diaphragm lost all their leverage for steady and controlled expiration. The *rectus abdominis* attaches in the middle and the *obliquus abdominis* at the sides to the lower ribs, and these bones should be held firmly in their elevated position while the heavy muscles of the belly, counterbalanced by the powerful diaphragm (the muscle of inhalation), smoothly maintain air pressure as the gas gradually escapes through the glottis. The lowering of the sides of the costal cage should come at the end, not the beginning of the phrase, as a final expenditure of the "complementary breath."

145   To put it more simply, take a deep breath, and then hold the chest high, *as if you were not expending any of the air at all*. Let inhalation be quick and intentional—studied—and exhalation be slow and subconscious—unstudied. That is, let the intercostals and the diaphragm resist the abdominals so that the exhalation will be so slow and steady you will scarcely be aware of it. This may involve some bulging of the epigastrium, a fetish of the "breath control" experts, but you may share the sensation of many singers of "sitting on the breath." It is like sitting on that beach ball I mentioned in Par. 132. I sometimes say inhaling is like inflating a doughnut-shaped rubber cushion, and sitting on it is the secret of breath control. This has been called "singing on the gesture of inhalation." In teaching this I sometimes make a fist and push it into the student's epigastrium while he attempts á long phrase. The muscular antagonism which he must set up in order to maintain a stiff epigastrium against my pressure often enables him to sing a considerably longer phrase. Some advocate "holding" the breath, a very descriptive misnomer. Be sure that the "holding" is done by the diaphragm and by the intercostals (or even by the shoulders, Par. 141) and *not by the larynx*. Rather than the latter it is better to be short-winded. For this reason breath control should not be taught until a free flowing tone is mastered. This may involve even waste of breath in the learning. (I refer to the "imaginary h" discussed in Chapter 3.) The expression *breath management* is preferred by many to *breath control* because it does not contradict the idea of freedom.

146   It is not only the amount of air in the lungs that determines whether or not you will be forced to take another breath; but also the purity of the air. When oxidization has progressed to a certain level, the phrenic nerve automatically contracts the diaphragm. As we all know, even when one holds his breath, not making a sound, his lungs full, sooner or later he will have to get rid of the carbon dioxide and replace it with more oxygen. In the excitement of singing, the lungs burn oxygen faster. This is why in learning a piece, long phrases are more difficult than they will be when they are more familiar. It also explains the shortness of breath one experiences before an audience. In concert, no matter how careful the singer is to take plenty of air with each inhalation, he finds himself mysteriously short if he is the least bit stage-frightened. It is not the air, it is the carbon dioxide content of the air.

147   To overcome the weakness of unfamiliarity the obvious solution is practice. The singer must be sure he knows his music thoroughly, and the difficult passages even more so. I am indebted to Frans Hoffman for an excellent psychological stratagem for teachers of breath control. He had his pupils learn long phrases backwards. That is, the last two measures are practiced first several times, then the last three, etc., adding to the length of the phrase until finally the student can begin at the beginning and go all the way through. The secret is that the last part of the phrase becomes so thoroughly familiar that in singing the whole thing in concert it becomes increasingly easy instead of difficult. There is no horrid memory of running short in the last measure, because throughout all the practice that part was always sung with plenty of breath.

148   The solution of the problem of stage-fright is more difficult. The singer should forearm himself against it by not planning on as long phrases in public as he can negotiate in private. If he can barely make a certain phrase in the studio, he should practice taking a breath in the best possible place in the middle of it. In concert he will need the breath, and if he has not prepared himself to take it, he may pass the place and be forced to gulp somewhere else where it will be

noticeable. In the case of the "Messiah" arias, it is accepted custom to breathe in the middle of words. In the case of lesser known works of the same period, the word can be finished and started again. The effect to the audience is that of a repetition for emphasis. The word must be worthy of repeating or it would not have been selected by the composer to be sustained so long. Incidentally, they breathed in the middle of some of those long runs even at the time they were written. Duey quotes three authorities from the Golden Age to this effect; Doni from the seventeenth, and Tosi and Manfredini from the eighteenth century (p. 75 and p. 78).

149   Vocalists and vocal pedagogs are overly conscious of phrasing. They notice how many breaths a performer takes, but the audience as a whole is not counting. If the singer heaves like an exhausted runner, they will notice it; but if the breaths are taken easily and in fairly reasonable places grammatically there can be many or few and it is of small moment artistically. The better the music, and the finer the dramatic sense of the performer, the more this is true. Many a fine singer continues to hold the concert stage long after the voice has passed its prime and the breath is short, simply by virtue of artistry.

Exercises for Breath Control

150   The following exercise is beneficial and often recommended: Inhale slowly, while counting five; hold the breath while counting ten; exhale slowly, while counting five; repeat indefinitely. This may be done while walking, a step for each count. Variations may be improvised, gradually increasing the length of time the breath can be held. However, the regular repetition is important. There is no virtue in abstaining for a minute and a half if you are gasping for the next ten.

151   The above should lead to a second exercise, taking the breath quickly and then spinning it out through partially closed lips making the expiration as long as possible. This is more comparable to the singing situation. The sudden inhalation is helped by imagining that you have just been pleasantly surprised. The "surprise breath" not only is quick and deep, but it also, by reflex action, usually produces the best adjustment of the throat. (Par. 247a) This is one of the "natural aids" to singing. However, if you find that a pupil, either through lack of imagination or through wrong habit, does not inhale "naturally" according to correct principles, better forget the whole thing and work the problem out some other way.

152   Finally, any exercise that improves the physique will make for better singing. There is probably no other skill in which general fatigue or debility will show more plainly. Of course, pursuits that build the body but endanger the organs involved in singing must be foregone. This applies to swimming, one of the best exercises physically, but injurious to the ear. Any book or article on calisthenics will furnish several technics of strengthening the abdominal muscles, and this is the foundation of breath control, indeed, of singing.

Chapter 3

ATTACK

153   Breathing *per se* is a dull subject, and even mastery of it will not insure good singing. Athletes frequently have enlarged their vital capacity to maximum, can hold their breath longer than most singers, and are otherwise superior in this department, but still sing poorly. Also fine singers can be found whose technic is unorthodox, even poor. The important part is coordinating the breath pressure with the vibrator, which Louis Bachner called "hookup." This is epitomized in the attack. A lesson on breathing should never consist of silent breathing exercises only. They should always be followed by practice in correct attack.

154   Much of the material of this chapter appeared first in The N.A.T.S. Bulletin, February 1961 and February 1963, and is reproduced by permission. To understand it we need to know some facts about the lungs and the larynx, though a fully detailed study of the latter will come in Chapter 4.

The Lungs and the Larynx

155   The channel through which the air enters the thorax is called the *trachea* or *windpipe*. It is a tube made up of rings of *cartilage*, or *gristle*, which keep it open for the passage of air. Cartilage is rather unyielding, though not quite as stiff as bone. The hose of a vacuum cleaner usually has rings in it which stiffen it in much the same manner as the cartilages of the trachea. The tube is both flexible and distensible. The rings are not complete, but are open at the back, and this space is filled with muscular and membranous tissue.

156   The muscles instinctively tighten and reduce the diameter of the windpipe somewhat on exhalation and relax on inhalation. There is nothing to be done about this, of course, but it is a part of a larger picture of tenseness throughout the vocal tract during exhalation, and hence during phonation. One of the big problems of teaching is the conditioning of this reflex as much as possible in the direction of release during singing. It gives meaning to the concept of "singing on the gesture of inhalation." We have already noted this idea with reference to breath control (Par. 145) and we shall be reminded of it when it comes to the adjustment of the resonators.

157   The trachea divides into two branches, known as *bronchi*, and the bronchi subdivide further into bronchial tubes which break into smaller vessels, etc., until we have a mass of spongy material so thin-walled that oxygen filters right through into the blood stream. This spongy mass is called the *lungs*. It is in two parts, or *lobes*, one for each bronchus. It has no muscular strength, and its form is determined by the shape of the *thorax* (ribs and diaphragm) and the pressure of the air which enters it. The only other major organ in the chest is the heart.

158   There is a valve at the top of the trachea, to retain the air as long as it is needed. This valve consists of two muscles that stretch from front to back of a cartilaginous structure, called the *larynx*. Each muscle has two folds. The two upper folds are called *ventricular bands*, or the *false vocal cords*. The primary function of the false cords, or *superior folds*, is to assist the *inferior folds* in closing the valve tightly. In normal phonation they do not close, but in whispering they assist the true cords, and sometimes they actually phonate. In this way a person may sing two pitches at once, one note with the true and the other with the false cords. However this

is rare, and control of either pitch or quality is even more so. Almost anyone can produce two or more pitches simultaneously with practice, but this is usually done by causing the vocal folds to vibrate in two portions simultaneously. In the laboratory of Janwillem van den Berg, Groningen, I have heard excised larynges producing diplophonia (two tones at once) even after the false cords were removed. Diplophonia is somewhat dangerous, by the way, and should not be practised, even though it is amusing.

Phonation

159   The lower folds are called by many names, commonly the *vocal cords*, but much more descriptively: *Vocal folds, vocal lips, vocal shelves, vocal bands*, even *vocal wedges*. The space between the two halves of the valve is called the *glottis*, and hence the lower folds are also called *glottal lips, glottal bands*, etc. It is well to understand at the outset that they are not "cords," and they do not function like the strings of a violin. The derivation of this unfortunate expression will be explained when I describe the larynx in greater detail, but for the time being let us think of the mechanism purely as a valve, since this is its primary use.

160   Singing is a secondary, or superimposed function of the larynx. All animals that breathe, whether they phonate or not, have a valve to hold breath and to keep food from entering the lungs. Above the muscular folds just described is a leaf-shaped cartilage, called the epiglottis, which folds down over the larynx to complete the closure when one swallows and to make sure that the food will go behind into the *esophagus*. When one is not swallowing, this lid of the voice box stands up more or less vertically, and holding of the breath is accomplished by the approximation of the muscular folds. (See Fig. 14)

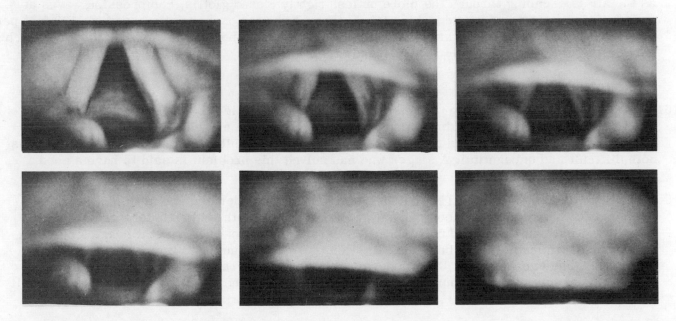

Fig. 14. Movement of Epiglottis
Bell Telephone Photographs, courtesy of Brodnitz. Epiglottis (lit.: over the glottis) comes down instinctively whenever there is any danger of a foreign body entering, and also whenever exertion reaches a certain level, as in loud singing. It can be seen how difficult it is to get good photos of the glottis, especially under certain conditions of interest to singers. Here the vocal cords are separated, forming an inverted V. For phonation the cartilages which are at the back ends of the cords (bottom of picture) are drawn together, closing the glottis (Fig. 17).

161   For various purposes, the valve must prevent movement of the breath. For one thing, whenever heavy work is performed, like lifting, the thorax must be immobilized to provide a better

fulcrum for the levers (arms) that operate. That is why men sometimes grunt when exerting physical effort; the grunting is the slipping of the valve. It usually happens not during the effort, but at the moment of relaxing. The valve is also needed for the important act of defecation. The combined action of the abdominal muscles and the diaphragm force the waste matter from the body, and the ascent of the diaphragm is prevented by inflating the lungs and holding the breath.

162   As a secondary function, many animals make noises with the valve. These sounds have purpose, and in man they become an art. Art is an improvement upon nature. I do not find useful the concept that singing should be "natural." First of all, no one knows what is "natural;" it is merely an expression that one applies to what is habitual. Second, there are many natural functions (in the sense that they are instinctive) that do not aid singing, and it is only as one learns to overcome these tendencies that one sings well. So I shall not try to justify my precepts by saying that they are natural. It is true that art is greatest when it "looks natural," but this is one of the most difficult accomplishments.

163   In phonation, the false vocal cords relax, and only the true vocal lips are brought together. The resistance they offer to the breath causes it to vibrate as it is forced through the valve by the action of the intercostal muscles plus the abdominals, controlled or steadied by the diaphragm. The objective here is a maintenance of pressure by a flow of breath. The actual rate of expulsion is faster than that of an oboist and slower than that of a trumpeter, and the difference lies in the resistence offered by the vibrator in each case. Guard against the misconception that breath carries the tone throughout the auditorium. The actual breath goes only a short way and is moving slowly, as has been proved by various scientific experiments. But as the air is escaping through the more or less tightly closed glottis, compression waves at audible frequencies are created which travel through the atmosphere at a speed of 1100 feet per second. It is the elasticity of air that determines this speed, not the flow of breath. That which travels is not air, but *energy* from released air *pressure*.

The Attack

164   The problem of the singer, then, is to make the most efficient balance between the contraction of the muscles of breathing and the tension in the muscles of the valve. Proper adjustment should be achieved at once, since readjustment while the tone is being produced is both difficult and unbeautiful. A singer who has solved this problem is said to have a good *attack*.

165   The two extremes of incorrect balance which must be moderated are *breathiness* and *tightness*. If the valve is too loose and allows a waste of breath, either before or during the tone, it will lack intensity and brilliance. A variable amount of rustling that creates no vibration but uses air rapidly will be heard. If it comes at the beginning it is recognizable as the letter "H." The two extremes, breathiness and tightness, correlate rather well with the two different concepts of embouchure discussed in Par. 54. It is now time to explain the Bernoulli Effect more fully.

The Bernoulli Effect

166   I am indebted to Robert Taylor for calling my attention to this fact of physics. He makes the point that in this age of science it is easier to convince students of singing not to use excess muscularity if one proves that the glottis can be vibrated by breath alone, that even the closing of the glottis can be accomplished partly by flow of air.

167   If Taylor has been somewhat of a voice crying "Bernoulli" in the wilderness of voice pedagogy, he has not been alone in the world of voice science. Van den Berg[3], *et al.,* wrote an

abstruse article on the subject for the *Journal of the Acoustical Society of America,* and others have mentioned the Bernoulli Effect in explaining vibratory phenomena (Moore[2], Timcke, von Leden).

168   The principle which Bernoulli enunciated has many applications. It is a lifting force in aviation, and it creates the suction needed in atomizers, as well as being a factor in the vibrators of wind instruments. An easy demonstration of it is illustrated in Fig. 15. If you will hold a letter-size sheet of paper against your chin (Fig. 15 A) and blow, the paper will rise to a horizontal position (Fig. 15 B). The reason for this is that when a gas (or a liquid, for that matter) is in motion it exerts less than its normal pressure upon its surrounding environment. In Fig. 15 A, atmospheric pressure (represented by the arrows) is normal on both sides of the paper, so gravity pulls it down. In Fig. 15 B, pressure is reduced above the paper by the motion of the air, and therefore the normal pressure below is sufficient to raise the paper.

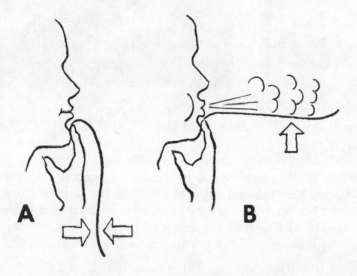

Fig. 15. Demonstration of Bernoulli Effect

169   Fig. 16 is a diagram of an atomizer. Air (or water, as in the case of the insecticide spray often used with garden hose) is moving from left to right in the drawing. The tube narrows, which causes the flow to be even faster in passing this point. Just here is the opening of a tube which goes down into a jar containing the liquid that is to be sprayed. Reduced pressure caused by the flow of air (or water) above draws the liquid up into the current, and it is blown out of the atomizer.

170   Now turn Fig. 16 on its side and see how the atomizer parallels the cross-section of the windpipe and larynx shown in the tomogram (courtesy of van den Berg). The under surface of the vocal folds is funnel-shaped. Indeed, the membrane lining it is called the *conus elasticus.* When the vocal folds (vocal cords) are fairly close to each other there is a narrowing of the air passage sufficient for the Bernoulli Effect to draw them together, if the breath is flowing at the same time.

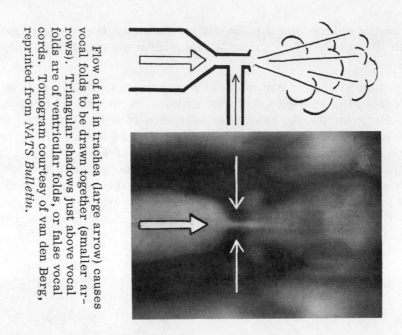

Flow of air in trachea (large arrow) causes vocal folds to be drawn together (smaller arrows). Triangular shadows just above vocal folds are of ventricular folds, or false vocal cords. Tomogram courtesy of van den Berg, reprinted from *NATS Bulletin.*

Fig. 16. Diagram of Atomizer Compared with Tomogram of Larynx

The Bernoulli Effect in Laughing

171   As a matter of fact, in laughter the vocal muscles are sucked together in just this way. Moore and von Leden[3] have published a careful study of the kind of laughter that is expressed in writing commonly as: "Ha-ha-ha." Fig. 17 shows frames from a high-speed motion picture taken by them of the closing of the glottis for one of these "Ha's." In these pictures the arytenoid cartilages are seen at the bottom and the vocalis muscles are at the top.

172   You may find the next few paragraphs a little technical if you have not studied laryngeal physiology before, and if such is the case you will want to reread them after you have absorbed the material in Chapter 4. Meanwhile, I believe you will still be able to follow the essentials of the present discussion. The vocal cords, as we call them, are complex structures the forward part of which is muscular (with ligamentous edges) and the rear part of which is cartilage. The muscles are always together at the front end (top of our pictures) since they arise from the angle of the thyroid cartilage, but the glottis is opened or closed by movements of the arytenoid cartilages, which are controlled by three sets of muscles other than the vocalis muscles.

173   In Fig. 17 A, the glottis is rather widely open, and throughout the series C-L the arytenoids are closing at a nearly constant rate, but the vocalis muscles are doing something else. The Bernoulli Effect is drawing them together more rapidly than the arytenoids are approaching each other. At D they almost touch. However, their elasticity is such that they pull apart again (E-H), after which the suction of the flow of air brings them toward each other again (I-L). In L the *muscular* glottis is closed, though the *cartilaginous* glottis is still partly open. Moore and von Leden report that actually the muscular glottis completed two more vibrations, closing tightly and remaining closed for a longer time than the open phase, *before the cartilages came together* (Fig. 18).

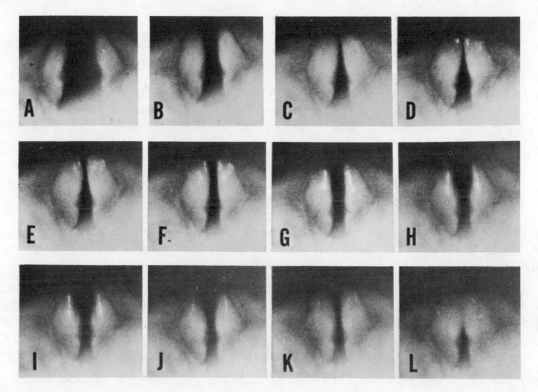

Fig. 17. Vocal Folds in Very Light Aspirate Attack
Fastax camera sequence by Paul Moore[2] and Hans von Leden, from *Folia Phoniatrica* and *NATS Bulletin*. Wide spaces between A, B, and C, indicate that frames have been omitted. From C to L pictures are roughly every other frame from movie.

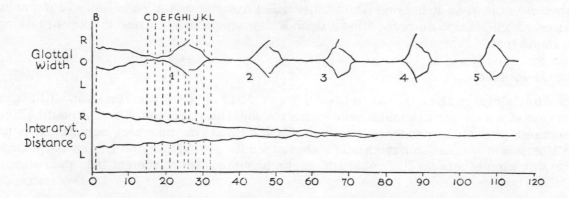

Fig. 18. Graph of Movements of Vocal Folds and Arytenoids in Aspirate Attack
Graph of movements taken from Fastax camera sequence represented in Fig. 17. Reprinted by permission from *Folia Phoniatrica* and *NATS Bulletin*. Number of frames 0-120 indicated at bottom. Distance between mid-points of muscular folds as measured in each frame is shown in upper graph. Five separate complete vibratory movements can be noted. Distance between arytenoid cartilages is shown in lower graph. Notice that there are three vibrations of the muscular (or ligamentous glottis) before the arytenoids are fully approximated. Fig. 17A is a frame that came before this graph. Vertical broken lines show where the other frames belong on this graph. Fig. 17B is frame 1; Fig. 17C is frame 15, etc.

Two Concepts of Vibration

174   This is how vibration is initiated by the aspirate [h]. Breath is flowing while the glottis is closing by action of the interarytenoid muscles. When the vocal muscles are nearly enough together, the Bernoulli Effect sucks them into vibration before the cartilages have fully closed. After the cartilages have been approximated (it may even be an imperfect approximation) the sequence of aerodynamic factors is as follows: first the flow of breath sucks the glottis shut; this stops the flow momentarily, whereupon breath pressure blows the glottis open again; air flow recommences and the cycle repeats.

175   This is rather different from the way the vibration has usually been described. In fact, I myself have written, Par. 54, "The lips hold back the breath until its pressure becomes greater than their tension. Then a minute puff of air escapes, reducing the pressure to the point where the lip tension can stop the flow of breath again." The concept here is one of muscle *tension* resisting breath *pressure*. No account is taken of *suction*. The old idea is part myoelastic; the new one does not deny the muscular factors, but neither does it depend upon them—it is completely aerodynamic, throwing the emphasis upon breath flow.

176   You can demonstrate purely aerodynamic vibration by holding two sheets of paper to your lips and blowing between them. Hold the sheets vertically, one in each hand. They may fall apart, but when you blow they will be drawn together and will begin to vibrate. The Bernoulli Effect brings them together. This stops the flow of air, so they are blown apart only to be sucked together again immediately, and the cycle repeats itself as long as you keep blowing.

177   Actually we must combine both of these ideas in our concept of phonation. Voice is a myoelastic-aerodynamic phenomenon (van den Berg[4]). But our teaching should emphasize *breath* rather than *muscle*. The difference of emphasis is epitomized in the two different ways in which it is possible to attack a vowel. This is one detail of singing upon which I allow myself to be a perfectionist.

178   There are two acts which must synchronize in attacking a vowel. The interarytenoid muscles must close the glottis (with cooperation from other laryngeal muscles) and the breath must flow. If the two acts synchronize perfectly, we have the perfect *simultaneous attack* or *instantaneous attack,* as it is sometimes called. But assuming that a student will not achieve perfection, which act should come first? Upon which act should he concentrate, breathing or closing the throat?

The Glottal Plosive

179   If the glottis closes first, and then breath pressure is applied, the vibration will begin with an explosion of air as the pressure overcomes the muscular tension. The Bernoulli Effect will then become a part of the process, it is true, but too late. The muscular adjustment is not the same. Moore and von Leden have also photographed the *glottal plosive* (which is the phonetic term for this kind of attack, Par. 428) and shown how much more violent it is than an aspirate attack.

180   Fig. 19 was prepared by Paul Moore. The first picture, A, corresponds roughly to Fig. 17 B, and shows the glottis closing. Notice that the arytenoid cartilages are not parallel and meet at the vocal processes first, Fig. 19 B. Friction is thus created between the vocal processes as the cartilages are further drawn together, and sometimes repeated glottal plosives actually produce contact ulcers between the cartilages. In Fig. 19 C the closing of the glottis is complete and its tenseness is shown by the fact that the laryngeal collar is closing over the glottis. The epiglottis (upper right) is descending and the cartilages of Santorini are moving in (bottom of picture). The false cords, or ventricular bands, are closing over the true cords on each side.

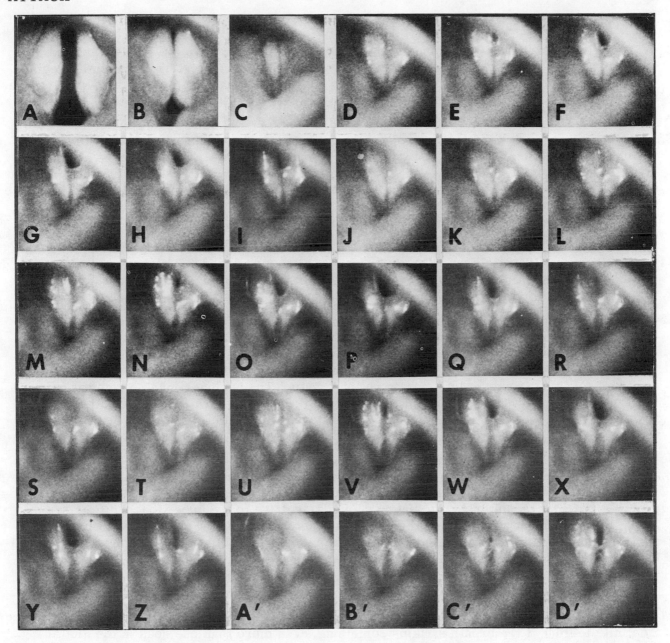

Fig. 19. Vocal Folds in Glottal Plosive
Fastax camera sequence by Paul Moore, *NATS Bulletin*. Wide spaces between first four
pictures indicate that frames are omitted. Beginning with D, frames are consecutive.

Dr. Moore writes that a few frames later the true cords were completely obscured. The
glottal plosive is really a slight cough. The whole larynx tenses for it. The explosion is one
which laryngologists agree is damaging to the delicate structures.

181   The remaining pictures in Fig. 19, beginning with D, are consecutive frames taken at 4000
per second, and they show the first $3\frac{1}{2}$ cycles of vibration. Notice the constriction. The glottis
opens only partially, the cartilages remaining tightly held. Only in the 4th cycle (just beginning
in the last picture, lower right) does the whole glottis open. Dr. Moore writes that in some
films in his laboratory as many as 22 cycles of vibration elapse before the full cords become
active.

The Imaginary Aspirate

182   The attack which develops freedom in the laryngeal adjustment is the one in which the flow of breath begins first, and then the glottis is closed to meet it. The vibration actually begins with the Bernoulli Effect, and the adjustment of the muscles that bring the vocal cords together need never be as tense as with the glottal plosive. The result is truly "singing on the breath." In the Bernoulli Effect, we find the scientific explanation of this classic empirical concept.

183   The objection is sometimes raised that an aspirate attack results in a breathy tone. I am willing to concede that in cases of extreme breathiness the glottal plosive may be a means of overcoming this fault, but it is a dangerous remedy. The glottal rattle, (Par. 195) or "fry" as the speech authorities call it, is better. However, the aspirate attack need not be breathy. Indeed, there can be a very complete reaction from the breathiness of the $[h]$ to the clarity of the vowel. Think of the laugh for a moment. Breath flows generously between the "ha's" but the vowel sounds themselves are loud and clear.

184   I believe in deliberately using an exaggerated $[h]$ in many cases. It makes sure of a relaxed valve. In contrast then it is followed by a sudden, firm, loud vowel. In staccato work the valve is then immediately loosened again before tenseness has time to develop.

185   Of course, an audible $[h]$ is only a crutch for learning the correct attack. Once there is a clear, crisp initiating of the vowel, the amount of time and breath that is wasted in the $[h]$ should be reduced until finally there is only an "imaginary h." Mynard Jones calls this the "unaspirated h." I am sure that insistence upon this kind of vowel attack is the most direct means of teaching freedom, or "singing on the breath." The beginner may not achieve a much more pleasing tone with the "imaginary h" than he does with a careless glottal plosive, but vowels initiated with the "imaginary h" have a future. The glottal plosive only leads to more tension.

186   The "imaginary h" is not limited in its usefulness to the attack alone. It promotes freedom wherever it may be needed. For example, one often hears a singer insert an aspirate in making an ascending leap on the same vowel. This is poor in performance, but profitable in practice. *Without* the aspirate the singer may simply drive to the upper tone with the same laryngeal adjustment as he had on the lower one, just be increasing the tension in it. *With* the aspirate the lower tone is released and a new adjustment is achieved for the higher one. When it has been learned, the aspirate becomes unnecessary, but it must still be *imagined!*

The Stroke of the Glottis

187   The attack by means of $[h]$ can be every bit as crisp as the glottal plosive. In fact, one has a definite feeling of the breath striking something, even more than one does in the glottal plosive. In other words, the closing by means of the Bernoulli suction may well be what was originally intended by the expression "stroke of the glottis." The connotation was not objectionable at first, but as the expression became corrupted to mean glottal plosive, it lost favor. For this reason it is well to avoid using the phrase "glottal stroke," because one can never be sure what it means to the other person.

188   Garcia advocated the *coup de glotte* and described it as a plosive, comparing it to the consonant $[p]$. However he also said: "It is very necessary to guard against confusing the articulation or stroke of the glottis with the stroke of the chest which resembles a cough, or the effort that one makes to expel from the gullet something that disturbs it." *(Il faut bien se garder de confondre l'articulation ou le coup de la glotte avec le coup de poitrine qui ressemble à la toux, ou à l'effort que l'on fait pour expulser du gosier quelque chose qui le gêne,* Garcia, p. 11). We can see with the aid of Fastax photography that the glottal plosive really is

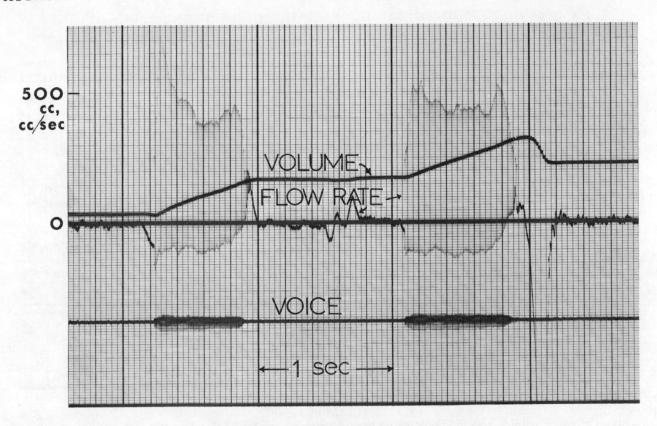

Fig. 20. Graph of Glottal Plosive
        Bottom graph, made by microphone, shows actual sound vibration patterns for two tones
attacked with glottal plosive. Middle graph, flow rate, actually records the individual puffs of air
corresponding to the microphone pattern, though this is almost too delicate to reproduce in print.
Upper graph, volume, shows the total amount of air exhaled. Gross flow rate can be computed
from this line also, since when there is *no* flow it will be flat, and when there *is* flow it will slope
upward, steepness of slope increasing with flow rate. From *NATS Bulletin*.

a cough, the difference is only one of degree. On the other hand, the "imaginary aspirate" when
seen with the unaided eye in the laryngeal mirror (which is all Garcia had) looks very much
like lips making a plosive.

189   I am convinced that Garcia did not mean the *glottal plosive* when he coined the expression
coup de glotte. The term has since been corrupted, and would best not be used. It is probably
impossible to restore the original meaning. The best we can do is to absolve Garcia from the
responsibility for its present usage. The expression "imaginary h" or "imaginary aspirate" is
recommended as pedagogically useful and accurately descriptive of the desirable attack.

Pneumotachograms of Various Attacks

190   Recently a *pneumotachograph* has been devised which measures the rate and amount of
breath flow accurately and registers it graphically so that it can be seen on paper and comparisons can be made between breath flow under different conditions. The principle of this
instrument is this: If resistance is offered to the air flow, by having it pass through a fine wire
screen, the pressure in the air on the near side of the screen will be greater than the pressure
after it has passed through. A subject sings into a tube which catches all of his breath. This is
insured either by having him hold his nostrils or by providing a face-piece like that of an in-

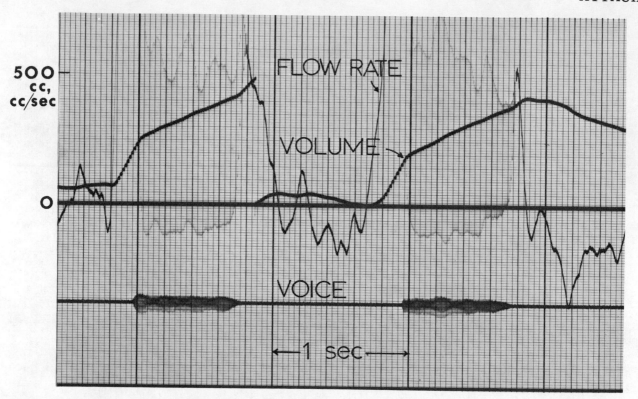

Fig. 21. Graph of Aspirate

Steep slope of volume graph shows rapid breath expenditure immediately before phonation. In the first case it is 140 cubic centimeters in 0.15 second (flow rate 940 cc/sec) and in the second case it is 180 cc in 0.25 sec (flow rate 720 cc/sec). Flow rate was high enough to cause turbulence of breath, which made aspirate audible. From *NATS Bulletin*.

halator which fits over both nose and mouth. The air passing through the tube goes through a 400-mesh monel wire screen, which is heated electrically to prevent condensation of moisture. Small tubes take air pressure from each side of the screen to a highly sensitive strain gauge transducer, which measures the pressure drop. The resistance is so small the singer is unaware of it. The result is reproduced on a moving strip of sensitized paper. The signal from a microphone is also reproduced on another channel on the same paper.

191   Nobuhiko Isshiki has constructed a pneumotachograph with which he was kind enough to record a variety of attacks as I produced them. Fig. 20 is the graph of a glottal plosive. The line representing breath expenditure is flat (indicating no expulsion) until the moment of the attack, as registered in the microphone tracing at the bottom of the figure.

192   Fig. 21 shows an aspirate attack, in which there is a rapid flow of breath for up to a quarter of a second before the beginning of the vowel sound. Air flow can be either *laminar* (smooth) or *turbulent*. When the flow rate increases beyond a certain point, other factors being constant, the flow becomes turbulent, forming eddies which are audible—in this case, the phoneme [h]. The phenomenon is heard when one turns on a gas jet. The flow is silent until it is great enough to produce turbulence.

193   Fig. 22 shows an "imaginary h." This comes nearer meeting the conditions described by Garcia for the coup de glotte than any other attack in this study. There is a flow of breath for a quarter of a second before the tone begins, but the ear does not detect an aspirate sound

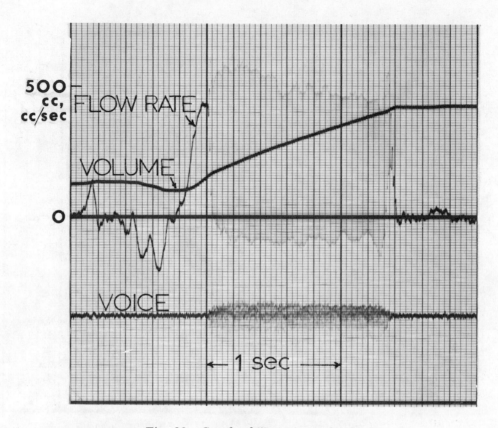

Fig. 22. Graph of "Imaginary h"
Similar to aspirate, except that breath expenditure is much less, 60 cc in 0.25 sec (flow rate 240 cc/sec). At this rate there was no turbulence and the [h] was inaudible. From *NATS Bulletin*.

because the rate is lower and the flow is smooth. This momentary flow sucks together the vocal folds so smartly that there is a sensation of the breath striking them. There is as much clarity in the beginning of the sound as in the case of most glottal plosives, and indeed the two attacks can easily be confused in the ear unless careful and discriminating attention is given. However, both the sound and the sensation of the glottal plosive are decidedly different from those of the "imaginary h." If one will note the clarity and actually percussive sound of each utterance in a laugh one is reminded of how definite such an attack can be.

194   It is interesting to note that following a plosive surd (like [t] or [p]) there is an "incidental h" (Judson and Weaver, p. 184). Fig. 23 shows the breath expenditure for the syllable [pa]. The flat line before the plosive is the same as in Fig. 20, and following this before the onset of the vowel itself (as seen in the microphone tracing) there appears a curve like that of the "imaginary h." Its duration is 0.08 seconds. Many teachers use plosive consonants to insure a good adjustment of the breath and the larynx. Indeed, for those students who may not have the patience to learn a good coup de glotte, a plosive consonant (other than the glottal plosive, of course) is a useful substitute. It is also useful for group work, under circumstances where it may not be desirable to attempt to teach a good glottal stroke.

The Rattle or Scrape of the Glottis

195   Coughing is an illustration of the wrong kind of "stroke," which has been called the "glottal shock." Garcia's formula for obtaining "the sensation of the glottic action" was: "Coughing

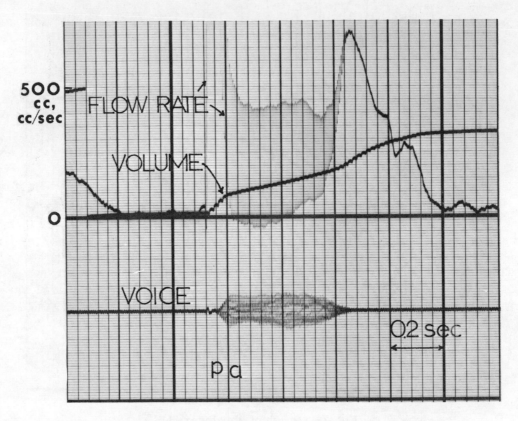

Fig. 23. Graph of Labial Plosive followed by Incidental h
The syllable [pa]. Note silent breath flow between [p] and [a] similar to "imaginary h."
From *NATS Bulletin*.

almost imperceptibly," (Garcia[2], p. 5). This gentle "popping," however, far from being a shock, is a beneficial exercise for the muscles of the valve. The single "pops," which must be very gentle and without apparent movement of any of the organs of speech, can be speeded into a "rattle," or "glottal scrape." According to Allan Rogers Lindquest, the "glottal scrape" or *scraspning* was a part of the method of Gillis Bratt, the great Swedish authority. This exercise is especially good for breathy pupils. A breathy tone can hardly be initiated by the tension required for the rattle. However, it is an ideal tension which adjusts the glottis without tightening the throat, and as such benefits students who are too tense. The voiceless rattle may rumble into a tone by adding phonation. This approach is the opposite of that described in Par. 182. The "imaginary h" is more suitable for attacking high notes, where tension is a danger, and the "rattle" is better for low notes, indeed it builds the low part of the range. It is especially beneficial for low voices.

196   As a transition from breathing exercises, you may care to have your pupils do panting exercises, followed by staccato attacks. Teach them to close the valve at exactly the right moment to meet the abdominal thrust. If they do not synchronize perfectly, let the error be on the side of too much [h] rather than not enough. Hope that they are not sophisticated enough to be confused by the "red herring" of the bouncing epigastrium. Follow the staccato work with combined staccato and legato work. I sometimes use this simile: The work is done by the muscles at the bottom of the lungs. They are like the bell-ringer at the bottom of the tower. He pulls the rope and the bell rings at the top. Make sure that your bell rings high in the head, or out in front of the mouth, not in the throat.

197   I ask singers to "blow out four candles" (which is another way to do panting) followed by four "imaginary h's." We establish a regular cadence, counting in fours and repeating indefinitely. After a little of this we add a sustained tone at the end of the exercise, attempting to get the feeling of "sitting on the breath," (Par. 145). The trick is to inhale for the sustained tone in the same manner as one would to blow out a candle, but not to make the wasteful ex-halatory gesture. A certain amount of breath may be wasted in learning the correct attack, but once the trick of singing "on the breath" has been mastered the singer will discover that his sustained tone is very efficient and can be prolonged satisfactorily. The law of the Bernoulli Effect is such that a timid application of breath can simply "leak" through, but a bold applica-tion sucks the glottis shut promptly and creates the needed pressure for the voice with neither excess muscle tension nor waste of air.

Mental Preparation for the Attack

198   Before leaving our consideration of the attack, we should note that of course the ear monitors the entire process. This means that the correct attack should be conceived in the ear *before* the act. Many teachers quite rightly lay great emphasis on the mental concept as a prerequisite of all technic. This includes all that has been said thus far, and also the matter of pitch. The deplorable habit of "scooping" is the result of not thinking ahead and hence having to tune the tone after it has begun. Actually, the entire musical phrase should be conceived in advance. With gifted students one may take for granted that mental preset will take place, but with others perhaps the most important responsibility of the teacher is to insist that they look before they leap, or rather, think before they sing.

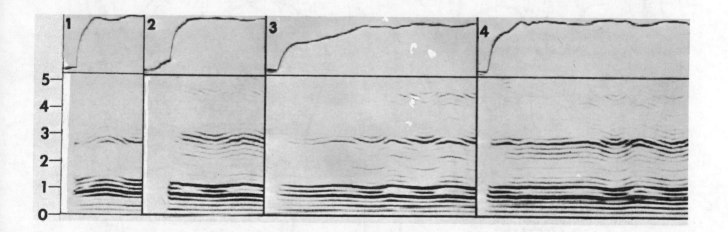

Fig. 23.5. Sonagrams of Different Attacks

From van den Berg[6] and Vennard, *NATS Bulletin*. Pitch E_3, bass clef. 1, Glottal plosive, 0.3 sec. 2, Aspirate attack, 0.42 sec. 3, "Imaginary [h]," soft attack, 0.77 sec. 4, "Imagi-nary [h]," with an attempt to make it as abrupt as the glottal plosive, 0.77 sec. Lines at the top record intensity. Sonagraphy is discussed in Par. 458.

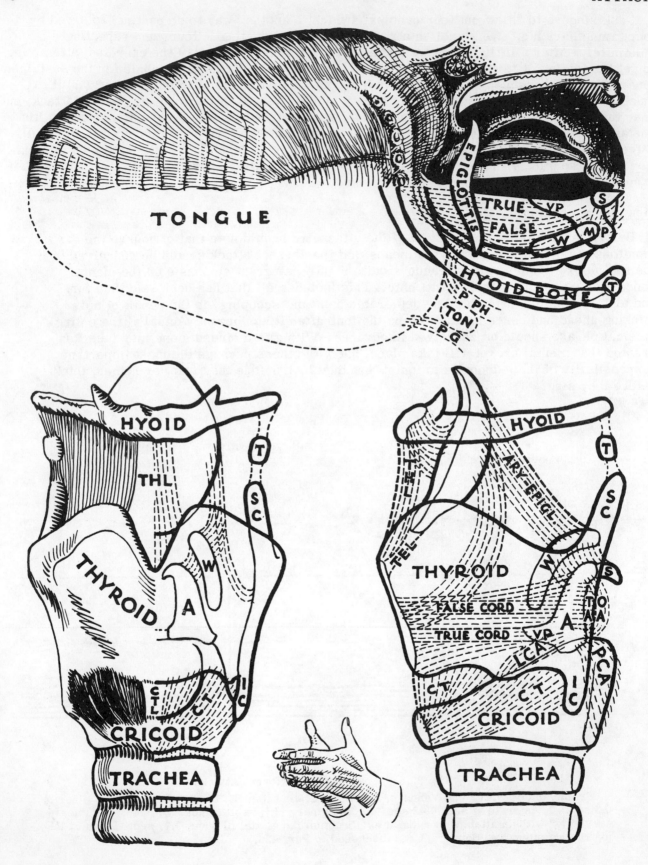

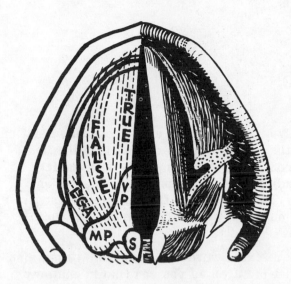

Fig. 24. Anatomy of the Larynx.

Above, left: Top view including tongue.
Above, right: Top view, hyoid bone and epiglottis
                removed, false cord cut away to show
                lateral cricoarytenoid.
Bottom, left to Right: Front, side, rear views.

In each drawing, right half of larynx is rendered
realistically; left, diagrammatically. Straightedged
mirror laid along midline will complete either rendering.
Cartilages are shown with solid lines, as if transparent,
lines being light when they are seen through a nearer
cartilage. Muscles, etc., are indicated by broken lines.
Glottis is shown open as in whispering or as it might be
when closing to begin phonation. Sketch between front
and side views shows how hands may assume shape of
thyroid.

A, arytenoid c.
CC, ceratocricoid m.
CT, cricothyroid m.
CTL, cricothyroid ligament
IC, inferior cornu
LCA, lateral cricoarytenoid m.
MP, muscular process
OA, oblique arytenoid m.
PCA, posterior cricoarytenoid m.
PG, palatoglossus m.
PPH, palatopharyngeus m.
S, c. of Santorini
SC, superior cornu
T, triticeal c.
TA, transverse arytenoid m.
TEL, thyroepiglottic ligament
THL, thyrohyoid ligament
TON, faucial tonsil
VP, vocal process
W, c. of Wrisberg

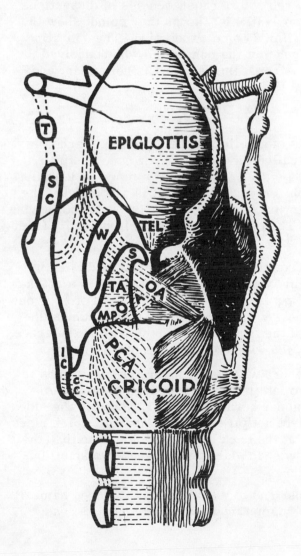

Chapter 4

REGISTRATION

199   So far we have thought of the larynx merely as a valve, and phonation as a secondary function resulting from the fact that when the valve holds back the breath imperfectly a vibration is produced. All this is true, but the phenomenon is far from being that simple. A wide variety of tones can emerge from the vibrator, depending on its adjustment alone and quite apart from any modification by the resonators which are above. In order to understand this important phase of singing, which is commonly called *registration,* we must study the larynx in greater detail. (See Fig. 24)

200   It is difficult to get a satisfactory concept of the larynx from words or even from two-dimensional pictures. I recommend that you study as many flat pictures as you can find in anatomy texts, and if possible see the beautiful Viewmaster stereo color transparencies of dissections by David L. Bassett. Good commercial models are also available, though they do not show the cricoarytenoid articulation too well. An instructional film, "Voice Production—The Vibrating Larynx," shows forty-two minutes of detail. The chairman of the committee who conceived it was Janwillem van den Berg, and the other members were D. Burger, C. C. Shervanian, and myself. Much of what follows is from the script of that film.

The Framework of the Larynx

201   We find the voice-box is composed of two large bits of gristle. At the top of the trachea is one more ring-like cartilage, larger than the others, called the *cricoid cartilage.* It is oval, with the long axis from front to back, and shaped like a signet ring, having a more or less flat rectangular plate extending upward at the back. It is the only cartilage that is a complete ring, closed at the back. The other large cartilage of the larynx is the *thyroid.* It is V-shaped, having two sides *(lamina)* or wings *(alae)*, fused at the front. The opening at the back is partially filled by the plate of the cricoid.

202   The point of the thyroid cartilage often protrudes under the skin of the throat and is called the *Adam's Apple.* When you feel yours with your finger, you may notice that there is a notch at the top, where the two wings do not join. If you will put the ring and little fingers of your one hand against those of the other, leaving a few inches between palms and extending thumbs upward your hands will roughly approximate the shape of the thyroid. The notch will be the space between index fingers. The thumbs will represent the *superior cornua,* or upper horns.

203   Unless you suffer the deformity of polydactylism, there will be no fingers on your hands to represent the *inferior cornua,* but you can imagine two lower horns extending downward, directly below your thumbs. They are shorter than the upper horns, and are attached to the sides of the cricoid by ligaments and muscles, forming a pivot not far from the flat plate which rises from the ring of the cricoid and partly fills the space at the back of the thyroid. Near the corners of this plate, on the top edge of the cricoid, one on each side, are attached two small but most important cartilages called the *arytenoids.*

204   Thus we have four important cartilages to remember and to visualize, having three names: First, *cricoid,* from a Greek word meaning "ring," a symmetrical, but single part. Second,

thyroid, meaning "shield," two halves that fuse at the front. Third, *arytenoid,* meaning "ladle," a pair of small cartilages that are ladle-shaped. But they are more irregular in shape than ladles. Each has three *processes* or prongs. Each has a prong extending forward toward the thyroid notch, called the *vocal* or *glottal process.* On either side, one extending to the left of the left arytenoid and the other to the right of the right arytenoid, are the *muscular processes.* The upward projection of each is called the *head,* or *apex.* Attached flexibly to the apex is another cartilage which curves backward like the handle of the ladle, or like a horn. They are called *corniculate* (horn-like) *cartilages,* and are named for Santorini, who discovered them. In pictures of the larynx we judge what the arytenoids are doing by what we see of the cartilages of Santorini. These and the vocal processes are all we see of the arytenoids in the laryngeal mirror.

205   In addition to these four elements of the framework should be mentioned the only bone. The *hyoid bone* can be felt by our fingers, above the thyroid, in the base of the tongue. It is U-shaped, with the opening at the back. The voice-box hangs from it. One additional cartilage we have already mentioned. It is the *epiglottis,* a leaf-shaped lid for the voice-box. It is hinged to the thyroid cartilage and muscles run down from it on either side attaching to the arytenoids and forming a kind of collar for the top of the larynx, called the *aryepiglottic folds.* Stiffening these folds, like whalebone in the collar of a woman's dress, are the *cartilages of Wrisberg.* They are near the arytenoids. In the ligaments that run from the upper horns of the thyroid cartilage to the tips of the hyoid bone are two lumps called the *triticeal cartilages.* Both these and the cartilages of Wrisberg are important in lower animals but only vestigal in man, serving no human purpose. If you don't like anatomical terms, don't bother to remember them.

The Cricoarytenoid Articulation

206   Like the bones of the body, the cartilages of the larynx are held together by ligaments. I just mentioned those that attach the hyoid bone to the thyroid cartilage. Each arytenoid is at-

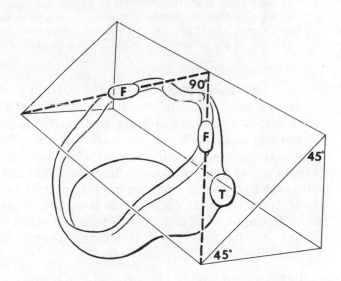

Fig. 25. Articulatory Facets on Cricoid
F, F, facets for articulation of arytenoids.
Diagram represents approximate angle of facets
to each other and their angle to the horizontal. T,
facet for left inferior cornu of thyroid.

tached to the edge of the cricoid plate by means of a *synovial joint,* that is, the whole articulation is enclosed in a ligamentous capsule, containing lubricating fluid. The joint is rather hard to visualize in flat pictures, but it is most important to understand.

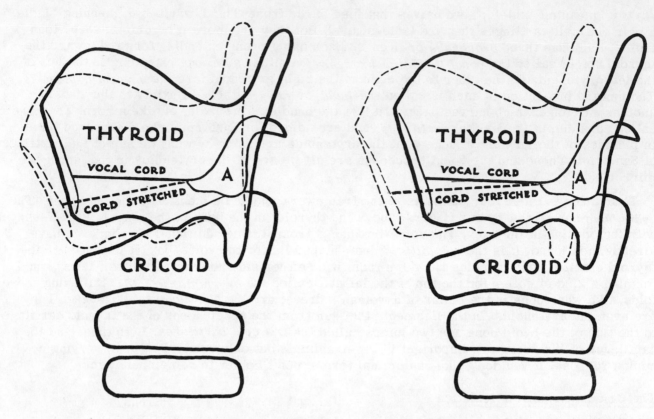

Fig. 26.   Articulation of Thyroid and Cricoid
A, arytenoid cartilage.
Left: Rocking. Broken lines show how contraction of cricothyroid muscles tips thyroid cartilage
upon cricoid, stretching vocal cords. This is recognized as a manner in which pitch is altered.
Actually both cricoid and thyroid move, but longitudinal tension is identical.
Right: Gliding. Sonninen presents X-ray evidence that in some cases lower horns of thyroid slip
from their facets on the cricoid and are drawn forward by cricothyroid muscles. This is not
possible in all cases. Its significance in contrast to rocking has not been evaluated.

207   On the sloping upper edge of the cricoid plate are two convex facets, having oval outlines.
Their surfaces are almost cylindrical, and the axis of each cylinder is about at right angles to
the other, and they lie in a plane about 45° from either horizontal or vertical, assuming that
the bottom of the cricoid is horizontal. (See Fig. 25) Now on the under surface of the big, blunt
muscular process of each arytenoid is a concave cylindrical facet to fit the convex one on the
cricoid plate. The arytenoids have two possibilities of movement, *rocking* and *gliding*. When the
two little cartilages rock together the vocal processes touch, but otherwise the arytenoids are
separated unless they also glide together. When they glide together so that their heads touch
(the cartilages of Santorini are together) they do not touch at the vocal processes unless the
proper rocking movement also takes place. This will become more meaningful as we study the
musculature (Par. 231, Fig. 31).

208   The lower horns of the thyroid are bound to facets on the sides of the cricoid near the back
by means of the *ceratocricoid* ligaments. There is some insignificant muscle tissue there also.

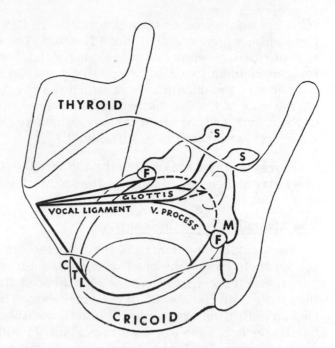

Fig. 27. Conus Elasticus
Outline drawing as if parts were transparent, somewhat distorted in order to make cone shape more obvious. CTL, cricothyroid ligament; F, F, facets on cricoid for articulation of arytenoids; M, muscular process; S, S, cartilages of Santorini.

This is basically a rocking articulation, much simpler than that of the arytenoids with the cricoid. However, calling it a "pivot" is an oversimplification, because in some cases (not all) the horns can slip out of their concave facets and the thyroid can glide forward. There is enough play in the ceratocricoid ligaments, sometimes, to permit a few millimeters of gliding. Either rocking or gliding of the thyroid increases the distance from front to back of the larynx, and stretches the vibrating cords. (See Fig. 26)

The Conus Elasticus

209   The most important ligament of all is the *conus elasticus*. The base of this distorted cone is the upper oval edge of the cricoid, and its apex is a firm attachment below the notch of the thyroid (Fig. 27). The conus also attaches to the under side of the arytenoids, including the vocal processes. It is split, and when the arytenoids are separated, of course, the slit opens. We already know this slit—it is the glottis. Part of the conus, thus, is like a heavy protective skin for the under side of the vocal folds. It meets the blast of air from the lungs. The conus is only loosely attached to the vocal folds above, like the skin on the back of one's hand. Notice that when your hand is relaxed the skin is loose. When the vocal muscles are relaxed, the conus vibrates rather independently.

210   The conus is not uniformly thick, and at points where it is thicker and tougher it has special names. It is important to know that these names refer to parts of the conus, and are not separate structures. The front part of the conus, running between the angle of the thyroid and the front part of the cricoid, is called the *cricothyroid ligament*. It prevents the cartilages from moving too far apart at the front. The edges of the glottis are also thicker than the rest of the conus, and are called the *vocal ligaments*. The vocal processes are cartilaginous, and fairly

stiff, but as they taper they become more flexible, and at their tips they merge with the vocal ligaments, which are still more flexible. The edges of the vocal folds are thus like bull whips, stiff at the back ends and increasingly flexible toward the notch of the thyroid. If you will imagine holding two such whips tied together at a point in front of you, you will begin to visualize some of the undulations of which the vocal lips are capable. These edges show white against all the pink of the larynx, which is covered with transparent mucous membrane like the inside of the mouth and throat. They have given us the name "vocal cords," and if we think only of the ligaments, this term is justifiable.

211   Fibres of the conus reach the top of the cricoid plate near the middle, between the arytenoids. They strengthen the capsule of the synovial joint at that point.

The Musculature of the Larynx

212   Fortunately, the names of the muscles are derived from the names of the cartilages, which makes them easy. The ones which will interest us most are the *thyroarytenoids*, the *cricothyroids*, and the *cricoarytenoids*. All three of these are *intrinsic* muscles of the larynx, that is, they have both their ends in the voice-box. There are also the muscles that operate the epiglottis (including the aryepiglottic folds), and those that approximate the hyoid bone and the thyroid cartilage, but these are less important. In addition to the intrinsic, there are also several *extrinsic* muscles that pull between the larynx and various outside points of attachment, such as the skull, the jaw, the breast-bone.

213   The thyroarytenoid muscles form the valve itself. They are the body of the vocal lips. Since they extend from the notch of the thyroid to the arytenoids at the back, merging with the vocal processes, they can completely close the top of the trachea if they come together. They are covered with a membrane that is continuous with the lining of the entire larynx. This pair of muscles is complex enough to produce different kinds of tone, even if there were not other factors involved.

214   First, the muscles form two distinct folds on each side. The upper pair are the ventricular bands, and the lower, the true cords. But it is far more complicated than that. Anatomists have dissected each thyroarytenoid into several *fasciculi*, or bundles of muscle fibre, each having its own origin and insertion like any big muscle, (Fig. 28). The fascicles which form the inferior folds, or true cords, have been named the *vocalis* muscles, or the *internal* thyroarytenoids. The heavier body along each wing of the thyroid is called the *external* thyroarytenoid. Also, fibres running across the main direction of the folds have been discovered, woven through the main fascicles, and it is thought that these may have some power to aid in the process of thinning the edges of the lips, which will be described later. These fibres are inserted into the ligamentous edges and are called the *aryvocalis* muscles, but they are really only an obscure detail of the thyroarytenoid muscles.

215   The complexity with which the various fibres of the thyroarytenoid muscles are woven together is confusing, and also tempting to enterprising thinkers who offer new theories about them. For example, Goerttler, in 1951, studied these muscles microscopically and advanced the belief that there were no fibres that ran the full length of the cord and that could be called *thyroarytenoid*. He said there were only *aryvocalis* (from arytenoid to the vocal ligament and lower parts of the conus) and *thyrovocalis* (thyroid to vocal ligament). This would mean that when the fibres contracted they would pluck the ligaments like the fingers of a harpist. This

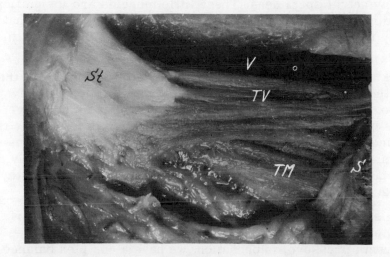

Fig. 28. Photograph of Left Vocal Cord
Courtesy of Janwillem van den Berg. About twice life size. Conus elasticus and other membranous covering removed. St, arytenoid cartilage (Stellknorpel); S, thyroid cartilage, cut through (Schildknorpel); TV, internal thyroarytenoid or vocalis muscle (Thyrovocalis, i.e., from thyroid to vocal process). Note several more or less independent fasicicles, or bundles of muscle fibre. TM, lower part of external thryroarytenoid muscle (Thyromuscularis, i.e., from thyroid to muscular process); V, ventricle.

fitted nicely the *neurochronaxic* theory of Husson, and these ideas created a great wave of interest in the early half of the decade. By now they have been largely discredited, and we return to the old-fashioned picture of mostly longitudinal fibres, running in different diagonals and woven together, with the mystery of certain transverse fibres still unsolved.

216   I recommend that we think of only the internal thyroarytenoids, which form the body of the true cords and are also called the vocalis or vocal muscle. The ventricular band is part of the big, bewildering external thyroarytenoid. The ventricular band resembles the true cord, having in it both muscular and ligamentous tissue, and so is called the "false cord," but it is not suitable for phonation, and as I have said (Par. 158), is not a part of normal voice production. Between the true and false cords, on each side of the larynx, is a pocket, called the *ventricle,* It is thought by some to be a resonator, and we shall consider that later. It also contains glands which secrete lubrication for the true cords—sometimes too much.

217   Just as a small boy can change the shape of his arm merely by tensing and relaxing his biceps, so the vocal lips can change their shape by the action of the fibers of the thyroarytenoids, but obviously change may also result from any movement of the arytenoid cartilages. These odd-shaped little levers to which the posterior ends of the vocal folds attach are operated by the *cricoarytenoid* muscles. There are two *lateral* cricoarytenoids that pull forward on the muscular processes of the cartilages; and two *posterior* cricoarytenoids that tip the cartilage back; four muscles in all. There is a single muscle, called the *transverse arytenoid* which can pull the tiny cartilages together. Also there is a pair of *oblique arytenoids*. Each fastens to the top tip of one arytenoid and crosses down to the opposite corner of the other. They form a

letter "X" at the back of the larynx which always looks impressive in drawings, but which is almost invisible in many actual specimens. These little muscles are insignificant compared with with the transverse, so much so that there is not much point in imagining what they could do independently. I usually refer simply to *interarytenoids*, which includes all three.

218   You remember that the thyroid cartilage is pivoted by the inferior cornua to the cricoid and rocks forward and back, increasing and decreasing the length and tension of the vocal bands. There are muscles at the front of the larynx that fill the gap between these two large cartilages. The *cricothyroids* fan out from the middle of the front of the cricoid cartilage, running backward and upward to the bottom edge of the thyroid. Their action is to pull the thyroid forward with relation to the cricoid, and downward, closer to it. Both of these motions stretch the thyroarytenoids (assuming that the cricoarytenoids hold fast), and conversely, the contraction of the thyroarytenoids pulls the two cartilages apart and stretches the cricothyroids (Fig. 26). This is another illustration of muscular antagonism.

219   However, it is not a simple case like the biceps pulling against the triceps. The pull involves the leverage of the arytenoids, and the little muscles operating them. In other words, when the valve closes against breath pressure, in phonation, we have a complex balance of the tensions of three distinct sets of muscles-cricothyroid, cricoarytenoid, and thyroarytenoid—none of which is simple. The balance may be either *static* or *dynamic,* a distinction which I wish to make because I think we shall find it important as we continue our discussion. If any muscle tightens so rigidly, or if any cartilage becomes so braced, that a new adjustment is impossible without "breaking" the tone that is being produced, I shall call it *static balance.* Such a condition can be recognized, even though our anatomical knowledge is not precise enough to define the rigidity specifically. The ideal for singing is *dynamic balance.*

220   When one's laryngeal function is so crude as always to be static, with breaks between different adjustments, we hear what are called "registers." The term is borrowed from that most elaborate of all wind instruments, the organ. It is commonly confused with the concept of *range,* that is, reference will be made to "high register" and "low register," etc.; but it is well to remember that on the organ, while some are very high and others are very low, different registers can also be for exactly the same compass. This is true of the voice as well. *Pitch* is a very important factor in registration, but the real distinction is in *quality* of tone, the result of difference in production.

Research in Laryngeal Function

221   As long ago as 1841, Garcia, the great singer and teacher, invented the *laryngoscope* to observe the vocal cords in vibration. It is only a little mirror fastened at the proper angle to a long handle, but until Garcia thought of it, there was no way to look down into the throat. Remember this the next time someone pooh-poohs vocal pedagogy as unscientific; it was a voice teacher who made this permanent contribution to science, used by all dentists and throat specialists today.

222   Recently a great deal has been learned about the different modes of vibration of the vocal lips, through the use of the *stroboscope*. This is a method of observing objects that are in rapid motion, too fast for the unaided eye to see clearly. The stroboscope consists simply of a flashing light, the frequency of whose flashes can be controlled. Suppose a wheel is revolving 500 revolutions per second. The eye sees only a blur. But with the stroboscope properly adjusted, the eye sees a series of short flashes, one every 500th of a second; that is, the eye sees the wheel only at the beginning of each cycle, and it appears to be standing still! Now, if the

stroboscopic light is adjusted to flash at a slightly lower frequency, instead of seeing the same moment of each cycle, we see a series which gives us the impression that the wheel is moving slowly, and we can see any irregularities in its revolving. This trick has been used for the study of delicate machinery for years, and in 1932 two French scientists, Husson and Tarneaud, applied it to the larynx. Still more recently the Bell Telephone Laboratories investigated the action of the vocal cords with a remarkable motion picture camera, capable of taking 4000 frames per second. The result is a series of beautiful movies that slow the motion to about one 200th normal speed, adding even to the information supplied by the stroboscope. The Fastax camera, as it is called, is now being used by various investigators throughout the world. Pictures taken by it are seen in Figs. 17, 19, 32, 34, 35, 36, 37, 38.

223   Ever since Ferrein, in 1741, experimenters have caused excised larynges to phonate by blowing air through them and simulating the action of their muscles. Van den Berg, with his associates T. S. Tan and later D. Berger, has brought this research technic to near perfection. An excised larynx can be made to produce all the registration effects of the living voice, with upper parts cut away for greater visibility, and with the muscles activated independently and under control. Van den Berg uses a stroboscope which, by means of a Delta-f Generator can be adjusted to any frequency the larynx produces, thereby slowing the motion or stopping it and causing it to move forward or backward by the turn of a dial (all this as an optical illusion, but a reliable one). Much has been learned about laryngeal function. I collaborated with Dr. van den Berg during the academic year of 1959-60, and from what he showed me I offer the following outline of five factors of laryngeal function.

The Power Factor—Breath Flow—Respiratory Muscles

224   We are aware that the actuator of the voice is the breathing apparatus, and we have already discussed how the breath should be applied to the larynx in the attack. The aerodynamic aspect of voice production should never be ignored. Given an adjustment in which the glottis is almost but not quite closed, vibration can be initiated and maintained by air flow alone, the final closing movement being caused by the Bernoulli Effect and the opening being a yielding to pressure as soon as the flow has ceased. This is singing "on the breath."

225   In an excised larynx, such as are found in the laboratory of van den Berg, increased flow of air will increase the loudness of the tone and also will raise the pitch. The pitch will go up because the greater flow of air will heighten the suction of the Bernoulli Effect, causing the glottis to close more quickly each time, and also because the greater flow will force itself through the glottis more quickly each time after the closing. Both of these factors will raise the frequency of the cycle. At the same time the resistance of the glottis to this greater flow will result in greater compression in each sound wave, making the tone louder.

226   This will always be the case with a lifeless larynx because the musculature can make no compensation for the increased flow. It is also sometimes true of a beginning singer. When he pours more breath into his voice, making a crescendo, he may reach a point at which he cannot compensate skillfully enough and he will sharp along with the crescendo. With experience, however, his ear will demand that he stay in tune, and he will learn to be satisfied with no more volume than he can keep on pitch. As his skill increases, his laryngeal musculature will be conditioned to enable him to achieve still greater loudness without sharping, (Rubin[2] *et al.*). *This must always be done by ear*, of course, and he should never think he is controlling the pitch by muscle. In general he should think of singing more loudly as pouring more breath, and depending on moderation and a good ear to keep him in tune. The higher the pitch, the more this is true, (Isshiki[2,3]).

The Pitch Factor—Longitudinal Tension—Cricothyroid Muscles

227   We have seen that the action of the cricothyroid muscles causes the distance from the thyroid notch to the cricoid plate to increase, thus stretching the vocal folds longitudinally, (Fig. 26). The increased tension causes them to return more promptly to the midline after breath has separated them, and this obviously raises the frequency or the pitch. For photographic evidence of this see Fig. 29. There are two simple experiments by which you can prove this to yourself. First, press inward upon your Adam's Apple while phonating, and then suddenly release the pressure. The pitch will go up. (This is a little like the patella reflex; it doesn't always work. But you will discover that the normal reaction is for the pitch to go up.) This is because your pressure works against the cricothyroids, shortening the folds and reducing the longitudinal tension. When you release, the cricothyroids are able to stretch the folds, and this raises the pitch.

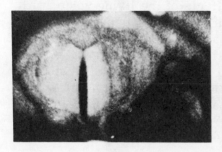 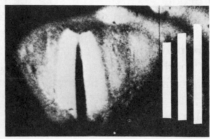 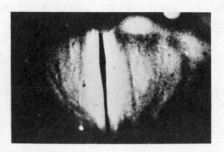

Fig. 29. Longitudinal Tension as Related to Pitch
Left: Low tone. Center: Middle tone. Right: High tone. Bell Telephone photographs, courtesy of Brodnitz. Assembled for comparison in center picture are white bars exactly equal in length to glottis in left, center, and right.

228   The second test is not quite as easy, because you must find the tiny space between the thyroid and the cricoid cartilages. You will be able to insert your fingernail, I believe. Now sing the interval of an octave upward. You will feel the space close and force your finger out. Here again we have the action of the cricothyroid muscles. Other tests, more scientific than these (for example electromyography, Faaborg-Andersen) have demonstrated that the primary function of the cricothyroids is to determine pitch.

229   Now tensing the vocal folds makes them more difficult to move, so as the pitch goes up greater resistance is offered to the breath stream, resulting in greater air pressure, (Rubin[2], et al.). So the raising of pitch and the increasing of loudness go together. This has been seen in van den Berg's experiments, and of course it is well known in singing. Beginners find it almost impossible to sing high tones softly, and even when professionals sing high pianissimos, these tones are louder than fairly loud tones at lower levels. We think of them as pianissimo only in contrast to the sound of a fortissimo on a high pitch. In a secondary way, then, the cricothyroids are used to increase loudness, but this is very subtle and indirect. Remember that muscles are controlled in terms of the effects they produce, and almost never directly (Par. 81). Pitch, like loudness, is controlled by ear.

230   Since change of pitch is a matter of changing the relationship of the thyroid and the cricoid cartilages, one can easily see that neck muscles which pull upon the larynx in different directions might assist the cricothyroids in creating longitudinal tension. As a matter of fact it is instinctive for the hyothyroid muscles to pull the thyroid up toward the hyoid bone as the pitch rises, and while this is happening, those muscles which raise the hyoid also tense themselves,

and the whole larynx rises. The cricoid plate, however, is partially anchored by the esophagus and by the weight of the trachea and lungs. This stretches the vocal folds. We shall consider this whole matter in greater detail in Chapter 5, but for now let us state that high larynx singing is poor, and shows an inability on the part of the singer to control pitch by the muscles of the larynx itself, the *intrinsic* muscles.

An Efficiency Factor—Adduction—Interarytenoid Muscles

231   The vocal folds must be brought together (or nearly so) in order for phonation to take place. They are together at their origin, just under the notch of the thyroid, but whether the glottis will be closed is a matter of the position of the arytenoids, which are at the back ends of the folds. The transverse arytenoid muscle draws the little cartilages together. It is assisted by the two less important interarytenoid muscles, the obliques. The movement is largely gliding, along the upper edge of the cricoid plate. Bringing the vocal folds toward the midline in this manner is called *adduction*.

232   The opposite movement is *abduction*, and is caused by the posterior cricoarytenoid muscles, which exert a downward and backward pull on the muscular processes. The arytenoids glide back down from their high perch together to the lower ends of the facets on the cricoid plate, and they also rock apart. This separates the vocal processes as much as possible. This position goes with normal breathing, and the more strenuous the inhalation the more widely the vocal processes are separated (Fig. 30). The posterior cricoarytenoids are active during silent breathing. They go quickly into action between singing phrases. Most physiologists will tell you that they go out of action during phonation, since their function is to open the glottis. Briess offers an interesting theory that they provide a subtle factor of muscular antagonism. Without them, he asserts, the adductory muscles might close the glottis too tightly, creating friction and damaging the voice. So the posterior cricoarytenoids (which are called the *posticus*, for short) pull gently against the adductory muscles during phonation. Briess offers some electromyographic evidence to support his theory, but it is not generally accepted.

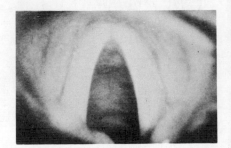 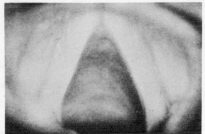 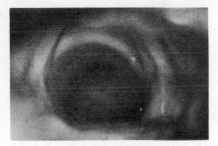

Fig. 30. Vocal Folds in Breathing
Left: Quiet respiration. Center: Breathing with moderate effort. Right: Breathing in extreme exertion. Bell Telephone photographs from Friedrich S. Brodnitz, *Keep Your Voice Healthy*.

A Second Efficiency Factor—Medial Compression—Lateral Cricoarytenoid Muscles

233   The interarytenoids are the primary adductory muscles, but they cannot close the glottis perfectly by themselves. A glance at Fig. 31 (third drawing from the top on the right) will explain this. As the cricothyroids (which are called the *anticus* for short because they are at the anterior part of the larynx) create longitudinal tension, this turns out not to be a direct pull from A to B, because the facets for the arytenoids are not at B. Instead there are two diagonal pulls (indicated by the broken lines AF, AF) because the arytenoids are shaped like a

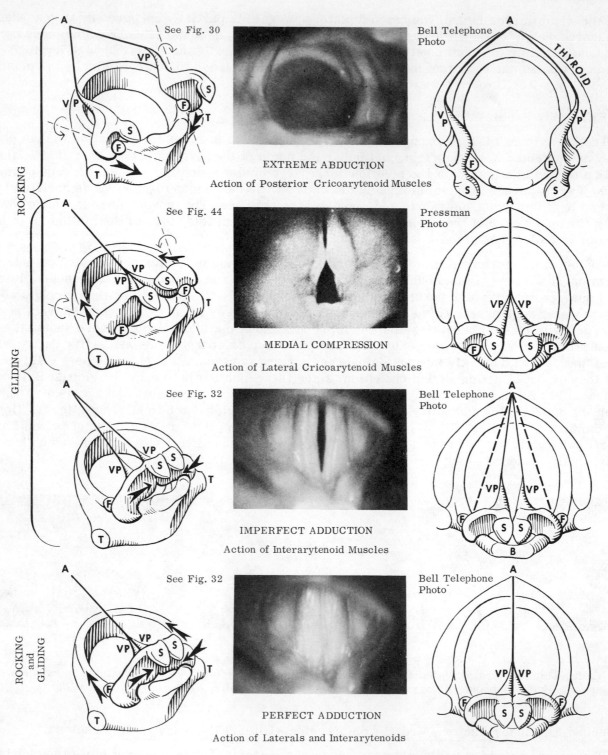

Fig. 31. Movements of Arytenoid Cartilages

Left: Drawings in three-quarters view to give some idea of movement in depth. Center: Photographs by means of laryngeal mirror. Right: Drawings of top view at same angle as mirror image.

A, angle of thyroid; F,F, facets for cricoarytenoid articulation; S,S, cartilages of Santorini; T,T, facets for cricothyroid articulation; VP,VP, vocal processes.

dog's hind leg, and attach at the sides instead of at the middle of the cricoid plate. The greater the longitudinal tension the more the vocal folds tend to assume the positions of the broken lines, and this means that the vocal processes will not touch. This is not just a geometrical theory, it has been demonstrated in actual specimens repeatedly.

234   To counteract the tendency for longitudinal tension to separate the vocal processes and make the glottis gap in the middle, it is necessary for the lateral cricoarytenoids to pull. They create a rocking in direct opposition to that caused by the posticus, and thus bring the vocal processes together. Whenever the glottis closes, then (as it does thousands of times) there is a beautiful coordination of the interarytenoids and the lateral cricoarytenoids (*laterals* for short) so that the vocal folds come together perfectly.

235   This pull of the laterals on the muscular processes, causing the vocal processes to press together is called *medial compression*. I have listed it as a separate factor, because it often happens that medial compression is adequate when the interarytenoid pull is inadequate. This happens in strong whispers, for instance. The position is shown in the second level from the top of Fig. 31, a photograph by Pressman of the glottis in whispering. Everything but the laterals is relaxed and air is blowing through all of the glottis, except at the point where the vocal processes touch. The laterals are holding them together. (I may add that the external thyroarytenoids parallel the lateral cricoarytenoids and probably assist them. They are bigger and exert greater leverage because they pull forward upon the whole arytenoid and not just the muscular process.)

236   During phonation, especially in falsetto, it often happens that the *muscular* glottis (the part in front of the vocal processes, also called the *ligamentous* glottis) vibrates cleanly, closing completely once in each cycle; but the *cartilaginous* glottis (the part bounded by the arytenoids) does not close at all. This is often the case with young voices, especially young women's. The gap between the arytenoids is called the *mutational chink*, because it is typical of singers whose voices are "changing." It represents a weakness of the interarytenoid muscles. The sound is that of a clear little voice, accompanied by the rustling of "wild air" through the chink. It is a characteristic sound of the breathiness of young voices, and usually just the normal exercise of the singer, plus maturity, strengthens the interarytenoids and empowers the voice. *Young singers should not be driven to eliminate this breathiness impatiently.*

The Registration Factor—Activity-Passivity—Vocalis Muscles

237   The fifth factor is the condition of the vocal folds themselves. Remember that we have the conus elasticus (like a skin on the under surface) with its thickened edges, the vocal ligaments, which form the edges of the cords. We have a flexible front part and a comparatively stiff back part, the arytenoids with their vocal processes. The body of each fold is the vocalis muscle, the internal thyroarytenoid. These complex vibrators are being acted upon by air flow, longitudinal tension, and two distinct adductory forces. Indeed, it is oversimplifying to call it a "three-way tug-of-war." If the vocalis muscles resist the forces which are exerted upon them we have one type of vibrator, comparable to the lips of a trumpet player. If the vocalis muscles relax they are like the lifeless vibrators of a reed instrument. Actually they never relax completely, and there are many intermediate degrees, but we may say that there are two extreme adjustments—active and passive.

238   Thus we have two extremes of vibration, two "registers" if you wish to call them that. One covers the lower two thirds of the compass and the other applies to the upper two thirds. I emphasize the fact that there is at least an octave which can be sung either way. If the singer is given to static adjustments, he will have "chest voice" and "head voice" and the overlapping area will be small; in fact, he may even have three or four "registers" with no overlapping,

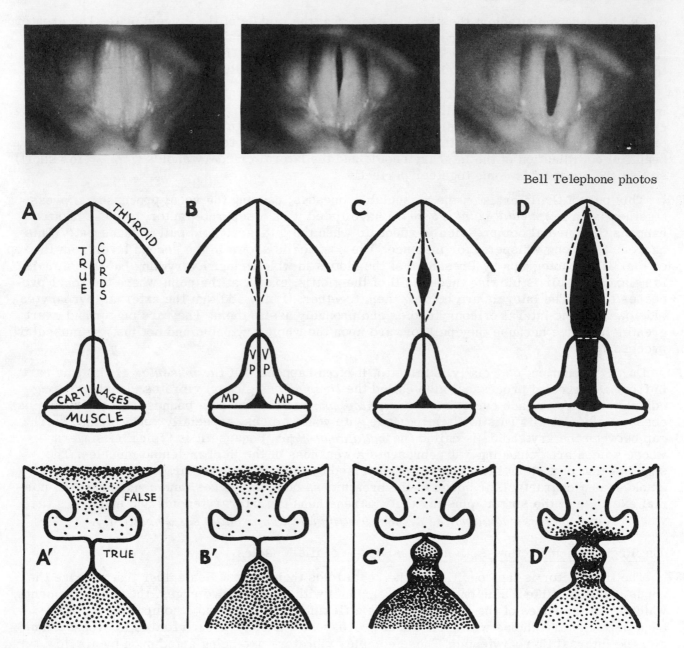

Bell Telephone photos

Fig. 32. Schema of the Heavy Mechanism
A to H, schematic view of vocal bands as seen in laryngoscope, in series of positions representing one vibration cycle. False cords not shown. Arytenoids indentified by word "cartilages"; VP,
vocal processes; MP, muscular processes. Cartilages of Santorini and Wrisberg, not shown.
Broken lines indicate how breath pressure is beginning to force bands open underneath, forming
vertical rippling. Broken white line differentiates between ligamentous glottis and cartilaginous
glottis. Note longitudinal undulation in these drawings. (Based on Bell Telephone Laboratory
Motion Pictures, and stills from the film in F. Lincoln D. Holmes, *A Handbook of Voice and Diction*
(New York: Appleton-Century-Crofts, Inc., 1940), opposite pp. 14 and 15).

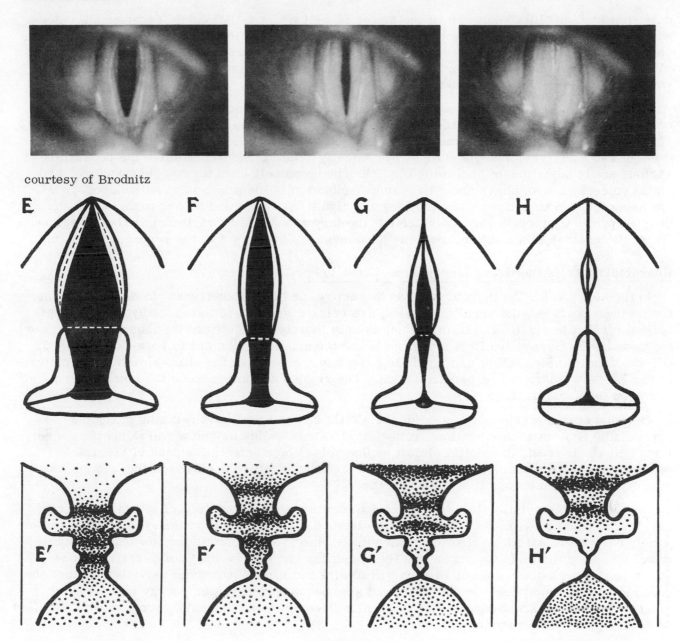

courtesy of Brodnitz

Fig. 32. Continued
A' to H', schematic cross sections corresponding approximately to the drawings above. Vertical
rippling is suggested on basis of Bell Telephone Laboratory Motion Pictures. Stippling represents
molecules of air (highly diagrammatic) indicating accumulation of pressure beginning with first
closure, G' and continuing through H', A', B', C'. Note compression phase is at least half of cycle.
Rippling of bands causes each puff to be irregular, producing wide range of partials. Irregularity
of puffs is indicated by stippling above glottis. (Based on X-rays by Canuyt and Gunsett in
J. Tarneaud, *Traité Pratique de Phonologie et de Phonialrie*, pp. 62-65. Drawing A' based on
diagram representing "chest voice," upon stroboscopic findings of Husson and Tarneaud in Robert
Curry, *The Mechanism of the Human Voice* (New York: Longmans, Green & Co., 1940), p. 75).
Bell Telephone photographs across top, from Friedrich S. Brodnitz, *Keep Your Voice Healthy*.

only "breaks" or "lifts" between. If the singer is well trained, the middle range of his voice will be produced with a dynamic balance whereby it will be difficult to call it either "chest" or "head." He will be able to make it heavy or light, smoothly and at will, and the compass in which this is possible will expand with the maturing of his voice until it includes most of the notes that he feels free to use in public.

239   The vocabulary of registration is as confused as the knowledge of its function. There is considerable prejudice against the use of the word "register," so it is just as well to speak of "heavy mechanism" and "light mechanism" as suggested by Wilcox, (pp. 9-10). I prefer to think of two extremes, *heavy* and *light,* dynamically related, and to minimize the possibility of various static adjustments according to pitch. The commonly used terms, "chest voice" and "head voice," probably have about the same connotation in the minds of most pedagogs, and I am using them in this discussion, but they are highly figurative and belong to an era when people apparently thought that the voice left the larynx and was "directed" into these regions. We shall consider this whole concept of "placement," when we get to the resonance system.

Characteristics of the Heavy Mechanism—Chest Voice

240   In the heavy voice the thyroarytenoids are active, and hence shortened. In the lowest tones the internal portions, the vocalis muscles, are relaxed and so are the cricothyroids. Longitudinal tension is small. The conus, which is only loosely connected to the muscles, is sucked together by the Bernoulli Effect at a point below the upper surface of the vocal folds (Fig. 32, G') and then its sides billow and ripple like flags in a breeze. In the ultra-slow-motion pictures of the Fastax camera it is a beautiful sight. The ripples continue across the mucous membrane on the upper surface.

241   Because of the thickness of the folds the glottis closes firmly and remains closed an appreciable time in each vibration, so that air pressure builds up below and fairly bursts out. Each puff of air opens the glottis almost explosively. Voice scientists speak of a *vertical phase difference* because the glottis closes at the bottom before it closes at the top, and also *opens* at the bottom before it opens at the top.

242   Another characteristic of the heavy mechanism is that the amplitude of vibration is great, that is, the vocal folds move a rather large distance from the midline, the glottis opens rather widely each time. All these characteristics make chest voice suitable for low tones (because it takes so long for them to happen that the frequency can only be low) comparatively loud (because compression builds up in each puff of air) and rich in harmonic partials (because the rippling creates complexity in the puffs, and also because the greater energy in each cycle makes possible the sounding of other frequencies beside the fundamental, some of which may be determined by the resonators).

243   The lowest tones of the voice are not very loud because the cricothyroids are not offering enough antagonism to the thyroarytenoids to create much resistance to the breath stream. The difference between soft and loud low tones is probably a matter of whether the internal portion (vocalis) is relaxed or whether it joins the external thyroarytenoid in contracting.

244   As the cricothyroids contract the pitch rises, as we have already stated (Par. 227). Because the thyroarytenoids are active in this adjustment the vocal folds do not elongate as rapidly as they would otherwise. The thyroarytenoids are opposing the cricothyroids. In the lowest tones the internal thyroarytenoids are relaxed and flabby (unless maximum volume is desired). As the pitch rises they enter the tug-of-war that the externals are already having with the cricothyroids. Longitudinal tension mounts without necessarily elongating the vocal folds, although of course eventually the full stretch of the ligaments will have taken place. The cords are still thick as the pitch rises because muscles thicken when they are working, but at the top of this

voice instead of being loose they are like rubber cushions striking together. It requires more breath power and more muscular effort, which probably communicates itself to the neck muscles as well. As we have already mentioned, such a tone will be very loud. The upper limit of this register is reached when the limit of muscular strength has been reached. Beginners who have discovered no other way to ascend the scale often "crack," that is, the thyroarytenoids give way, allowing the cricothyroids to win the tug-of-war, and an involuntary falsetto is heard. The singer feels pain from the sudden stretching of the vocal ligaments, and embarrassment at the loss of control, and he stops singing, but if he were to continue he would be in light registration.

Characteristics of the Light Mechanism—Falsetto

245   In the light voice the thyroarytenoids are not entirely passive, but comparatively so. This is not only the conclusion of logical speculation, but it has been proved by electromyography (Faaborg-Andersen, Katsuki). With the vocalis muscle relaxed it is possible for the cricothyroids to place great longitudinal tension upon the vocal ligaments. The tension can be increased in order to raise the pitch even after the maximum length of the cords has been reached. This makes the folds thin so that there is negligible vertical phase difference, no such thing as the glottis opening at the bottom first and then at the top. The vocalis muscles fall to the sides of the larynx and the vibration takes place almost entirely in the ligaments.

246   Such a vibration can take place at high frequencies because there is very little mass to be moved, and the amplitude of movement is small anyhow. The folds offer much less resistance to the breath. It requires great breath expenditure to produce a loud tone, except in the highest parts of falsetto, where the tension has been raised to the point where it offers resistance. A tone sung in chest voice is always louder than the same pitch sung in falsetto. Because the edges of the folds are so thin in light mechanism each puff of air is comparatively simple. The relative weakness of each puff also produces a more flutelike tone, with fewer partials. The closure is brief at best, and often the glottis does not close completely. Because of the great longitudinal tension, great medial compression is also needed to make the closure complete, and often this is lacking. This leads us to a discussion of a mysterious phenomenon called *damping*.

Damping or Dampening

247   Until the vibrations in falsetto were studied by stroboscope and Fastax camera it was assumed that the vocal lips puckered like the lips of a whistler for the highest tones. Indeed the highest register in a woman's voice was called the "whistle register." In rare cases a true whistle does occur through an opening between the arytenoid cartilages (the mutational chink) but this is not very loud, and is not useful for singing. We may ignore it. But we can understand that when the larynx is vibrating at high frequencies it may not have time to open fully in each vibration. It may also not close completely at any time either. The result will appear to the unaided eye as a puckered opening through which whistling might be taking place. Early drawings, as in Behnke, Proschowsky, Shakespeare, and others, illustrated this concept.

248   In each vibration cycle (in either chest or falsetto) the air bubbles through first at the point which is weakest or most flexible. This is always in the ligamentous portion, never between the arytenoids. In most cases it is midway between the vocal processes and the angle of the thyroid, but in some larynges it is at the forward end of the glottis, right at the angle. Even in chest voice the opening appears there first and then undulates to the back ends and separates the arytenoids. At low frequencies it will be apparent that the entire glottis is in vibration, but as the frequency rises there is less and less time for the glottis to open. So for low falsetto the entire glottis will open as a tiny slit, but in middle falsetto range only the forward half of the glottis has time to open, and for the highest tones there will only be a brief opening at the

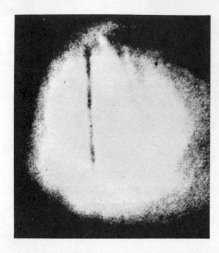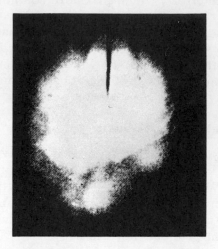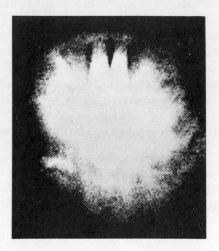

Fig. 33. Early Photographs of "Damping"
Left: Low falsetto. Center: Middle falsetto. Right: High falsetto. Taken in 1942 by Joel
Pressman and Arthur Hinman. These are perhaps the earliest photographs of the phenomenon. They
have appeared in various publications and are here by courtesy of Brodnitz and Pressman. Fastax
camera study by Henry Rubin, Fig. 35, confirms the evidence. See also photographs in William E.
Ross, *Secrets of Singing,* p. 81.

forward end which will close again before there has been time for any more of the glottis to
open.

249   Joel Pressman, who with Arthur Hinman pioneered in photography of the larynx, showed this
phenomenon in three still pictures which are reproduced in Fig. 33. Without the aid of the
Fastax camera this was interpreted as "damping" or "dampening." These words apply to
holding a string so that it cannot vibrate, and they implied a comparison with the finger of a
violinist moving along the string in order to raise the pitch. It was assumed that somehow the
glottis was pressed together at the back end, and that as the pitch rose the damping was increased until finally only a small part of the "strings" was allowed to vibrate. This was
regarded as a pitch mechanism by which the "cords" were shortened to raise the pitch. The
aryvocalis fibres (Par. 214) were thought to have something to do with it. We now know that
actually the vocal folds are *lengthened* (by stretching) to raise the pitch, and this illusion of
damping is an *effect* of longitudinal tension, rather than a *cause*. We also know that damping
occurs only in some singers, not all.

250   The factor of medial compression undoubtedly enters the picture. Remember that as longitudinal tension increases, medial compression becomes more and more necessary (Par. 233).
The young singer, who sings largely falsetto and who has a mutational chink, has it because
the laterals are holding the vocal processes together, but the interarytenoids are not holding
the rest of the arytenoids together. Such a falsetto can be seen in the Henry Rubin sequence in
Fig. 34. Notice that the ligamentous glottis is opening and closing completely, but the triangular
space between the arytenoids never closes. Such a voice sounds clear but weak, because compression waves instead of passing out of the mouth are simply sucked through the chink by
the rarefaction below. The condition is like a loud-speaker without a baffle.

251   Now suppose the singer does not increase medial compression but learns to use his interarytenoids enough to close the chink. His voice will sound clear and strong. The entire glottis will still open in each vibration, but it will also close completely in each cycle. But suppose in tightening his interarytenoids the singer also increases medial compression. He will hold his arytenoids together so tightly that they will not open at all, and all of the vibration will take place between the vocal ligaments. This will indeed be a damping of the posterior end of the glottis. Rubin also shows Fastax pictures of this (Fig. 35). Fig. 36 is a series of schematic drawings, similar to Fig. 32, showing what seems to be happening in Rubin's sequence. A few frames from Fig. 35 are included to emphasize the comparison. It has been thought that damping always characterized falsetto production, but this is not correct.

252   We know that falsetto with a mutational chink is inefficient, but we are not able to make any further correlations. Some trained singers exhibit damping and some do not, and both phenomena also appear with untrained singers. It is still one of the mysteries, though perhaps not quite as puzzling as it once was.

253   There are three pedagogical approaches to registration, each espoused by respectable authorities, and in such a case I believe that one should try to have an appreciation of all three approaches. The following outline appeared first in Music Journal and was later incorporated in an article which I wrote for "Voice and Speech Disorders—Medical Aspects" edited by Nathaniel Levin.

The Idealistic Approach—One Register

254   The idealistic concept is that of "one register." The voice, if possible, should produce all the pitches of which it is capable smoothly and consistently, without "breaks" or "holes" or radical changes of technic. This is the goal toward which all teachers are striving, and many believe that the best way to make an ideal come true is simply to assume that it *is* true, and never admit anything to the contrary. They hold, as a principle of pedagogical psychology, that one should never suggest to a student the possibility that he might have a register problem, but that one should begin in the middle of his potential range with the best technic possible, and expand this area until it includes all the tones that can be expected.

255   In approaching the upper tones of a voice, such a teacher gives instructions to "let go," to "supply more breath support," etc., but he does not suggest that there is a new register to be entered. He may say that women "color" their voices at the bottom and men should "color" their's at the top, and he may use such expressions as "covering" and "approaching the high tones from above," which indicate that he knows more about the problems than he thinks the student should be told. He is likely to say, "There is no such thing as a 'high' tone; all tones radiate high and low in all directions; the 'high' tones should be placed on the same shelf as the 'low' ones." The psychology of this is simply that the student will somehow subconsciously make the necessary adjustments and sing the high tone if he does not fear it. All this has a great deal more to be said for it than may be implied by my cursory treatment.

The Realistic Approach—Three Registers

256   The realistic philosophy, however, is that of "three registers." If one goes by the facts of vocal experience, be they ideal or not, one recognizes distinct qualities of tone, produced by distinct adjustments of the larynx, without recourse to which the full potential of the voice cannot be sung. (In many cases this full compass, three octaves or so, is not usable professionally but this does not alter the major proposition.)

257   The more sensitive one becomes register-wise, the more registers one is likely to isolate, but we may generalize and say there are three. In a man's voice these are most frequently

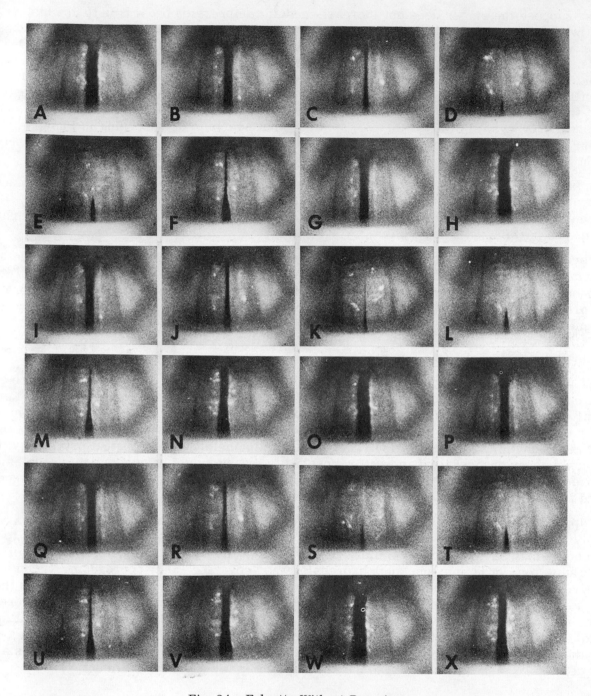

Fig. 34. Falsetto Without Damping

A little more than three vibrations. The great longitudinal tension (cricothyroid muscles) in falsetto is accompanied by great medial compression (lateral cricoarytenoid muscles). The vocalis muscles are comparatively relaxed, and the interarytenoids in this case are also relaxed so that the back part of the arytenoid cartilages (bottom of picture) never closes, even in D, K, and S. The triangular opening in E, L, and T, is a typical "mutational chink." Medial compression is enough to achieve efficient closure of the muscular (or ligamentous) glottis in each vibration, but it can be seen that the entire glottis is vibrating in this variety of falsetto. Compare with "damping" (Fig. 35) in which only the anterior (front) part of the glottis vibrates. Fastax camera sequence by Henry Rubin, from *The Laryngoscope*, Sept. 1960.

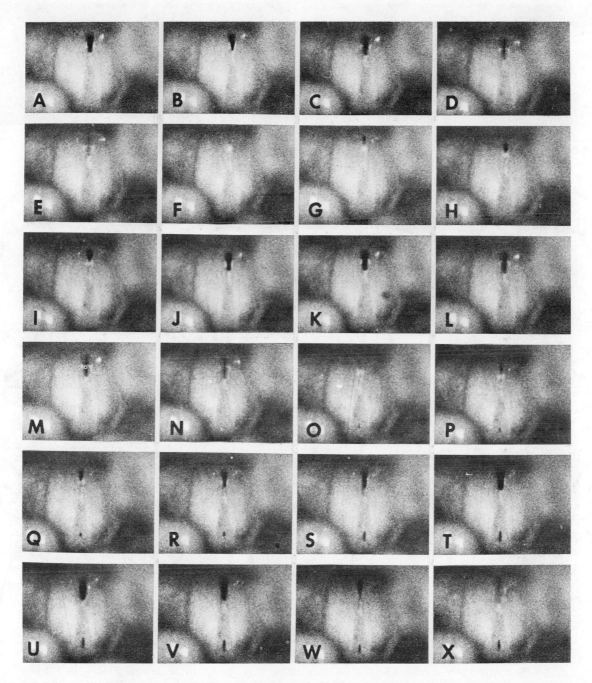

Fig. 35. Falsetto With Damping

Roughly two and one half vibrations while the singer is making a descending portamento from high falsetto. Note that the opening appears at the forward part of the glottis (top of picture) and increases toward the back (toward the arytenoids). Since pitch is descending, the maximum opening in each vibration is increasing: A, K, U. Interarytenoid and lateral cricoarytenoid muscles are contracting so strongly that the arytenoid cartilages do not separate during the vibrating sequence from A to O. However, the descent in pitch is accompanied by progressive relaxation, and from O to X the relaxation of the interarytenoid muscles can be seen in an increasing opening between the arytenoid cartilages. This chink could increase to resemble Fig. 34, E, L, T. Damping thus appears to be an extreme adduction, particularly extreme medial compression. Fastax camera sequence by Henry Rubin, from *The Laryngoscope*, Sept. 1960.

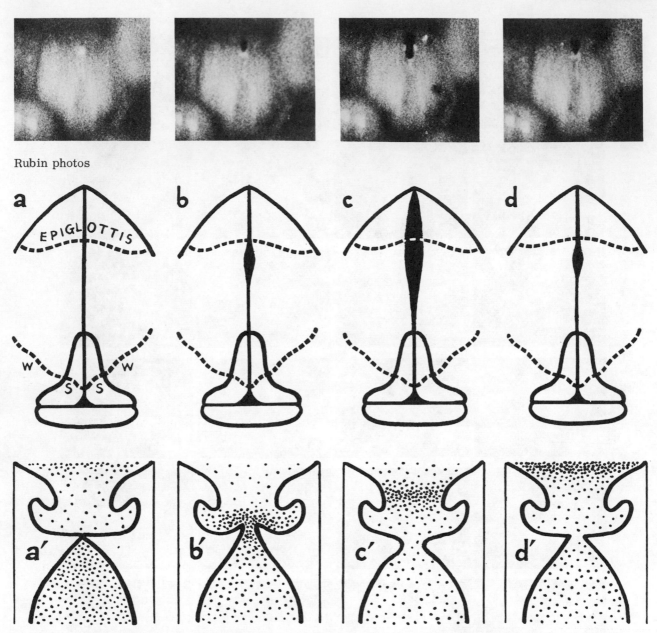

Rubin photos

Fig. 36. Schema of Light Mechanism with Damping
    Top: Frames from Fastax camera sequence in Fig. 35.
    a to d, schematic view of vocal bands as seen in laryngoscope, in series of positions representing
one cycle of vibration, octave higher than heavy tone diagrammed in Fig. 32. Heavy broken lines
indicate extent to which epiglottis above and cartilages of Santorini and Wrisberg below may
encroach upon view. Read discussion in Par. 247-251. Damping does not always occur in light
registration.
    a' to d', schematic cross sections corresponding to drawings and photos above. Note thinning of
edges, eliminating vertical phase difference. Breath pressure at moment of closure, a' , is indicated
as same as at G' in Fig. 32, but since compression phase is only a brief portion of falsetto cycle,
there is no time for it to accumulate. Note weakness and simplicity of puffs as indicated by
stippling above glottis. (Based upon same sources as for Fig. 32. Drawing "a" based upon
diagram of "falsetto" by Husson and Tarneaud in Robert Curry, *The Mechanism of the Human
Voice*, p. 75.)

called "normal, or chest," "head," and "falsetto." In a woman's voice they are "chest," "middle," and "head." Teachers who use this vocabulary set about "blending the registers," or helping students through the "passage" or "bridge" from one register to another.

258   Most authorities agree that basses sing largely in "chest," with some use of "head" for very high tones, but that their falsetto is acceptable only for comic effects and that there is probably no transition to it without yodeling. Tenors sing in "chest" up to F_4 or F_4 sharp, passing into "head" which they carry at least to A_4, above which theorists dispute. Some call the quality from there on up a "reinforced falsetto," others deny the use of falsetto. The baritone, of course, is midway between, but more like a bass in quality.

259   Teachers agree that most women beginners need to "find their middle voice." Sopranos sing largely in "head" and contraltos largely in "chest," but when they discover the "middle" and how to get into it, their vocal development really begins. Many will say that the soprano should never sing in "chest," while others will say that she may occasionally but should never carry it higher than F_4 (at the bottom of the treble staff) and preferably not higher than D_4 (above Middle C). The mezzo soprano or dramatic soprano sings in all three registers throughout a very wide range with considerable smoothness.

The Hypothetical Approach—Two Registers

260   Between the idealistic concept of "one register" (or "no registers," or "each tone is its own register") and the realistic concept of "three" (or more), there is an hypothesis of "two registers," that may be an oversimplification but which offers a rationale for explaining the multiple voices and how they may be combined in one. Baldly stated it is that every voice has a potential of roughly two octaves of "light mechanism" and two octaves of "heavy." These compasses overlap by one octave; that is, one octave can be sung in either laryngeal adjustment. In this area ("find the middle voice") it is possible to achieve a production that combines the best properties of both (*voix mixte*). The most radical proponents of the philosophy argue that at the bottom of this middle octave the light mechanism can taper off and the heavy take over, providing a transition to the bottom; or, conversely, the light can take over at the top. Thus every singer should have three octaves (Stanley). More realistic authorities will say that many dramatic sopranos can do this, but only exceptional voices in other categories manage it. They say that basses and contraltos have such fulsome and rewarding heavy mechanisms (chest voices) that the use of this mechanism prevails in all tones, even at the top. They may mix light mechanism with the heavy so that the upper part becomes more fluent and the range extends higher than would be possible with pure chest voice, and they also learn the trick of *mezza voce* (half voice) for special artistic purposes. However, in public performance these singers never drop out the chest voice completely, and never emerge singing with the light mechanism except for comic effect. Lyric and coloratura sopranos, on the other hand, sing in all light mechanism, "thickening" it at the bottom by mixing it with heavy voice. The quality in the pure chest voice below may not be usable in public.

261   The "two register" philosophy yields certain practical concepts. One is that of the "unused register" and another is that of "dynamic" as opposed to "static adjustment."

The Unused Register

262   Most beginners tend to sing either all heavy or all light. If they are conscious at all of the other register, they are schizophrenic about it. The *unused register* (a phrase I wish to coin because I think we will find it useful) is like a different personality to the beginner, something into which he lapses only by accident. He must be taught to use what I like to call *full voice*, a blending of both heavy and light quality.

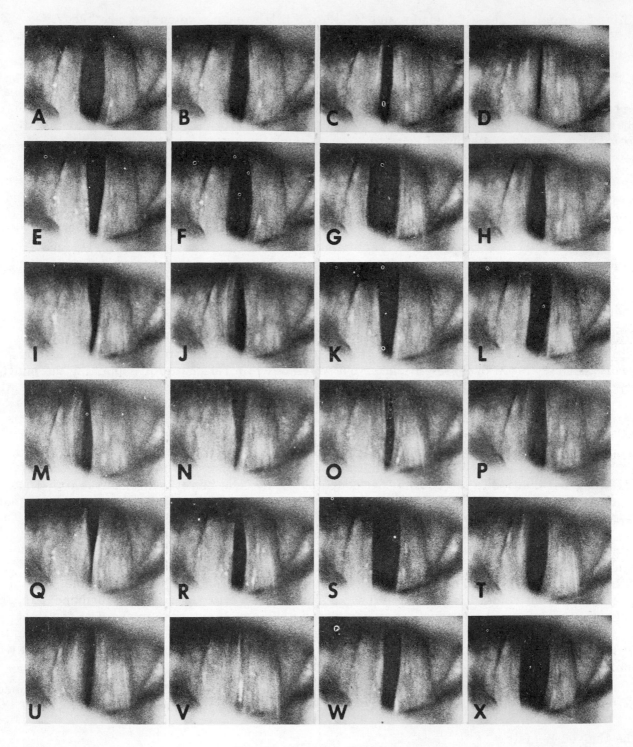

Fig. 37. Register "Break"

Roughly five vibrations at the moment of abrupt transition from heavy to light registration. The vocal folds are not under control and vibrate without any definite pattern. The duration of the different vibrations is irregular and the amplitude of maximum opening also varies: A, G, L, P, S, X. The folds almost close at D, I, N, and Q, but they do not achieve complete closure till V. Fastax camera sequence by Henry Rubin, from "The Falsetto, a high speed cinematographic study," *The Laryngoscope*, Sept. 1960. The motion picture is available from the author upon request.

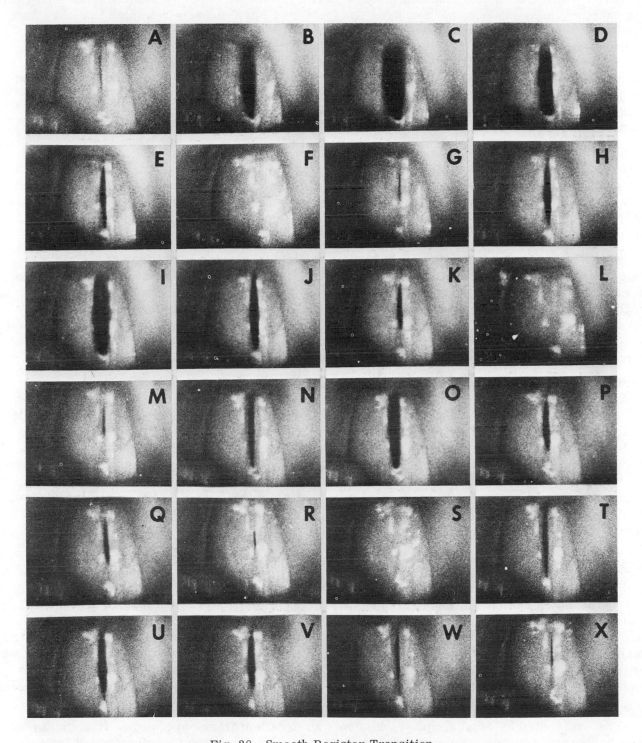

Fig. 38. Smooth Register Transition

Roughly four vibrations while singer is making a portamento from heavy to light registration without a "break." Mode of vibration is gradually changing. Note progressively decreasing amplitude of maximum opening in each cycle: C, I, O, U. Compare with the irregularity of the vibrations shown in Fig. 37. Fastax camera sequence by Henry Rubin, from "The Falsetto, a high speed cinematographic study," *The Laryngoscope,* Sept. 1960.

263   With men, the unused register is *falsetto*. Ever since their voices changed, most men (with the exception of some tenors) have been so afraid they might sound effeminate that they have cultivated a tense, heavy production. Take them up the scale and they will lighten their production only in the abrupt misfortune of "cracking" into falsetto. With women, the unused register is *chest*. With the exception of some contraltos, they have so carefully avoided masculinity as to sing entirely in light production. It is true that many women speak with "chest quality," and this is an advantage to the teacher, but he will find that women are averse to making their singing voices sound "coarse" like their speaking voices. Men both sing and speak in the same register, usually.

264   The development of the "unused register" produces two good results. It builds muscular strength somewhere in the vocal instrument, which I shall not venture to identify, but which I am sure is valuable to the singer. The laryngeal musculature is given a special kind of exercise in one extreme register which the opposite extreme will not provide, but which would be generally beneficial. Second, this practice gives the singer a "feel" of something that he should be doing but which he probably does not when he uses only the other mechanism.

265   Specifically, when a man sings in falsetto he overcomes some of his fear of high tones, and he gets the feel of relaxation of the vibrator and activation of the breath that he does not achieve in chest voice. It may be the means of discovering his "head voice," *voix mixte*, or *mezza voce*. In the adjustment known by these names, the vocalis muscles are not as relaxed as in falsetto, but they are much less active than in chest. The relaxation makes possible greater longitudinal tension and higher pitches, but the partial activity gives a continuity with the quality of chest voice. It is as if the singer had gone partway into falsetto, but still retained some of chest.

266   Similar statements can be made conversely about the woman's chest voice, but there is this very important consideration: it does no harm for a man to develop his falsetto downward, *but forcing the female chest voice upward is dangerous if not actually malpractice*. It is this mistake more than any other thing that has brought the two-register philosophy into disrepute. Hyperfunction (overuse) eventually leads to hypofunction (Froeschels), resulting in the loss of the upper tones of the voice, especially creating difficulty in bridging over into the light upper voice. A woman's chest voice *can* be extended upward over a long period of time, just as a man's can, but I have never felt any necessity to attempt this. She gains enough benefit simply from using the lower part of the chest as she will always, in combination with the upper registers.

Dynamic Versus Static Adjustment

267   I have already mentioned the difference between static and dynamic balance of the larynx (Par 219). When one cannot change the quality or leave the compass without a "break," this is a static adjustment. According to this definition, a bass has a "static falsetto," but he has a "dynamic adjustment" between chest and head; that is to say, there is a smooth transition from pure chest into a voice in which a great deal of falsetto is mixed. The dramatic soprano has a dynamic voice from top to bottom though she may perhaps slip into static adjustments occasionally. It is a question how many voices can hope to achieve the ideal of completely dynamic registration.

268   Otto Iro (quoted by Moses, pp. 45, 46) gives an excellent figure of speech. Imagine a test tube having earth in the bottom and water in the top. These are the two elements of the voice, chest and falsetto. In some voices they are separate, with only a scum of mud between. In others the water has penetrated the earth forming clay. The ideal is complete homogenization, with smooth clay all the way, a little thinner at the top and a little thicker at the bottom. Many voices have "static" earth at the bottom; many have pure water at the top; but it is the clay mixture that is useful for artistic purposes.

269   The multiple register concept has a tendency to work itself out in static adjustments related to the development of range. Such terms as "low register," "middle register," and "high register," illustrate the point. Psychologically this leads to problems of transition points. The great teachers have always recognized the overlapping of registers and the possibility of going from one to another on the same pitch, while making a crescendo or decrescendo. This is the essence of the *messa di voce*. Garcia (p. 8) recognized that a woman's chest voice overlaps her middle voice (which in his early writing he called "falsetto," which is rather confusing because "head" was still higher) and he proposed that she change on different notes for different artistic purposes. He also noted an overlap in men's voices and pointed out (Garcia[2], p. 39) that tenors, especially, benefit from passing from one register to another while singing certain single tones in the area of the overlap. He said, "It is very difficult, but once mastered, of great use." F. Lamperti and Shakespeare also pointed out these things. But most of the exponents of the multiple register concept overlooked these important matters. It is necessary to think of registration not only with reference to pitch, but also with reference to other properties of tone.

270   Three generalizations may be offered, one as to pitch, one as to intensity, and a third as to quality. First, to develop the widest possible range without a break, the adjustment must be heavy in the lower part of the voice, and the balance should shift smoothly toward the lighter production as the scale is ascended. Second, on any given pitch, the softer it is, the lighter must be the production without breathiness; and the louder, the heavier. Third, to produce "rich" timbre the adjustment should be heavy; to produce "sweet" timbre, it should be light. We have seen that the differences in timbre are differences in degrees of regularity and irregularity in the pattern of each vibration.

271   I have said that the vocal lips ripple like cloth. Imagine two Indians making smoke signals with blankets over a fire. If they let the blankets be loose and wave them, the smoke will rise in irregular, undulating puffs. This is like heavy registration. Each vibration is complex. If the Indians hold the blankets taut and merely open and close over the fire, the puffs will be simple, but could be produced at higher frequency. This resembles light registration.

The Lift of the Breath

272   Talented beginners often approximate the desired results by availing themselves of what Witherspoon (p. 90) and others have called "lifts of the breath." They do not make as violent a change in registration as I have described as "cracking," but they do make definite shifts. At certain places in their ranges they feel that the tension is becoming too great, and they consciously and audibly change to lighter production. As we have seen, the lighter the production the less the intensity for the same amount of breath pressure. Therefore, in order to keep the volume from dropping off, the singer feels the need for an extra surge of breath at the point of shifting. The expression, "lift of the breath," is very descriptive.

273   I daresay every singer feels a certain amount of "lifting" in going toward high notes. The more gradually he lightens, the less perceptibly will he "lift." The more abruptly he must make the change, and the more introspective and selfconscious he is about it, the more he is likely to locate definite notes upon which the lifts take place. Choirmasters sometimes place voices not by discovering the extremes of their ranges (which due to lack of development might not be singable) but by locating their lifts. Authorities do not agree as to precisely where certain voices can be expected to shift, but the method nevertheless can be used for practical purposes. It is most useful with unsophisticated voices. A clever singer can make a lift on any one of several notes, and a suggestible one will probably give you one on whatever note you lead him to believe is right for his voice. Some force, by singing with heavy mechanism up beyond the point where they should have begun to use a lighter adjustment.

274   Some authorities believe that there are several places in every voice where changes in registration take place, and these correspond to intervals in the harmonic series. I feel that probably the notes have been chosen arbitrarily, or at best that the relation to the partials is only coincidence. It is a mistake to explain registration on the basis of overblowing. Instrumental overblowing is a matter of the physics of the resonance system, while vocal registration is a matter of the physiology of the vibrator. Overblowing occurs most readily in a tube whose diameter is very small in comparison with its length, as in the brasses. The dimensions of the vocal resonators are exactly the opposite.

275   It is sometimes argued that A_3, top line, is a "lift note" for basses. Does this mean that A_3 is the first overtone? If so, A_2, bottom space, would be the fundamental, and most basses can sing much lower than this. If A is the second overtone, then low D_2 is the fundamental. This is the bottom of some bass voices, but not the bottom of all, but even passing that, we find D_3, middle line, as the first overtone, and I daresay no bass is conscious of a "lift" there.

276   I prefer not to locate specific notes upon which a voice will change, because this tends to make the student self-conscious when he sees these notes in songs. The emotional stimulation of a well written phrase should carry the singer through without worries such as: "That F is my 'changing note.' I know I won't be able to get a good tone on it."

The Classification of Voices

277   No statistics are available, but it may be expected that most voices have medium ranges. That is to say, most men are baritones and most women mezzo-sopranos, but we must remember that because of the unused register, the facts are disguised. Most untrained baritones have not discovered how to sing their top tones, and hence consider themselves basses. Most untrained mezzos dislike the category, and because they have a satisfactory head voice consider themselves sopranos. A good many teachers are so pleased with the fresh lightness of a young girl's talent and yield so readily to the temptation to work on repertoire instead of building the voice, that they try to make coloraturas of all their feminine students. If the girl happens to be a potential contralto, it will be discovered only if she also happens to be completely unashamed of her chest voice. Meanwhile she may strain her voice working for high notes that are not hers. The only girls who really benefit by cultivating the falsetto exclusively are the true coloraturas, who are rare.

278   The unusual voices are the extremes: bass, tenor, alto, and high soprano. In most choirs, the tenor and alto sections are filled out with a selection of high baritones and low mezzos. Such are the exigencies of reality and the facts should be recognized. The choirmaster should guard against demanding too much from these people; permanent injury can be done to their voices. Of course, among those who undertake a professional singing career, the extreme voices are in greater proportion than they would be found in the general population, should such a census be taken. Competition eliminates a greater number of mezzos and baritones.

279   I never feel any urgency about classifying a beginning student. So many premature diagnoses have been proved wrong, and it can be harmful to the student and embarrassing to the teacher to keep striving for an ill-chosen goal. It is best to begin in the middle part of the voice and work upward and downward gradually until the voice classifies itself. Students of better than average talent will probably have a certain amount of coordination of light and heavy in this area, and it is merely a matter of extending it. Avoid the fallacy of thinking that the middle is good enough and that it is the extremes that need work. When technic has been perfected in the middle, where it is easiest, its application to the extremes will make them easier, but at the top or the bottom is no place to practice technic. It is difficult enough and hard enough on the larynx to sing there at all, and until one has mastered the easy notes, the high and low ones will get no better. However, high and low tones should be vocalized a little in each session. The extremes will not come unless they are claimed.

280   The ideal is to develop both heavy and light production as *one* voice without involving the discussion of registers. The material of this chapter is offered for the instruction of teachers rather than the confusion of students. In most cases, however, the beginner will have questions to ask, or will have an unused register to develop.

281   A well trained voice of professional calibre will probably have a compass of two octaves. Wider ranges are not uncommon, but in order to generalize we may hold to the interval of the fifteenth. The bass voice is roughly from E_2 below the bass staff to the E_4 above it. The baritone octaves are a third higher, and the tenor should be able to reach C_5 above Middle C. Altos may be thought of as an octave above bass; mezzo, above baritone; soprano, above tenor. Generally the women's voices are a tone or so higher than this, but these boundaries are arbitrary anyhow. Endless embellishments are made upon this outline, because no two voices are identical.

282   But voices should not be classified entirely by range. Many singers have wide ranges—more than two octaves—and the important criterion is *tessitura*, that is, that part of the range in which the voice performs best, both as to sound and as to ease. Basses and contraltos sing largely in chest voice, but tenors and sopranos use the light voice as well as the heavy. To the extent that they prefer light production we call them *lyric*, and their high tones will be their best. All young high voices should be classified lyric, regardless of potential. As they mature some of them will learn to use the vocalis muscles more actively in the upper range. This is called "pushing" and is dangerous, but nothing ventured nothing gained. The Italians actually dignify it by recognizing it as a classification, *spinto* (literally, pushed). A *lyrico spinto* is an essentially light voice that sings more powerfully in dramatic climaxes.

283   A spinto may acquire enough stamina, with patience, to sing full voice all the time. The *dramatic soprano* is either a spinto who is now able to "push" relentlessly, or a mezzo who has learned to carry her full production (or nearly so) clear to the top of the soprano range, say high C_6. The *heroic tenor (Heldentenor, tenore robusto)* may develop from a spinto, but is more often "a pushed-up baritone." This kind of singing is only for rare voices, and probably not before the age of thirty-five. It is foolhardy—and a little ridiculous—for a young singer to classify himself as "dramatic."

284   Of course, these distinctions are relative. In opera workshops one often hears young singers in dramatic roles. This is not as dangerous as some may believe, providing the young voice is not pitted against mature professionals who have genuinely big voices. True, the orchestration is likely to be heavy, but the important consideration is the balance of the voices on the stage, and if this is satisfactory the orchestra can be held down, given favorable acoustics. Also, a spinto can give extravagantly for a few workshop performances judiciously spaced, and this is not the same as singing a professional season at the same dynamic level. In rehearsals all wise singers save their voices by "marking the part," that is, singing lightly or dropping the high tones an octave.

Chapter 5

RESONANCE

285   It is with the reluctance of leaving an unfinished chapter that I leave our discussion of the function of the larynx. There are many unresolved questions, and all I can say is that in no book that I have read, in no remark of any colleague that I can remember, in no experience or observation of my own have I found satisfactory answers. The healthy activity of the muscles in the voice box lies below the level of consciousness, in a realm that still awaits new technics of investigation. Only when something is painfully wrong do we become conscious of the function and never do we control it directly.

286   If you take a bite of toast, it is voluntary. You may chew it consciously for as long or as short a time as you like, and in any manner. Of course, the act becomes habitual, and thus subconscious, but still you can at any time analyze the process consciously. Even the act of swallowing is voluntary. But from there on the process is both involuntary and unconscious. You cannot learn how to digest your food; the most you can do is learn how to provide the best conditions, emotionally, etc., for the thing to take place. If you become aware of food in your stomach, it means indigestion. So it is with the voice-box. If you feel that you are manufacturing the tone in it, you are feeling something that is wrong. It is only when you seem to "let go" in the larynx, and the tone begins to seem as if it were in the resonators, that production will be right.

287   This is the reason that so much emphasis has been laid upon various ideas of resonance. The resonators can be controlled consciously, by careful training. It is like forming habits of taking and masticating food; laborious and inept at first, but finally a skill that has become so habitual the performer can forget it. Registration was first thought of in terms of resonance, as shown by the persistence of such terms as "head voice" and "chest voice." And it is just as well, because we control registration indirectly, largely in terms of just such imagery. That is why vocal pedagogy is so much more intangible than instrumental pedagogy. The voice teacher cannot say, "Put your index finger on this valve and your middle finger on *this* one, and for this note press down the first one and for *this* note press both of them." Even a thing like singing falsetto instead of full voice is done indirectly, on the basis of past experience, controlled by the ear, suggested by imagery. Learning to sing is a slow and patient undertaking, in which a good ear is the prerequisite, the imagery is an aid supplied by the teacher, and the experience is gradually accumulated until it is so powerful that merely calling up the memory will reproduce it.

288   There are probably more matters that have their seat in the larynx but their apparent controls in the resonators. Some laryngologists tell us that with every superficial change in the resonators there is a change in the vibrator. They would have us believe that the whole art of singing lies in this subconscious region, with the implicit conclusion that there is little point in learning the control of anything else. This, however, is contrary to experience. Most singers have improved their voices by learning what to do with the pharynx, the mouth, the tongue, the jaw, etc., and hence this chapter. But I want to guard against thinking that resonance tells the whole story. There is good evidence that when we are learning the shaping of the cavities above the larynx, we are training the vocal cords unconsciously at the same time.

Two Theories of Vocal Resonance

289   Helmholtz founded the present science of acoustics, and few of his basic ideas, for all their age, have been repudiated. He elaborated the concept of vocal resonance originally suggested by Wheatstone in 1837, and the one that has been advanced thus far in this book. This theory may still be considered as the most apt generalization. It is that the vocal lips produce a tone with a definite desired pitch, considerable volume, and of complex timbre, having the possibilities of beauty. As this tone passes through the throat and mouth, these cavities encourage those partials which make for power and beauty, and muffle the undesirable ones; or, in the case of the unskillful singer, the opposite occurs.

290   Some authorities argue that the laryngeal tone is raucous and even louder before the purifying process. They argue that the walls of the resonators are fleshy and tend to absorb and dampen. Others feel that there is not only a filtering but also an augmentation of the volume of that part of the tone which the resonators let through. Some of the sounds of an excised larynx are disappointing in volume, and it is also true that when experiments are made with the co-operation of a patient whose cancerous larynx is about to be removed and who (under local anesthetic) is able to phonate a little directly through the incision without the aid of his normal resonators, the tones are weak. These facts are cited to show that resonators enhance the volume of the tone. But we must remember that under such abnormal conditions the singer is also unable to avail himself of the help of his extrinsic musculature. It is practically impossible to test the volume of a sound made without resonators in any way that can be related to normal phonation.

291   In 1906, another authority, Scripture, proposed quite a different idea, which perhaps goes as far back as Willis, 1830. He said:

> According to Wheatstone, Grassman and Helmholtz the glottal lips vibrate after the manner of strings and produce a series of partials of which the first (or fundamental)—that is, the tone of the voice—is the strongest. The series of cavities above the glottis reinforce certain of these partials; for each vowel the cavities are readjusted and a different set of partials is reinforced. . . . The overtone theory of vowels cannot be correct, (Scripture, p. 109).

Scripture argued that the larynx produced no overtones, but only a series of puffs. These determined the pitch of the tone and at the same time excited the air in the resonators so that they sounded their own frequencies in much the same way that a bottle gives forth a tone when you blow across the mouth of it. This theory made the larynx comparatively unimportant, like the vibrator of a reed instrument, or of the flute, whose only function is to set into vibration the column of air. In this case the quality of the laryngeal tone would be negligible, and its volume, insignificant; both power and beauty would be overwhelmingly products of the resonators.

292   Scripture influenced the thinking of serious teachers of singing at the time. Lilli Lehmann, for example, wrote of *Wirbeln* created in the larynx and passing through the resonators, where the tone was considered to be "placed." (This word *Wirbeln* has been translated "whirling currents," whereas "eddies" would be preferable. The word *Wirbeln* gave rise to the so-called "vortex" theory, accompanied by drawings of little tornados, like corkscrews, twisting upward from the larynx into the throat, mouth, sinuses, etc.) Marafioti (p. 125) acknowledges his indebtedness to Scripture, but it is not likely that Scripture would ever have supported his statement, "Voice is speech, and is produced by the *mouth* and not by the *vocal cords*," (p. 69).

293   In the case of a reed instrument, even the pitch is determined by the air cavity, (Par. 57). The important difference between the voice and a woodwind is that the player must make his reed vibrate in tune with the pipe, whereas the frequency or pitch of a vocal tone is determined

primarily by the vibrator, and usually only the timbre is modified by the resonators. In some cases resonators that are hopelessly out of tune may affect intonation; this explains how singers with good ears but poor technic can sing "off key."

294   Wheatstone and Helmholtz availed themselves of the Fourier theorem which analyzed vocal tone into harmonic partials. Scripture admitted the possibility of this theoretically, but insisted that while it was true to the nature of strings, it was only a mathematical trick with reference to the voice. He utilized the formulae of another calculator, Hermann, to show that most Fourier spectra of vocal tone could be analyzed still further to show the presence of *inharmonic* partials, and he was convinced that this was a better explanation of the facts.

295   At first it would seem that these ideas are incompatible, but it is believed today that both principles probably operate simultaneously. We may assume that the voice is more akin to the brasses than to either the reeds or the strings. (Incidentally, this is true to Helmholtz, Scripture notwithstanding.) The resonators function selectively with reference to the laryngeal tone, which is of primary importance, but they also add frequencies which are generated in themselves, and which may not exist in the laryngeal vibration at all. These added frequencies would depend on the size and shape of the respective resonators and might not belong to the harmonic series for the fundamental pitch being sounded. These frequencies tend to compromise with the nearest frequency in the harmonic series; however we have not a simple case of the augmentation of overtones, but the actual addition of new pitches. In some cases the result is objectionable, and the singer must find a way to correct it by reshaping the resonators. Mackworth-Young (p. 73 ff.) is convinced that a good singer always tunes his throat in harmony with his vocal cords. Vocal pedagogs sometimes speak of "fundamental" as being produced in the larynx, and of "overtone" as being produced in the resonators. From what has been written here, it can be seen that while this is careless usage of the terms, it expresses a concept that is not entirely incorrect. More about all this later (Par. 417).

296   If it seems that my explanations of vocal resonance are confusing, I can only say that the reality I am trying to describe is even more so. Those pedagogs who offer simple generalizations resemble the fabled committee of blind men who went to "see" the elephant. One felt the trunk and reported, "The elephant is like a snake." Another felt the tusk and insisted, "The elephant is like a spear." Even if you never heard the fable, you can easily imagine the other reports, The members of the committee differed radically in their conclusions and yet each was correct on the basis of his own observations.

297   Certain principles may be accepted as a basis for understanding. First, any resonator is a secondary vibrator. Second, the vocal resonator is a column of air. It is not a sounding board of some sort, as comparisons with stringed instruments would make it. Third, the shape of the resonator is not only complex, but highly variable. Thus it may vibrate as a whole or in any of its parts. It should not be too hard to think of it as vibrating several ways at once. Indeed most vibrators do this, otherwise we would not have timbre, which consists of several frequencies of different intensities sounding together. Air is fully as capable of this as any other medium; indeed, the sounds of many diverse instruments are carried to the ear by the same air, are funnelled into the same tiny canal, and can still be heard as one sound or as sounds from the individual sources, depending upon the manner in which we give attention.

298   Not all sympathetic vibration contributes to the acoustical product of an instrument. We shall see that some of it is wasted, in that the audience never hears it. The singer may be aware of such vibration, and whether or not it helps him depends upon how he adjusts to it. It may help him psychologically (in terms of "placement" Par. 431-436), or it may deceive him into preferring a tone which sounds good to him but not to the listeners. In some cases, as we have seen (Par. 55, 56) sympathetic vibration produces a *wolf tone* that does more harm than

good, and this can happen in the voice, (Par. 313). There are three kinds of vibration in a musical instrument. First, there is the primary vibrator; in the voice this is the larynx. There is also a secondary vibrator which we call the "resonator"; in the voice this is a body of air chiefly in the throat and mouth. Third, there is the wasteful vibration I have mentioned. Strictly speaking it, too, is resonance, though dictionary definitions include the idea of *reinforcement* or *prolongation* which do not apply to this third type of vibration. I shall use the word "resonance" only for the secondary vibration which enhances the voice.

299   The quality of the vocal tone will be a product of the original glottal sound, minus those overtones which were discouraged by the resonance cavities, plus the augmentation of overtones that were encouraged, plus possible inharmonic frequencies which were generated simply by virtue of the fact that the air in certain cavities was set in motion. To the extent that the resonators are subject to conscious control, then, we should be interested in their pitch and what are the factors that determine the pitch.

The Size and Shape of the Resonators

300   The larger anything is, the less frequent will be its vibrations. The larger the body of air, the lower its pitch. If the shape is that of a cylinder in which the diameter is small in proportion to the height, this latter factor will be the determiner. This is the case, for example, with the resonators of a marimba or xylophone, or with some organ pipes, indeed most wind instruments. The pitch is fairly easy to compute, because we know how fast sound waves travel (1100 feet per second) and thus how far apart compression waves will be. For example, in the pitch A-440, there are 440 waves in every 1100 feet, so they must be 30 inches apart, and 30 inches is the *wave-length* of A-440. If a 440 tuning fork is near a $7\frac{1}{2}$ inch tube, a compression wave will go to the bottom and be reflected back out (a total of 15 inches) in one 880th of a second, just in time to make room for the rarefaction wave to go in and out during the second half of the cycle. If the pipe is longer, the compression wave will not emerge in time, and a rarefaction wave will start down into the pipe too soon. The two waves will cancel each other out. If the pipe is shorter, the compression wave will get out all right, but the rarefaction wave will be late and the motion of the air will have subsided and will have to be started all over again. The comparatively inaudible action of the fork will be timed exactly for a $7\frac{1}{2}$ inch pipe, and the air contained in it will be put into strong vibration, just as a child giving weak pushes to a swing at the right moments will make its motion more and more ample. Notice that for closed pipes, the length is one fourth the wave-length of the pitch it will resonate, or that it will sound if it is blown.

301   With the exception of the trachea and possibly the pharynx, the bodily cavities are not cylindrical, and the problem becomes much more difficult. We still have the general indication that the greater the volume, the lower is the pitch. Where we have spherical cavities, like the Helmholtz resonators, the larger the opening, the higher is the pitch. On the other hand, if the opening has a neck, the pitch is lowered. When the shape approaches that of a cone, it is more likely to respond equally to all frequencies, and the greater the diameter in ratio to the altitude, the more this is so. For instance, in the megaphone we have a resonator that tends to amplify all pitches indiscriminately. The old-time Victrola horn utilized this principle.

The Combining of Resonators

302   When cavities are connected their pitches are not the same as they would be separately. Pagel, who did many experiments trying to reproduce vocal sounds with artificial resonators, joined a large resonator having the pitch 645, with a front orifice 24 mm. in diameter, to another resonator, smaller and having the pitch 812, the opening between them being 22 mm.

When a tone, representing the laryngeal tone, was sounded through them, passing from the 812 resonator first, the overtone resonated by the second one was not 645, but ten semitones lower, almost an octave! In another case, a small resonator with a large opening, 20 mm., and the high pitch of 2298, was coupled with a large one, 512, the orifice between them being only 8 mm. The pitch of the small resonator fell a full tone and the pitch of the other dropped a fourth.

303   Paget set forth the following laws:

> The effect of joining two resonators, the one with larynx attached at one end and the other end open, and the other with both orifices open, is in general to lower the resonance of each, but in different proportions according to their relative capacities, and to the relative areas of the common central orifice and the front orifice of the front resonator.
>
> For a front resonator, the maximum fall occurs when the front resonator is large and the back resonator small, and the central orifice is large compared with the front orifice.
>
> The minimum fall occurs when the front resonator is small compared with the back resonator, and the front orifice is large compared with the central orifice.
>
> For a back resonator the maximum fall is produced by a large back resonator and small front resonator, with a large central orifice and small front orifice.
>
> The minimum fall is produced by a small back resonator combined with a large front resonator. In this case the size of the central and front orifices is practically immaterial, (Paget, pp. 762-763).

304   You have doubtless recognized that the two cavities represented are the throat and the mouth, but our laws cover only two. What happens when the nasal passages are shunted in?

The Composition of Resonator Walls

305   There are other considerations beside size and shape. Miller performed interesting experiments in the *composition* of resonator walls, following a suggestion in the writings of Schafhäutl (Munich, 1879). He made three organ pipes having exactly the same cavity dimensions. The first was quite ordinary, made of wood, and gave the tone G_3 (top space, bass clef). Another was made of zinc and had hollow walls, leaving a space 2 cm. thick that could be filled with water. Here is Miller's account:

> While the pipe is sounding continuously, the space between the walls is slowly filled with water at room temperature. The pipe, with the dimensions of a wooden pipe giving the tone G_4, when empty has the pitch of F_4, and when the walls are filled with water the pitch is E_4; during the filling the pitch varies more than a semitone, first rising then falling. While the space is filling, the tone quality changes conspicuously thirty or forty times, (D. C. Miller, p. 181).

306   The third pipe had single walls of zinc. Of it, we read:

> Using the single-walled pipe one can produce the remarkable effect of choking the pipe till it actually squeals. When the pipe is blown in the ordinary manner, its sound has the usual tone quality. If the pipe is firmly grasped in both hands just above the mouth, it speaks a mixture of three clearly distinguished inharmonic partial tones, the ratios of which are approximately 1:2.06:2.66. The resulting unmusical sound is so unexpected that it is almost startling, the tone quality having changed from that of a flute to that of a tin horn, (D. C. Miller, P. 181).

307   Russell quotes these two passages and adds that he did similar tricks with a lead-tin, round walled, open organ pipe, pitched at D_5 sharp (treble staff) "which gives what is probably as passable an imitation of the vowel α (ah) as can be had by such mechanical means."

> If while this pipe is sounding, it is grasped just above the exit (letting it fall into the soft crotch between the thumb and forefinger which are then pressed against it laterally) it speaks αu-αu-αu as plainly as any other mechanical vowels the author has heard. At the same time its

pitch is not lowered more than a fraction of a semi-tone. . . . . The vowel quality change must therefore have been due to changed partials, (Russell, p. 68).

If it is possible to make a lead-tin pipe say "Ouch!" merely by squeezing it, not enough to change its shape, can we wonder that muscular tension in a singer's throat spoils the quality, and makes his vowels unrecognizable? We should specify in passing that the resonator is still the body of *air,* but that its vibration is conditioned by the *container* which defines it.

The Surface of the Resonators

308   *The hardness or softness of the surfaces* of the container encourage or discourage high overtones. Soft walls absorb the rapid, short-wave vibrations, making the quality sweeter, mellower. Hard walls make the tone more brilliant by reflecting the high partials, unimpaired. In the vocal resonators we have various surfaces. Most of them are fleshy and therefore soft, but the hard palate has a bony structure near enough to the surface to make a difference. Indeed many have erroneously called it a "sounding-board." Finally, just before the tone emerges, it may pass either a soft, fleshy orifice (as in the vowel "oo") or a sharp, hard-edged orifice (as in the vowel "ee," especially when it is "smiled"), (Par. 472). The teeth are as hard and sharp as we are likely to find in any resonator. The cartilages of the trachea have an interesting effect, (Par. 313).

309   Scripture experimented with resonators of different materials, some brass like the Helmholtz resonators, and some softer texture like flesh (meat over a wire frame) and water (saturated cotton over a frame). He did this to refute the Wheatstone-Helmholtz theory. He showed that a hard resonator will respond only when the vibrator contains an overtone that is exactly in tune with the resonator, while a soft resonator permits a wide range of fundamentals to pass through undampened but adds its own frequency as an overtone, harmonic or inharmonic as the case may be.

> Helmholtz supposed the vocal cavities to act as a series of resonators which respond to definite overtones in the glottal tone. Such a proposition would be appropriate if the cavities were made of metal or other hard substances. The vocal cavities have, however, soft or moderately hard walls lined with moist membranes. The laws of resonance for soft cavities are different from those for brass resonators. The experiments on resonance. . . . show that cavities with soft walls will respond to a range of tone which increases as the softness; for example, a cavity with walls of water will respond to any tone, a cavity with flesh walls to a considerable range of tone, etc. . . . The process of vowel production must therefore differ completely from the theory that compares it to the response of hard resonators to overtones, (Scripture, p. 110).

310   In justice to Helmholtz, however, we must record that he anticipated this discussion, for after enunciating his basic theory, he wrote:

> Moreover vowels admit of other kinds of alterations in their qualities of tone. . . Flaccid soft walls in any passage with sonorous masses of air, are generally prejudicial to the force of the vibrations. Partly too much of the motion is given off to the outside through the soft masses, partly too much is destroyed by friction within them. Wooden organ pipes have a less energetic quality of tone than metal ones, and those of pasteboard a still duller quality. . . The walls of the human throat, and the cheeks, are, however, much more yielding than pasteboard, (Helmholtz, p. 115).

The Chest as a Resonator

311   Having examined the factors which determine the function of a resonator, we should now count and evaluate the cavities of the body with this in mind. One often hears the expression, "chest resonance," and as a relic of a former day of pedagogy it may be tolerated, but we must

not allow ourselves to include the chest seriously in our list. Let us not forget that the resonators are cavities of *air*, and while there is air in the lungs it certainly is not free to vibrate
as an integral mass. The chest is not a resonator because it is not a cavity! The thorax is
filled with a soft, spongy material similar to that used artificially for insulation. It would tend
to absorb, not augment. As a fifth argument against clavicular breathing (in addition to the
four I gave in Par. 112) it is sometimes said that the chest must be kept expanded so that it
will provide good resonance. I think we must resist the temptation to use this argument; the
poor quality of the flat-chested is due to their poor breath support which results in excessive
laryngeal tension. If the chest were a resonator it would be constantly changing its pitch, because even though the ribs may remain fixed the volume is decreasing because of the ascent of
the diaphragm. The capacity of the thorax cannot remain constant during exhalation, and there
cannot be phonation except with steadily controlled exhalation.

312   To refer to the chest as a "sounding-board" is even worse. No instrument maker would use
a cage for a sounding-board, and even supposing he did, he certainly would not fill the spaces
and cover the framework with a soft material like flesh. If the chest were a sounding-board,
singers would have more volume if they exposed their bodies. No instrument maker would
cover his sounding-board with an insulator, and yet we all know that Siegfried sings just as
loudly wrapped in a bear-skin as he does in any other circumstances.

The Trachea and Bronchi as Resonators

313   It must be admitted, however, that the trachea is a clear tube with fairly hard surfaces. The
fact that it is below the larynx and that the tone does not pass through it on its way to the audience makes no difference. Every time a compression wave is created above the glottis, the
pressure below the glottis is decreased: that is, a rarefaction wave is formed: and *vice versa*.
The pattern which goes up also goes down. The fact that it is in reverse makes no difference,
the frequencies are all the same. The trachea connects with two bronchi which subdivide further, forming an inverted hollow tree. Van den Berg[4] has measured the resonance properties
of these tubes and the frequencies are shown in Fig. 39. Oddly enough this resonance is more
of a hindrance than a help.

314   To understand this we need to repeat an experiment first done by Weiss in 1932 and one
which you will find amusing. He used glass tubes 27 to 28 mm. in diameter, 100, 84, and 50 cm.
in length. If you will take such a tube in your mouth and sing a scale from low to high you will
discover that the quality is greatly changed by the long artificial resonator, but what may come
as a surprise is that when you get to a certain pitch your voice will probably sputter! With a
little effort you can go on up beyond the place where you sputtered, but the quality of your voice
will be different. The critical frequency, at which the sputter occurs, will be found to be the
natural frequency of the air in the vocal cavities *plus the glass tube.*

315   Now I have described what will *probably* happen the first time you try the experiment. However, with a little practice you will discover that you can compensate and by anticipating the
transition to a new quality you can get past the critical frequency without sputtering. This is
remarkably like the experience of every singer who has learned to overcome difficulties of
register transition. The learning is a subconscious adjustment monitored by ear and by "feel,"
but it is a muscular adjustment. In other words the basic problem of registration is myoelastic.
I wish to emphasize this point. Bronchotracheal resonance is an interesting detail to be added
to what we were considering in Chapter 4, but it does not amount to a revolutionary discovery
that changes all our broad concepts of register.

316   The reason that this happens is that a resonator with hard walls will assert its own frequency
strongly enough to compete with the strength of the larynx. As I have already mentioned (Par.

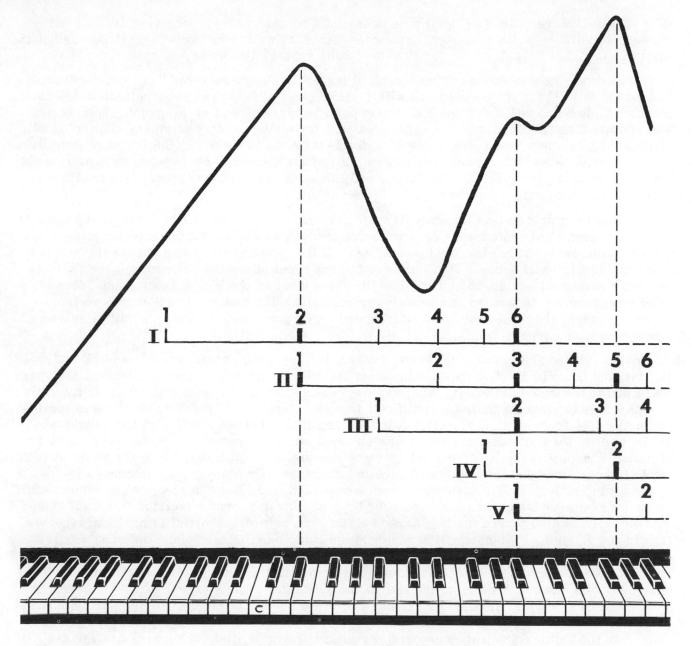

Fig. 39. Chart of Bronchotracheal Resonance
Graph at top from van den Berg,[4] *NATS Bulletin*. Below are spectra of possible tones in human voice. II is most important, since it can be sung in all voices, male and female, and its fundamental is affected. Where only an overtone is affected this is probably only of theoretical interest. V involves the fundamental, but concerns only high sopranos.

55), for ideal resonance one vibrator must dominate the other, and normally the larynx dominates the air in the vocal cavities. The Weiss experiment was not fully accepted as an explanation of registration because the facts were applied to the resonators above the glottis—after all, the glass tube was simply an extension of the supraglottal resonators—and glass has properties that make it so different from the natural resonators that conclusions drawn about one may not be applied to the other. We have already seen that Scripture pointed this out

(Par. 309). However, the subglottal resonator—the bronchotracheal tree—very likely does create interference at its resonant frequencies, since its walls are harder. Cartilage is not as hard as glass, but it is much harder than the fleshy supraglottal walls.

317   In van den Berg's experiments with excised larynges this phenomenon has been duplicated. If a larynx is in chest voice (low pitch with vertical phase difference) and longitudinal tension is increased, the pitch will go up until a certain point is reached, and at this point a sputtering will occur. If the conditions of the experiment are maintained at this point, the sputtering will continue for a moment, and then a new vibrational pattern will be set up (higher pitch with little or no vertical phase difference) resulting in midvoice or falsetto. Often this new vibration cannot maintain itself for long, and the larynx will fall back into the chest tone. This oscillation between registers will repeat itself.

318   Van den Berg proved by various tests that the critical frequency at which this will happen is that of the subglottal system—the tank and tubes through which the compressed air passes on its way up to the vocal cords. Change the length of the tubing and you will change the pitch at which the sputter will occur. There are two factors which make the phenomenon very noticeable. First, the tubing has hard walls like the glass tubes of the Weiss experiment. Second, a dead larynx cannot "learn" to compensate for acoustical impedance. The Weiss experiment catches a singer the first time because it takes him by surprise, but later the singer makes slight muscular compensations.

319   Another glance at Fig. 39 will remind you that the resonance peaks are at about E_4 flat, B_5 flat, and G_6. The first of these is the most significant, since both men and women can sing tones whose fundamentals are on this pitch (represented by Spectrum II), and most individuals of both sexes experience their most difficult register transition here. Note that this is located on an absolute scale, just as Garcia located the registers, and not relative to the individual voice, that is, the difficult transition (between chest and the register above) is in the upper part of a man's voice and the lower part of a woman's voice. In fact, this is about the same tone on which Garcia advocated leaving chest voice in both sexes. (In his early writing he called the upper register "falsetto" in both sexes, which caused him to place "head voice" in women still higher, a confusion which he corrected later by renaming her middle register "medium voice."). The old Italians also placed the boundary at E flat or E natural, though it is not clear whether they meant E_4 or E_5. Numerous later authorities could be cited who place the most difficult register transition just a little above Middle C_4 in both male and female voices. Some teachers say that men "color" their voices at the top and women at the bottom. The sex of an individual does not make much difference in the size of the subglottal system except that a smaller individual will have slightly smaller tubes, and this will move the pitches up somewhat. Of course these are not the only points of interest with reference to registers, and myoelastic factors enter into the picture. Sopranos report a transition around B_5 flat, which also fits van den Berg's findings for the bronchotracheal tree, but few singers can get high enough to test the G_6. I have suggested how upper partials of some tones might be interfered with, but this is not likely to be worth much consideration.

320   I should like to point out that what we are discussing here is due to sympathetic vibration, but it is not the kind of "resonance" singers speak of as a desirable property of the tone. Instead it is analogous to a "wolf tone." It is not a case of the air column sounding in one register (like the *chalumeau* of the clarinet) and then "lifting" or "overblowing" into a higher register (like the *clarino*, Par. 58). The air column in the Weiss experiment is merely passing on the primary vibration to the outer air, except at the critical frequency, at which point acoustical impedance rises rather suddenly to a point which demands a laryngeal readjustment. The resonance which truly contributes to the acoustical product of the voice is found in the supra-

glottal cavities still to be considered in this chapter. The air in them transmits the fundamental frequency of the glottis without interference and resonates various harmonic partials.

321   Except for the possibility of high impedance at the pitches shown in Fig. 39, the resonance of the trachea and bronchi is the same for all the sounds any given voice can produce. It is impossible to "add chest resonance" to some tones and not to others. The only way resonance of the trachea could be eliminated would be to plug it, and needless to say, this would end not only the tone but the singer as well. Stanley implied that tracheal resonance could be used in low tones of the voice, and eliminated in higher tones, thus providing a resonator of a more appropriate length. He thought the cavities resonated the fundamental. Wilcox, who in "The Living Voice" wrote an interpretation that I find more acceptable than Stanley's own books, included this idea in a long quotation in his first edition (pp. 7, 8 derived from Stanley[2], pp. 83-85) but significantly eliminated it from later editions. A footnote in Stanley[2] (p. 72) indicates that he was aware of his error at least to some extent. It is entirely possible to add heavy registration, which is sometimes called "chest quality," but this is not "adding chest resonance."

The Larynx as a Resonator

322   We are accustomed to think of the larynx as merely the vibrator, since it is the site of the vocal bands, but after all it is also a cavity. Startling as it may be, our most prized resonance may be here! Bartholomew (pp. 145-147) reports investigations at Peabody Conservatory which show that the "ring" of the voice is the presence of a strong overtone averaging around 2800-2900 cycles for men (about F_7 to F_7 sharp at the top of the piano), and higher, about 3200 cycles, for women. The actual frequency varies and is not reported as the same by all investigators, but since "2800" is convenient to remember I shall use it in quotation marks hereafter to mean any of these high frequencies which give "ring" to the voice.

323   This "ring" has various characteristics that associate it with the larynx. It is not always heard in the falsetto, but its intensity varies with the extent to which the full voice is used. This we know to be a function of the vibrator. The absence of the "ring" in falsetto is due to the fact that there is less muscular resistance in the larynx and most of the breath pressure goes into the fundamental, leaving not enough energy to sound upper partials. This is another way of saying that falsetto is comparatively breathy and "hooty." We know, of course that some falsetto productions are stronger than this, and in such cases a ring can be heard. (Incidentally, the contention that women use more of the falsetto than men parallels the fact that women have less of this "ring" we are discussing, especially in the highest ranges.) Also, the "ring" is intermittant, and sounds only with the high intensity phase of the vibrato. This will be discussed later, but here again it is probably laryngeal.

324   Above the glottis is a space which is defined by the aryepiglottic folds, which, stiffened by the cartilages of Wrisberg and held open by the epiglottis, form a kind of collar for the larynx, (Par. 205). We may assume that when there is the right kind of tension in the vocal lips, a certain partial of about the frequency mentioned above is produced, and at the same time the collar shapes itself to tune the air space accordingly; or we may assume that if the collar is shaped correctly the air in it will vibrate at the frequency of "2800" providing there is enough strength in the laryngeal vibration to sound it. Russell attributes great importance to the function of the epiglottis and also intimates that the cartilages of Wrisberg may be more significant than we have supposed.

325   Because there are so many complex factors involved it is difficult to say how well adapted this cavity is to resonate the frequency of 2800 cycles per second. There are other cavities in the same general region. Russell has called attention to the space between the tongue and the epiglottis which is called the vallecula. The same conditions as are outlined above would apply

to this cavity. The spaces between the collar of the larynx and the thyroid cartilage, known as the *pyriform sinuses,* might also qualify. Eijkman suggests that the spaces between the faucial pillars and the back of the pharynx could be adjusted to resonate "2800." This could easily cause it to be associated with nasality; and might account for the fact that many singers think "2800" is to be gained by "putting the tone in the nose." I am much more impressed by Paget's ideas concerning "twang," (Par. 411).

326   In any case, it appears that what is commonly called "getting resonance in the voice," is really getting "2800," and this is fully as much a matter of proper vibration as it is proper resonance. Also, even if it is really resonance, it is in some small cavity below the level of consciousness, which is only controlled indirectly, largely by ear. We cannot relegate it to indifference, however, because it does appear in some tones and not in others, and any means that will build it, no matter how indirect, must be taught. To the extent that the epiglottis is involved, the tongue will influence it, because movements of the two are intimately related. This may explain why various exercises for the tongue are used for "resonance," or "ring." The latter is a much better word for this quality. The idea that head cavities have anything to do with it can only be imaginary, or figurative.

The Ventricles as Resonators

327   The little pockets between the false and the true cords (Par. 216) have fascinated many thinkers on the subject of voice. In howling monkeys, there are pouches connected with the ventricles which can be inflated with the breath, and when this impounded air is then forced back out it produces a sound. Vestiges of such pouches are found in some humans, and although no one has demonstrated any correlation between their presence and vocal talent, it is tempting to imagine them as resonators, (Kay).

328   In 1703 Dodart proposed an idea that they created eddies as the expired air passed them, thus making the larynx a kind of whistle. This idea has roots as far back as Galen, in the 2nd century, and has persisted even since Ferrein in 1741 proved the primary importance of the vocal fold vibration. Theories of *Wirbeln,* cyclones, whirling currents, and vortexes continue, (Par. 292).

329   In the late 19th century a number of authorities speculated on the possibility of closing the false cords and inflating the ventricles to provide a cushion which would support the true cords against the pressure below them. Myer[2] (pp. 49-53) called this "the true point of resistance" and said that correct tone production began as the false cords opened, thus laying a foundation for the belief that this was meant by Garcia in his phrase *coup de la glotte.* It was the beginning of the corruption of this expression to mean its opposite, glottal plosive, (Par. 187-189). The idea was vigorously refuted by Browne and Behnke (pp. 128, 129) and in his later writings Myer did not refer to it.

330   The monumental authority on the larynx, in both animals and humans, Victor E. Negus, attributes no significance to the ventricles as resonators. Van den Berg[2], however, has tested their acoustical properties, and while agreeing in general, he describes them as possibly being low-pass filters. This means that when they are distended they could possibly trap very high frequencies which might be in the glottal tone and muffle them. Thus they would tend to make the voice more mellow, but only when they are distended. Zimmerman reports that "good voices of every type revealed a widely gaping sinus Morgagni." I believe this is an evidence of their relaxation more than it is of their possession of better resonators.

331   Tomographic studies (Husson[2], Landeau, Luchsinger[2], van den Berg[2]) show clearly that in soft tones and falsetto tones the ventricles are the largest (Fig. 40). In medium tones they are

Tomograms
from
van den Berg,[4]
NATS Bulletin.

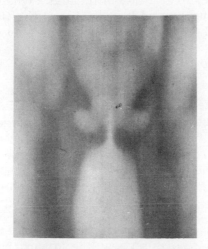 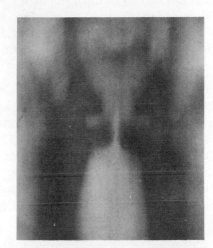

Bass, Ah, F_3, mezzo-forte   Bass, Ah, F_3, forte

See
discussion
Fig. 44

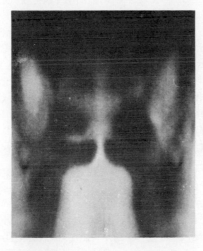 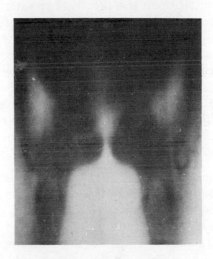

From Landeau
and Zuili,
NATS Bulletin.

Tenor, Ah, B_3, piano   Tenor, Ah, B_3, forte

More
tomograms,
Fig. 44, 53, 65.

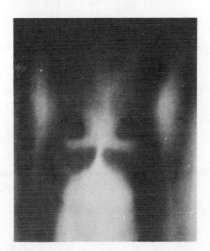 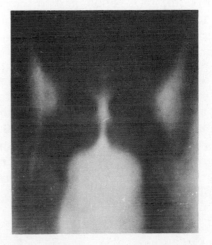

From Landeau
and Zuili,
NATS Bulletin.

Tenor, Ah, G_4, falsetto   Tenor, Ah, G_4, full

Fig. 40. Changing Size of Ventricles

smaller, and in loud high chest tones they are often obliterated. When the larynx closes tightly to hold the breath, as in straining, both upper and lower folds of the thyroarytenoids are thickened tense muscles, pressing firmly together with no space between. The more strenuously we sing, the more nearly we approach this condition, in which there are no ventricles.

The Pharynx as a Resonator

332   Immediately above the larynx and extending upward behind the mouth and the nose is a cavity that is called the *pharynx*. For convenience it is thought of as in three parts, *laryngo-pharynx*, *oro-pharynx*, and *naso-pharynx*. The latter, uppermost section can be shut off from the rest of the throat by the arching of the soft palate, combined with a sphincter action of the upper pharyngeal constrictor, one of three large muscles that form the walls of the pharynx. The laryngo-pharynx can be shut off from the upper parts by constriction between the back of the tongue and the throat wall, but this closure is seldom complete.

333   Since the pharynx is subject to rather accurate control if the singer is patient enough to learn it, this resonator is most important. Also, it is so near the larynx that it has the first, and therefore the most potent effect upon tone quality. There is more agreement among teachers of singing upon the fact that the pharynx must be as open and free from constrictive tension as possible than upon any other principle of singing. Even those teachers who do not speak of the throat, and who minimize its importance, still have empirical suggestive methods that indirectly achieve the same end. In 1945, Ross[3] analyzed questionnaires from 940 voice teachers on various topics. Those who avowed a belief in the pharynx as a resonator were only 434, as opposed to 170 who gave no opinion, 492 who mentioned the mouth, and 636 who believed in "head resonance." However, 547 believed in a "relaxed throat," and 213 in "throat or pharynx firmness." Paradoxical as it may seem, I am convinced that both of the latter groups are striving for what I call an "open throat," and Bartholomew makes an excellent case for the idea that those who emphasize "head" resonance, are indirectly achieving pharyngeal resonance.

334   Garcia[2] (pp. 12, 13) said, "The real mouth of the singer ought to be considered the pharynx . . . because it is in the pharynx that is found the causation of timbres. The facial mouth is but a door through which the voice passes. Still, if this door were not sufficiently open, sounds could not issue freely." I believe that this somewhat confuses the mouth *orifice* with the mouth *cavity*. Stanley[2] (p. 78) took an even more extreme position to the effect that *only* the pharynx should be used as a resonator, and he made a great point that if one attempts to use the mouth as such one defeats the use of the pharynx. He admitted, however, that the mouth cavity inevitably imparts resonance to the acoustical product, and his reasons were more pedagogical than scientific. Shakespeare emphasized the "open throat" throughout his books. Mackworth-Young attributes primary importance to the throat (pp. 73-90) but also recognizes the role of the mouth (pp. 91-97).

335   The pharynx, when it is large enough, strengthens the lower partials of the voice, giving it mellowness and fullness. It is likely that when singers think they are "adding chest resonance," they are really adding heavy registration, resonated by a deeper pharynx. Bartholomew[2] estimates that its pitch is from 400 to 600 cps in the male voice. Mackworth-Young (p. 115) gives 330 and 660 cps as the extremes. Coffin (p. v) indicates 350 to 750 cps. We shall see when we consider the vowels that the pharynx is constantly interacting with the mouth, and changing its capacity and consequently its pitch. We shall find that we must think of one highly complex and variable *buccopharyngeal resonator*.

The Mouth as a Resonator

336   The mouth, also called the *oral* or *buccal cavity*, obviously can be controlled as consciously as the pharynx. These two cavities work together to alter the quality of the laryngeal product so that it is recognized as any given vowel sound. The boundary between the oral and the pharyngeal cavities is marked by the soft palate at the top, the pillars at the sides, and the tongue at the bottom.

337   The position of the tongue determines whether the mouth and the throat will function principally as one large air chamber, or whether there will be two resonators, and how the cavities will vary in size. The size is also influenced by the position of the jaw, and the shape and dimensions of the orifice are, of course, a function of the lips and teeth. In general, this is the explanation of difference in vowel quality, and therefore of all vocal quality, apart from the vibrator itself.

338   The parts of the mouth are also used in the production of consonants. Therefore, the function of the mouth is to shape the tone into words, and the skill one must acquire is that of articulating without spoiling the quality which has been generated in the larynx and resonated by the pharynx. A tone that is muffled by the tongue, or that for any similar reason cannot get through the mouth is called "swallowed," or "throaty." (The latter term is also applied to tones from a constricted pharynx, but I prefer the term, "tight," or "strained.") A tone that is clear and bell-like is often said to be "in the mouth."

The Nose as a Resonator

339   As has been mentioned, the naso-pharynx, and thereby the whole nasal resonator, can be shut off by a sphincter action of the soft palate (also called the *velum*) and the superior constrictor muscle of the pharynx. The part of the superior constrictor which presses against the velum to produce this closure is called "Passavant's cushion." The cavity itself is not adjustable, so the control consists entirely of shunting it in or out of the resonance system. There is considerable dispute as to which is desirable, or assuming that the passage can be only partly open, to what extent it should be.

340   The nasal passages are adapted to the filtering and warming (or in rare cases, of cooling) incoming air, so that it will be cleansed of dust particles, etc., and will be of such a temperature that it will not injure the lungs. The surface is irregular, having fins, or *turbinates* in the sides like the fins of any mechanical radiator, and it is also fleshy and full of blood vessels, for the purpose of exposing the air to as great a body-temperature area as possible. All this results in two things: While the passage is ideally suited to its function, it is a poor means of taking breath quickly, and it is a poor resonator for either improving or building the tone. For these reasons, most singers both inhale and sing through the mouth.

341   The quality of tone as resonated by the nose is well known even to the layman. It is a "honky," muffled sound, which should not be confused with what is sometimes called "nasal twang." A good illustration of it is heard in the speech of those unfortunates whose palates are defective and cannot shut off the nose from the other resonators. Anyone can make a cruel imitation of such speech simply by allowing his velum to drop so radically that the mouth is largely shut off and the tone must exit through the nostrils. No matter how well the pharynx is distended, the tone cannot emerge unimpaired except by way of the mouth.

342   How much of this quality is admissible to singing? I lean toward the opinion that it should be eliminated entirely; that the closure of the naso-pharynx should be complete. As a demonstration that nasal resonance is of negligible value, I sometimes sing a sustained tone for my students while alternately closing and releasing my nostrils with my fingers. There is practi-

cally no change in quality. If you sing with a bell-like, "mouthy" timbre, you can undoubtedly do the same; indeed, it may surprise you, if you have never tried it.

343   In 1954, Wooldridge attempted to isolate the contribution of the nasal passages to the singing voice by comparing the vowels produced by six professional singers under two conditions: normal, and with the nasal passages filled with cotton gauze. He was unable to find significant differences between the spectra of the vowels produced under the two conditions, and a jury of expert listeners was unable to distinguish the two conditions by hearing tape recordings. Wooldridge concluded, "The term 'nasal resonance' is without validity in describing voice quality in the singing voice," (p. 39). A repetition of this experiment by five male singers, including myself, confirmed the original findings, (Vennard[8]). However, this does not apply to the nasal consonants or the French nasal vowels, (Par. 509).

344   You can readily test how much breath passes through your nostrils while singing by holding a mirror under them and noting how much it clouds. I find a tiny bit of fogging under perhaps one nostril, whereas when I sing a French nasal most of the mirror clouds. A more arduous experiment consists of filling the nose with milk by means of a syringe. As I sustain an oral vowel I see a fine trickle of milk escaping into my throat, but when I pause for breath I must swallow the large quantity that was retained till that moment.

345   Croatto and Croatto reviewed thirty-six authorities and summarize the matter thus, "On the whole, radiological research has lead most of the authorities to favor complete occlusion (of the nasal port) in the oral phonemes. Some of them meanwhile present evidence that it is not always produced in hermetic fashion," (p. 137).

346   However, Russell points out that in many of his X-rays, the velum sags away from the wall of the throat, and he insists that no more nasality was apparent in these tones than in the others. This may be explained if we remember that in the 19th century Passavant performed an experiment (since confirmed by others) in which tubes were inserted in the nose to keep open the space between the soft palate and the muscular cushion which bears his name. He found that an opening 12 sq. mm. in cross-section had no reaction upon vowel quality, but one 28 sq. mm. resulted in distinct nasality, (Rousselot, p. 268). Bartholomew puts it another way; that if the nasal resonance is only a small part of the tone, it is not objectionable and is called "head resonance," but it becomes objectionable when the other resonators are either constricted or shut off, (p. 148).

347   Of course, a small seasoning of nasality is sometimes desirable to give the voice a "velvety" quality. It is the *sine qua non* of the French nasal vowels, though the rest of the language is no more nasal than any other. Also, nasality is the characteristic of certain consonants, represented by the letters "m," "n," and "ng." Teachers frequently make use of these consonants to "place" vowels in vocalizing. But here the nasality is a means to an end and should not persist in the tone. Jean deReszke is said to have remarked, "The tone should be in the nose, but the nose should not be in the tone." I take this to mean that a good tone will be felt in the nose, but that it should not be nasal. The sensations which give rise to the illusion of "placement" (Par. 431-436) may be based upon sympathetic vibration in the nose and/or the sinuses, but this is not the same as resonance which enhances the acoustical product of the instrument.

The Sinuses as Resonators

348   The only cavities remaining to be evaluated are the sinuses. It used to be the fashion to attribute the presence of high partials, or "resonance," to the singer's ability to "direct the tone" into these pockets. It is now recognized that the sound vibrations cannot be directed at all. They enter every nook and cranny possible, and also set all the bones into vibration. Where

they reach a mass of the right natural frequency, be it air or be it bone, it will be agitated by sympathetic resonance, and may produce a sensation of which the singer will be conscious. But these vibrations add nothing to the tone that reaches the ears of the audience.

349   Various great singers, like Caruso, have reported feeling a response from certain sinuses when producing certain tones, and these evidences were taken to prove an elaborate theory of "tone placement." Lindsley made scientific measurements of such vibrations in such places as larynx, chest, top of head, front sinus, left and right sinuses, side of nose, pharynx, cheeks, occipital lobe, etc., during the phonation of "ah," "ee," "oo," and "m." The results were rather as would be expected, but I mention the experiments because of the fact that it was necessary to use an "electrical stethoscope" which greatly amplified the vibrations in order to measure them. Obviously they could be no part of what is heard by others. These experiences may be useful to the singer to prove the presence of desirable overtones, but they are not the overtones themselves, nor the cause of them. Lindsley states, "My research does not embrace a method of approach that will afford any evidence as to the relationship to voice quality of changes within the resonance cavities," (p. 33).

350   Perhaps the one startling discovery he made was that the falsetto voice, for all its high pitch, excites more response from the chest than from the cavities of the head.

> If the conventional theories concerning head resonance and the function of the sinuses are true, it would be logical to expect falsetto tones to incite the greatest response in the small resonators. The tenor who served as a subject was able to sing and sustain beautiful falsetto tones and I had a very good opportunity to measure the relative amounts of vibration produced thereby . . . . The actual amount of vibration measurable at the point of the sinus was very small, particularly for a and u, and . . . the amount of chest vibration was correspondingly large, approximately the same as produced by the first four tones in his natural singing range. The maximum intensity of vibration was recorded at the point of the larynx and the trachea. This latter finding conforms to our knowledge of how the cords vibrate during the production of this sound, and relates to the general position derived from this study; namely, that voice quality differences are conditioned primarily by the structure and functioning of the vocal bands, (p. 90).

351   This would bear out the contention of Bartholomew that there is no "2800" in the falsetto. The fundamental frequencies, which compose the major part of the flute-like falsetto quality, are not high enough to excite the small sinus cavities, so paradoxically, it is only chest voice, which contains the high "2800" frequency, that can produce true sinus resonance.

352   In the experiment on nasality to which I have referred (Par. 343) we not only filled our nasal passages with gauze but also had our maxillary sinuses more than half filled with water, (Fig. 41). These are the largest of the sinuses, and putting water in them would change their reso-

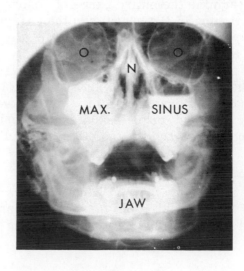

Fig. 41. X-Ray Negative of
Maxillary Sinuses
Occipito-frontal x-ray negative of a subject in the experiment referred to in Par. 343, 352, at an angle known as Water's view of the sinuses. Maxillary sinuses are more than two-thirds full of Hypaque, a harmless solution which will leave a shadow on the negative. Subject sang as well under these conditions as normally. N, nasal septum; O, O, orbits.

nant properties noticeably if they were of any importance. Our singing under these conditions was compared with our normal singing by 86 vocal authorities from the United States and 25 from Holland. The Dutch judges were included because Europeans frequently judge American speech to be nasal but they were no more able to detect the difference between the normal and the abnormal singing than were the American listeners. Our conclusion was that neither "nasal resonance" nor "sinus resonance" has validity.

353   To dispose finally of the idea that these tiny air spaces, with their minute openings into the other resonators, could be of any value other than as indicators to the singer himself, let me quote a typical scientific authority, Schaeffer.

> It is very unlikely that the paranasal sinuses exert any influence upon vocalization. The ostia of the sinuses are so small and not infrequently encroached upon by neighboring parts that one naturally wonders how the chambers can have any modifying influence on the sound waves. Moreover, the great variations in the size and arrangement of the sinuses would preclude any constancy of influence. The theory that the paranasal sinuses impart resonance to the voice must doubtless be abandoned.

Recapitulation of the Possible Resonance Cavities

354   It seems that several cavities which have been thought important as resonators, either are inadequte as such, or are subject to no control, so that it is useless to bother our heads about them. The chest is full of a spongy material which would dampen rather than resonate. The sinuses have such small openings that they cannot be considered a part of the resonance system. The trachea may cause register difficulties, but these are corrected by acquiring laryngeal skill, not by adjusting the trachea.

355   Two cavities are subject to partial control. One is the nose, which cannot be altered, but which can be shut off entirely or which can be joined with the other resonators, the ratio of its influence to that of the others depending upon how *they* are controlled. The other is that cavity which produces "2800," the frequency of that partial which has been recognized as giving "ring" to the voice. This priceless ingredient is probably produced in the space formed above the vocal lips by the epiglottis and the aryepiglottic folds, or in some other part of the pharynx, and it is energized properly only when the vibrator is functioning properly. This resonator, enigmatic as it is, nevertheless can be controlled in the same manner that laryngeal function is controlled, namely by the ear, the memory of past experience, and poetic suggestion. The student must learn to listen for "2800," and then to keep it in every tone he produces.

356   The two remaining resonators are controllable to such a great extent that it may be said that they determine the entire range of resonance effects. Even nasal resonance is delimited by the conditioning of the buccal and the pharyngeal cavities. In combination with the factors of registration, the mouth and throat produce all the differences possible in vocal quality. These differences include various degrees of beauty and ugliness, and also the spectrum of vowel colors. We shall devote a chapter to the vowels, but before we leave this one, we should consider how the throat and mouth may be controlled in order to achieve the most pleasing timbre, assuming that the vibrator is doing its work well. We shall assume wherever necessary that the vowel is Ah. The tongue assumes different shapes for different vowels, but otherwise, what makes a good Ah is good for the others as well. I think of them as modifications of Ah.

Pronunciation and Production

357   We must remember that the same muscles which shape the resonators exert pulls upon the larynx. This is probably even more important, because there is nothing the resonators can do to make satisfactory a vibration that is wrong at its source. As we go on to our study of the

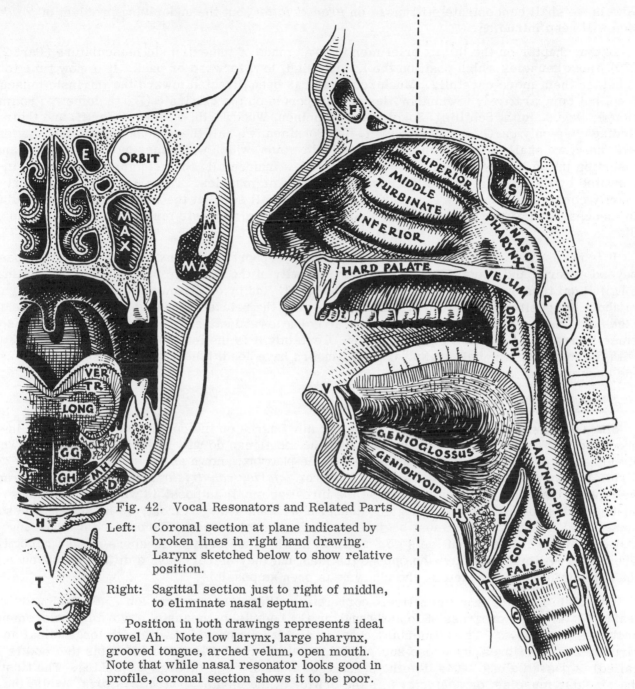

Fig. 42. Vocal Resonators and Related Parts

Left: Coronal section at plane indicated by broken lines in right hand drawing. Larynx sketched below to show relative position.

Right: Sagittal section just to right of middle, to eliminate nasal septum.

Position in both drawings represents ideal vowel Ah. Note low larynx, large pharynx, grooved tongue, arched velum, open mouth. Note that while nasal resonator looks good in profile, coronal section shows it to be poor.

A, arytenoid c.; C, cricoid c.; D, digastric m.; E, epiglottis, ethmoid s.; F, frontal s.; GG, genioglossus m.; GH, geniohyoid b.; LONG, longitudinal m.; M, malar b.; MA, masseter m.; MAX, maxillary s.; MH, mylohyoid m.; P, Passavant's cushion; S, sphenoid s.; T, thyroid c.; TR, transversus m.; V, vestibule of mouth; VER, verticalis m.; W, c. of Wrisberg. (b, bone; c, cartilage; m, muscles, s, sinus) Pillars are seen on either side of abbreviation "oro-ph."

vowels we shall concentrate still more on *pronunciation*, but the underlying problem of *production* will keep intruding.

358   In our chapter on the larynx brief mention was made of the extrinsic musculature (Par. 212, 230), those muscles which position the larynx, high, low, forward or back. It is now time to consider them more carefully. Much research has been directed toward the intrinsic musculature, but comparatively few authorities have reported on the extrinsic (Bartholomew, Frommhold, Hoppe, Negus, Ruth, Schilling, Sokolowsky, Sonninen, Woodworth, Zencker, Zerffi) and their findings are only partly harmonious. If, like Sonninen, we call these muscles *external* instead of *extrinsic*, we shall include with them the cricothyroids, which while they have both origin and insertion in the larynx are after all on the outside. Incidentally the cricothyroids are not innervated by the same nerve as the rest of the intrinsic muscles. The cricothyroids are primarily concerned with pitch (Par. 227-230) and we shall see that the whole external musculature influences pitch also. The higher the pitch, the more the extrinsic musculature comes into play.

359   It is necessary for the extrinsic musculature to support the larynx and this probably goes beyond synergy and actually supplements the activity of the intrinsic musculature in creating longitudinal tension. Zenker and Zenker (pp. 19-31) find by electromyography that the larynx is in about the position of rest for tones at the level of the relaxed speaking voice, that as the pitch rises extrinsic tension increases, and that in going toward extremely low tones there is also some increase, except in the genioglossus. Certainly it is instinctive for this to happen. I agree with the majority who believe that trained singers have conditioned the reflex so that they use the neck muscles far less.

The Large Throat

360   Singers differ as to mouth adjustments, but most agree on the open throat. If the tone is produced in a constricted throat, nothing that the mouth can do will make it satisfactory. There are three large muscles that form the wall of the pharynx, known as the *upper* or *superior constrictor*, the *middle constrictor*, and the *lower* or *inferior constrictor*. By their names we may well guess that their function is to make the throat as small as possible when one swallows, squeezing the food into the esophagus. Hence, if we want a large throat, we must relax these muscles. I am sure that to most beginners, getting a good tone is accompanied by a feeling that everything in the throat "lets go," and this is why a majority of teachers preach relaxation. There is a militant minority who oppose the idea, but they merely have a different approach to the same thing, namely, getting the pharynx as open as possible.

361   The Bible is more than figuratively correct in calling man a worm (Job 25:6; Psalm 22:6; Isaiah 41:14). The progress of food throughout the body is by means of a wormlike movement known as *peristalsis*. The alimentary canal is a long tube provided with both longitudinal and circular muscle fibres, by whose successive wavelike contractions the *bolus* (as the food is called) is passed along. It is like the passage of a darning egg through a stocking. The first of the circular muscles, or *sphincters*, is the orifice of the mouth, *orbicularis oris*. While the food is between the cheeks *(buccinators)* it is masticated by the action of these muscles, the tongue, and the jaws. We use these muscles for making vowels and consonants, but it is well to remember that they are not primarily speech organs, but chewing organs.

362   The buccinator muscles attach to a ligament which extends between the upper and lower jaw on each side, back of the teeth, and is called the *pterygomandibular raphe*. The superior constrictor attaches to this raphe, as well as to the upper and lower jaws, and continues circularly to the back, where the two sides join at another seam, called the *median pharyngeal raphe*. This is like a long tendon suspended from the skull at a point called the *pharyngeal tubercle* just in front of the backbone. It extends downward almost to the esophagus, and all three pairs of constrictors attach to it.

363   After the food has been chewed the tongue rises and is drawn back by some of the longitudinal muscles I mentioned above, which work with the circular ones. We shall discuss these muscles before long, since most of them happen to be extrinsic laryngeal muscles. The food is thus pressed into the oropharynx, which is bounded by the upper constrictor. The soft palate prevents its going into the nose, and when the upper constrictor tightens the food passes downward.

364   The middle constrictor arises from the greater horns of the hyoid bone and the lower part of the *stylohyoid ligament.* There is a rather sharp bony projection from the base of the skull on either side of the neck bones, between the ears, just back of the jawbone, called the *styloid process.* Several important muscles extend from these processes (more longitudinal muscles) as well as the ligaments just mentioned, one on each side, which attach to the lesser horns of the hyoid. The middle constrictor, being a circular muscle, carries around from the hyoid bone and joins at the pharyngeal raphe. Its fibres fan out so that its insertion on the raphe is much wider than its origin at the horns of the hyoid, and the upper point at the back covers the superior constrictor. The lower point goes inside the upper part of the inferior constrictor, into which the bolus is passed when the middle constrictor contracts.

365   The lower constrictor will be very interesting to us because of its relation to the cricothyroids. It arises from a diagonal line on the thyroid cartilage known as the *oblique ridge,* and from the parts of that cartilage which are back of that line, including the lower horns and some of the lower edge. This part of the lower constrictor is called the *thyropharyngeus muscle.* A glance at Fig. 43 will show you that the cricothyroid attaches at the same lower edge and continues on around to the front of the larynx. The fibres of these two muscles are running in the same direction, and indeed some of the thyropharyngeus fibres attach to the fascia which covers the cricothyroid. We might imagine that they cooperate, and indeed such is the case. The cricothyroids are innervated by the external branch of the superior laryngeal nerve, twigs of which also reach thyropharyngeus. The lowermost part of the inferior constrictor is called the *cricopharyngeus muscle,* because, as you can guess, it arises from the cricoid cartilage. Like all the other constrictor muscles, it meets its twin at the median raphe. Its lower fibres mingle with those of the esophagus. It is the successive contraction of these constrictors that creates the peristaltic wave which is continued by the circular fibres of the esophagus. You can see how the various longitudinal muscles are also essential to the process. Outside the circular fibres of the esophagus there is a layer of fibres running up and down. More about them later, (Par. 376).

366   When the thyropharyngeus muscles contract they exert a considerable pull upon the wings of the thyroid. When there is not too much ossification in this cartilage, it is flexible enough to change its shape, especially in the case of young singers. This may explain why older singers lose some of their top tones. There is considerable X-ray evidence that the wings of the thyroid can be drawn closer together, (Fig. 44). This has the effect of moving the notch of the thyroid forward, (Fig. 45). Thus we have a cooperation with the cricothyroids, since by pulling up on the front of the cricoid they cause its plate to move backward. The combined action of these two muscles produces the greatest possible distance between the thyroid notch and the cricoid plate, and hence maximum longitudinal tension in the vocal folds.

367   Zenker and Zenker find that in the position of rest the space between the wings of the thyroid is greatest and that in singing it may be a centimeter less. The tomograms presented by Husson and Djian and by Landeau and Zuili show differences of only a few millimeters, but since they do not show the rest position we may gather that any phonation induces some thyropharyngeal activity, more in some cases than in others. Husson[2] (p. 131) and Landeau (p. 11) agree that it remains unchanged in chest tones from low to high pitch. This may well be because in chest voice the thyroarytenoids are active, and would oppose not only the cricothyroids, but the thyropharyngeus as well. However, in falsetto the wings are drawn closer together, especially in

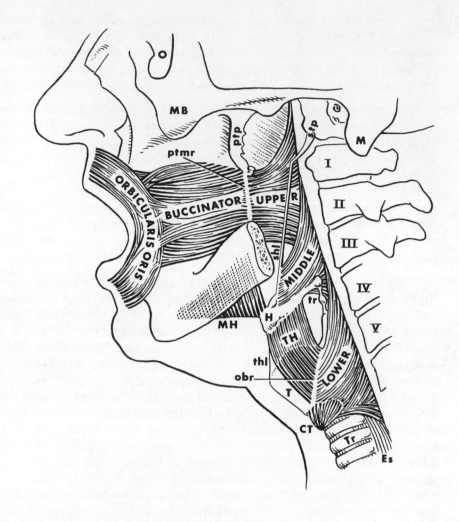

CT, cricothyroid m.
Es, esophagus
H, hyoid bone
M, mastoid process
MB, malar bone
MH, mylohyoid m.
O, orbit
obr, oblique ridge of thyroid
ptmr, pterygomandibular raphe
ptp, pterygoid plate (internal)
shl, stylohyoid ligament
stp, styloid process
T, thyroid c.
TH, thyrohyoid m.
thl, thyrohyoid ligament
Tr, trachea
tr, triticeal c.
I-V, cervical vertebrae

Fig. 43. Circular Muscles of the Resonators
Semi-realistic drawing from left side. Main circular muscles
identified with words, other parts with initials. Jawbone is
severed at the angle, and is shown as if transparent to make all
of the mylohyoid visible. External pterygoid plate not shown.

going from low to high. (Little thyroarytenoid opposition, if any.) Husson found the wings approaching each other in going from soft to loud. Both he and Landeau found a narrowing of the larynx when it was in a higher position in the throat. This is related to "covering," and I shall discuss it again in our chapter on the vowels, (Par. 541-548).

368   It is clear that movement of the larynx is involved in swallowing, and that the action of the cricothyroids is instinctively associated with that of the constrictors. We have a conflict in which the higher we wish to ascend in pitch the greater there is an instinctive tendency for the throat to constrict. As a matter of fact, the pharynx relaxes instinctively only upon inhalation, in harmony with an even deeper reflex which we have already noted in the windpipe, (Par. 156). Activity in the intrinsic musculature of the larynx is joined synergistically by the muscles that would reduce the diameter of our first really essential resonator, and as we shall see, by other muscles which would reduce its depth also. This is clearly not a point at which Mother Nature is a willing ally. However, one can condition reflexes to desired behavior, and the acquiring of most artistic skills begins with muscular independence.

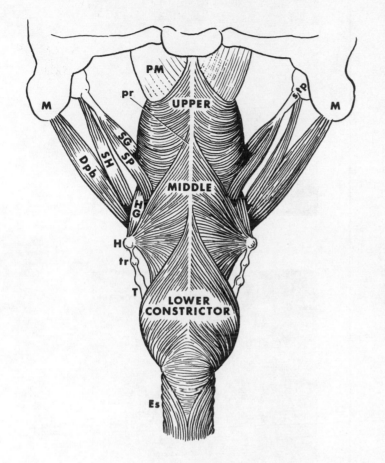

Dpb, digastric m., posterior belly
Es, esophagus
H, hyoid bone
HG, hyoglossus m.
M, mastoid process
PM, pharyngeal membrane
pr, pharyngeal raphe
SG, styloglossus m.
SH, stylohyoid m.
SP, stylopharyngeus m.
stp, styloid process
T, thyroid c.
tr, triticeal c.

Fig. 43, continued
Semi-realistic drawing from back, spine eliminated, skull sectioned. Main circular muscles identified with words. Initials
identify several longitudinal muscles shown as they are related
to the constrictors. Compare with Fig. 46.

The Low Larynx

369   Several longitudinal muscles lie in the walls of the throat, working with the constrictors, and
these attach to the larynx to raise it. They are the upward pulling group of extrinsic laryngeal
muscles. Thus, along with the constricting of the pharynx, we have the lifting of the voice-box,
and not only the diameter but also depth of the resonator is reduced. Add to this the fact that all
this tension in the walls makes the pharynx a poor resonator also, in the manner of Miller's
organ pipes, (Par. 305). A sound that passes through a tense throat is different from one that
comes from a relaxed throat. Some writers deplore the use of the word "relaxed," as if the
many teachers who use it meant "flaccid." It is perfectly true that one never relaxes completely until he is dead, but in poor singing of an all too common variety certain muscles are
too tense, and the feeling that such singers have when they produce a correct tone is that the
throat has relaxed. They often feel as if the tone is no longer being produced in the larynx at

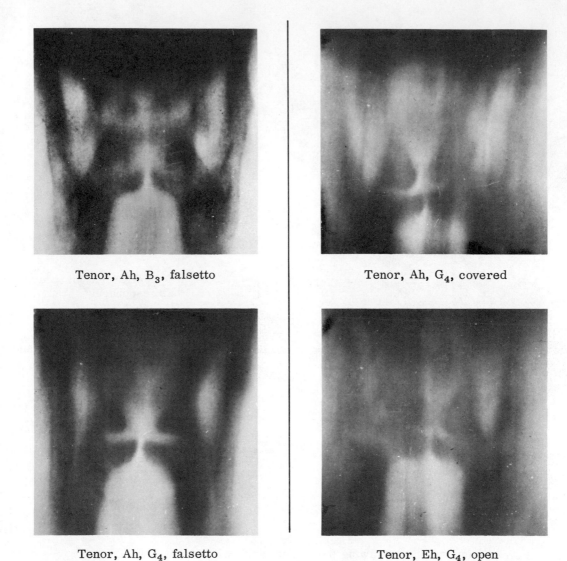

Tenor, Ah, B_3, falsetto   Tenor, Ah, G_4, covered

Tenor, Ah, G_4, falsetto   Tenor, Eh, G_4, open

Fig. 44. Tomograms Showing Action of Thyropharyngeus Muscles

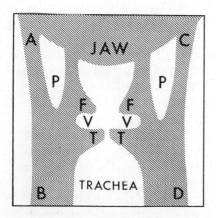

From Landeau and Zuili, *NATS Bulletin*. To understand a tomo-gram one must know that this is an x-ray technic in which both the x-ray tube and the photographic plate move during the exposure. This makes everything disappear in the final picture, except the part that is at the axis of the rotation of the equipment, and even this part will have somewhat blurred outlines. Moving parts, like the vibrating edges of the vocal cords, will naturally be even less distinct, but the firmness of their closing can be judged by the width of this gray area. In the accompanying diagram we have a shadow roughly corresponding to those in the tomograms. The shadow of the jawbone is at the top and the vertical shadows AB and CD are of the wings of the thyroid. Com-pare distance between them in tomograms placed one above the other here. Distance can also be judged by size of pyriform sinuses, P, P. F, F, false vocal cords or ventricular bands; T, T, true cords or internal thyroarytenoids; V, V, ventricles of Morgagni.

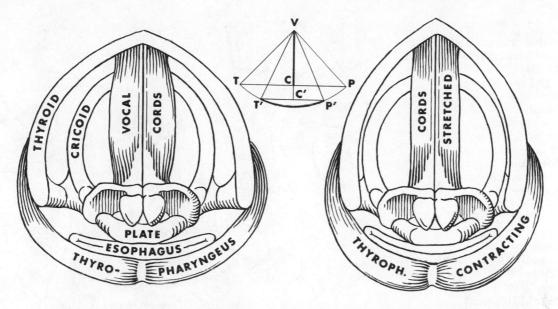

Fig. 45. Schema of Thyropharyngeus Action
Semi-realistic drawings of the larynx. Thyroid cartilage is sectioned at about the level of the glottis. Only muscles shown are thyropharyngeus and vocalis (internal thyroarytenoid). Diagram in center shows principle involved. TP, relaxed thyropharyngeus; T'P', contracting thyropharyngeus. VC, vocal cords; VC', vocal cords stretched.

all, and it is this illusion that has given currency to the very descriptive misnomer, head tone. As long as it continues to be effective pedagogy, I shall continue to ask my pupils to relax their throats. The effect of the change in muscle tonus in the walls of the resonator may be negligible; I leave this question to the scientists, but I know that when throat or tongue stiffens something happens somewhere that produces a harsh quality in the voice. The purpose of the pharynx is to give mellowness to the voice, and this comes from adding strength to low partials (which calls for a large resonator) and from muffling undesirable higher partials (which calls for softer walls in the resonator).

370   Another reason why the high larynx is undesirable is perhaps even more important than the one just mentioned. To understand it we need to consider the extrinsic musculature in somewhat greater detail. There are three groups of these muscles. Those that pull upward and backward, toward the base of the skull, we may call the *swallowing muscles*. Those that pull upward and forward, toward the point of the jaw, we may call the *tongue muscles*. Since these are all above the larynx and their combined effect is to raise, they are called *suprahyoid* or *supralaryngeal*. There are not as many *infralaryngeal muscles*, but they are larger, and they have gravity to assist them. In fact the lowering of the larynx is regarded as a passive motion resulting from relaxation of the supralaryngeals. It is this relaxed position that the singer needs. Excessive lowering of the voicebox is almost as poor as raising it.

371   Most of the suprahyoid muscles are for swallowing. I have already mentioned the styloid process, (Par. 364). Three muscles descend from it on each side: the *stylohyoid* which goes to the body of the hyoid bone; the *stylopharyngeus*, which enters the pharynx between the upper and middle constrictors and reaches the thyroid cartilage, its fibres also mingling with those of the lower constrictor; and the *styloglossus* which enters the side of the tongue. This latter muscle of course helps to raise the larynx, since the tongue is attached to the hyoid by various ligaments and muscles. Indeed, the hyoid is the "tongue bone." *Palatopharyngeus* and *salpingo-*

Dab, digastric m., anterior belly
Dpb, digastric m., posterior belly
Es, esophagus
GG, genioglossus m.
GH, geniohyoid m.
H, hyoid bone
HG, hyoglossus m.
hp, hammular process
LC, lower constrictor m.
LP, levator palati m.
M, mastoid process
MB, malar bone
MH, mylohyoid m.
O, orbit
OH, omohyoid m.
PG, palatoglossus m.
ptp, pterygoid plate (internal)
SG, styloglossus m.
SH, stylohyoid m.
shl, stylohyoid ligament
SP, strylopharyngeus m.
StH, sternohyoid m.
stp, styloid process
StT, sternothyroid
T, thyroid c.
TH, thyrohyoid m.
thl, thyrohyoid ligament
TP, tensor palati m.
tr, triticeal c.
V, velum
III-V, cervical vertebrae

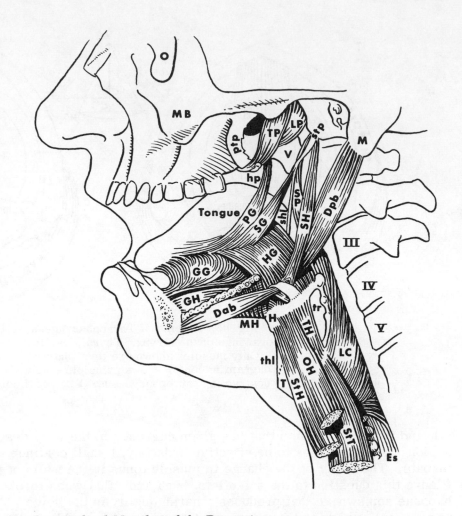

Fig. 46. Longitudinal Muscles of the Resonators
Semi-realistic drawing from left side. Lower constrictor only remaining circular muscle,
(Fig. 43). Most of left side of jawbone is removed, and mylohyoid is shown severed.

pharyngeus extend downward from the soft palate to merge with the stylopharyngeus. Their fibres diffuse in the inner lining of the pharynx at the bottom, where it attaches to the larynx. *Palatoglossus* enters the side of the tongue, merging with styloglossus. I shall discuss these further when we consider the action of the soft palate, (Par. 404-415).

372   Outside the styloid processes and a little behind are two large blunt processes called the *mastoids*. They can be felt behind and below the ears. A large and interesting suprahyoid muscle arises from the mastoid process. It is called the *digastric* because it has two bellies, or *biventor* because that word also means two-bellied. The front part of this double muscle attaches to the jaw bone, near the point, and the two are joined by a slender tendon just above the hyoid bone. There is a loop of tendon attaching to the middle of the greater horn of the hyoid, and the tendon of the digastric muscle passes through it. It also passes through the lower part of the stylohyoid. Sometimes it can slip freely and sometimes not. In any case, the larynx is suspended from this sling that is just inside the jawbone. The back part, which comes from the mastoid process, belongs in the swallowing group clearly. The front part, to the extent that it may be independent of the back part, pulls forward and belongs to the group of tongue muscles.

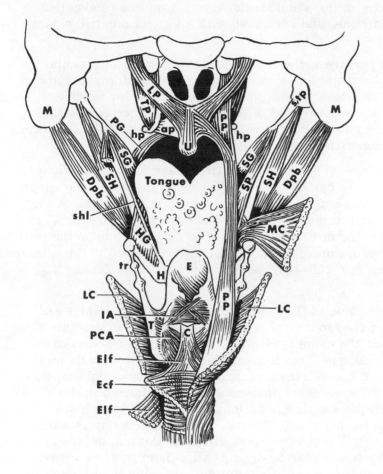

ap, aponeurosis of tensor palati
C, cricoid c.
Dpb, digastric m., posterior belly
E, epiglottis
Ecf, esophagus, circular fibres
Elf, esophagus, longitudinal fibres
H, hyoid bone
HG, hyoglossus m.
hp, hammular process
IA, interarytenoid m.
LC, lower constrictor m.
LP, levator palati m.
M, mastoid process
MC, middle constrictor (fragment)
PCA, posterior cricoarytenoid m.
PG, palatoglossus m. (front pillar)
PP, palatopharyngeus m. (back pillar)
SG, styloglossus m.
SH, stylohyoid m.
shl, stylohyoid ligament
SP, stylopharyngeus m.
stp, styloid process
T, thyroid c.
TP, tensor palati m.
tr, triticeal c.
U, uvula

Fig. 46, continued.
Semi-realistic drawing from back, spine eliminated, skull sectioned. Lower constrictor
opened by vertical slit at back. Only a fragment of right middle constrictor shown. Longitudinal fibres of esophagus cut on left side and reflected to show circular fibres. Left stylopharyngeus severed to show stylohyoid ligament. Left palatopharyngeus removed to show palatoglossus.
These are the pillars of the fauces.

373   Another muscle in this group is the *geniohyoid*. It lies beside its partner under the tongue.
It arises from the inside of the point of the jaw and is inserted in the body of the hyoid bone,
pulling it forward. Between the geniohyoid and the anterior bellies of digastricus on each side
are the two *mylohyoids*, which form the floor of the mouth, or the *diaphragm of the mandible* as
it is sometimes called. A central raphe extends from the inside of the point of the jaw to the
hyoid, and the two mylohyoids come from the sides of the jawbone to be inserted in this raphe.
Some of the fibres attach directly to the body of the hyoid.

374   The infrahyoid muscles are in four pairs. Pulling downward upon the thyroid cartilage is
the *sternothyroid* on each side. It arises from the inside of the breastbone and is inserted in the
oblique ridge of the thyroid, overlying the lower constrictor, which you recall attaches to that
same ridge. Another muscle attaching to that ridge goes upward to the hyoid bone. It is the
thyrohyoid muscle, also called *hyothyroid*. Partly overlying the sternothyroid is the *sternohyoid*, whose attachments are implied by its name. Finally we have the *omohyoid*, another two-

bellied muscle. It arises from the upper edge of the shoulderblade, has a middle tendon that passes through a loop arising from the collarbone, and continues with a second muscular part that draws the hyoid downward.

375   The longitudinal muscles mentioned thus far are rather distinct from the tube of circular muscles which form the walls of the buccopharyngeal resonator. Some are outside and some inside. Some are part outside and part within. Most of them can be brought under voluntary control, and this makes them interesting since a great deal of the technic of voice production consists of this reeducation of the chewing and swallowing muscles. In the case of the esophagus the muscles are involuntary, but they are interesting for a related reason.

376   The muscles of the esophagus are in two layers. The circular fibres are inside, and there is a complete outer layer of longitudinal fibres. As can be seen in Fig. 46, at the top of the esophagus the longitudinal fibres diverge and go around to where they are attached to the top of the cricoid cartilage, between the posterior cricoarytenoid muscles. Since the supralaryngeal tension is all exerted upon the thyroid cartilage, the downward drag of the esophagus upon the back of the cricoid is of assistance to the cricothyroid muscles in pulling the front part of it up toward the thyroid, as has been pointed out by Negus (pp. 380-383), Sonninen (pp. 80-87), Zenker and Zenker (pp. 8-10).

377   Furthermore, Negus tells us that the upper tips of the arytenoids (really the cartilages of Santorini) hook backward and are attached to the front edge of the mouth of the esophagus. This is primarily a mechanism for helping to open the esophagus when the sphincteric action of the collar of the larynx closes the larynx for swallowing, but it also makes possible a crude method of holding back the arytenoids in phonation. If the extrinsic muscles of the larynx tighten, they pull up on the hyoid bone and the thyroid cartilage. Since the esophagus is attached to the stomach, which is anchored below the diaphragm, the esophagus pulls down on the arytenoids, and the higher the larynx goes, the tighter the valve becomes. Notice, however, that this is a different kind of tension from that produced by well developed intrinsic musculature, unaided by extrinsic pulls. For one thing, pulling on the tops of the arytenoids tilts them in such a way that the vocal processes are raised and the maintenance of medial compression to balance the mounting longitudinal tension places a strain upon the lateral cricoarytenoids, (Par. 233-235).

378   Two extreme positions of the larynx and the normal one for good singing are shown in X-rays of myself in Fig. 47. Electromyograms taken by Faaborg-Andersen showing energy potentials in convenient suprahyoid and infrahyoid muscles are correlated with the X-rays. In normal production there is less activity shown in the musculature than in either of the other adjustments. Faaborg-Andersen remarked that he had seldom seen such a relaxed mylohyoid. The larynx is in a comfortably low position, the hyoid being at the level of the bottom of the third cervical vertebra. Apparently no effort in the sternothyroid is needed to keep it there. Considerably more activity in these muscles is seen in the "depressed larynx" production, which I shall discuss in greater detail in Par. 420. But for some idea of how much activity is really possible in the sternothyroid see Fig. 48, which shows its maximum in yawning and its minimum in swallowing. It is interesting also to note that the mylohyoid is almost as energetic in yawning as in swallowing, considerably more so than in producing an Ah in any of the three technics.

379   The high larynx production shows so little increase in mylohyoid activity that we must assume most of the work is being done by the back swallowing muscles arising from the palate and the styloid process. It is not so convenient to place electrodes for studies of these muscles. However, the hyoid is raised appreciably, and the thyroid even more so. The movement appears to be upward rather than forward. In fact the larynx is near the back wall of the throat in all

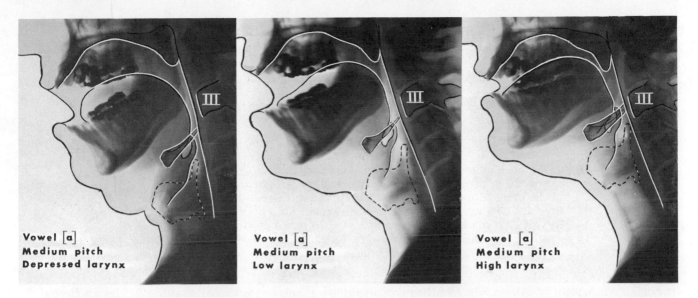

X-rays of the author, from van den Berg[6] and Vennard, *NATS Bulletin.* Fleshy parts have been retouched from visible evidence in the negatives. Not all the outline of the thyroid cartilage photographs, but it is indicated in broken outline. Its position is accurately located by portions which *do* photograph. Note space between thyroid and hyoid is greater when they are lower. Elevation of the larynx can be gauged with reference to third cervical vertebra, III.

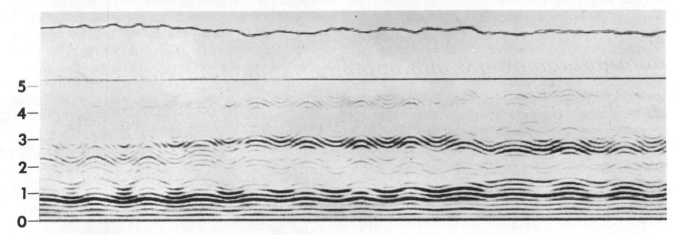

Sonagrams from van den Berg[6] and Vennard, *NATS Bulletin,* corresponding to the positions shown above in x-rays. Pitch, E_3 on bass staff. Time, 2.2 seconds. Scale of kilocycles at left. Note surprising lack of "ring" (at 3 kilocycles) for depressed larynx production, which always seems "resonant" to the singer. Sonagraphy is discussed in Par. 458.

Electromyograms from Faaborg-Andersen[3] and Vennard, *Annals of Otology, Rhinology and Laryngology.* See discussion in Par. 378, 379. Note preparatory tensing of mylohyoid which is released before attack of vowel. This may be only an idiosyncrasy.

Fig. 47. Three Positions of the Larynx for Ah

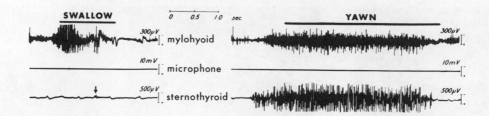

Fig. 48. Electromyograms of Swallowing and Yawning
From Faaborg-Andersen[3] and Vennard, *Annals of Otology, Rhinol-ogy and Laryngology*. Duration of each act is indicated by length of black line at top. Swallow is about 1.25 sec.; yawn, 3.25 sec. Sterno-thyroids are inactive in swallowing, except for a flicker (arrow) at the moment larynx begins to descend. Other peaks in sternothyroid myo-gram are produced by heartbeats. Note that mylohyoid is almost as active in yawning as in swallowing.

three productions of Ah. Only in other vowels does it move forward, making a "large throat." It seems that *deep* throat is more important. After all, the pitch of a resonator can be lowered by making it deep and giving it a small opening at the top as effectively as can be done by mak-ing it large with a large opening, (Par. 301).

380   The thyrohyoid muscles should perhaps be listed with the supralaryngeals rather than the infralaryngeals, because they seem to contract only when the larynx is rising. Of course, these muscles, and the ligaments between the thyroid and the hyoid are an effective connection, so that when the sternothyroids contract, their downward pull is also on the hyoid, but the connec-tion seems not to be an active one. There is an upward pulling chain of which the thyrohyoid is an active link, and the cricothyroid is another. They all pull together, raising the hyoid, drawing the thyroid toward it, and also drawing the cricoid to the thyroid, stretching the cords. The synergy seems to be instinctive. (The logic of this ought to make us reverse the names so that they would become *hyothyroid* and *thyrocricoid*, since the first part of a muscle's name refers to the origin—which is relatively fixed—and the second part refers to the insertion—relatively mobile. Indeed, Sonninen uses the term *hyothyroid*, but no one has made bold enough to abandon the term *cricothyroid*.)

381   Stanley[3] advocated a technic of separating the hyoid bone and the thyroid cartilage by insert-ing fingers between them. It seems to me that this begins at the wrong end of a long chain of cause and effect. He did say that "the pupil must relax so that the teacher can make the ad-justment," (Stanley,[3] p. 84); but he also said "the tension may be so great that it requires all the effort the teacher can exert," (p. 85). A dozen years later he confessed, "I have encountered a shockingly large number of voice students who have been seriously hurt through the incorrect use of the manipulations I have described—some of them were so badly injured that the training of their voices thereafter was impossible," (Stanley,[4] p. 358). I know of some instances in which manipulation has helped pathological voices, but this is in the province of a physician. It is more appropriate to the speech clinic; singing is too delicate a process.

382   In most animals, and in most untrained singers, phonation is always initiated with a general tightening process and an elevation of the larynx. This is aided slightly by the upward breath pressure in the trachea. But the tone produced is poor. It could be recognized by a stone deaf observer simply by the throat tension which accompanies it. While all our authorities offer ex-planations why extrinsic tension is an instinctive way of stretching the vocal folds, none says it is artistic. Studies of professional singers (Frommhold, Hoppe, Husson, Ruth) show that they keep their voice boxes low and near the backbone.

383   Forcing the larynx down is futile, but at the same time I am convinced that the student must be conscious of its position, because it is a clear indication of how nearly the intrinsic musculature has achieved.independence of the extrinsic. When the pupil has learned how to sing, not while forcing the larynx down, but while *letting it remain down,* he will have cured both the symptom and the disease. He will have the vocal lips functioning freely, and he will have the best possible resonator for them. Once again we see how intimately the two are related, and once again we see that singing is an art—not a "natural" process.

384   I must guard against creating the impression that the larynx should never rise in singing. It is bound to follow the motion of the tongue in forming vowels and consonants, for example, because the thyroid is suspended from the hyoid bone which is in the root of the tongue. Also, the larynx may rise for high notes. Almost all singers need the assistance of the extrinsic musculature for the highest and loudest tones in any register, although one's objective should be to avoid it. However, if the pharyngeal resonator is smaller under these circumstances it is not so serious, since a low pitched resonator is not as necessary when the fundamental is higher.

385   There are three ways of lowering "naturally" a larynx that is pulled up under the jaw. With inhalation, with yawning, and after swallowing, the larynx descends by reflex action.

386   The first is a link between breathing and singing. Nature wants us all to get plenty of air with each inspiration, so she has prepared us to open our throats when we inhale. This is especially true of inhaling through the mouth. She doesn't care whether we sing or not; that has little to do with the preservation of the species, so she does not make us sing by reflex—we have to learn that ourselves. But, after we inhale, if we take care to phonate with the same open throat, without immediately constricting the pharynx, we will find that nature has laid the foundation for good tone. In the case of tight-throated singers, I believe in having them place a finger on the Adam's Apple to locate it, and then notice how it drops as they inhale diaphragmatically. The whole thing becomes an advanced breathing exercise and emphasizes the importance of correct respiration. I also ask them to sing still feeling the protuberance of the thyroid cartilage, to notice whether it pops up as soon as phonation begins. With practice they learn how to "breathe a tone right back out" without raising the larynx, or at least without raising it as much. Some singers insist that while they are singing a free tone they seem to be inhaling! The teachers who say to begin to sing "on the gesture of inhalation" may have this in mind, though they also have "breath control" as an objective. I sometimes suggest that the singer should take a deep breath and then, just before the attack, take "an added sip" of air to relax the valve.

387   A second aid to dropping the larynx is yawning. You can speak of yawning and get results whether the pupil is inhaling or exhaling. Of course, when he is singing he is not inhaling, but he can still think of a yawn and thereby open his throat. So after you have tried to establish the low larynx production by coordinating it with breathing exercises, and the pupil is still singing with much the same poor quality, you continue to attack the problem by suggesting a yawn. This may be with the word, or with actual oscitation. I sometimes gape all through a lesson, and the power of suggestion is such that it makes the pupil do likewise. Of course I tell the students what I have in mind.

388   A word of caution about yawning must be inserted. It is only at the beginning of this act that the throat is right for singing. In an extreme yawn the throat is just as tense as before, only different muscles have tightened. Some teachers oppose teaching the low larynx, because they fear going to this extreme, but the same kind of argument can be brought against any good thing. The reason a yawn feels so good is that the pharynx is habitually constricted, and the action of opposing muscles relaxes this tightness. It is a part of the general pandiculation, or "stretching" before and after sleep. Pandiculation stretches and relaxes the postural or "anti-gravity" muscles. We hold the larynx up against gravity all day long, and it feels good to loosen this tension

by yawning. At the moment before these opposing muscles become tense there is an ideal balance in which no muscles are straining. This is the way a singer's throat should be. Note, this is another example of muscular antagonism.

389   Italian masters of the fabled Golden Age used to tell their neophytes that singing a tone felt like taking a drink of water. They spoke of "looseness of the neck," and the "tone floating on the breath," and they made the analogy to swallowing. As has been described, swallowing itself is opposite to opening the singer's throat. The collar of the larynx closes, helping to open the esophagus and at the same time preventing food from entering the "Sunday throat." The tongue humps up, and the epiglottis folds down to cover the larynx, which has risen high. Almost everything is as it should *not* be in singing. After swallowing, all these motions are reversed—the larynx drops, the tongue flattens, the epiglottis lifts—three movements that are conducive to good tone production. Now the advantage of this approach to the problem is that of conscious control. One swallows consciously and voluntarily. With a little concentration one can reverse the process also at will. If the pupil will swallow and then as the larynx drops again afterward, will prolong the act, he will be opening his throat. After all, if an adolescent can bounce his necktie by moving his newly protruding Adam's Apple, surely any adult singer should be able to control it.

390   In case you smiled when you read "reverse the process" of swallowing, let me add that many a teacher has instructed his pupils to "vomit the tone!" The metaphor is highly expressive and useful. It is also literally true that when a person with a sensitive gag-reflex opens the throat well, his uvula may touch the back of the pharynx and cause him to feel momentarily nauseated. Learning to sing is a strenuous exercise, not for the squeamish!

391   Some sopranos have such small larynges that they can't find them. They can't feel what is happening. However, if they will look into a mirror they can see the back of the tongue drop, the soft palate rise, the throat open.

The Grooved Tongue

392   There is not nearly as much agreement among singers as to the correct position of the tongue, or *glossus,* as there is on the matter of the large pharynx, or "open throat." Also, some teachers argue that it does no good to speak of the "unruly member" (as Saint James wrote in his Gospel), because if a pupil becomes self-conscious the law of reversed effort enters in, and the tongue becomes more unmanageable than ever. However, the teacher should know what he wants in this matter, and use his own discretion about how much he discusses it with the student. I have found that many singers can control the tongue consciously with a little patient, optimistic concentration, and I should like to describe what seems to me to be the best conduct of the tongue for good tone production.

393   A tennis player has a certain spot on the court that he knows is his best defensive position. In singles it is on the center line, a few feet forward from the service line. During the play it is impossible for him to remain rigidly in that one place, but he returns to it continually. If he runs up to the net to return a short one, he must run back again or his opponent will lob the ball over his head to bounce on the back line. It is much the same with the tongue. To pronounce consonants in singing, even to pronounce some of the vowels (Ay, Ee, etc.), the tongue must do things that would spoil a good Ah. But there is one place to which it should habitually return, and which it should occupy as much of the time as possible. In vocalizing, this habit should be formed by keeping the tongue in this position, even exaggerating.

394   The upper part of the tongue, which we see, is made up of layers of muscle fibre, some lengthwise, some across, some vertical. They are partially interlaced. The action of these

fibres can make the tongue thick and high in the middle, short and bunched toward the roof of the mouth, or flat with very likely a groove lengthwise—this last being the preferable position for singing. Below this, and forming most of the tongue are the *genioglossus muscles*, separated by a tough thin *septum* which also divides the upper part. The genioglossus fans out from its origin just above the geniohyoid as shown in Figs. 42 and 46. The front fibres of the genioglossus pull the tip inside the teeth. The back fibres pull the tongue forward, and under the right circumstances, protrude the tip. In this it is assisted by the geniohyoid. The tongue is attached to the hyoid bone by folds of muscular and tendonous tissue, and there is also a connection with the epiglottis. So movements of the geniohyoid and genioglossus influence the larynx. There is also the *hyoglossus*, a flat, rectangular muscle on each side arising from the greater horn of the hyoid. Finally we should mention again the palatoglossus and styloglossus muscles.

395   It is a good idea for singers to practice all kinds of tongue movements before a mirror, to bring it under conscious control. The mirror is a great help. In fact, some voice scientists believe that we could control even our laryngeal muscles more specifically if it were convenient to see the glottis. One good exercise is to hook the tongue behind the lower teeth and then alternately extend it out of the mouth in a ball and retract it again. Some authorities favor this exercise because they think the tongue should be drawn out of the throat in singing. Stanley[3] invented a stainless steel instrument, something like a hoe, which he inserted in the mouth so that the student could exercise the "genio-hyo-glossus muscles" against it (p. 76 ff.). This was because he advocated the "large pharynx." Other authorities like the exercise of protruding and retracting the tongue for an opposite reason because they feel that after the organ has been loosened up in this manner it can then relax into the retracted position. Its merit, actually, is simply that it brings the tongue under voluntary control.

396   An X-ray study by Hoppe and Frommhold of singers ranging from beginners to stars of the Berlin Opera shows that it is the beginners who pull the tongue forward. Zerffi[2] agrees. Russell was the pioneer in X-ray studies of singers and others as they were producing tone. His evidence led him to suspect that the size and shape of the mouth cavity might not be of great importance in changing the quality of the vowels. From the viewpoint of a phoneticist this is doubtless true. In fact some vowels can be pronounced after the tongue has been removed, as has been the case with certain rare cancer patients, (Negus, p. 418; Brodnitz[3]). But it is also true that when a cancerous *larynx* has been excised, the patient can actually speak by esophageal substitution, (Curry, p. 172). So we must return to the normal conditions of the voice studio, and observe healthy singers. There we will find that changing the formation of the oral cavity unquestionably changes the vowel, and controlling the tongue is a basic factor.

397   The phoneticist concerns himself more with whether the vowels are recognizable or not, and less with their desirability for singing. We all know that there are half a dozen recognizable Ah's, but the problem is to select and cultivate the one that is most pleasing to the ear. In several cases, Russell has told us which of his vowels were best, musically. In Fig. 49 I have drawn two profiles similar to Russell's X-rays. The one on the left resembles Figs. 83, 98, 103, and 130 in "Speech and Voice." The jaw and larynx are comparatively high and the tongue fills the mouth. To Fig. 98, Russell applies the words "flat," "metallic," *"voix blanche"* (p. 145), and to Fig. 130, the words "piercing," "barbaric," (p. 151). The outlines I show on the right in my Fig. 49 resemble Russell's Figs. 56, 66, 75, 86, 123, etc. Of these, 66, 75, and 86 were made by professional singers, soprano, tenor, and baritone. Fig. 86 was made by the baritone using "forward placement" in contrast to "pinched, tight tone," (p. 128), by the same singer (Fig. 83 above). According to Russell, the soprano's voice was "soft," "mellow," "resonant," (p. 150). Fig. 123 was of a child whose voice was "piercing," but the tone was better than that of Fig. 124 in which the tongue was higher, (p. 111).

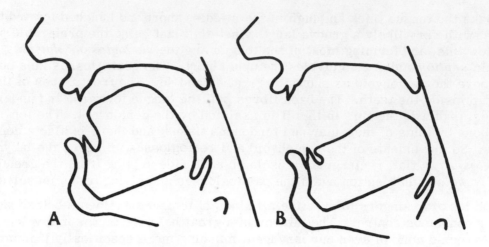

Fig. 49. Contrasting Tongue Positions
Generalized outlines based upon X-rays by G. Oscar Russell, *Speech and Voice* (New York: The Macmillan Company, 1931).
    A resembles various X-rays to which are applied the words: barbaric, flat, metallic, piercing, pinched, tight, *voix blanche.*
    B resembles various X-rays of professional singers and others, to which are applied the words: forward placement, mellow, resonant, soft.
    See discussion in paragraph 397. Note that "large pharynx" does not seem to be as important as deep pharynx, or low larynx.

398   The tongue in Fig. 49B assumes the position most voice teachers advocate. It resembles the outline drawn by Lilli Lehmann (pp. 57, 100). This same position of the tongue was used by Caruso, according to Marafioti (p. 113), who was the personal physician of the great tenor and whose book was endorsed by him.

399   We are discussing the vowel Ah. Most of the X-rays represented in Fig. 49 are of this vowel. Different tongue positions are usual for Ay and Ee, just as the lips usually change for Oh and Oo. Consideration of the vowels and their interrelation will come later. Many teachers, especially the old Italian masters, have placed Ah centrally in their pedagogy, and this coincides with the findings of both physiology and acoustics. We are thinking now only of tone production in general, as in ordinary vocalizing.

400   Let us define this Ah position of the tongue. It is reasonably low in the mouth, lower in front than in back, making the buccal cavity somewhat megaphone-shaped. If we were to continue our analogy between the voice and the trumpet, in which we have already likened the glottal lips to the lips of the trumpeter, we might say that in the vowel Ah, the mouth is the "bell" of the instrument. The tip of the tongue is not raised, it lies flat behind the lower teeth. For vocalizing it may even loll out, or rest against the lower lip, as a discipline; but under no conditions should it go back farther than the gums, never up, closing the mouth opening, as in Fig. 49A. A tongue that writhes about while the pupil is vocalizing is bad. It should not keep changing its shape, first round and thick like a sausage, next flattened but twisting sideways, etc. Such a tongue is out of control but a little patience plus a little Coué treatment ("Every day in every way, my tongue is getting better and better!") will accomplish much.

401   Viewed from the front, the effect is that the tongue drops out of the way, leaving plenty of room for the pharyngeal tone to emerge unmuffled. When the larynx descends, it pulls down on the tongue at the back, and this is what our hypothetical soprano of the previous section could

see in the mirror. In a deep yawn, the tongue is pulled far back, and the tip usually flies up. This stoppage, plus the muscular tension of the walls of the resonator produces the characteristic quality of the "yawny" tone. The pupil must be told that only the "beginning of a yawn" is good, and that the tip of the tongue must remain against the front teeth.

402   This extending often results in the formation of a deep groove running the length of the tongue, the sides perhaps being lifted by the styloglossus and palatoglossus muscles. Lilli Lehmann and other authorities favor the appearance of this groove, improving as it does the megaphone-shape of the mouth, although most people agree that the groove is not absolutely necessary. Indeed some individuals lack the power to form this trough. It must be one that originates in the back and extends to the front, rather than one that the singer initiates by curling the blade of the tongue. Efforts to produce the desired concavity by putting the finger into the mouth, or by depressing the tongue by any other mechanical means are not likely to succeed. The groove must result from the tongue's self-extension at the same time that the downward pull of the yawn is being exerted upon it. Sometimes the control comes only by "ear," that is, instead of giving attention to the tongue, the student concentrates on getting better tone, and the groove appears at the same time the tone improves, and to the same extent.

403   One caution must be added. In keeping the blade of the tongue forward, touching the lower teeth, there should be no pressure against them. If the tongue becomes tense, the tension will sound metallic in the tone. Here again I do not hesitate to use the word, "Relax." In all work with the tongue, the teacher should use positive suggestions, and avoid heckling. "Don't let your tongue get stiff!" "Stretch your tongue forward—No, No! Not like that! Put a groove in it!" These negatives and nervous admonitions are the worst kind of psychology. Instead say, "*Let* the tongue come forward. It will if you keep patient and cheerful and have a little faith in it." "That's much better. It will have more and more of a groove as you bring it under control." "Takes time, doesn't it? But it's worth it." Use the mirror for this. With many pupils you will not have to mention the tongue or the larynx all the time. The same result is obtained by saying, "Let's give that tone a little more room." That after all is what the groove is for.

The Arched Palate

404   We have already mentioned twice an imaginary coloratura soprano who cannot feel her larynx with her finger because it is so small, and who looks into her throat by means of a mirror to see what is happening. At the same time that she sees her tongue lower itself at the back, with a groove forming from root to blade, she will probably also see an arching of the velum, or soft palate.

405   I include two sketches of widely opened mouths, showing the tongue as it frequently looks in a yawn and should never be in singing Ah (Fig. 50A), and as it looks when the tongue drops and the velum arches (Fig. 50B). Notice that the edges of four upper teeth are visible, that the tongue is V-shaped, having formed a deep trough, that the soft palate is stretched rather high, making an opening into the pharynx that is roughly heart-shaped, because of the dangling of the uvula. The singer who sees this picture in the looking-glass when he opens his mouth can expect to produce a truly open-throated Ah, provided he does not lose the position the moment he begins to phonate. Fig. 50C shows the mouth as it frequently is in poor production, with both jaw and tongue raised.

406   Extending downward from the underside of the skull to about the level of the teeth, and a short distance behind the upper wisdom teeth, are two irregular-edged bony processes. The outer one is called the *external* or *lateral pterygoid plate*. Inside on each side is the *internal* or *medial pterygoid plate*. The tendonous upper part of the pharynx attaches to it. At the bottom of the internal plate is a bony hook, called the *hammular process*. The pterygomandibular ligament ex-

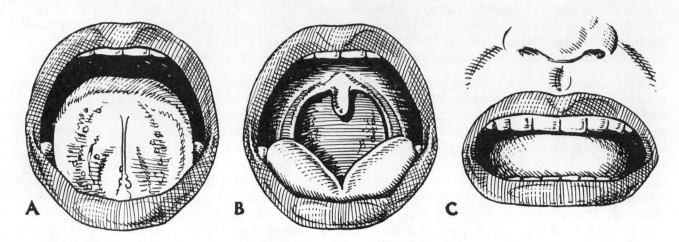

Fig. 50. The Mouth from the Front
A, Yawning
B, Singing with open throat
C, Tight singing

tends from this process to the lower jaw and we have already considered it, (Par. 362). Now behind these bony projections, outside the uppermost part of the pharynx, are two interesting
muscles on each side, which pass through just above the upper constrictor and exert pulls upon
the velum. Descending from the under surface of the skull is *tensor palati*. It tapers to a tendon
which goes around the hammular process and then spreads out into a sheet that joins its fellow
from the other side. This is the flexible framework of the veil of the palate and it attaches to the
back edge of the hard palate. When the tensors pull, this aponeurosis is stiffened. The *levator
palati* originates on either side of the base of the skull, behind the tensors, and forms a loop.
That is, some of the fibres of each merge with those of the other. The remaining fibres attach
to the tendonous sheet formed by the insertion of the tensors.

407   When the tensors work alone the soft palate is stretched from the level of the hard palate to
the level of the upper teeth, and the pharynx is separated from the oral cavity. In some animals
to whom the olfactory sense is indispensible the velum and the epiglottis actually overlap, so
that the odor of food which may be in the mouth will not prevent the animal from smelling the
approaching danger which may be downwind. When the levators contract they are opposed by the
tensors (another case of muscular antagonism) and the velum forms a double arch extending
from the hard palate to the upper constrictor. This causes the throat and mouth to be one continuous cavity, and closes the nasal port; that is, it separates the pharynx from the nasal cavities. A band of fibres in the superior constrictor (called Passavant's ridge) completes the
closure. The soft palate is thus a two-way valve, opening the pharynx either into the mouth or
into the nose. When it relaxes it is in an intermediate position. I am convinced that it should be
up.

408   Attached to the aponeurosis of the soft palate are three thin flat muscles whose fibres twine
together like ropes at the sides. The ones in front go into the sides of the tongue. You may call
them *palatoglossus* or *glossopalatinus* depending upon which way you think they pull. When the
larynx is low and the palate high there is considerable stretch in the palatoglossus muscles and
they stand out from the walls of the throat, forming an arch over the back of the tongue. They
are called the *anterior pillars*. The other two muscular layers of the palate enclose the slender
(and apparently useless) muscles of the uvula, which arise from a point at the middle of the edge

of the hard palate. These same layers also enclose the insertions of the levators, and their fibres rope together to form the *palatopharyngeus*, or *pharyngopalalinus muscles*. They form another arch and are called the *posterior pillars*. Between the front and rear pillars are the well-known tonsils, which are only two of a whole ring, including the adenoids, and similar glands on the back of the tongue and in the pharynx.

409   There is likely to be stretch in both pairs of pillars, increasing as the pitch rises and the extrinsic musculature comes into greater play along with the mounting activity of the cricothyroids. This is the one exception to my reiteration of the word "relax" throughout this discussion. I think this is what is referred to by those teachers who prefer "throat or pharynx firmness" (Par. 333). A good many refer to a feeling of stretch, (Lehmann, p. 98). Lawson tells us, "It will feel almost as if the vocal cords were attached to an elastic stretched from the hard palate to the diaphragm," (p. 34). If we remember those longitudinal fibres of the esophagus his statement is borne out almost literally.

410   When the desired adjustment has been achieved the overtone I have called "2800" comes into the voice just about to the extent that the posterior pillars are stretched. Since they are a part of the soft palate, the "2800" formant is often miscalled "nasal resonance."

411   The sound to which I refer is "twang," which is a characteristic of "Yankee" speech. Nasality may be mixed with it, because if the velum drops enough in achieving it, the "honky" quality of the nose will sound, but this is only a byproduct. Paget[2] reproduced this overtone by constructing "a resonator formed of a rubber tube (about 1 inch in diameter) attached to an organ reed and fitted with a cork tongue." His account continues:

> It was found that if, while the reed was sounding, the tube was suitably pinched, near the opening from the reed, . . . an appreciable twang was added to the vowel-sound. This experiment indicates that a part, at least, of the so-called nasal quality . . . is probably due to a constriction of some part of the pharynx, so as to produce an additional resonator of high pitch, though the presence of nasal resonance seems also to be indicated, (pp. 95, 96).

Paget estimated the frequency of the resonator to be 2732, which certainly agrees with Bartholomew's "2800." Russell also tells us that exaggerating partials above 2500 in frequency gives typical New England "twang," (p. 172). There is a resemblance between the experiment just described and those of Miller and Russell in squeezing pipes, (Par. 306, 307). Perhaps "twang" can be explained in terms of muscular tension (including the posterior pillars) without locating a new cavity. Nevertheless, there are two cavities to be mentioned, formed by the pillars. Paget also reports that according to Eijkman a pair of small resonance chambers is formed between the palatopharyngeal pillars and the back of the pharynx, which produces the frequency of "twang."

412   This quality of "twang" is a needed ingredient of tone, like salt in a cake. Too much is ruinous, but none at all is equally undesirable. This is probably the real reason for the pedagogical success of the hum and such consonants as m, n, and ng, which exercise the velum. They produce nasality, but they also call into play the pillars, and once the "twang" is induced, the "honk" can be eliminated by arching the velum. Between "twang" at one extreme and "honk" at the other we hear the sounds of the French nasal vowels (Par. 513).

413   A somewhat contradictory theory is offered by Bartholomew. He calls attention to the fact that the pillars are part of the group of swallowing muscles which raise the larynx, making the pharynx a poor resonator. Relaxing the velum tends to relax the swallowing muscles, and hence, producing nasal sounds tends to drop the larynx, which everyone agrees is essential to good

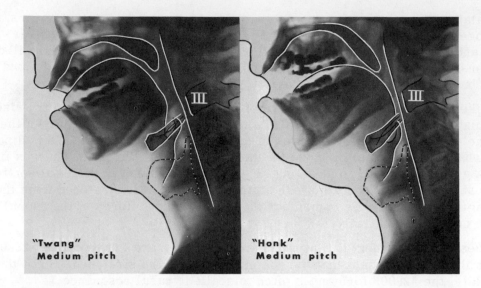

X-rays from van den Berg[6] and Vennard, *NATS Bulletin*. Fleshy parts have been retouched from visible evidence in the negatives. III, third cervical vertebra. In "twang" openings to mouth and throat appear equal, throat larger in diameter. In "honk" larynx is lower, but opening to mouth is almost closed. See Par. 513.

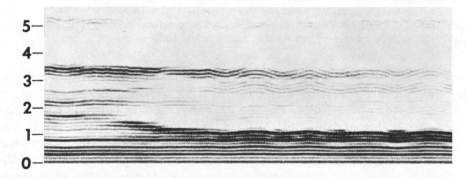

Sonagrams from van den Berg[6] and Vennard, *NATS Bulletin*, corresponding to the adjustments shown above in x-rays. Pitch, C_3 on bass staff. Time, 1.5 sec. Scale of kilocycles at left. Note that "twang" shows formants up to 3500 cps., "honk" shows little above 1000 cps. Sonagraphy is discussed in Par. 458.

Fig. 51. Twang and Honk

singing. Bartholomew continues,

It is quite possible, after the ability to secure the enlarged throat has been acquired, to learn to lift the velum just enough to close off the naso-pharynx and destroy the head resonance while still maintaining the enlarged throat and the relative relaxation of the swallowing group. And, yet, one of the most effective ways of first learning how to secure that throat setting is by use of some such imagery as "head resonance." Thus, one should not condemn this imagery, (p. 153, see also Bartholomew[2]).

414   We see a relationship between the initial "h" in staccato vocalizing, and the initial "m" or "n" in legato work. The one begins with deliberate breathiness in order to relax the valve, and then goes into a distinctly contrasting, clear vowel, in which the breathiness is discarded, but the freedom of the valve is retained. The other begins with deliberate nasality to relax the swallowing muscles, and then the nasality is discarded, arching the velum and bringing the pillars into position. Nasality is not dangerous in a beginning singer, if it is only a means to an end. If it is accompanied by tension in the sneering muscles and seems to "bring the tone forward," it can be relaxed, and the tone will "drop into the mouth."

415   How much nasal resonance should be carried into the finished product it a matter of taste. Some is doubtless good, though I feel that there is considerable danger of muffling all the "2800" in the tone, thereby defeating the real objective. Indeed, I have heard otherwise good singers whose voices lacked power and sounded breathy just for this reason. In some cases I have had the pleasure of persuading them to forego most of the nasality, and when they sang "more in the mouth," they gained in clarity and sounded distinctly better. The singer who uses too much nasality is probably going to the extreme in relaxation, and it is no coincidence that his tone becomes breathy at the same time.

The Loose Jaw

416   The lower jaw, or *mandible,* has two symmetrical parts, fused at the front. We have enumerated the laryngeal and tongue muscles which attach to it, and perhaps we should consider those muscles which hold it to the skull. The bones turn upward just in front of the ears and separate into two processes. The one at the back is like a knob and is called the *capitulum* or *condyle,* and the one in front is called the *coronoid process.* The condyle fits into a loose socket, but the jaw is held by several ligaments (we have mentioned the pterygomandibular ligament) and can move freely in various directions, providing the muscles are not too rigidly held. Whenever a student complains that opening his mouth causes a "grinding" in his jaw with "bumps" at various points, this simply means that he has not learned to loosen it, or that he is too introspective or selfconscious. It is easy to be concerned about normal bodily sensations the first time we notice them.

417   A large muscle called *temporalis* is located in the temple (named for it) and sends down a ligament to the coronoid process. There is a bony arch over this attachment, called the *zygomatic arch.* You can feel it as an extension of the cheekbones. The large powerful *masseter* muscles arise from this arch and cover the angle of the jaw on the outside. Coming from the external pterygoid plate (Par. 406) is the *lateral pterygoid muscle* which pulls the coronoid process forward, and there is a *medial pterygoid* arising nearby and going down diagonally to the corner of the jaw on the inside.

418   The jaw muscles, of course, do their main work in chewing, but we forget that they work all day long without weariness just overcoming gravity. They are postural muscles, and just as the back postural muscles synergize with breathing (Par. 97), the jaw muscles synergize with the extrinsic laryngeal musculature. Indeed, the digastric muscles assist in opening the jaw against resistance. This may explain why some teachers do not ask for exaggerated opening; they have found that some students tighten the muscles under the jaw in doing so.

419   Much has been said about the position of the jaw, but its *freedom* is of greater importance. A tight jaw is a symptom of a tight throat. If the extrinsic laryngeal muscles pull, their tension must be resisted by those muscles that lift the mandible. It may become fixed in almost any position, and in no case is it good. Asking the student to drop his jaw may help, but asking him to "relax" it is almost asking the impossible. Explain to him that he must relax the throat, and that he will be able to tell that it is relaxed when he discovers looseness in the jaw. The same

is true of speech, (Perkins, *et al.*). Rigidity of the jaw is a symptom, just as is elevation of the larynx, and the same considerations apply. The singer must learn the kind of singing in which the jaw is free. Before singing he may loosen it, but unless he phonates correctly it will immediately set again. A useful psychological strategem is to imagine that the jaw is made of lead and hangs down of its own weight. It also helps to wiggle the jaw from side to side while vocalizing.

420   One's posture should be such that the head is a little forward, so that dropping the jaw will not compress the larynx, (Frommhold[2] and Hoppe, Sonninen; Par. 79). Notice the X-ray of the adjustment designated "depressed larynx" in Fig. 47. The neck is more nearly vertical than in the other productions, the head held back and tipped down. A wide opening of the jaw thus produces an excessively low larynx with the hyoid bone depressed so that it is no longer parallel with the plane of the glottis. (Compare with the other X-rays in this group.) The digastric and geniohyoid are tense. Some teachers actually stand their students against the wall and press against their jawbones to produce this! The tone is sometimes impressive, and I shall say more about it under the topics of "covering" and "throaty production," (Par. 541-554).

421   Some of the neck muscles are also postural muscles, and maintain the position of the head. Extrinsic laryngeal tension is hence reflected in them. For example, a pull of the suprahyoid muscles forces the jaw to set, but this is of no avail unless the face is held up. This means that the back of the head must be pulled down, so the straining sternocleidomastoids, between the breastbone and the ears, will be seen standing out in the neck. (This, by the way, is a good reason for not using these muscles in breathing. Every part of the instrument affects all the others.)

422   Sometimes when a teacher asks a student to open more widely, or to "give the tone more room" (a very good way to put it), the student tips his head backward. Instead of lowering the lower jaw, he raises the upper! This defeats the teacher's purpose because the mandible is still in the same position and still exerts the same undesirable pull upon the larynx. The position is commonly called "reaching for the tone," (Fig. 64).

423   Some singers do very well with an almost closed mouth. However, I think that for most the results will be better if the jaw is dropped rather far. Many fine singers open so widely that the temporals and masseters can be noticed standing out. They are not working necessarily, but their position is changed. There is no set rule for it, such as being able to put a certain number of fingers between the teeth, though this is a good means of helping some students to realize how little they are actually opening. The mirror is also a help. One whose jaw is inhibited is always surprised how far he can open it without looking strange. We "feel" things (a tooth cavity, for example) to be bigger than they appear when we see them. The hinge of the jaw is not a simple pivot and the jaw is capable of sliding in several directions for the act of mastication. As long as it is opening simply by relaxing the temporals with the condyles in their sockets, it will not open far. The maximum opening requires the mandible to "slip out of joint." This can be felt by placing a finger in front of each ear, near the bottom. Here one can feel the *ramus*, or upward projection of the jaw-bone on each side. When the mandible really drops, the *rami* are pulled forward by the lateral pterygoids, making it possible for the fingers to sink into a pocket in front of each ear. In Husson's[3] X-rays of members of the Paris Opera in changing from speech to song the jaws drop and move forward.

424   A good reason for dropping the jaw as far as possible is that this pulls the tongue farther out of the pharynx, increasing its size and at the same time improving the megaphone shape of the buccal cavity. For vowels other than Ah, it is necessary to put the tongue in other shapes, and this necessitates other jaw positions as well. Even so, it is interesting to discover how far the jaw can be dropped while still making a good Ee or Ay. These vowels are much improved in

quality by this process. Experiment is the only way to settle the question of how much to open the mouth. I often ask a student to sing all the vowels with his thumb-joint held vertically between his front teeth. Didn't Demosthenes practice with pebbles in his mouth?

425   When students are vocalizing, I sometimes suggest that they drop the jaw a little more when approaching a difficult note. This is only a means to an end. The act of opening is likely to prevent a tightening of the throat and a lifting of the larynx. The additional space in the mouth is valueless.

The Lips and Teeth

426   The last conditioner, for better or for worse, before the tone is finally on its way to the audience, is the orifice of the last resonator. If the lips are pursed, they lower the pitch of the resonators by decreasing the diameter of the orifice, giving it soft edges, and perhaps adding a "neck" to the resonator. This results in a deadening of the tone, and unless a sombre effect is desired, it is not good. I admit that a certain amount seems necessary for the "dark" vowels, Oh and Oo. I shall say more about it in discussing "covering." Trumpeting of the lips is usually associated with a violent, strenuous type of production, which is also undesirable.

427   If the lips are drawn back, as in an exaggerated smile, the edge of the orifice becomes the teeth, which encourage high partials. If the opening is made larger, this would raise the pitch of the resonator. The acoustic effect is the exact opposite of "darkening," and is called "whiteness," or "*voix blanche*." The hard edges of the teeth are sometimes employed to give brilliance to an otherwise breathy tone, as for example, the falsetto. Girls who have not learned to use their full, ringing voices often try to improve their tone by smiling, which may improve the appearance but is not good for the tone.

428   The singer should learn to smile with his eyes. For the most part, the lips should be relaxed. In some cases, however, they may be too flaccid, and muffle the tone. There must be a little life in them. If four of the upper teeth show (just the edges) it will be about right to give animation to the expression and to preserve whatever good high partials have been generated in the tone. The mouth should be opened as if to take a bite out of an apple. I do not believe it is necessary to shape Ee and Ay with the lips. All this does not mean that the lips have no part in singing. They have plenty to do in the formation of consonants.

The Essentials of "Good Resonance"

429   There are two requirements for resonating a tone well. It must have the quality usually called "ring," which seems to mean the frequency "2800." This means that some small resonator, possibly the collar of the larynx, must function properly, and that there will be nothing about the shaping of the rest of the air passages that would muffle and destroy this brilliance. At the same time we must strengthen as many low partials in the tone as possible, to keep it from being shrill. The high partials alone would make the voice "reedy" like an oboe or clarinet (see their spectra in Fig. 9); but low partials add "mellowness" such as is found in the tone of a horn (also shown in Fig. 9). Low frequencies need large resonators, and so the opening of the pharynx is essential to mellowness of tone. The voice, to be well produced, needs both of these qualities.

430   Until the student realizes this fact, he will be confused. One moment his teacher will be demanding brilliance, and as soon as the student gives him a strident tone, his teacher will demand the opposite. When the poor pupil tries to supply this request, the teacher will tell him not to "swallow" the tone. It will seem as if the instructor cannot make up his mind, unless the point is clear that these are not extremes to be comprised, but polarities to be included in one fully rounded voice. It should be the objective of every singer to get as much brilliance as pos-

sible and as much depth as possible in the tone at the *same* time. They are the hemispheres of production.

The Illusion of "Placement"

431   It is easy to see how "mellowness" is associated with "depth." It is produced by a well actuated pharynx, and it is perfectly accurate to say that it is *in the throat*. The expression *full throated* is not figurative. Tones of this kind awaken sympathetic resonance more forcibly in the bones of the thorax, and so they are also spoken of as being "in the chest." This is misleading, since the term *chest voice* has connotations of registration, and should not be used with reference to resonance. But we may as well face it, people are going to continue talking about "deep tones that go all the way down to the diaphragm." It has a certain psychological value.

432   If "2800" is resonated in the collar of the larynx, it is puzzling why "ring" should be imagined elsewhere, but such is the case. We must remember that the larynx is below the level of consciousness, so any sensations will have to be associated with some other part of the mechanism. Lindsley (Par. 350) has shown us how sympathetic resonance would cause this effect to be concentrated in the region of the sinuses. It is an illusion, but one upon which many singers agree. There is also that muscular connection via the levator palati and palatopharyngeus, (Par. 409). Furthermore, a poorly produced tone gives the sensation of much strain in the region of the voice box, whereas good production releases all this. When this happens, the throat seems completely relaxed, and it is hard to believe that the tone is being produced there. At the same time, the ear becomes aware of more tone reaching it through the outer air, and the illusion is that the tone is "singing itself, out in front of the mouth."

433   When Garcia literally illuminated the larynx a hundred years or so ago, everyone became excited and there was a flurry of research on the subject of registration, some of it superficial and most of it confusing. Scientific knowledge of voice physiology has always tempted teachers into direct methods of manipulation and "local effort," which are often questionable. The "resonance school" of pedagogy was a reaction which projected the facts of laryngeal physiology elsewhere, in terms of changing bodily sensations, some of which might truly be called "resonance," although only in the manner that I have discussed in Par. 298. This school of thought was implemented by the findings of Scripture, and found its expression in the writings of Lilli Lehmann, Marafioti, Fillebrowne, and others.

434   Thus we see that a good tone will seem to be anywhere except in the larynx. The more mellow it is, the more there will be the feeling that it goes *"down"* and *"back."* The more brilliant it is, the more it will seem to go *"up"* and *"forward."* The important point to remember is that it must go in *both directions at once*.

435   A friend of mine has studied with a good many different teachers. He sang for one of them and was told that what he needed was to "place the tone where it could get the resonance of the turbinates in the nose." For one reason or another he was unable to continue his work with this pedagog for more than a few weeks, and began studying instead with a man who advocated opening the throat well, "keeping the tone back of the mouth, and getting the resonance of the trachea." The good thing my friend is able to report is that whatever the worth of the theory, this teacher was a good judge of tone and progress was made. My friend followed instructions and got his voice "down into the trachea," and the results were so pleasing that when the former teacher heard him, she congratulated him generously with the words, "You see how much benefit there is in getting the tone into the turbinates?" In my thinking, this story does not make either of the teachers ridiculous. Both methods have the merit of freeing the vibrator. There are many who say, "Placement is a myth. You cannot direct a tone anywhere; science tells us that every tone goes into all the cavities it can and vibrates the bones of the head and most of the bones of the

upper body." All of this is true. Some of the scoffers go on to make sarcastic remarks about how impossible it would be to resonate a tone in the head unless one's brain pan were an empty cavity. I cannot share this attitude. I think it is better to admit the validity of imagery as a teaching aid, although one should avoid the pitfall of literalism and not make the mistake of locating the placement in terms of anatomy.

436   I think I may risk the generalization that the Italian tradition of pedagogy is to emphasize "forward placement," which makes for great brilliance and flexibility; whereas the Germanic teachers have been more likely to emphasize a "deeper" production, the "stroke of the glottis," which makes for fuller tone and more power, such as Wagnerian opera demands. The fault of the Italian singer, when it appears, is likely to be "shallowness," or "whiteness"; and the fault to be heard in some Germanic singers, is "throatiness," or "darkness." These, of course, are extremes to be encountered only in superficial exponents of the pedagogies. The truly great and thoroughly schooled products of either method have pursued their development to the point where the best qualities of both are theirs. When we have arrived at a few facts about vowel formation, we will be ready to consider more fully this matter of resonance imagery, (Par. 474).

The Correlation between Resonance and Registration

437   We have a resonance dichotomy: "forward brilliance" as opposed to "mellow depth"; and we have a registration dichotomy: "light" as opposed to "heavy." There is always a temptation to correlate the two. For example, light registration is called head voice; there is a sensation of "getting the tone out of the throat," so we tend to correlate light registration with "forward placement." It is true that these two often do go together, but there is no necessary connection between them. All the variations of resonance effects can be produced in either falsetto or full voice. The vowels are merely different timbres produced by different adjustments of the resonators, as we shall see in the next chapter. Some are classified as "brilliant" and other as mellow," and yet all of them can be pronounced with varying adjustments of registration, thereby varying the timbre still more.

438   In individual voices, however, correlation can often be made, at least in the early development. Frequently, when a man begins his study he is guilty of a tightness that produces two faults, constriction of the resonators and static heaviness of registration. Since the two faults are correlated, the two cures will also be connected in his mind. As he learns to lighten the registration by making more "falsettoish" tone, he will free the "ring" in his voice and, not feeling it in his throat, will get the sensation that his voice is more "forward." At the same time he will be working to open the resonators so as not to "swallow" the tone. The whole process will be wrapped in one package, while in reality two distinct mechanisms are involved.

439   With a woman's voice it is usually the opposite. She has been singing a breathy falsetto tone which is lacking in the necessary power to produce high partials. She may have been "whitening" the tone with her teeth, or if she is a mezzo, she may have considered it more refined and cultivated to "bottle up the tone" in the pharynx. In either case she lacks the true "ring of the voice." Frequently she will discover the "ring" at the same moment that she discovers her chest voice. Ask her to use her "speaking voice," to shout, as she would at a football game. She will tell you that the tone is "horrid," and "nasty," and that she "can't stand it"; but if you can persuade her to experiment with it until she discovers a more dynamic adjustment of this voice, she will never be satisfied with pure falsetto again, except perhaps for extremely high notes.

440   The only generalization we can make, then, is that the "unused register" is likely to be correlated with "forward placement," which is another way of saying the obvious, namely that the deficiency in registration is likely to be associated in the experience of the student with his resonance deficiency, and both difficulties will be overcome together. In more talented or advanced students

it will not be as simple, because the deficiencies will not be as crude. There will be no completely unused register; the problem will be more a matter of coordination than of discovery. I find that both men and women benefit from the suggestion, "Sing it the way you speak it," or "Don't sing it so beautifully, *shout* it." And also, both male and female voices profit from exercises such as the "yawn-sigh," in which there is a portamento from a high quasi-falsetto into a low deep chest tone, because it is much easier to coordinate the registers in that direction than it is to begin with heavy low tone and lighten it while ascending a scale.

Chapter 6

VOWELS

441   Up to this point we have considered vocal tone in general, except for a few places where it has been necessary to specify that what was being said applied more to the vowel Ah than to the others. The various vowels may be considered different qualities or timbres, and as such they are the product of the vibrator and the resonators. However, the chief influence of the vibrator upon tone color is the registration, light or heavy; all the vowels can be pronounced clearly in either falsetto or full voice. So the consideration of the vowels is largely a continuation of our discussion of resonance and concerns the vibrator only to the extent that the two are coordinated.

442   Those who argue that the vowels are really formed in the larynx base their opinion upon the fact that laryngologists observe slight differences in the position of the arytenoids when the vowels change. This is particularly true of whispered vowels. Negus tells us that for the vowel Ee the vocal processes of the arytenoids move toward each other, and in strong whispers actually touch, (pp. 428, 429). That is, in whispering the arytenoid muscles relax a little, allowing the glottis to be partly open, but for the vowel Ee the lateral cricoarytenoids pull upon the muscular processes, swinging the vocal processes closer together. In loud whispers the part of the glottis which is formed by the muscles actually closes, while the part which is formed by the arytenoid cartilages is open. Fig. 52 shows this.

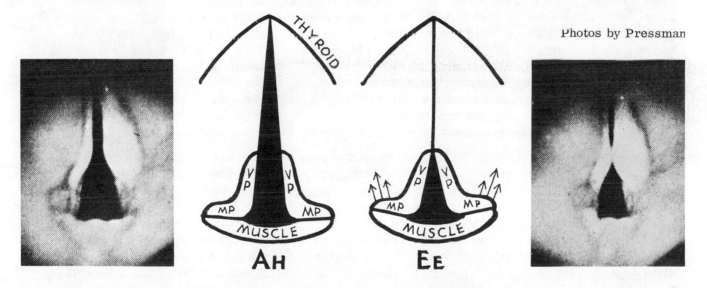

Photos by Pressman

Fig. 52. Glottal Formations in Whispering
Diagrams of glottis in whispering Ah and "round vowels" and Ee and "pointed vowels." (Based on
V. E. Negus, *The Mechanism of the Larynx* pp. 428, 429. Similar drawings appear in P. J. Rousselot,
Principes de Phonetique Experimentale p. 468. Photos from Brodnitz, *Keep Your Voice Healthy*.
VP, vocal processes; MP, muscular processes. Arrows indicate pull of lateral cricoarytenoids.

443   Fig. 53 shows tomograms of the larynx in producing different vowels with the same loudness. The ventricles are largest for Ee. Tarneaud (pp. 60-65) shows similar evidence taken by the pioneers of laryngeal tomography, Canuyt, Greiner and Gunsett. Landeau's evidence shows little difference between open production of Ah and Eh, but if the Ah is covered the ventricles are considerably larger, (Fig. 44 and 65; Par. 544).

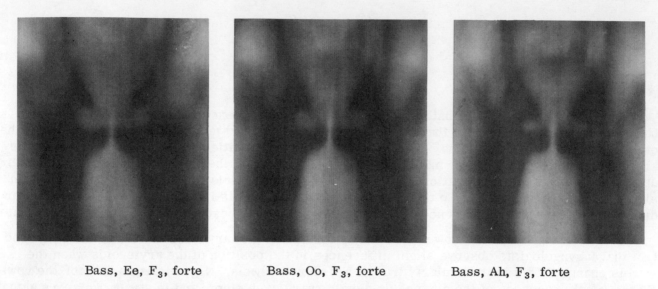

Bass, Ee, F₃, forte   Bass, Oo, F₃, forte   Bass, Ah, F₃, forte

Fig. 53. Tomograms of Larynx in Production of Different Vowels
From van den Berg,[4] *NATS Bulletin*. See also Fig. 44, right-hand side.

444   Isshiki found that if a singer is asked to phonate Ee, Oo, and Ah at the same loudness he will
actually make the Ah much louder than the other two. This is because he gauges loudness by the
effort he is using, and in this experiment the subglottal pressure was the same for Ah and Oo,
but the Ah was louder because the mouth was more open. Subglottal pressure for Ee was a little
higher, even though the subject intended it to be the same. This probably means that we have
learned to give a little more energy to this vowel, partly because the mouth is likely to be more
closed, and partly because it must have a high overtone, as we shall see. Isshiki asked the same
subject to phonate the three vowels while looking at a decibel meter to keep them uniform in
loudness. In this case Ah required much less pressure, and the Oo slightly less than the Ee.
A similar unpublished experiment by Rubin and myself confirms these findings.

445   The experiment by Isshiki shows that the differences in laryngeal *production* of the vowels
may be due to differences in the amount of laryngeal exertion demanded by the different *pronunciations*, (Par. 357). It is easy to see that the glottal formations in whispering show greater
adductory effort for Ee. The difference in the ventricles is contradictory, and baffling. In most
cases, lowering the larynx opens the ventricles, but here we have the reverse. However, we
shall see that the vowels have specific effects upon laryngeal function, through the extrinsic
musculature. The glottal rattle, or fry (Par. 195), requires a loose glottis, and is much more
difficult to perform on either Ee or Oo than it is while the resonators are forming an Ah.

446   If you have ever been to a throat specialist, you remember that when he wants a good look at
your vocal cords, he asks you to say "Ee." He is pulling your tongue out of your mouth at the
same time, so that you cannot actually pronounce the vowel, but he gets a better closure of the
glottis, apparently, than if he had asked for Ah, as when a doctor wants to see the pharynx from
the front of the mouth. I think the real reason for this is that in saying "Ee" the tongue is
allowed to go farther forward, as we shall see. With other vowels, the tongue, and with it
the epiglottis, bunches back in the throat, and partly obscures the larynx as viewed in the
laryngeal mirror. In other words, this is not so much a function of the voice box as of the
buccopharyngeal resonator.

447   With this much acknowledgment of one more secret hidden in the larynx, we proceed to our study of the vowels, on the assumption that much more is to be learned by thinking of them as a resonance phenomenon. From here on, we shall consider only the effect of the resonators upon vowel quality. I believe that those teachers who instruct their pupils to "form the vowels in the throat rather than in the mouth," overlook a good many important facts.

Two Theories of Harmonic Structure

448   In Chapter 1 we discovered that differences in timbre can be shown in acoustical spectra, and in Fig. 9 we have a few typical examples. No matter what the fundamental may be, the spectrum remains essentially the same, provided we are still in the same register of the instrument. This is illustrated in the top half of Fig. 54, which shows flute tones on middle C_4, E_4, and G_4 sharp, respectively, and while there are slight changes in the relative strengths of the partials, the second predominates in each case. This is in accord with what is called the *Relative Pitch Theory* of tone quality, which stipulates that the strength of the partials is always *relative* to the fundamental.

449   In the lower half of Fig. 54 we see three more spectra, on D_3 sharp, F_3 sharp, and A_3 sharp, respectively, all representing the voice singing the vowel Ah. But the predominating partial in each case is *not* relative to the fundamental, but instead is always the same pitch, in this case A_5 sharp above the treble staff. For the fundamental, D_3 sharp, it is the sixth partial; for F_3 sharp, it is the fifth; and for A_3 sharp, the fourth. This violates the Relative Pitch Theory, and it has been explained by what is called the *Fixed Pitch or Formant Theory*. This second hypothesis is that some part of the instrument will have a fixed pitch, which by sympathetic resonance will augment whatever partial in the tone is in tune with it. This part of the instrument, and also the frequency band in which the exaggerated partials will be found, are called the *formant*.

450   Most instruments have formants. That is, an analysis of all their tones will show certain regions where overtones are likely to be disproportionately loud. In other words, the Relative Pitch Theory explains only eighty or ninety per cent of the phenomenon. For example, if you will examine closely the flute spectra in Fig. 54, you will see first that the second partial is always strongest, and this bears out the Relative Pitch Theory; but you will also notice that in the C_4 spectrum the first partial is weaker than the third, while as the pitch of the tone rises, the first partial grows in strength and the third diminishes. This can only be explained by the Formant Theory; that is, there could be discovered in the flute a formant whose pitch was fixed somewhere between the first and third partials, so that as the first moved up toward it, that partial was augmented, and as the third moved away from it, that partial was diminished.

451   To the extent that formants are detrimental to the tone, instrument makers strive to eliminate them. In the case of the violin, a formant causes a *wolf tone*, and we have seen that the bronchotracheal formant creates vocal problems, (Par. 313-321). The supraglottal formants, however, are essential, and the story of vocal timbre reverses that of instrumental timbre. Here eighty or ninety per cent of the proportioning of the harmonics is controlled by formant, and the rest is relative to the fundamental.

452   A relationship will be seen between these theories and the two that were set forth in the preceding chapter. The Formant Theory, since it emphasizes the importance of the resonators, correlates with the Willis-Scripture Theory; which would imply that the Wheatstone-Helmholtz Theory parallels the Relative Pitch Theory. However, all four hypotheses are needed to explain the harmonic structure of vocal tone, and they should not be thought of as incompatible, but rather as differing aspects of the same complex phenomenon.

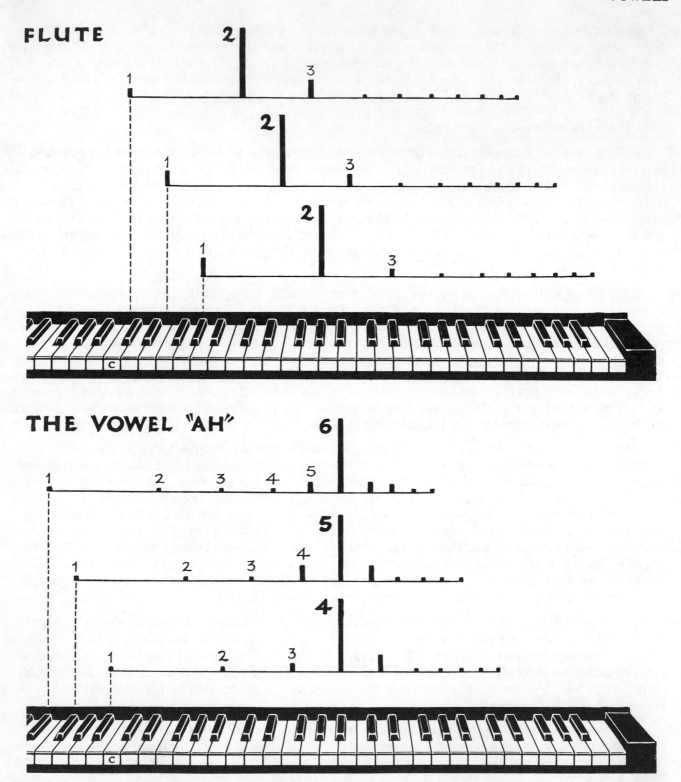

Fig. 54. Spectra of Flute and Vocal Tones
From Dayton C. Miller, *The Science of Musical Sounds.*, Copyright, 1916 by the Macmillan Company and used with their permission, p. 256.

Acoustical Findings as to Vowel Formants

453   Fig. 55 shows the formants for the five "pure" vowels, as derived from various acoustical investigations. Each line in the five spectra represents the finding of some physicist for that parti-

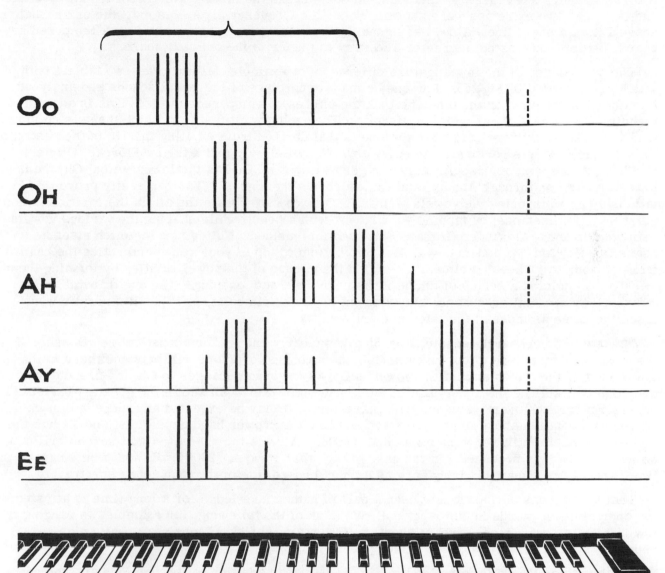

Fig. 55. Vowel Formants as Located by Early Investigators

Based on the following sources:

I. B. Crandall, "A Dynamical Study of the Vowel Sounds," *Bell System Technical Journal*, Vol. III, No. 2, 1924, pp. 232-7.

Harvey Fletcher, *Speech and Hearing* (New York, Van Nostrand, 1929).

M. H. Liddell, "Physical Characteristics of Speech Sound," *Purdue University Bulletin 16*, March 1924, p. 20.

R. J. Lloyd, "Genesis of Vowels," *British Association Paper*, 1896, p. 251.

Dayton C. Miller, *The Science of Musical Sounds* (New York: The Macmillan Co., 1916).

Sir Richard Paget, *Human Speech* (New York: Harcourt, Brace & Co., 1930), p. 42.

Brace at top indicates approximate range of soprano voice. See Par. 565-571.

cular vowel. The six authorities consulted are Crandall, Fletcher, Liddell, Lloyd, Miller, and Paget. They agree in principle but not in detail, that is, as to specific pitches. This, I believe, is due to the fact that no two people pronounce a vowel exactly the same way, and also that no two researchers used identical methods. In some cases the investigator recorded an "average" and in others two extremes were shown. Where the frequency given was extreme or unusual, I showed it as a short line. Also, I assigned the frequencies to specific notes on a tempered keyboard. Anyone interested in greater accuracy can refer to the original sources.

454   The procedures of the investigators differed. For example, Miller gives two tables, both of which are included in Fig. 55. For one he made recordings of the vowel sounds and analyzed them harmonically. For the other he took the pitches of whispered vowels. This is an interesting technic. It consists of carrying the Hermann Theory to its ultimate, in which there is no vibrator tone (or practically none) and the only tone is that derived from exciting the air in the resonators. This experiment was performed as early as 1780 by Hellwag, and later by Flörcke, Olivier, Donders, Aiken, and others. All agree in general; that is, Oo has the lowest pitch, Oh, the next lowest, and so on through Ah, Ay, and Ee, which has the highest. You can easily prove this relationship by whispering the vowels yourself. Or, you can vibrate the air in the cavities in some other way, for instance, by tapping your larynx with a pencil while shaping the various vowels with your mouth. Alexander Graham Bell used this method. Notice how the pitch rises as you shape Oo, Oh, Ah, Ay, and Ee. Whistle from bottom to top of your range and notice the change from "Whoo" to "Whee." Helmholtz verified the pitches of the vowel cavities by forming them silently and holding a series of tuning forks near the mouth opening. The one that was in tune awakened sympathetic resonance and sang out loudly, (Helmholtz, p. 107). His results were much the same as those of the later authorities.

455   Whatever the research technic, Fig. 55 gives clearly enough the acoustical relationship of the vowels. Regardless of the fundamental, the strongest overtone will be somewhere in the lower part of the treble staff if the vowel is Oo. If the vowel changes to Oh, the predominant overtone will shift to the upper part of the treble staff. Since Ah shows the greatest variety of possible color, the overtone which will characterize it may be expected anywhere within the octave immediately above the treble staff. Ay has a narrower band above this, and Ee has the highest formant of all, reaching as high as "2800." This is the one vowel that sounds brilliant no matter how it is produced. In the case of the other vowels, "2800" will sound only part of the time, and I have shown this frequency as a short broken line in the four upper spectra.

456   That all this has unconsciously been a part of human knowledge for a long time is attested by the onomatopoeic words in our language. We think of the following, for example, as ranging from low to high in pitch: moan, groan; shout; yell; scream, shriek. Lions roar, while pigs squeal and mice squeak. Doves coo, but chicks peep.

457   Another thing that will be noticed in Fig. 55 is that in addition to its high formant, the vowel Ay has a lower formant in the upper half of the treble staff; and the vowel Ee not only has the highest formant of all, but also the lowest, at least as low as the bottom of the treble staff. These vowels have two formants each. Of the authorities represented in Fig. 55, Crandall, Lloyd, and Paget found two formants for all the vowels. With modern electronic analyzing equipment all present day investigators find two, even three or four formants, for all the vowels, which makes possible refinements in our understanding, but which does not deny the original findings.

458   The Sonagraph is an example of such modern instrumentation. It makes a graph in which time is shown from left to right (2.4 seconds in a complete sonagram) and the formants appear from bottom to top, their respective blackness indicating their strength. Special devices in the Sonagraph make it possible to show the relative strengths of the partials more exactly, or to

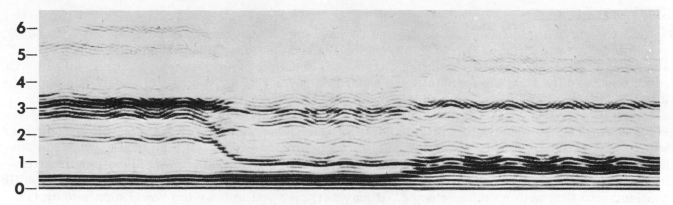

Fig. 56. Sonagram of Ee, Oo, Ah [i, u, ɑ]

show the variation in overall intensity, or loudness. Sonagrams have appeared already without comment in Figs. 23.5, 47, and 51, because I thought you would like to have them with the X-rays and other data on the same page. You may care to refer back to them.

459   In Fig. 56 we have another sonagram correlated with X-rays. The bottom line (at zero) is merely a base line. The next above that is the fundamental. I was singing E_3 flat, about 150 cps. Note that it is not strong. The nature of the ear is such that it will recreate the fundamental and recognize it, even though it is weak. Amplification of any of the partials makes the whole tone stronger; so it is not necessary for the voice to create a resonator big or deep enough to resonate the fundamental. The next two lines, rather black, are the low formant of Ee, about 400 cps. Above and below 3000 cps. are two more strong partials. The older authorities would have heard them as one high formant.

460   Between the partials of the tone, white spaces can be seen. As the frequency of the fundamental changes, the space between the partials does also, and the difference is more noticeable at the top of the sonagram because musical intervals involve greater differences of frequency, numerically, at the top. For example, the octave from A_2 to A_3 is from 110 to 220 cps., while from A_4 to A_5 is from 440 to 880 cps. The higher octave will thus occupy four times as much space on the sonagram. The white spaces, hence, will show the rate and degree of smoothness of the vibrato, and this will be more visible in the upper partials, but the exact pitches cannot be read directly.

461   As the voice shifts to Oo the low formant becomes much stronger. The two upper formants drop, one of them all the way to 1000 cps. This is the second Oo formant, not strong enough for the early investigators to have discovered it. The third formant turns out to be our old friend "2800," which is the "ring of the voice," (Par. 322-326, 410). Note that it runs more or less horizontally throughout all three vowels in this graph. It shows only weakly, if at all, in graphs of the speaking voice. Denes and Pinson, in a table of formant frequencies for nine English vowels (p. 118) show the third formant moving from 3101 cps. to 2390 cps. for men, and from 3310 cps. to 2780 cps. for women. While some vowels (especially Ee) are more "ringing" than others, older scientists may be forgiven for saying that vowel color is defined by the two lower formants, and that the "ring" is something which may or may not be superimposed. Its presence in strength marks the fine singer.

462   The vowel formants in our sonagram move up and cluster in the neighborhood of 1000 cps. for Ah. The ring is higher in pitch than for Oo, and a little stronger but not as strong as for Ee. You will see other less important components in the sonagrams, but our present discussion need not concern itself with them. They give the voice its individuality, its "personality."

The Vowel Triangle

463   Our vowels fall into two groups. Oo and Oh have one strong overtone each, or two not widely separated. Ay and Ee have two each. I originally used an old-fashioned terminology: "double" and "single" formant vowels. Delattre[2] has shown that in synthetic vowels, at least, this is still good; that is, only when the formants are separated do they affect the ear as such. The clustered formants appear to be heard as a single overtone at a frequency between the two formants as detected by electronic analysis, (p. 205). Ah partakes of the nature of both, belongs in both series: Ah, Oh, Oo (descending pitch) and Ah, Ay, Ee (ascending *and* descending pitch). Another way to say it is that when one sings Ay, he is really singing Oh, plus a high partial which is not heard in the Oh; and when one sings Ee, he is really singing Oo, plus a still more ringing overtone. You can test this readily by singing Ee loudly and putting your hand over your mouth while continuing to sing with no other change. It may surprise you to hear the vowel turn into an Oo. Your hand muffles the high overtone and leaves only the low formant. Try turning Ay into Oh by the same experiment. It works almost as well.

464   This brings us to our first statement of the Vowel Triangle, arriving at it upon purely acoustical grounds.

		Ee (highest and lowest formants)
Separated (double) formants:	Ay	
	Ah	
Clustered (single) formants:	Oh	
		Oo (lowest formant)

465   This arrangement has been agreed upon by practically everyone who has studied the subject, different though their theories and approaches may have been. Russell[2] shows a fascinating series of variations on the triangle by Hellwag (1780), Chladni (1809), Du Bois-Reymond (1812), Brücke (1856), Lepsius (1863), Techmer (1880), Trautman (1884), Passy (1890), Carhart (1910). Other names might be added. The differences are negligible, appearing in the elaborations which were made upon the basic outline.

The Mechanism of the Formants

466   Thus far we have discussed the vowel triangle entirely on the basis of what the ear recognizes as the differentiation between the vowels. We have found that vowels are simply different timbres of the instrument, in which the overtone structure varies. Emphasis has been laid upon the Fixed Pitch or Formant factors in the phenomenon, which are salient, though we must remember that these are modifications of the primary glottal tone, which contains many partials, depending upon the registration. Changing the vowel is comparable to changing the tone color of, say, a trumpet, by putting a mute into the bell. By changing the shape of the resonator, the quality of the sound is altered.

467   The only variable resonators in the voice are the throat and the mouth. These are capable of many subtle changes. Probably the tongue is the most important factor in varying the size of the chambers, and so it may be called the "mute." It could be compared to the right hand of a horn player as he places it in the bell of his instrument. I am convinced that directly or indirectly the control of the tongue is the most important factor in good vowel formation. However, as Russell argues, all the vowels can be produced independently of the tongue position. It is possible to sing all the vowels with the jaws widely separated and the tongue touching the outer skin of the lower lip, or with mouth almost closed and tongue tip held between the teeth, etc. Ventriloquists demonstrate that speech sounds can be produced or at least simulated with no

visible adjustments. All these exercises promote muscular independence, and sometimes help
to build singing technic, but we must realize that they involve special muscular compensations
inside the mouth. The tongue is still the important factor.

The Mechanism of the Separated Formants

468   Of the five vowels, Ah is probably the nearest to the original glottal tone. That is, it makes
the least modification of the sound produced by the vocal bands. The pharynx is distended
comfortably, the jaw is dropped, the tongue is low and grooved, if possible. The formation
resembles an old-fashioned Victrola horn, or the bell of a saxophone, inverted. Both of these
are comparatively non-selective resonators—they tend to resonate all tones, their function being
primarily to amplify./ This is why Ah is the loudest vowel. Ay and Ee are more penetrating: but
for sheer volume, Ah is the most efficient. Authorities tell us that the glottal tone is probably
more neutral than Ah, more like Uh. Ah may be considered an Uh that has been beautified by
proper resonation.

469   Of course, the resonator for Ah is not entirely megaphonic, or non-selective, for we know
that it has a pitch varying within the octave above the treble staff and that it augments whichever
partial in the basic glottal tone comes nearest to that frequency. Early investigators found one
strong overtone in any given Ah, but present researchers find two or more. This means that
the oro-pharynx is functioning as two distinct cavities. The most active differentiator between
mouth and throat is the tongue. The velum is there also, but normally it should be arched out
of the way, otherwise a third cavity, the nose, enters to complicate the picture.

470   We may say that the vowels Ay and Ee are formed with the tongue. It is almost impossible to
pronounce them without moving it. The farther forward the tongue arches, the smaller the cavity
formed in front of it and the larger the cavity behind. With the position for the vowel Ee we have
the smallest possible anterior chamber, and hence the highest possible formant; and at the same
time the largest possible posterior chamber, and hence the lowest possible formant. With Ay, the
tongue partition is farther back; so the front formant is larger and lower, while the rear formant
is smaller and higher. It does not seem hard to see how the forward cavity of the vowel Ee should
have a frequency near that of the collar of the larynx, which is said to produce "2800." Incidentally, this is also the pitch of the chamber of the outer ear, which means that this overtone need not
be very loud to sound loud, since the ear itself amplifies it by sympathetic resonance.

471   Before continuing I must admit that assigning the high formant to the space in front of the
tongue and the low to the space behind, while not entirely incorrect, is an oversimplification.

> It is good to realize the limitations of this simplification. Actually, both resonators are
> coupled and they interact. This interaction has several aspects. For example, the formants
> push each other apart, i.e., the low formant becomes lower and the high formant becomes higher.
> When the cavities are of about the same size, as for the [ɑ] it is impossible to ascribe the form-
> ants to "their" cavities. A result of practical importance to exact theory is that two formants
> never coincide. When the two cavities are tuned to exactly the same frequency, their interaction
> will provide two formants with different frequencies. Also, the formants will never cross over
> when the cavities are gradually changed. Moreover, the simplification is unable to provide an
> explanation of the higher formants. Roughly speaking, every non-nasalized vowel has five form-
> ants below 5000 cps., or four below 4000 cps., i.e., one formant per 1000 cps., the location of the
> formants depending on the shapes of the cavities. To a certain extent, these high formants may
> be regarded as overtones of the various cavities, (van den Berg,[6] p. 12).

Delattre notes that we are studying *movements* of the speech organs, and changes in the opening
of the mouth and the orifice between the mouth and the throat, (Delattre,[4] p. 99). This harks
back to Paget,[3] (Par. 577-583).

Vowel [i]   **Vowel [u]**   **Vowel [α]**

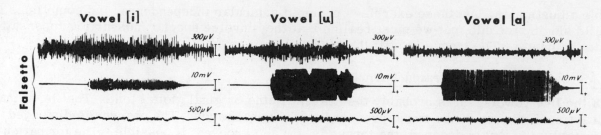

Falsetto production on C₅, octave higher than chest tones in this study, shows much the same muscular effort as normal chest production (facing page). I attempted to keep a constant volume, that is, to maintain equal subglottal pressure. However, microphone shows considerably more volume for [α]. Similar subglottal pressure produces greater volume with wide open mouth, as in [α], than half open mouth as in [i] and [u]. This accords with findings of Isshiki that intention to phonate with equal loudness produces equal subglottal pressure but unequal loudness, while phonation controlled by seeing decibel-meter requires greater pressure for [i] and [u] than for [α]. Falsetto [u] is louder than normal [u] (facing page). Falsetto [i] is weak.

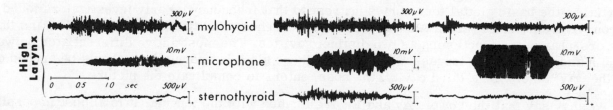

High larynx production shows less activity of the mylohyoid than normal (facing page) which is surprising until one remembers that the jaw is raised for this production, making it easier for tongue to be raised. [i] is weaker in volume than in normal production because there is less mouth opening. See x-ray of high larynx [α] in Fig. 47.

Depressed larynx production shows increased activity in sternothyroid, as might be expected, but also increased activity in mylohyoid, especially for [i]. This shows that the tongue muscles must be differentiated from the backward pulling supralaryngeal muscles. In yawning also the mylohyoid coordinates with the sternothyroid, (Fig. 48). See x-ray of depressed larynx [α] in Fig. 47.

Fig. 57. Electromyograms of different Resonator Adjustments for [i, u,α]
From Faaborg-Andersen[3] and Vennard, *Annals of Otology, Rhinology and Laryngology.*

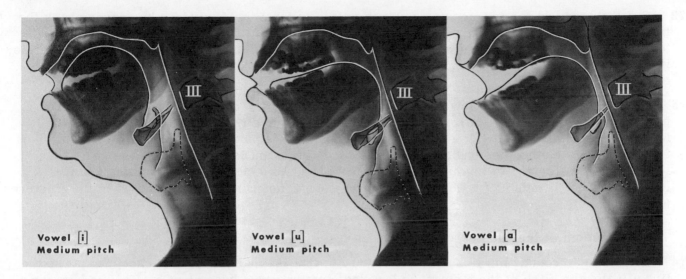

X-rays of the author, from van den Berg[6] and Vennard, *NATS Bulletin*. Fleshy parts have been retouched from visible evidence in the negatives. Vowels are produced normally. Elevation of larynx can be gauged with reference to third cervical vertebra, III. Note space between thyroid and hyoid is greater when they are lower. Mouth is more open for [ɑ].

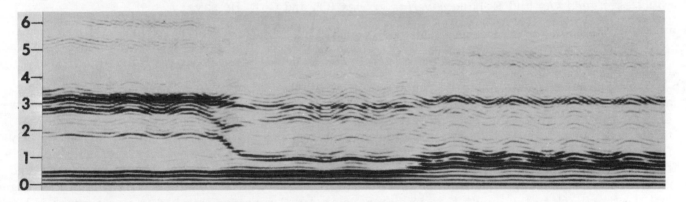

Sonagrams from van den Berg[6] and Vennard, *NATS Bulletin*, corresponding to the adjustments shown in above x-rays. Pitch C₃ sharp, bass staff. Time 2.2 seconds. Note strong "ring" (near 3 kilocycles) for all three vowels. This is the same sonagram shown in Fig. 56.

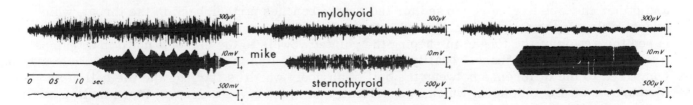

Electromyograms from Faaborg-Andersen[3] and Vennard, *Annals of Otology, Rhinology and Laryngology*. Normal production on C₃, bass staff.

There seems to be a preparatory tensing of the mylohyoid in all production, which is relaxed before singing [ɑ], but which is increased for [i] and maintained with some diminishing for [u], due to the tongue position required for these vowels. In the sternothyroid muscle there is a moderate increase which is greatest for [u] and least for [i].

Fig. 58. Normal Production of [i, u, ɑ]

472   Some singers whose tongues are sluggish prefer to form the Ay and Ee by drawing back the lips in a smile. I have already expressed my disapproval of this practice. It makes the high formant too strong for the low, and makes the tone shrill, thin, or "white." It is easy to see how it can be a substitute for "2800," and why singers whose tone is too nearly falsetto employ a toothy production.

473   Delattre tells us that the low vowel formant is tuned by the overall opening of the bucco-pharyngeal resonator, (p. 868). When the tongue and jaw are raised, as for Ee and Oo, the low formant is at its lowest point; and as the jaw drops and the mouth opens, the low formant rises toward Ah. He further demonstrates that the second formant is tuned by what he calls "cavity lengthening," referring to the mouth cavity. This has two factors, tongue backing and lip rounding (p. 872), either of which will lower the second formant. This brings us to the clustered formant vowels.

The Mechanism of the Clustered Formants

474   If the singer rounds his lips over the vowel Ah, that is, changes nothing except to purse the lips a little, the pitch of the formant is lowered, and the vowel becomes Oh. This is because a cavity with a smaller aperture has a lower pitch. Most singers instinctively or by habit that was formed unconsciously in childhood, drop the larynx a little in going from Ah to Oh and from Oh to Oo, which would tend to lower the frequency of the pharyngeal resonator. Indeed, Rousselot noted the position of the larynx as one of the mechanistic criteria differentiating what he called *voyelles aiguës* (Ay and Ee) and *voyelles graves* (Oh and Oo). He says:

> According to the measurements taken on me by Dr. Natier the average position is that of the *Ah*; from there to *Oo* the larynx lowers, and to *Ee* it rises. . . . This progressive elevation of the larynx corresponds to the division of the vowels into deep and sharp, (p. 721).

475   I prefer that students form the round vowels with the lips, but there are some teachers who argue that there is no more reason for doing this than for using the lips to form the pointed vowels, Ay and Ee. These are the teachers who say to "form the vowels in the throat." I feel that this results in a "throaty" or swallowed pronunciation, a dangerous pitfall for all and especially for beginners. However, the acoustics of such production should be explained. Russell suggests that in such a case, the narrowing of the aperture occurs between the tongue and the palate, and produces the same lowering of pitch as we have discussed. Here we have a bunching of the tongue still farther back in the mouth than in either Ee or Ay. I consider this bad in itself, since it leads to stiffness of the tongue, one of the most serious faults. I reiterate my conviction that the tongue should be low in the mouth as much of the time as possible.

476   In changing from Oh to Oo, the process is more extreme. The larynx is lower, if it can be, and either the lips are more pursed, or the tongue bunches farther back in the throat, which is undesirable. If the Oo is being formed with the lips the jaw will probably rise a little. We compared the action of the tongue in shaping the pointed vowels to the use of a mute in a trumpet, which gives it a more "nasal" quality. The action of the lips in shaping the round vowels may be compared to the difference between the bell of an oboe, which is flaring, and the bell of an oboe d'amore or an English horn, which is spherical, and which gives a deeper, more mellow quality.

477   All this might be summarized in the vowel triangle, with mechanistic rather than acoustical commentaries.

High larynx:	Ee	(Most likely to be "toothy")
Formed with the tongue:	Ay	
Glottal tone simply resonated:	Ah	Greatest modification of glottal tone
Formed with the lips:	Oh	
Low larynx:	Oo	(Most likely to be "throaty")

Vowels other than the "Five"

478   Of course, there are many vowels not shown in the basic triangle, all necessary for good
pronunciation. Some are easy to relate to the five "long" vowels (or Latin vowels). For example, if one sings Ah and begins to arch the tongue, he will sing Eh (as in "pep") before the Ay is
reached. It might be called a "half-hearted Ay." Also there is Ih ("pip") between Ay and Ee.
Or, in the other direction, as one rounds the lips, Aw comes between Ah and Oh. The vowels Ee,
Ay, Oh, and Oo are considered *tense vowels*, and their *lax* counterparts are the vowels in "bit,"
"bet," "bought," and "put," (Wise, p. 61). If you will feel your tongue muscles from below you
will notice the floor of the mouth relax as you go from "beet" to "bit," "bate" to "bet," etc.,
(Kenyon, p. 83). The only lax vowel in our triangle is Ah. Wise says that all the vowels with the
tongue low are classified "lax," though he says that the vowel in "bat" may be tense but this is
"not socially approved of, and so is felt to be harsh, flat, and unmusical, and subject to objectionable nasalization," (p. 62).

479   Also there are the European vowels, the *umlauts, ö* and *ü* in German, paralleled by *eu* and *u*
in French. These are formed by both rounding the lips and arching the tongue, seldom done in
English. Sometimes the instruction for pronouncing *ö* is: "Round your lips as if you were going
to say Oh, and then try to say Ay." This is all right, but with most American singers, it results
merely in their singing Ay. They unconsciously say to themselves: "That looks like an Oh, but
it isn't; I'm supposed to try to say 'Ay'," and they do. A better instruction is: "Round your lips
for Oh, shape your tongue for Ay, and then say something that is a combination of both." I think
it is best to teach all these sounds as new pronunciations, not be found in English at all. Tell a
pupil that *ö* is like the *u* in "church" or in "murmur," and he will be unable to divorce the *r* from
the vowel sound, and will fall into the common error of pronouncing "Goethe," "Gertie."

480   Phoneticians will distinguish between an *ö* that has the tongue in the position for Ay and one
that has the tongue in the position for Eh. One of these is the tense *ö* [ø] as in *Röslein*, and the
other lax [œ] as in *Rösschen*. I am not sure that singers, especially Americans can be expected
to differentiate these. There is also the tense *eu* [ø] as in *feuillage*, and the lax *eu* [œ] as in
fleur. Americans are likely to pronounce *eu* incorrectly as [ʊ]. Anglicizing French words
usually follows this pattern, for example: "amateur," "entrepreneur," and "saboteur," all of
which are pronounced with [ʊ] in the final syllable. It sometimes helps to point out to a student
that one French word which has been in our language perhaps longer than most is pronounced
almost as the French would pronounce it: "chauffeur." Give the syllables equal stress and
English pronunciation here is almost correct French.

481   Americans should also guard against the fault of pronouncing *ü* as if it were Ee, which comes
from "rounding the lips and then trying to say Ee." There is a tense *ü* [y] in *Tür*, and a lax *ü*
[ʏ] in *Hütte*. This may be a difficult distinction in singing, but the vowel in German should be
nearer to Oo than to Ee or Ih, whereas the French *u* [y] is nearer the Ee, and has no lax form.
This latter distinction is possible for most American singers, and all should try to make it.
However, Ay and Oh are not as far removed as Ee and Oo, and it is difficult to make two different sounds between them. In other words, it is too much to expect singers to whom the languages
are foreign to differentiate between tense and lax *ö* and *eu*. Perhaps they should in speaking, but

not in *singing*. We come back to the difference between phonetics and music. There are more distinctions in speech, which is not always beautiful, than there are in song, which is supposed not only to be recognizable, but also euphonious.

482   In order to pursue this subject in greater detail it will be helpful to learn the International Phonetic Alphabet, because it becomes increasingly difficult to represent the different sounds with makeshift spellings, like Ah, Aw, Eh, etc. The following are the common vowels:

Ee [i] as in beet	Oh [o] as in tone
[ɪ] as in bit	[ʊ] as in foot
Ay [e] as in pay	Oo [u] as in boot
Eh [ɛ] as in pet	[ɜ] as in word (with silent r)
[æ] as in back	[ɝ] as in word
[a] as in bask	[ɚ] as in per
Ah [ɑ] as in calm	[y] French u or German ü (tense)
[ɒ] as in hot	[ʏ] German ü (lax)
Aw [ɔ] as in bawl	[ø] French eu or German ö (tense)
[ə] as in the	[œ] French eu or German ö (lax)
[ʌ] as in cut	

483   The vowel triangle is a venerable concept, but modern phoneticians find it inadequate. When the vowels are plotted by locating imaginary dots at the center of gravity of the tongue for the different positions, more of a rectangle is likely to emerge (Fig. 59). The triangle is still there, with [ɑ] at the bottom, and off center. The vowels can also be plotted according to the frequencies of their formants. The lower strong partial can be represented by locating it on a frequency scale from left to right, and the upper strong partial on a scale from bottom to top. The result is Fig. 60. Oddly enough, not only can the triangle still be seen, but the other vowels fall in much the same relative locations as in our tongue chart.

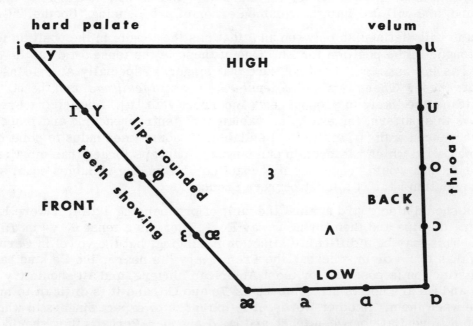

Fig. 59. Chart of Tongue Positions for Vowels

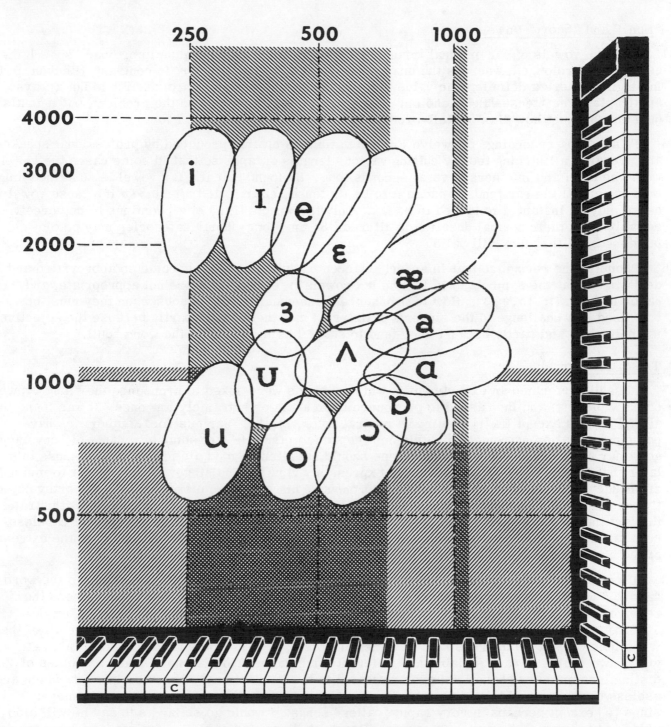

Fig. 60. Formants of English Vowels

Based on data from Denes and Pinson, Fairbanks, Peterson and Barney. Low formant frequency plotted on graph from left to right. Second formant frequency plotted from bottom to top. Average locations indicated by IPA symbols. Egg-shaped overlapping areas based on Peterson and Barney, showing that there is wide latitude in frequencies the ear will accept for a given vowel under differing circumstances, and same acoustic signal may be perceived as one vowel one time and a different vowel at another. Shaded areas show the easy range of the soprano voice, and narrow bands suggest upper limit at C₆. Only vowels [ʊ, ɑ, a, æ] can be produced normally in soprano's upper voice, (Par. 565-571).

"Long" and "Short" Vowels

484   The five vowels of our original triangle have been called *long* because in ordinary speech they usually are prolonged, whereas the unaccented vowels are called *short* in contrast, (Kenyon, p. 86). In singing, where a definite time value is given every syllable, the word "short" is not always applicable. The "tense-lax" dichotomy is a more modern approach to the problem, but it is also questionable just how "lax" a well-produced singing tone should be.

485   Tiffany took recordings of twelve English vowels as clearly produced by professional speakers and prepared a listening test by cutting various lengths of tapes so that in some cases the vowels would be brief and in others several seconds long. He found that if a lax vowel is sustained longer than is normal the ear tends to judge it to be its tense relative, and *vice versa* if a tense vowel is heard only an instant it is judged to be lax. Only the vowels [i, u, æ, ɜ] continue to be perceived reliably when their normal duration is altered. So the "long-short" categories may be old-fashioned, but they are still valid.

486   Phoneticians recognize that in speech unaccented syllables often become so abbreviated and devitalized that the symbols used for the lax vowels [ɪ, ɛ, ʊ, ɔ] etc. are not appropriate, and they have another set: [ʌ, ə, ɜ]. How to pronounce these usually brief sounds when they must be sustained is a challenge to the singer's artistry. I call them "dull" partly because the adjective is applicable, and partly because they tend to sound like the vowel in the word "dull."

The "Dull" Vowel

487   Russell performed an experiment in which subjects were asked to pronounce the "long" vowels on easy pitches, and then asked to pronounce them again on extremely low ones. It was found that all the vowels except Ee [i] acquired a neutral color, Uh [ʌ]. Various vocal authorities have pointed out that on extremely high pitches the same is true; in fact some advocates of "covering" go so far as to say that for high notes one should not attempt good diction. I shall discuss this later, but for the moment am content to express my view that no singer should resort to methods of production in which it is impossible to pronounce his language, merely for the unworthy objective of eking out an extra high or extra low note. I mention the matter now simply to illustrate the fact that neutral vowels are the result of poor voice production, either because of carelessness (as in the unaccented syllables of speech) or from extraneous difficulties (as in the extremes of the singer's range).

488   There are two phonetic symbols for the "dull" vowel, [ʌ] and [ə]. We find them in the word "above," which is transcribed [əbʌv]. In speech they may be distinguished by the stress they receive. The [ʌ] is long enough and tense enough to place on our acoustical chart, (Fig. 60). The [ə] is called the *schwa* vowel, and has been described as "the dumping ground for all of the variations caused by unstressing," (Kantner and West, p. 83). I defy anyone to sing "above" giving two counts to each syllable and differentiating them. This is one of many examples of distinctions made by phoneticians, as reflected in the International Phonetic Alphabet, which are useless to singers. If this is too strong a statement, then we must say that an artist never sings [ə] except perhaps in very rapid "patter" songs. I would go so far as to say he will also avoid [ʌ] and some other speech sounds. Research discovers what *is*. Artists (and their teachers) attempt only what *should be*. Phonetics is descriptive; pedagogy, prescriptive.

489   In another experiment by Tiffany[2] he asked his subjects to speak various vowels under three different conditions. They were pronounced in isolation. They were pronounced in carrier sentences spoken with such meaning as to place stress on the word containing the vowel, and spoken in the same sentence with the stress elsewhere. For example, "But *he'd* never *had* the warning," and "But he'd *never* had the *warning*." In the first case we have [i] and [æ] stressed,

and in the second we have them unstressed. It was found that when the sounds made by professional speakers were analyzed acoustically and plotted on a graph, they tended to make rough
quadrilaterals, one inside the other, (Fig. 61).

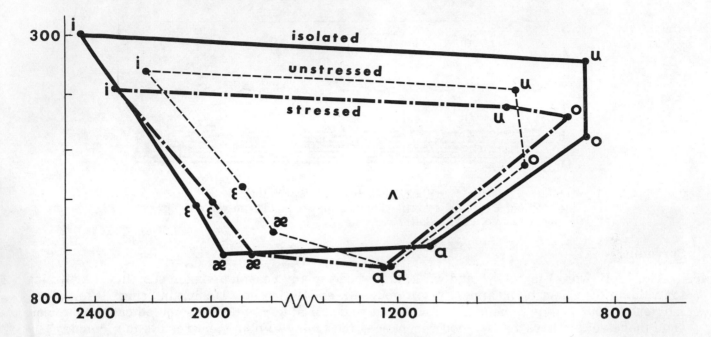

Fig. 61. Migration of Vowel Formants

Modified version of chart in Tiffany.[2] [ɪ] and [e] have been omitted because they would obscure the
principle demonstrated in the other vowels.

490   Tiffany[2] comments, "Vowels seem to move toward a neutral, or at least a central, point on
the vowel diagram as they lose energy in context. The trend is somewhat less obvious for [ʌ]
and [ɑ], as one might expect, and is to some extent reversed for [ɪ] and [e]," (p. 314). The untrained speakers made a somewhat similar graph, only smaller; that is, they did not make such
noticeable differences in stress and even when speaking the vowels in isolation, did not separate
them acoustically as widely as did the professionals.

491   The less carefully and effectively one pronounces the vowels, the more nearly they all merge
in the neutral vowel [ʌ], or its even more vague variant [ə]. The same thing happens even
more drastically in different forms of the same word. When "contract" is a noun it is [kɑntrækt];
as a verb it is [kəntrækt]. "Able" is pronounced [eɪbl] but "ability" is [əbɪlɪtɪ]. Consider also
"battle" [bætl] "battalion" [bətæljən] and "illustration" [ɪləstreɪʃən] "illustrative" [ɪlʌstrətɪv].
Kantner and West give all these examples and then state, "The vowel [ə] has no typical position.
It represents a tendency rather than a position, a tendency of vowels to lose their identify by
moving toward the neutral position," (p. 85). Kenyon (pp. 106, 107) makes similar comments.

492   A lazy tongue is the source of our problem. It takes energy to arch the tongue for an [i] and
generate enough compression in the larynx to sound the high partial the vowel demands. It even
takes energy to keep the tongue low for an [ɑ]. The "dull" vowel is the easiest to make, and
that is why it heard so often in unaccented syllables. One more vowel, [з], should be mentioned.
It is the vowel in "fur" when the "r" is not pronounced—another example of lax pronunciation, as
far as English is concerned, though this is close to the umlaut sound, [ø]. When the "r"
sounded, the symbol is [ʒ] or [ɚ], (Par. 482).

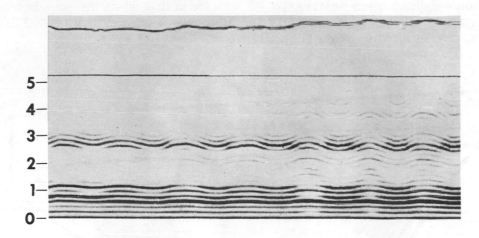

Fig. 62. Sonagram of "Spreading"
Pitch, E_3 on bass staff. Time, 1.5 second. From van den Berg[6]
and Vennard, *NATS Bulletin*.

Spreading

493   The "dull" vowel is "gray" and weak, and when for any reason a singer sustains it and tries
for volume the effect is unhappy. Try it yourself, and notice how lacking in "ring" it is. The
moment "2800" begins to sound, you will find yourself singing [ɑ], or some other Latin vowel.
Only these vowels have really good resonance, and trying to blur them results in a "muddy"
quality which becomes worse as it becomes louder. The most commonly used expression for
this fault is "spreading."

494   Fig. 62 is a sonagram of the vowel [ɑ] being allowed to "spread." It begins as a "dull" [ɑ]
(almost [ʌ] as shown by the lower formant). The increase in volume shows in the line at the
top. Note that the added energy does not increase the blackness of the vowel formants, but is
literally spread between and above them. The existence of this figurative expression in singers'
vocabularies shows that the ear instinctively anticipated what the Sonagraph finally made visible.
Maybe the language of singers is not as empty-headed as non-singers sometimes appear to think!
Another illustrative sonagram is to be seen in Fig. 64, Par. 543.

495   Spreading is related to breathiness. In Fig. 63 we see an [ɑ] becoming breathy while the
singer attempts to keep the volume at the same level. This requires considerable effort, and
was fairly successful as can be seen by the graph of volume at the top. Note that vowel formants
fill up; in other words, spreading is taking place. It is likely that breathy, "dull" and "spread"
tones form a continuum in which the only difference is in loudness. All are inefficient and simply
show differing degrees of misdirected effort. Note also that the breathy tone is without vibrato.

496   Winckel has analyzed the tones of many singers, trained and untrained. He says;

An essential fact, to my knowledge never observed, is that the number of overtones, within
limits, stay the same for each individual singer. A well trained, male singer, singing a normally mezzo-forte tone in the middle range, shows in most cases, between 9 and 14 partials, sometimes between 8 and 33 partials; female singers between 7 and 12, sometimes between 5 and 15
partials. A similar distribution of the partials, with a little greater scattering, is also noticeable in an advanced voice student. Likewise in some popular singers, who have less voice training, but a better diction and expression, the same observation could be made. Also the trained
speaking voice of a qualified actor shows approximately the same number of partials as the
singing voice. But in comparison, the untrained speaking voice has more overtones and the
fluctuation is wider. . . . The reason why bass voices often sound rough is because the number

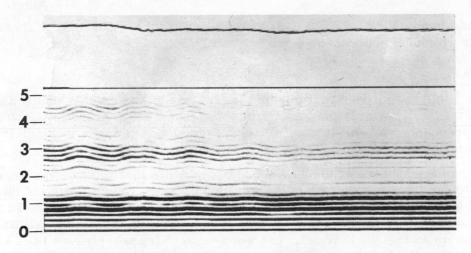

Fig. 63. Sonagram of Breathiness
Pitch, E₃ on bass staff. Time, 1.5 second. From van den Berg[6]
and Vennard, *NATS Bulletin*.

of partials is too great and the higher partials create a dissonance with the fundamental tone. The beauty of a tone depends on the limitation of the partials, which indeed also can be attained by a bass singer."

497   Ruth[2] quotes the above and makes the point that when a good singer concentrates the energy of his crescendo in a comparatively few partials, these vibrations are so intense as to awaken response in the bones of the face, giving rise to the illusion of placement, (Par. 298, 431-436). The opposite of spreading or diffusion is concentration or focus (Par. 532-536). At the end of Chapter 7 are sonagrams of speech and song compared, (Fig. 66). It was found that the strong vowel of each syllable averaged 6.34 visible formants in the speaking voice and only 5.07 in the singing. Furthermore, song was about ten decibels louder than the speech. The added power was focussed in fewer partials, actually only two or three.

498   "Dull" or "spread" tones, as well as "straight" tones are often under pitch. This is because of their inefficiency. It may well be also that the diffusion of the overtones confuses the ear so that it is difficult to tell what pitch the fundamental may be. I have already mentioned that our resonators do not amplify the fundamentals of low voices. It is important musically, therefore, that they should in addition to defining the vowel be harmonically related to the fundamental. Mackworth-Young has discussed this at length, (p. 73 ff). A "spread" tone cannot readily be assigned to a definite pitch. It is like trying to point to a period with the thick end of a billiard cue. But if the singer tries to come up to pitch without correcting the timbre, he will simply sharp. Poor production can be defined in terms of vowel formation, and often when nothing else helps, a singer whose tone is dull can correct it simply by being told that he is singing [ʌ] instead of [ɑ], or perhaps still another vowel may be suggested.

499   The neutral vowel, obviously, is not as useful musically as the other vowels. Singers are torn between singing "naturally" and prolonging unmusical sounds, or making beautiful tones and seeming "affected." The popular singer, who is primarily an entertainer, and to whom intelligibility is indispensable, chooses to sing poorly and be understood. The classical singer makes the opposite choice and is not understood. The middle course is a process of making sure of good production first, and then modifying it enough to make it sound colloquial but avoiding a sloppiness in which all the unaccented sounds become [ʌ]. For example, the word "pleasant" should not be "plea*sahnt*" [plɛzɑnt] but neither should it be "plea*sunt*." [plɛzʌnt]. The word "and" becomes an affectation if it is pronounced "*awhnd*," [ɔnd] "*und*" [ʌnd] is too dull, but a Midwest-

ern twang [ænd] is no better. The ideal is a compromise among the three. This brings us to another matter which helps us to solve our problem.

The "Bad" Vowel [æ]

500   I have coined this designation partly from the fact that this is another unpleasant sound (the counterpart of the "dull" vowel) and partly from the fact that it is heard in the word "bad," (bæd), especially as pronounced by uncultivated voices. Other English words in which it is found are "as," "act," "at," etc.

501   This vowel has a tenseness in the walls of the resonators that produces an unpleasant result in the same manner that sqeezing the walls of a pipe makes it change from the quality of a flute to that of a tin horn. It is the opposite of the mellowness characteristic of low-formant vowels. It decidedly is related to the [i ɪ e ɛ] series; indeed, the [ɛ] frequently has the same strident production as the "bad" vowel. The word "exact" [ɛgzækt] leaves little choice as to which is the "bad" syllable. As we drop the tongue from the [i] position without letting it fall back the tone becomes progressively strident.

502   There is often a raising of the jaw and a retracting of the lips, "adding teeth to the tone." And as climax of all the vocal sins, in the worst production of these vowels the high larynx completes the picture. This reminds us again of the intimate relation between vibrator and resonators. What we are describing in terms of resonance very likely involves faulty function of the vocal cords themselves. Since the cords are below the level of consciousness, we resort to concepts of pronunciation as a means of indirect control.

503   Kenyon (pp. 95, 96) gives us an interesting historical comment on the relationship between [æ] and [ɑ]. In 16th century English [ɑ] was prevalent in many words now pronounced differently. The Cockney pronunciation of "make" [mɑɪk] is a remnant. In the 17th century [ɑɪ] became [æɪ] and even [eɪ]. The vowel [ɑ] went out of fashion and was even considered poor. Sheridan's pronouncing dictionary (London, 1780) did not include it; nor did phonetic transcriptions by Benjamin Franklin (1789); and Hale (1799) shows [æ] in such words as "aft," "balm," "carve," and "gaunt." The latter two authorities are American. Present General American keeps [æ] in many strong words, and this is actually 17th and 18th century English! The more euphonious [ɑ] has come back into British pronunciation since then, and its influence is heard in Eastern and Southern American speech. Both the Webster and the Oxford dictionaries in the 19th century proposed [a] as a compromise, (Kenyon, p. 100). See also Par. 638.

504   In the Purcell excerpt shown in Fig. 66 at the end of Chapter 7, the word "man" occurs twice, and sonagrams of the spoken [æ] may be compared with the [a] which is used in singing the same word. (I hope no one will argue that since Purcell is 17th century English we should sing as many [æ] vowels as possible throughout his works!)

505   I should say that if the "dull" vowels may be considered clustered-formant vowels, poorly produced because of passivity, the "bad" vowels bear a counter-relation to the separated-formant vowels, poorly produced because of over-activity. Here we have a key to our problem of how to pronounce in singing those sounds which in speaking are unpleasant but are passed so quickly that they are not noticed. The "bad" vowel must be relaxed or "dulled" a little, and colored with [ɑ] The "dull" vowels must be energized with a little "badness." Carrying them all the way to [ɑ] is affectation, but a little "twang" brightens them up nicely. "Thinking" [ɑ] or some other clear vowel brings the needed brilliance. You can see how impossible it is to build a two-dimensional vowel triangle to include all the unclassifiable sounds. It would have to be a pyramid or a prism to show the presence or absence of a ringing third formant on top.

506   In the same Purcell excerpt I have just mentioned we have several schwas. In speech "mindful of" is [mɑɪndfəl əv], but in singing "mindful" is improved by making it [mɑɪndfʊl] and there is time to hear the [ʊ]. The word "of" is sustained in the singing, and we may not do violence to the music of a great composer. I was trained for years to sing [lɔv] for "love" but to relax the [ɔ] a little and at the same time concentrate on brilliance of production. This is what I did with the word "of" in the Purcell. I was surprised upon analyzing it sonagraphically (Fig. 66 continued), to find not [ɔ] but the formants of [ʌ]: 650, 1200, and 2000 cps roughly. The 2000 cps, however, is weakened, and a strong 3000 cps "ring" appears.

507   In examples of "twang" the letters "m," "n," and "ng," are often involved, as in "am," "man," "and," "angry," "hang," etc. This leads to the impression that the sound is essentially nasal. However, such is not the case, though nasality increases the undesirability of the tone. Contracting the sneering muscles and wrinkling the nose is really just a means of exposing the upper teeth, and not of producing nasality. Constriction of the nares is often associated with activating the pillars, but the velum can be quite independent. You can demonstrate this by pinching your nostrils with your fingers and then producing either nasal or oral vowels at will, simply by controlling the soft palate. This is a variation of the experiment mentioned in paragraph 342. The same can be done while wrinkling the nose, without the aid of the fingers. The nasal sounds of the English language are produced by the aid of consonants. The only true nasal vowels are in French, in which care often must be taken *not* to sound the consonants.

508   The position of the soft palate in the production of the oral vowels has been studied by Croatto and Croatto (p. 142) in Italy and by Hiroto *et al.* (p. 37) in Japan. Both investigations showed that the velum arches most forcefully to close the nasal port in the vowel [i] and the order of elevation for the remaining vowels is [u, o, e, ɑ]. Whitworth (p. 34) in Iowa found the series for three vowels to be [i, o, ɑ]. Croatto and Croatto point out the *rapport* with arching of the tongue. We might say that there is a correspondence with the amount of energy required to shape the buccopharyngeal resonator.

The Nasal Vowels

509   The nasal vowels are produced by adding another resonator, the nose. Paget reports a new formant which appears in the analysis of these vowels, with about the frequency of G_4 sharp on the treble staff, rising to as high as B_4 for the vowels in *bon* and *main*, French pronunciation. Howie and Delattre (p. 7) locate the nasal formant at 500 cps., B_4, and also another an octave lower, both of them weak, especially the one at 250 cps. May Laird-Brown tells us:

> The nasal vowels are produced by lowering the soft palate so that the breath passes simultaneously through nose and mouth. In singing it is usually sufficient to direct the thought to an increased breath pressure in the post-nasal cavities. There must never be contraction of any sort. Pupils under supervision of a competent teacher may practise alternating the "oral" and the corresponding nasal vowel on one breath, taking great care to keep the jaw relaxed, and remembering that the vowels must not be moved from their forward position in the mouth. Students who cannot nasalise readily may try the following simple exercise: Sound the vowel (ɑ) in its correct position; stop the tone, and inhale with the mouth open. The veil of the palate will be felt to drop. Then repeat the vowel, (p. 35).

510   There are four French nasals. The IPA symbol for the first is [ɑ̃], the [~] being the mark for nasalization. The second is usually shown as [ɔ̃] but the well-known French baritone and pedagog, Bernac, advises Americans to think it [õ]. This is another example of the different approaches—phonetic and vocal. Intellectual students who have brought the vocal mechanism under conscious control will pronounce these two sounds simply by saying the parallel English vowels with the velum relaxed. Others, who prefer to rely upon pronunciation habits formed

unawares in childhood, will prefer to use "ng," singing "ahng" and "ohng" and later making sure that the "n" does not actually become audible, though there will always be danger of falling into that error.

511   Another nasal vowel is found in the second syllables of "*chacun*" and "*parfum.*" It is sometimes described as nasalization of the lax German *ö* or the French *eu* [œ̃], but I think it is easier and just as successful to think of the sound as Uh with the velum lowered, [ʌ̃].

512   With the fourth sound we grapple the problem of "pinched," or "twangy" nasality. In the words, "*vin*," "*timbre*," "*lynx*," "*nymphe*," "*Rheims*," "*main*," "*faim*," we have different spellings of the vowel. It also appears in combination with the "Y sound" in "*chien*," "*bien*," etc. May Laird-Brown says,

> As heard in ordinary speech, (this vowel) is a sound resembling a nasal form of the English vowel in "sand." As such it is an impossibly ugly sound for singing, especially in the high range, and French singers open and darken it a little by lowering the tongue toward [a] (the vowel in "*lac*," (p. 36).

Notice the relationship between it and our "bad" vowel. The usual symbol is [ɛ̃], though the sound is nearly [æ̃], (Wise, p. 328). In singing, French artists substitute [ɑ̃] or nearly so. To summarize, the first two of these French vowels are nasalizations of [a] and [o]; the second two are nasalizations of our two embarrassing English sounds—they are "honky dull" and "twangy bad." And so we come back to our former conclusion that nasality is undesirable in English, and its chief use to Americans is in vocalizing, where it is only a means to an end.

513   Howie and Delattre show strong formants above the two weak ones mentioned in Par. 509. For [ɛ̃], [œ̃], and [ɑ̃], these are approximately the upper partials of the non-nasal analogues, [ɛ], [œ], and [ɑ], which apparently are not muffled by nasalization if the velum does not drop too far; but the upper formant of [ɔ] is 1000 cps., and drops to 700 cps. for [ɔ̃]. This defines the distinction between "twang" and "honk,"(Par. 411-415). At the dull end of the nasal spectrum we hear no partials above 1000 cps. because the formants of [ɔ̃] are all below that point, but at the opposite end we have a strong high partial at about 1800 cps. Extreme "twang" has a strong formant still higher. Fig. 51 shows "twang" changing to "honk."

Consistency of Vowel Color

514   If we appraise our vowel colors in the light of what we have found to be the essentials of "good resonance," we find that the clustered formants, and with them the "dull" vowels, are rich in mellowness or "depth," and the separated formants, including the "bad" sounds, are strong in brilliance, or "ring." Indeed, if we substitute the expression *low formant* for clustered formant, and *high formant* for separated formant, the acoustical reasons are even more apparent.

515   We have said, however, that a well-rounded tone contains both hemipsheres, and the objective of the singer should be to get as much as possible of both extremes in his voice. How can he get both when singing a vowel that belongs distinctly in *one* hemisphere? This is a musical requirement demanded much less, if at all, in speech, and is another factor in the problem of intelligibility in singing, (Cornut and Lafon). The vowel [a], of course, belongs in both, and is the most fully resonated sound in the language. Fortunately it predominates in our literature, and whenever one sings it, one can hope to achieve maximum brilliance and maximum depth in the one sound. Lilli Lehman offers the startling suggestion that it is possible when singing [a] to sing the other vowels, [i] and [u], at the same time! This principle she applies throughout her book, "How to Sing," showing us in *black* the vowels to be *sung*, and in *red* those to be *thought* at the same time.

516   The brilliant vowels, [e] and [i] should not offer too much problem when we remember that they are actually [o] and [u] with added high formants. The chief difference between them and the vowel [ɑ] is in the proportions of their overtones. In [ɑ], "ring" and mellowness are equally balanced, while in [i] the "ring" is higher pitched and may overpower the lower partial. This is what happens when the [i] sounds strident, "white," or nasal. In such a case the [u] which is underlying the [i] sound is being muffled by a tongue that arches too high, or is being obscured by a forward resonator that is too strongly activated. The tongue may be too stiff, or the teeth may comprise too great a part of the aperture, either of which conditions would encourage high partials at the expense of low ones.

517   To produce an [i] that has a satisfactory balance of the antipodal components of good tone, the jaw must be as far down as possible, and the lips must be comfortable, not retracted. It will probably be necessary to raise the jaw somewhat from the [ɑ] position, in order to get the tongue high enough to make the front cavity, but the tendency should be moderated. Until the attempt has been made, most singers do not realize how much opening is possible without loss of characteristic [i] flavor. Of course the effect of this opening is to permit the low partial to emerge in equal proportion with the high. If the sound is still too brilliant for its intended purpose (for example, in a sad song) rounding the lips a little will soften the high overtones. This is the beginning of the French *u* or German *ü*, indeed it is largely by connotations that the mind distinguishes between a partially veiled [i] in English, and an *u* in French.

518   An [e] that is too strident can be corrected by giving it some of the pronunciation of the *ŏ*. All that has been said of the relation between [i] and [ɑ], could also be said in lesser degree of [e], because of its intermediate position. This should be enough to illustrate my premise that the vowels [e] and [i] can profitably be considered modifications of the vowel [ɑ]. One criterion of good singing is that all the vowels should have enough uniformity to sound as if they belonged together. They must be consistent. It should be possible to make them all sound brilliant, or all sound mellow, depending upon the requirements of the song. The color of the production should not change with the vowel. Of course, it is unavoidable that the [i] will sound more brilliant than the [u], but the differences should be moderated. If a singer has a well rounded [ɑ], and does not allow the other vowels to depart too far from it, he has solved the problem of consistent, uniform production.

519   With clustered formant vowels it is just as necessary to achieve brilliance as it is necessary to give mellowness to the separated formants. The upper partial can be strong enough to give the needed sparkle. I sometimes make an analogy with the technic of the *pointillistic* painters, who invented the trick of painting entirely with applications of pure color, producing all their blended effects by the juxtaposition of tiny dots of complementary colors. Suppose we compare [u] to deep purple. We paint in an area with this color, and then we stipple it with tiny dots of orange or gold. At a little distance, the effect is a purple that instead of being dull and lifeless has fire. The gold stippling in this figure is "2800," the "third partial" which does not show in two-dimensional charts. If the singer is using his instrument correctly, this high partial is being formed, perhaps, in the collar of the larynx, and all that is necessary is to make sure that it is not muffled by too much constriction. This means that the lips must not purse more than absolutely necessary, and above all that the tongue should not bunch in the back of the mouth, narrowing the pharynx and crowding the aperture into the mouth.

520   If the [u] sounds too "swallowed" the solution is to "let it out of the throat," by "giving more room." Specifically, this means that the jaw must drop as far as it can. The same considerations apply here as in the case of the [i]. Also the lips must relax more nearly to the [o] position. An [o] that is too muffled must be sung more like [ɔ]. In other words, while the extreme quality of the [e] and [i] vowels is best moderated by changing them in the direction of [o] and

[u], the process should not be reversed, lest it destroy the formant quality which is character-istic of the [ɔ], [o], [u] series, but instead they should be altered in the direction of [ɑ]. If the word "Gloria" does not sound sufficiently glorious, have the singer pronounce it [glɔrjɑ]. This principle is even more applicable to choral ensembles. An individual must be subtle about it, but in a group, the ones who are unresponsive to suggestions will offset those who follow too literally.

Emotional Connotations of the Vowels

521   There are various theories of the origin of language. One that illuminates the study of articulation I shall mention in our next chapter, Par. 577-581. Another theory involves the con-cept that the vowels are instinctive expressions of emotion, from which other, more specifically communicative expressions have evolved. There are two vowels, the "dull" and the "bad," that go a long way toward bearing out this theory. These vowels are extreme. In fact, in those European languages which we most commonly sing, neither [æ] nor [ʌ] can be found. Neutral sounds are heard in final syllables, but [ʌ] as a stressed vowel is not found in Italian, German, or French. The umlauts are nearest to neutral sounds used in stressed syllables. [ʌ] is Eng-lish, of course. The [æ] pronunciation is avoided in British English, and of course in the other three tongues.

522   The "dull" vowel is the sound that emerges when we are not at our best. Punch someone in the stomach and the unpremeditated sound that will come out is "Uh!" While groping for words we unconsciously intersperse with "uh's." Ask a stupid person a question and he will reply, "Huh?" Such a person uses the vowel over and over; his affirmative is [ʌhʌ] and his negative is [hʌʔʌ]. ([ʔ] is the symbol for the glottal plosive.) The spastic, who cannot shape his resonators efficiently, uses [ʌ] repeatedly. By extension, the "dull" vowel has found its way into many words for things that are blunt, bumpy, or bulbous. It is likely to be applied to unpleasant things, espe-cially in a dumb, or grubby, grumbly way. Of course, the vowel is occasionally found in words of opposite connotation. "Love" and "mother" are prime examples. Incidentally, most singers manage to substitute a better vowel, such as [ʊ] or [ɔ], (Par. 455). A Freudian etymology ex-plains "mother" when we recognize that [m] is both a sucking and an encompassing gesture. Many words which at first glance appear to be exceptions have migrated only a short distance from a circular or bulging connotation. For example we munch lunch or supper on the way to the gullet, stomach, and gut, stuffing ourselves with gustatory appetite. I resist further exposi-tion and submit a list of "dull" words, the mere reading of which should convince one that [ʌ] is a vulgar sound.

523   Also it does not seem like coincidence that [æ] is found in many words expressing aggres-siveness or unpleasantness, or both. The list of "bad" words is even longer than the "dull" list. Here again there are exceptions, for instance "glad" and "happy," but are they not "exceptions that prove the rule?" Again, good singers substitute [a] in these words. The [æ] sound is one that children make instinctively when they are trying to pick a fight, (Par. 813, Fig. 75). The word "anger" is more than a symbol of the emotion; it is a sample.

524   The vowels between these two extremes are more ambiguous in emotional tone, and hence have migrated farther from their original expressiveness. However, it can still be said gen-erally that the high formant vowels are more elated, whereas low formants are more sombre. The principle is involved in a kind of onomatopoea, in such words as "gloom," "groan," "moan," "mourning," "sorrow," and "happiness," "gaiety," "radiance," "glee," "spree," etc. This results in two advantages for teachers. A student frequently will be benefited by a psychological approach when mechanistic instructions fail. If he swallows his tones it may help to suggest that he sing them more "gaily," more "happily." If he sings too "whitely," tell him to make them

abut	buttock	cunctation	flux	hubbub	lunge	nuzzle	ruff	slump	sunk
adulterate	button	cunning	frump	huck	lush		ruffian	slush	sup
adunc	buxom	cup	fubsy	huckster	lust	pluff	ruffle	slut	sus-
amuck	buzz	curmud-	fudder	huddle	lustrate	plug	rugged	smother	
annul		geon	fuddle	huff	luxury	plum	rum	smudge	thrust
	chubby	cuss	fuddy-	hug		plumb	rumble	smug	thud
blood	chuck	custard	duddy	huh	much	plumbeous	rummage	smuggle	thug
blubber	chunk	custody	fudge	hulk	muck	plumduff	rump	smut	thumb
bluff	club	cut	fug	hull	mud	plummet	rumple	snub	thunder
bludgeon	cluck		fumble	hum	muddle	plump	rumpus	snuff	ton
blunder	clump	disgust	fundament	humble	muff	plunder	runt	snug	tough
blunder-	clumsy	doldrum	fungus	humbug	muffin	plunge	rupture	sough	trouble
buss	clunk	double	funk	humdrum	muffle	plush	rust	spud	truckle
blunt	cluster	drub	funnel	humdudgeon	mug	pub	rustic	sputter	truculent
bluster	clutch	drudge	fuss	hummel	mugget	puck	rustle	stomach	trudge
brunt	clutter	drug	fustigate	hummock	muggy	pud	rut	struggle	trull
brusque	conundrum	drum	fusty	hump	mugwump	pudder		strumpet	trumpery
bub	corrupt	drumly	fuzz	humph	mulch	puddle		strut	truncate
bubble	crepuscle	drunk		Humpty-	mulct	pudsy	scrub	stub	truncheon
buck	crumb	druxy	glum	Dumpty	mull	puff	scruff	stubble	trundle
bucket	crumpet	dub	glut	humstrum	mum	pug	scrunch	stuck	truss
buckle	crumple	dud	glutton	hun	mumble	pulse	scuff	stuck-up	tub
bud	crunch	dudgeon	grub	hunch	mumbo-	pulverize	scuffle	stuff	tuck
budge	crupper	duffer	grudge	hunger	jumbo	pulvinate	scullery	stultify	tuft
budget	crush	dug	gruff	hunk	mummy	pumice	sculpin	stum	tug
buffer	crust	dull	grumble	hunkers	mump	pummel	scum	stumble	tumble
buffoon	crutch	dumb	grummet	hunks	mumps	pump	scut	stump	tumbril
bug	cub	dump	grumpy	husk	munch	pumpkin	scuttle	stun	tunnel
bulb	cuckold	dumpling	grunt	hussy	mundane	punch	shrub	stunt	tussle
bulk	cud	dun	gulch	hustle	muscat	punish	shrug	stutter	tut
bum	cuddle	dunce	gulf	hut	mush	punk	shuck	su-	
bumble	cudgel	dung	gullet	hutch	mushroom	punt	shudder	sub-	udder
bump	cuff	dungeon	gullible		muss	punty	shuffle	succise	ugh
bumpkin	culch	dunk	gulp	jumble	musty	pup	shun	succose	ugly
bun	cull	duck	gum	jumbo	mutt	puppet	shunt	succumb	uh
bunch	cully	dust	gush	jungle	mutter	pus	shush	succursal	ulcer
buncombe	culm		gust	junk	mutton	putt	shut	sucker	un-
bung	culpable	emunctory	gustatory	jut	muzzle	putter	skulk	suds	under
bungle	culprit		gut			putty	skull	suffer	
bunion	culvert	flood	gutta	lubber	nothing	puzzle	sloven	sulk	vug
bunk	cumbent	flummery	gutter	luctual	nub		slubber	sullen	vulgar
bunny	cumber	flunk	guttle	lug	nudge	rough	sludge	sully	vulnerable
bunt	cumble	flunkey	gutturize	lull	nugget	rub	slug	sulphur	vulture
bust	cummer-	flush	guzzle	lumber	null	rubber	sluggard	sultry	
but	bund	fluster		lump	numskull	rubbish	slum	sump	wonder
butt	cumquat	flutter	hub	lunch	nut	ruck	slumber	sunder	wuff

Words Containing the Dull Vowel [ʌ]

more "sober," more "profound." On the other hand, when a singer lacks the imagination to enter into the mood of a song, technical suggestions may make the tone more appropriate. A sad song might be sung as if the [e]s were ŏ's [ø] and [i]s were ü's, [y]. In an exultant song, [o] becomes [ɔ], etc.

525   Robson refers to what he calls the *striking power* of speech sounds. In the case of vowels this corresponds with the pitch of the second formant; that is, the higher the overtone the greater the striking power. He analyses many phrases, like, for example, Winston Churchill's "blood, sweat and tears" in which the vowels [ʌ], [ɛ] and [i] are in ascending order of formants, (pp. 113-115).

526   Poets, of course, are sensitive to these values, and expressive words find their way into songs. An artistic interpreter is equally sensitive and "paints" his words in the way he pronounces them.

Resonance Imagery

527   Scientific language is inadequate in teaching an art, and we fill out the deficiency with poetic imagery. As long as we do not confuse fancy with fact, this can be a means of finding truths

ab-
Abaddon
abandon
abash
abaxil
abstract
accent
accident
acerate
acerbate
acetabulum
acetose
achillian
acid
ack-ack
acrid
acrimony
acrobat
act
actual
acupunc-
  ture
ad-
adamant
add
adder
addict
additive
addle
adequate
adhere
advance
advantage
affricate
aggrandize
aggravate
aggress
aghast
agile
agitate
agonist
agony
alack
alacrity
amass
ambition
ambush
ammunition
amorous
ample
an-
anathema
anatomize
andro-
anger
angina
angry
anguish
angular
animad-
  version
animal
animated
animus
ant-

antagonist
ante-
anthro-
anti-
anxiety
aphthong
apoplexy
apparatus
appetite
applicant
apposite
apt
arrow
ash
asp
assassin
asthmatic
athlete
atlas
attraction
attribute
avalanche
avarice
ax
babble
bacchanal
back
back-lash
bad
badger
baffle
bag
bamboozle
ban
bandit
bandog
bang
banish
banner
banter
bash
bastard
bastion
bat
battalion
batter
battle
battle-ax
blab
black
blackcap
blackflag
blank
blasphemy
blast
brabble
brack
brad
brag
bramble
brand
brash
brass
brat

brattice
braxy

cabal
cabaret
cabble
cachinate
cackle
caco-
cad
cadaver
cadger
caffeine
caffre
calamity
calc-
Caliban
callous
caloric
caltrop
calumny
camp
can
cancan
cancel
cancer
candent
canker
cannibal
cannon
cant
cantank-
  erous
captain
captation
cantilever
captious
captor
caravan
caricature
carrion
carry
cast
castigate
castle
casualty
casuistry
cat-
cata-
cataclysm
cat-and-
  dog
catapult
cataract
catas-
  trophe
catcall
catch
categor-
  ical
caterwaul
cath-
cavil
chack
chaff

challenge
champ
champion
chancre
chasm
clack
clamor
clamp
clandes-
  tine
clang
clank
clap
claptrap
claque
clash
clasp
clatter
climax
combat
compact
crab
crack
crackle
craft
crag
cram
cramp
crank
crapulent
crash
crass

dab
dagger
damage
damn
damp
dandy
dank
dash
dastard
dazzle
demand
drab
drag
dragon
drastic
drat
dynamic

ejaculate
emphatic
eradicate
erratic
exact
exaggerate
exasperate
expand

fabricate
faction
factor
fad
fallacy

famine
fanatic
fang
fantastic
fascinate
fast
fat
flabby
flaccid
flack
flag
flamboyant
flang
flap
flash
flat
flatter
flatulent
fractious
fracture
frantic
frazzle

gab
gad
gadder
gadfly
gaff
gag
gallant
gallivant
gallop
gallows
galvanic
gamble
gambol
gang
gas
gash
gasp
ghastly
gladiator
glamor
gnash
grab
grand
grapple
grasp

hack
hackney
hag
haggard
haggle
hallelujah
hammer
hamshackle
handle
hangman
hanker
harangue
harrass
hash
hatchet

inflam-
  mable
intract-
  able
iracible

jab
jabber
jack
jackal
jackass
jacktation
jag
jagged
jaguar
jam
jamboree
jampacked
jangle
jazz

knack
knag
knapsack

lacerate
lachrimose
lack
lackland
lag
lampoon
lance
languid
laniary
lank
lash
latch
lazaretto

Mab
machinate
maculate
madcap
madman
mag
maggot
magic
magistrate
magnate
magnet
magnify
magpie
majesty
mal-
malady
malice
malleate
mallet
mammon
mammoth
manacle
manage
mancipa-
  tion
mandate

manducate
manful
mangle
manhandle
manic
manifest
manifold
mansion
mantis
manufac-
  ture
masculine
mash
mass
massacre
master
masticate
mastodon
mat
matador
match
maximal

nab
nag
national-
  ism
nasty
natty

organic
orgasm
orgiastic

pach-
pack
pad
palisade
pamper
pan-
pander
pang
panic
pant
panther
paragon
paramount
paranoia
parapet
parasite
parody
paroxysm
parry
passion
patho-
patter
practical
pragmatic
prance
prank
prattle

quack

rab

rabble
rabid
rack
racket
radical
raffish
rag
ram
ramify
rampage
rampant
rampart
ramshackle
rancor
randic
rank
rankle
ransom
rant
rap
rapid
rapture
rascal
rash
rasp
rat
rat-
  catcher
ratchet
rat-tat
ratten
rattle
rattletrap
rat-trap
ravage
ravel
ravenous
ravish
razzle-
  dazzle
recalci-
  trant
refractory
rhapsody

sabotage
sac
sack
sacrifice
sadism
sagittary
salacity
salivate
salutary
salvation
salvo
Samson
Samurai
sanction
sanguinary
sap
sarcasm
satanic
satire
satisfy

saturate
Saturn
satyr
savage
scab
scabbard
scaffold
scalp
scalpel
scamp
scamper
scandal
scatter
scavenge
sciatica
scrag
scramble
scrap
scratch
shabby
shack
shackle
shadow
shallow
sham
shamble
shatter
slack
slag
slam
slander
slang
slap
slap-dash
slash
slattern
slaver
smack
smash
snag
snap
snatch
spank
spasm
spat
spatter
spavin
splash
splatter
stab
stagger
stamina
stamp
stampede
stand
straddle
straggler
strategy
swagger

taboo
tachy-
tack
tackle
tactic

tag
tag-rag
tally-ho
talon
tamp
tang
tangle
tantalize
tantara
tantivy
tantrum
tap
tarantism
tarantula
tariff
tatter
tattle
tattoo
tax
thanat-
thank
thrash
track
tractor
tragedy
trajectory
tramp
trans-
transact
trap
trash
travail
travel
travesty

vacillate
vacuity
vagabond
valiant
valid
value
vampire
van
vandal
vanity
vanquish
vantage
vapid
vapulate
varangian
varicose
volcanic

wag
wamble
wax
whack
wrack
wrangle
wrath

yammer
yank
Yankee
yap

Words Containing the Bad Vowel [æ]

which are as yet beyond our understanding, but which may nonetheless have practical usefulness. The only thing to avoid is word magic. To worship the image instead of the Reality is idolatry, and yet in our profession there are many such worshippers. Pupils have a superstitious faith in the language of their teachers and decry other teachers who say the same thing with other figures of speech. They are so devoted to the literal meaning of words which were not intended literally, that they lose the kernel and carry away the shell.

528   From here on in this chapter I wish to mention a few things in the experience of singers for which I have found no complete explanation, and yet which are valid. To provide a background I wish to evaluate a few figurative expressions used generally by authorities on voice, and to establish working definitions. My only objection to the use of such language is that often it is used so loosely and with so little consistency or reference to objective facts, that it becomes meaningless. I have no respect for mumbo jumbo, for incantation used by the teacher to impress the student, or the critic to hide his lack of discernment. In the Thesaurus at the back of this book I have elaborated the process still further. I have tried to recognize differences of usage, and to make a dictionary that would be applicable to all of the literature on this subject.

529   Most of the legitimate imagery used in teaching people how to sing is related to resonance. I have already mentioned how the illusion of "placement" grows out of real sensations of sympathetic vibration. We see still more reason why brilliance should be imagined "in front" when we think that the anterior chamber of the double formant vowels is what gives them their ringing quality. The vowels [o] and [u] seem "farther back," especially when they are produced by bunching the tongue far back near the soft palate. Although some scientists now discredit the categories, phoneticists classify these sounds as "front vowels and back vowels," referring to tongue positions.

The "Pear-shaped" Ah

530   When a comedian undertakes a comic impersonation of a singer, his face assumes an agonized expression and he sings, "mee, mee, mee," a few times, after which he superciliously begins a discussion of "pear-shaped" vowels. This analogy, which seems to have originated with Lilli Lehmann (p. 55), is not as absurd as it sounds. It summarizes the idea that a good vowel will have "forward placement," and at the same time fill the entire throat. The stem of the pear is at the teeth; it is the "focus" of the tone, which we shall see is a means of getting desirable quality. The stem itself is undesirable, and used only in vocalizing. It is nasal and "twangy" in its most extreme form, but the whole fruit grows from it. The small part of the pear is in the mouth; it is the brilliance of the tone, the front resonator in the case of the double formant vowels. But the pear is not limited to this; it swells into something large and mellow, that can be felt throughout the entire pharynx and is limited only by the singer's ability to enlarge this organ.

531   This description fits the vowel [ɑ] most aptly. The [o] has less of the mouth resonance, and is more "like an orange." The [e] is even more "cone-shaped" than a pear, and the [i] is still more "pointed."

The Concept of "Focus"

532   Related to the concept of "placement" is that of "focusing." Teachers talk about "focusing the tone out here," accompanying the instruction with some kind of forward moving gesture. As long as the gesture is vague and makes no pretense at being scientific, it is useful. One author gives a diagram showing a cone shape, the base of which encircles the oro- and naso-pharynx and the apex of which is in front of the mouth and nose, with a legend to the effect that it was the point of "focus." This would be bad were it not for the admonition of the authority, on the same page, that such charts should never be taken seriously. The relationship between the concept of "focus" and

the illusion of "placement" (Par. 431-436) should be clear. As soon as one accepts the idea of "focus" the next logical question is, Where? The classic statement of the answer is by Lilli Lehmann, who shows a staff, curving with a singer's profile, which is drawn with X-ray detail, (p. 81). On the staff is a scale, and running from the larynx are red dotted lines to each note supposedly indicating the exact region of the head through which each tone was to be "projected," or where it was to be "focused." I am sorry to say that this drawing has been copied without giving credit to its author in the works of various successors.

533   The first use of the concept of "focus" is to overcome breathiness. A tone in which the glottis closes inadequately has a "diffused" quality comparable to the light of a projector on a wall before it has been focused. When the singer achieves a good attack and maintains a clear tone, having no rustle in it of escaping breath, the effect is as pleasing in contrast as when the picture on the screen comes into focus. Sonagrams of "spread" tones and "focused" tones bear this out almost literally, (Fig. 62, 64). When the "glottal stroke" is correct, the singer seems to be ringing a bell, and the bell will not be in the throat, but "up" and "forward," "in front of the mouth."

534   Thus, the second use of the concept of "focus" is a resonance concept, one of "forward placement" or brilliance. A tone will seem to "focus" where the most energy is felt. If the throat is tight, the tone will "focus" where the tightness is; if the tension lets go, there will be no sensation in the larynx, and the "focus" will be a matter of resonance. The double formant vowels, [i] and [e] "focus" in front because a great deal of vibration can be sensed in the forward resonance chamber just behind the teeth. These vowels seem to help breathy pupils to overcome their fault; the two phases of the concept seem to merge, functionally.

535   One should guard against trying to use the word "focus" in its scientific connotation. Light and heat are both focused either by lens or by reflector. A glass lens will focus the rays of the sun so that its light will be more intense and paper can be ignited by the heat at the focal point. The reflector of a search light, and the reflector of an electric heater, illustrate how these waves can be focused without a lens. Sound is another series of waves, and as such can be focused. A balloon containing a gas of a different density from the air will act as a lens, so that if you place your ear at the right spot you can hear a watch ticking on the other side. Any reflector that will focus light or heat will focus sound, and the principle can be applied to the construction of buildings. Of course, "good acoustics" demands that the sound should *not* focus at any one place in an auditorium, but in other structures, for example in domes, we have interesting reflection effects in which sounds are loud or soft depending upon where they are focused, rather than upon how distant they are from their source. I digress to this extent merely to orient the word "focus" in the science of physics, and to make it clear the since there is no lens or reflector in the vocal mechanism, we must not think of "focus" as something literal. Some have tried to make the velum fit the role of reflector, saying that it catches the laryngeal vibration and focuses it at the opening of the mouth, or some such place. This could not be true, even if we assume that the velum would make a good reflector, because if the sound were actually focused at any one place it would not be audible elsewhere. On the contrary, the correct shaping of the mouth more nearly approaches the megaphone, which embodies an opposite principle.

536   But if we hold to the figurative use of the word, we are able to grasp something valuable to singers, a sensation, illusory perhaps, that when the tone is well produced it "comes to a point," either in front of the mouth, at the teeth, or even as high as the bridge of the nose. (Let's not mention the sinuses!) This quality of "point" or "focus" is the prime essential of good tone. It overcomes both breathiness and "spreading." It is the direct opposite of the diffused quality of the "dull" vowel, [ʌ]. The "twangy bad" vowel epitomizes it. I often ask students whose voices are either breathy or swallowed to wrinkle up their noses and say, "Angry hangman," making the

tone as "nasty" as possible. When they get it, much to their discomfort, I ask them to relax a little and sing [ɑ], but *"keep the focus."* Sometimes I have them vocalize with [e] before trying [ɑ].

Analogies with Color and Temperature

537   Another comparison that is often implied between acoustics and optics is in the use of the word "color." Helmholtz called timbre, "klang-farbe," which is best translated "tone-color," instead of "clang-tint" as Ellis rendered it. In either case it is a metaphor in which sight and sound are paralleled. The correlation of music and color appeals to the imagination and many have toyed with the idea.

538   Helmholtz himself recognized the fact that both hue and pitch are functions of frequency. He went so far as to record that if F sharp could be raised some twenty octaves or so, it would no longer be a sound but would have the frequency of the color red. The entire rainbow would lie within this octave, violet having double the frequency of red, that is, corresponding to the F sharp above, (p. 18).

539   But comparisons of this sort, while they may be mathematically correct, are of little value to the vocabulary of vocal imagery. On the other hand, both colors and timbres awaken similar psychological responses. We may expect, therefore, that a timbre that is depressing because of its lack of high partials would be called "dark," "dark brown," "gray," or "muddy." Analogies with the art of painting are used, like my mention of *pointillism* (Par. 519). Tones that are pleasing will be compared to pleasing colors; singers who produce them will be said to have "golden voices." High partials in a tone will be called "brilliance," "sparkle," "brightness." Many of these terms imply intensity of color more than hue. This is logical, since high partials tend to disappear in most musical tones when the intensity drops, and so we may expect ringing tones to be compared to colors of high intensity, and dull tones, to low. It is a good singer who can keep "2800" in his voice while singing softly. Those who get high partials at the expense of low ones are guilty of "white" production. The French expression, *"voix blanche,"* carries this connotation.

540   Much of what I have said about the relation between sound and color could be said with reference to temperature. At any rate, we add to our vocabulary such words as "warm" for tones rich in partials, especially low ones, and "cool" for simpler, high tones, such as those of a coloratura. Such figurative language is so far from scientific as actually to reverse the relationship.

The Concept of Covering

541   In 1840, two French physicians, Diday and Pétrequin, wrote an important treatise describing the technic of a member of the Paris Opera, Duprez, which he had learned in Italy, and which the two scientists called *une nouvelle espèce de la voix chantée.* Rivals of Duprez were not happy, and de la Madelaine wrote a sarcastic chapter (pp. 128-144) heaping scorn on the technic, which he insisted was undesirable and at least as old as Porpora if not *aussi ancien que le deluge,* (p. 131). Diday and Pétrequin were probably wrong in thinking Duprez had something new, but their analysis of it is the first scientific account of "covering," and while the concepts of de la Madelaine never got far beyond Dodart, Diday and Pétrequin's paper is still a classic worth reading.

542   According to the two scientists, most singers allow the larynx to rise with the pitch of the voice, but Duprez intentionally kept his at a low level throughout his singing. It was not felt that this enabled him to sing any higher, but that the high tones were esthetically acceptable, so that his professionally usable range was increased. Tones with a high larynx had a sound of strain

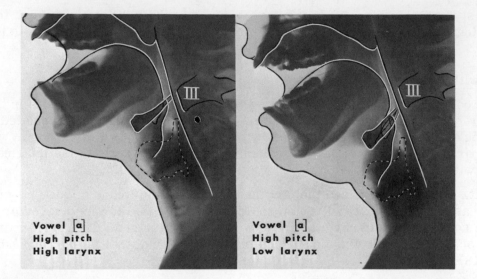

X-rays of the author, from van den Berg[6] and Vennard, *NATS Bulletin*. Fleshy parts have been retouched from visible evidence in the negatives. Elevation of larynx can be gauged with reference to third cervical vertebra, III. Tilting of head upward and backward in high larynx production is called "reaching for high tones." Larynx in right-hand picture is as low as normal larynx position in Fig. 47, but hyoid bone is tilted somewhat in the manner of depressed larynx, same figure. This may be characteristic of covering to some extent.

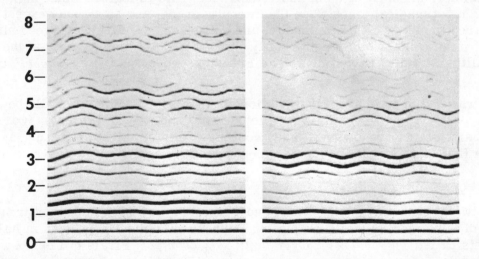

Sonagrams from van den Berg[6] and Vennard, *NATS Bulletin,* corresponding to the adjustments shown above in x-rays. Pitch E_4, above Middle C. Increased space between partials is characteristic of sonagrams of higher pitch, has no reference to timbre. Note "spreading" in high larynx production of high tone, left. Compare with Fig. 62, 63.

Fig. 64. High and Low Larynx Production of High Tones

which made them unusable. Two words were assigned to low larynx technic, *voix sombrée* and *voix couverte*.

543   Garcia, writing at about the same time, states that the voice has two timbres, *clair* and *sombre*, (p. 5). When *timbre clair* is exaggerated, he says, the voice becomes white, shrill, and screeching *(blanche, criarde, glapissante)*. The term, *glapissante* may also be translated "yelping," that is, it is applied to the way animals instinctively produce high pitches. When *timbre sombre* is exaggerated the voice is covered, choked, muffled *(couverte, étouffée, sourde)*. However, he adds that from E_4 on up to B_4 both men and women can carry up the chest voice in *timbre sombre* creating an illusion that they are not covered. Such tones Garcia called *voix mixte*. His pupil, Salvatore Marchesi, used the same vocabulary, making "covering" and "mixing" synonymous. As to the physiology of these timbres, Garcia agrees with Diday and Pétrequin, stating that for "clear" or "open" timbre the larynx is high and the soft palate low, whereas for "dark" or "covered" timbre the larynx is low, and the velum high, and the pharynx vigorously rounded. Fig. 64 shows [ɑ] sung on a high pitch with the larynx first high, then low.

 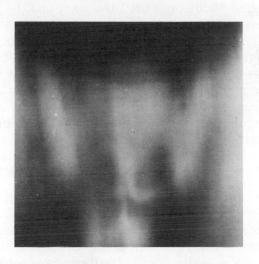

Tenor, Ah, F_4, forte, open   Tenor, Ah, F_4, forte, covered

Fig. 65. Tomograms of Larynx in Production of Open and Covered Vowels
From Landeau and Zuili, *NATS Bulletin*.

544   Fig. 65 shows tomograms of open and covered tones (Landeau and Zuili). Note the difference in the elevation of the larynx and the fact that the ventricles are larger in the low, or covered position, which implies that the thyroarytenoids are more relaxed. Looking back to Fig. 44, (Par. 366), we see that the difference between "closed" and "open" vowels is related to covering. The open [ɛ] shows constriction both in the ventricles and in the space between the wings of the thyroid, and the larynx is higher, in comparison with the "darker" [ɑ]. Pronunciation may thus be an approach to production. It is especially useful to cover the high formant vowels, such as [i] and [e] which tend to be shrill or "white" and which go too easily into the nose. We see that covering is related to "umlauting," for when we "darken," (by mixing in the pronunciation of [o] or [u]) [e] and [i] become ö [ø] and ü [y]. If we only suggest the "dark color," so that we do not produce the true German sound, we have merely "covered" the [e] and [i], and as such they will be easier to sing and will sound better. I know of no more reliable trick for helping a student sing a high tone on the vowels [i] or [e], than to suggest that he simply substitute [y] or [ø]. On

high pitches the substitution is completely acceptable to the ear. In the sense in which I am using the term in this paragraph, the "round" vowels, [o] and [u], and also the composite vowel, [ɑ], should not be covered. The lips need not be rounded any more in ascending the scale, and they can be "open," that is, pronounced the same, all the way to the top. Witherspoon's rule is related to this. He says that the open vowels modify toward closed and closed vowels modify toward open, (p. 78). In other words, all vowels move toward [ɑ], (Par. 514-520, 565-571).

545   Garcia[2] recommended that students sing all the vowels in every shade of timbre. In going from light to dark he gave the following table:

> A approximates to o.
> E approximates to eu in French.
> I approximates to u in French.
> O approximates to u in Italian, (Garcia,[2] p. 12).

546   If one sings clear to the top of the scale with the same coordination of the laryngeal muscles, he is singing "wide open" all the way, and the tone becomes more tense and strident until the moment when it strangles him. Such a singer will probably sing all vowels with the same crude production. However, he may have learned in childhood by unstudied trial and error to drop his larynx more when saying [u], than for any of the other vowels. We know that a low larynx is under less extrinsic tension because it is not subjected to the downward drag of the esophagus, and hence such a pupil as we are considering may produce better tone with [u]. Singing the "round" vowels tends to lower the voice box, and therefore they may sound better and actually rise to higher pitches than the "pointed" vowels. Therefore we have the familiar exercise of starting with [ɑ] at the bottom of a scale and shifting to [ɔ], [o], or even [u] for the top. This is used to teach "covering." We also have the expression "the groove of Oo," which has been used to describe the correct "placement" for high tones.

547   The correct adjustment can be achieved in terms of pronunciation, but I believe that we should also tell the student frankly that he must sing differently at the larynx. No matter how he pronounces the tone, he cannot sing well at the top of his range with the same muscular balance in his voice box that he has at the bottom of his range. Pronunciation can help only as it tends to adjust the vibrator. In fact after a student has been substituting ü [y] for [i] and ö [ø] for [e] for a while, he will become aware of something subtle in his voicebox which can be done on *all* vowels with very little change in pronunciation. The teacher may prefer not to discuss either anatomy or registration, but it is possible to suggest to a singer that he should "lighten" his tone as he ascends the scale. "Sing it like a falsetto, but not quite!" "The higher you go, the more the tone must have this quality (demonstrated)." In doing *messa di voce,* tell the pupil that when he initiates the tone it must "feel like a falsetto, but have just enough 'edge' or 'focus' so that it can crescendo to a full-throated tone without a break." This matter of laryngeal coordination affects gradations in volume as well as in pitch.

548   Some teachers feel that getting lightness of registration is easier with the vowel [u] than with the others, possibly for the same reason as I have mentioned. Clippinger recommends using it in developing what he calls the head voice, (p. 19). I much prefer to begin with [ɑ], and to work as long as is necessary in getting a well rounded production with both "forward placement" and "depth." However, I also use the other vowels to induce these qualities in the [ɑ]. I have the student sing [i, e, ɑ] to "focus" the [ɑ], and I use [o] and [u] to "free" it. It is said that Lamperti used [ɑ] primarily, but considered [u] "the medicine of the voice." A useful vocalise is the descending octave diatonic scale, on "lu, lu, lu," etc., sung as softly as possible, almost falsetto and perhaps breathily. This may be transposed freely. It is then followed with this melody on the

vowel [ɑ]:

The low three-tone scale is sung loudly in chest, or nearly so in the case of women's voices. Then there is a portamento to a pianissimo head tone at the top with a crescendo as the singer returns to heavy registration at the bottom. The student should "place the high head tone where he felt the [u]." Transpose freely. Finally the vocalise can be repeated with a crescendo on the top tone before coming down. This must be done with some caution, and not transposed too high. It is an adaptation of an exercise by Stanley[2] (p. 143), and reminds us of one by Lehmann which she called "breaking the tone," (p. 146). I sometimes use a more radical form, developed by Wilcox (p. 27), who was an interpreter of Stanley. In this exercise the leap is two octaves, going into falsetto and descending a two-octave scale with as little break as possible into chest. High voices, especially tenors, benefit greatly from it, and usually can do the two octaves without a break.

Throaty Production

549   It is my opinion that the expression "covering" is born of an old-fashioned conception, and its use is more likely to confuse beginners than to aid them. In the case of advanced singers who have learned to associate the word with a correct experience, the word is more useful. A much more serious indictment I would bring against "covering" is that it is likely to lead to throaty production. This we have already introduced as "depressed larynx" technic, (Par. 420, Fig. 47). There is a school of production that emphasizes "depth" and "roundness" at the expense of "ping" and "focus." Disciples of this teaching speak of "covering" the entire voice. They work primarily for the low larynx, the large throat, and a big, "chesty" tone. Their objective is operatic power, and they have no tolerance for a "thin" or "nasal" voice. That is, they work for fullness and "color" and hope that brilliance will be a by-product. As long as they sing loudly, the voice will ring, and therefore they stress loud production and reiterate the fact (which is correct) that the voice functions at maximum efficiency at the level of mezzo forte or stronger.

550   The danger is that when they sing softly they will merely "swallow" the tone, or allow it to become breathy. Also, the "dark" pronunciation spoils the diction, so that the words become unrecognizable. There is great tension in the throat, which exponents of this method often insist should be "rigid," and while this muscular tension does give high partials to the tone, I feel that such strain cannot be beneficial. The stiffness of the pharynx and the forcing down of the larynx is usually accompanied by a retraction of the tongue, which bunches in the back of the mouth, giving the characteristic muffled quality to the tone. I have mentioned the stainless steel instrument which Stanley used to push the tongue into this position, while asking the pupil to sing, (Par. 395).

551   If enough force is used, the tone which emerges is ringing to the point of being metallic. The stiffness of the throat and root of the tongue is apparent. If you wish to imitate the sound for the

benefit of some student who should be shown the difference between it and correct production, press the sides of your tongue against your upper molars and at the same time try to distend your pharynx as violently as possible. We might call this "tonsillar tone." The word "hyoid" is equally applicable. Diday and Pétrequin wrote at length about the dangers in the pressure that the technic can generate. The reason blood vessels can be seen standing out in the neck is that they are being pinched at some point where they pass between straining neck muscles.

552   Now after all this abuse, I must admit that many fine singers employ much of this technic. It must be conceded that the voice so produced has great power and fullness. There is a tendency to "scooping," because such a tone always seems to "come from the throat," and hence seems to originate "below" somewhere and frequently has to be tuned up to pitch after the attack. But this is only a bad habit, and perfect intonation is entirely possible with throaty tone. (Ironically, some of the foremost advocates of this kind of singing would call it anything but "throaty." They apply the term "throaty" to the constricted, high-larynx voice which I prefer to call "tight.") And another merit of this "hyoid" vocalizing is that it will reach some high tones that cannot be reached in any other way.

553   To attain these altitudes, the tongue including its tip, goes back and up into the position I have described unfavorably as a way of singing [u]. To keep the throat open, the geniohyoid and kindred muscles usually tighten rigidly. The pharynx is thus made into a deep cavity with a small aperture at the top. Through this resonator a tone is driven with considerable power, and unless the singer is unusually expert, the vowel must be as near [o] or [u] as it can be. A fairly reliable symptom in the diagnosis of throatiness is the inability to differentiate the mouth vowels, [e] and [i]. One gets the impression that the voice is squirted out of a nozzle. By this method, it is possible to sing notes a tone or so higher than will be possible if one insists on "getting them into the mouth" where most of the vowels have their characteristic pronunciation. Vowels which are sung too far "forward" on high notes are said to be "wide open" and they can easily have the unpleasant forced quality of a yell. In other words, the advocate of "covering" surrenders unconditionally to the idea that the higher one sings the less it is possible to distinguish between the vowels.

554   I realize that I am giving an unsympathetic account of this philosophy of voice production. I cannot change my point of view; I can only admit as tolerantly as possible that some singers do arrive at good production at maturity in spite of having come by the road of "covering." I myself think the dangers are too great for the advantages, and I prefer to lead my pupils by another route. Eventually they arrive at some of the same things that are products of the "covering" school, but their approach and their philosophy are different.

"Focusing" rather than "Covering"

555   I align myself with the many pedagogs who believe that "focus" or "ping" is the *sine qua non* of good singing. One should not strive at first for a beautiful, "rich," or even big voice. Rather one should work for complete freedom of the mechanism. The tongue must be loose and relaxed in the floor of the mouth. The first exercises I give are always for "freedom" and we use a yawn approach. When this concept is prepared we begin work on "focus," which I also call "intensity," partly with power in mind, but also admitting the psychological element, (Par. 17, 18.) The brilliance must come from the kind of "twang" we associate with the "bad" vowel [æ], call it "nasality" if you will. It must not come from any conscious muscular tension in the pharynx, or any stiffness of the tongue. This tone is "thin" at first, and perhaps not too pleasing, but it is the "stem of the pear," and luscious fruit will grow from it. Once this "core" is established, all that is necessary is to "give more room" in which the quality can develop. As much depth as possible should be added, but without losing the "ring."

556   I realize that much of what I am saying is hard to justify scientifically, but it comes from the subjective experience of many singers. It is one of the things that must be said in figurative language, but nonetheless it must be declared. The way to build a voice is from the front into the back, and not from the throat into the mouth. A means to this end is that synthetic consonant which I have called the "hum on the tongue," and which is described at the end of Chapter 8. This is an implement for achieving the correct "placement" of the tone, and thereby insuring its healthy development.

557   The student who begins with a tone that is "focused" somewhere in front can add plenty of "opulence" as he continues to build his voice. This refers us back to the yawning exercise. He will soon begin to feel the sensations that accompany the technic of "covering," including the feeling of stretch, (Par. 409) (Lehmann, p. 98, Lawson, p. 34). It will be easy for him to lower the larynx, because of the low position of the tongue. As he adds "yawn" and "depth" to his production he will achieve the desirable open throat, and will feel a certain firmness of the pharyngeal wall, but instead of having to overcome excess muscularity, he will simply be adding it in whatever measure is needed.

558   As he works to improve his range upwards, he will gradually find himself doing the same things that a singer who advocates "covering" will do, but it will be with the feeling that he releases the tone and sings it more like a falsetto. Oddly enough, he will seem to "focus" the high ones even more to keep them from "spreading." His progress in adding high notes to his compass will perhaps not be as rapid, but the tones that he does add will be more generally usable, and the vowel color will be recognizable.

559   Paradoxically, while the throaty tone begins as a sound of great fullness and force, frequently beginning and ending with a grunt, it is limited as to the amount of power it can develop. It seems gorgeous to the singer, but much of its quality is "bottled up" so that the audience never hears it. The more "reedy" voice has the advantage of the oboe; it may be small, but it carries. And as the student begins to "round" the throat "behind" the "point," the "cone" grows in diameter until eventually it has more power than could have been achieved otherwise. Incidentally, while this kind of development may not make high notes too easy, the lower tones will be better. They may not *sound* as low, because of their brilliance, but they will be louder.

560   Probably, both "focus" and "cover" are approaches to the same ultimate ideal. There is merit in both. The feeling of stretch in the pillars of the throat comes from both the nasal approach (because the palatopharyngeus muscles arise from the palate) and from the lowering of the larynx (because they are inserted in the bottom of the pharynx). I feel sure also that in some indirect way the intrinsic musculature of the larynx is facilitated by the process, as suggested in Chapter 5, though complete scientific data is not available. In Fig. 65 we see tomograms by Landeau which show that when the larynx is in a low position (which Landeau calls "covered") the ventricles are larger. It all ties in with the connotations of falsetto, or mixing, and the use of "covering" for register transition. Both men and women benefit from "darkening" the voice in any *passaggio*.

561   Both "focus" and "cover" are needed in equalizing the voice. Consistency of vowel color demands that the low formant vowels be "focused," and that the high format vowels be "covered." How much is a matter of taste. Husson[3] has treated this in an article on "singing with power," presenting X-rays (Par. 423) to show that spoken vowels are comparatively shallow, while singing demands an adjustment we might well call "covered." Delattre has commented upon this evidence, explaining how "vowel color" can be preserved while "voice quality" is altered for artistic purposes.

562   Frequently a sad, or a devout song is improved by "covering," and a gay, or a naive ditty is improved by singing it, "in the mouth" or "on the lips." All the qualities I have listed for the

[i], [e], [ɑ] series (they are "bright," "cool," "forward," "pointed," "high") should be true also of the [u], [o], [ɑ] group, only to a lesser degree. And the opposite qualities ("dark," "warm," "back," "round," "deep") should be cultivated in the separated formant vowels. A teacher who emphasizes "ping" first will teach [ɑ] as if it belonged in the "pointed" series, and he may use [i] and [e] as a means to that end. Proponents of "covering" use [u] and [o].

563   It is only fair to say that while guttural tones may begin and end with a grunt, the "forward" tones sometimes begin with a whine. "Swallowing" is a failing of low voices, in an effort to make them sound lower, but "nasal" production is more tempting to high voices, particularly tenors. Some of them are guilty of whining into all their initial vowels. They cultivate this to make them sound more "tenorish." I urge all basses to imitate tenors, and all tenors to imitate basses. I believe that for any given pitch there is an ideal quality, and that this standard should not be different for different voices. It is unfortunate to talk of "bass quality" and "tenor quality." A tenor and a bass singing the same note, say middle C, comfortable to both voices, should sound alike. It may even be said that a tenor and a contralto singing the same note should sound alike. This is an extreme statement, but it slants in the direction of truth rather than error. There will of course be small differences; no two voices are identical, they are like fingerprints, but the bass should not be attempting to "darken" his voice, nor the tenor to "whiten" his.

564   All voices should be trained alike, if possible. Certainly a high voice must vocalize on higher pitches, and a low voice on lower; but there is *one* ideal of voice production. The teacher who thinks of "bass quality" as different from "tenor quality" is the same who makes the mistake of classifying voices prematurely and working to fill out predetermined ranges instead of working for correct production in the middle of the voice where it is easiest. Compass will take care of itself. I am also unsympathetic to the idea of "finding the natural quality of the individual voice," because this "natural" quality will only be whatever is habitual to the singer, and it is the business of the teacher to inculcate *correct* habits, most of which will be new. "When the student takes his first singing lesson what does the teacher hear?" asks Clippinger. He answers his own question: "He hears the tone the student sings, but what is far more important, he hears in his own mind the tone the student ought to sing. He hears his own tone concept and this is the standard he sets for the student," (p. 44).

Vowel Problems for the High Soprano

565   After all I have said about not allowing high notes to merge into one neutral vowel, I find it necessary to mention an exception. The high soprano finds it difficult to differentiate the vowels for an entirely different reason. If you will glance again at Fig. 55, you will see a bracket at the top of the chart embracing the two octaves from middle C_4 upward. This is approximately the soprano range. The fact that some sing higher only adds force to what we are to discover about the acoustics of these voices. Notice that more than half of the soprano tones are above the [u] formant, and that the most effective part of her voice is also above the [o]. This means that she cannot pronounce these vowels in the same way as lower voices.

566   Try this experiment. Ask a soprano to sing [u], [o], [ɑ], on some fairly high pitch, say G_5 above the staff. As a matter of fact she normally sings all those vowels alike, but you have now challenged her to differentiate them, so what will she do? She will probably "swallow" the [u], and "whiten" the [ɑ]. The [o] will be the best, because it will have her best production, and the others will differ from the standard only by embodying some fault. What you actually will hear is a series of [ɑ]'s, one "dull," one very good, and one "bad." If she is singing words, the audience imagines the vowel differentiation and she can use a good round [ɑ] in all cases. She could probably sing "I loathe you," and unless ears caught the difference between "th" and "v," everyone would take it for "I love you." On high pitches it is simply impossible for her to

sound the overtone which is recognized in other voices as characteristic of the low formant vowels. Her fundamental is already too high. It is only in singing that she has this problem, because in speaking she probably uses a low pitch, perhaps even heavy registration.

567   According to Delattre[2] the first formant is as important as the second in determination of the vowel. Since the high-formant vowels [i, ɪ, e, ɛ] also have low first formants, this means that they too suffer as the fundamental rises, though perhaps not as much as [u, ʊ, o], (Coffin, p. v). This is suggested by shading in Fig. 60. Triplett found that a soprano can emphasize the upper formant of [i] as she attacks high C_6 so that the ear will recognize the vowel. However, the tension this requires is unkind to the voice, and she is likely to relax her throat and prolong the tone as an [ɑ]. Anyone hearing the tone from the beginning retains the illusion of [i]-color all through the tone, but if a tape is played from which the attack has been deleted, the tone is identified as [ɑ].

568   Actually some sopranos can also give the illusion of singing [u] on very high pitches. Most find this very difficult, but some teachers believe that a soprano voice benefits from making the attempt. Galli-Curci is said to have worked years to achieve this. When a soprano makes an [u] above the treble staff that convinces the listener it is an extremely flutelike tone, containing few strong overtones. It is this simplicity in comparison with her [ɑ] on equally high pitches that creates the illusion. Such an [u] must be a pure head tone, or falsetto, and this may be its pedagogical virtue—it can only be achieved by freeing and simplifying the production.

569   The higher a soprano sings, the more her resonators simply reinforce her fundamental and the less they function as vowel formants. Thus the higher she sings, the more instrument-like her tone, (Fig. 71). Since she is largely in falsetto she sounds flute-like and many a composer has recognized this by giving her a flute obbligato. She is also not required to sing words in such passages.

570   For this reason she should not be badgered about pronunciation, but should be encouraged to use [o] instead of [ɑ], if it results in a more liberated tone. I gladly make this concession to the principle of "covering." "Whiteness" is her besetting sin; she is unlikely to get any tones too "deep." This will be true of the vowels [i] and [e]. The upper formant will be safely out of her reach, but it is likely to sound so strongly in these vowels that they will be strident or shallow. It is more necessary for her to round her lips over these sounds, and to relax her jaw, than it is for other singers. The lowest formant she can get will be the fundamental itself, and she should "let it out" to offset the high formant, and round her lips to muffle high partials. Showing teeth is dangerous. She must cultivate as "full" a tone as she can, both in resonance and in registration. It is easy to see why coloratura arias usually abandon all words and simply turn into vocalises. The words are hard to understand at best. The high soprano is the one voice that is justified in choosing the most convenient vowel for her high notes, and using it throughout.

571   We should remember the wide latitude of frequency within each formant, and also the fact that the ear will accept compromise pitches, (Delattre[2] et al., p. 205). Tiffany[3] experimented with lowering the frequencies to see how this affected recognizability. He found that lowering the pitch of a man's vowel soon destroys it, but that women's could be lowered more without loss. This is because the ear accepts higher vowel formants in a woman's voice. Drop all the pitches and it sounds masculine, but the vowels are still there. Peterson and Barney find different formants for the same vowel in men, women, and children, (p. 183). It appears that the vowel is a Gestalt in which the pitches of the formants play a large role (as has been expounded in this chapter), but in which relationships between the formants also contribute to recognizability. Hence the illusion of a certain vowel sound may be possible with unorthodox formant frequencies. What we know scientifically about vowels is derived almost entirely from studies of the speaking voice. There is still much experimentation to be done with reference to vowel formation on the upper tones in the soprano range.

Chapter 7

ARTICULATION

572   Up to this point we have discussed the voice as a musical instrument. We have considered it a machine for the production of vibrations having pleasing and controllable pitch, duration, intensity, and timbre. This last factor has interested us enough to fill two chapters, since only the voice is capable of such subtlety and variety of usable tone colors. The average instrument produces one quality which is ideal, and the others are more or less ignoble tones resulting from the introduction of mutes, or outright poor playing. Piano music, as I sometimes teasingly remind my pianist friends, is monochrome. At the hands of a master it is comparable to a fine etching or lithograph, but to many musicians it is simply the charcoal with which a composition is sketched before the color is added. If, as has been suggested in Par. 41, we enlarge our definition of "color" so that it is not merely a synonym for "timbre," but also includes sonance, then certainly a great pianist produces different colors. This may be the semantic resolution of a long-standing debate between pianists and physicists on this point. What the ear percieves as color is a Gestalt of all the properties of tone. The ear does not report frequencies, intensities, etc., to our consciousness, but we are aware of combined effects which we call "qualities," "vowels," etc.

573   The voice has many limitations, but they are not with reference to timbre. In fact, the vocal range of vowel production, constitutes a differentiation not only in degree, but in kind. The singer is capable of expressing not only music, but also literature and drama. It is at this point that the vocal instrument transcends mechanism and becomes human.

574   The vowel sounds are not sufficient for this in themselves. The voice more than any other instrument utilizes the fifth property of tone: sonance, Language is the succession of different vowels, the fluctuation of timbre, and it is also the combination of these sounds with consonants, the admixture of noise. Other instruments have noises, but they are necessary evils. Even though they do help us subconsciously to differentiate their sources, we train our ears to ignore them. In the voice, however, the noises are intentional. They have symbolical meaning. It is by means of them that we express not merely the emotion or pattern of the moment, but events of the past and aspirations of the future.

575   It is this human aspect of the voice that causes difficulties in the mechanistic approach. I should be the last to argue that voice production can be taught solely by these methods. There are infinite subtleties which defy explanation on the basis of our present scientific knowledge. There is the underlying difficulty of the fact that the vibrator, doubtless the most important element of the voice, functions below the level of consciousness and must be controlled indirectly through the resonators and by means of resonance imagery. This subjectivity differentiates the voice from the instruments and makes vocal pedagogy highly personal. Even here, however, it is possible, I hope, to achieve some agreement as to definitions, and that is why I have devoted several paragraphs (527-540) to figures of speech in common use.

576   To surrender to "naturalism" is anarchy, unless we define what is "natural," and how can we do this, except by analyzing the mechanism objectively? To provide a background for this, may I review the "natural" origins of song? We shall see that vocal music emerges from communi-

cative phonation, which is superimposed upon the more elementary function of respiration; and that articulation, which is essential to communication but not to music, is superimposed upon the function of mastication. Speech is thus a sublimation of vegetative functions, an escape from the "natural," and the art of song is still more removed from "nature." In achieving the ability to sing, man has acquired what is to the comparative anatomist "a degenerate larynx," (Negus, pp. 469-483), that is, one which because of the comparatively short arytenoid cartilages is no longer well adapted to its original use. But there are still many instincts in us that must be denied in order to sing well.

Racial Origins of Speech

577   Paget has given us a fascinating theory of the origin of speech, which he has documented impressively. It is that language is a refinement of gesture. Gestures are common among primitive peoples, and among civilized people to whom speech is denied. Deaf mutes can make themselves understood by other mutes the world over by a kind of sign language akin to that used by the Indians of this continent. There is also much in common between these symbols and those devised by monks who have taken a vow of silence. True, local codes evolve which cannot be understood by outsiders, but wherever men are without speech there seems to be a universal language of bodily movements to which they have recourse.

578   At first there will be gestures which have obvious concrete meaning, and from these there will develop abstract and more symbolical meanings. Paget makes the observation that a primitive person concentrating intensely upon the mastery of a muscular act for a specific purpose will also duplicate the act with other muscles. For example, a child learning to write will "write with his tongue" at the same time, or, learning to tie his shoe strings, will all but knot his tongue in a parallel process. If at the same time he happens to make a sound, either with vocalized or unvocalized breath, he will be speaking a word.

579   In order to command attention to his gesture, the primitive man would undoubtedly phonate loudly. Suppose he is making a gesture for "high" by raising his arm and unconsciously raises his tongue at the same time. He will say "AL." A person inside a tent or cave, not seeing him could still recognize the gesture. It does not require much imagination to see how the word "AL" might eventually become a substitute for the arm movement, because it would be possible when the arms were occupied (as in hunting or fighting), and it could be recognized by ear instead of by sight (as in the dark, or behind an object).

580   As a matter of fact, "AL" does mean "high" in many languages. I quote Paget;

> In the Aryan languages, AL meaning up is found in the Latin word ALTUS, meaning high, from which we get our word ALtitude. In the Latin ALA, wing, the tongue-gesture is first upward (AL) and then downward (LA), and therefore means literally up-down or, as we might say, something that flaps. In Semitic, AL, ALE, mean to ascend. In Melanesian and Polynesian AL means to climb up, to rise; it also has the same meaning in some of the languages of North America, e.g. the Kwakiutl word ALLELA (where LL represents an unvoiced L, somewhat as in Welsh) meaning up. On the other hand, in ancient Sumerian AL meant to protect, which suggests that the tongue-gesture here corresponds to the arm-and-hand-up-gesture, signifying protection. . . . .
>
> All over the world this root AL, or its gestural variants ATL, AT, or AN—all made by raising the tongue tip to touch the palate—are associated with that which is up. The names of many of the great mountain ranges have it, as for instance, the ALps, ATLas, ANdes, UrAL, ALaDagh (Asia Minor). HimALaya, ALdan (East Siberia), TALa (Abyssinia), ALaska, ALLeghenny, NepAL, ChitrAL, ALtyn Tagh (Tibet), ALa (Bokhara), etc. ARARat, like TARARua in New Zealand are probably both members of the same family. . . . .
>
> The root AL, or its vowel variants EL and IL, which differ from AL only in starting from higher initial tongue-postures, are found in many words for God or Heaven. The German word

HIMMEL (heaven) is probably derived ultimately from the same original gestures as Himalaya, both words primarily meaning something enclosed (or surrounded)-up, (Paget, pp. 32-34).

581   In the various writings of Paget there are many other equally interesting illustrations of his theory. The importance of it is the emphasis it places upon articulation. It is not making of sounds that is basic, but the *movement* of the speech organs. That is to say, not the musical elements, but the non-musical. (Delattre emphasizes that shifts in vowel formants indicate movements more than they identify cavities, p. 865.)

582   There are, of course, other hypotheses that place more importance upon the tone. For example, the idea that vocal communication grew out of cries that expressed emotions will account for vowels, (Par. 521-526), but will it take us to the level of expressing concrete ideas? How much of a language has one without consonants? Also, there is the possibility that onomatopoeic imitations were the first words. These concepts must doubtless be accepted along with Paget's gesture theory, but there is nothing about any of them that pictures primitive man as a "naturally" singing creature. True, children instinctively intone some words, especially if they are going to repeat them many times. "Johnny has a sweetheart," is likely to be chanted on a minor third, with perhaps the article, "a," a step higher. We may imagine primitive man making music, especially rhythm, but when we think of song, in the sense of words combined with music, we think of something that demands artistic refinements. We conceive a man who can make beautiful sounds by phonation, trying to preserve their beauty and sonority while making movements and noises that will have meaning.

583   Whatever our theory of speech origins, it is likely that articulation is primary, and that phonation, while it coexists, serves the secondary function of providing audibility. Many of our languages, even today, are "whispered languages," that is, they do not depend upon phonation. The addition of vocalization is only to force attention, or to project the symbols across a distance. Even the different vowel colors might almost be dispensed with, but to the extent that they are necessary, they too are more articulation than phonation; that is, they are a function of the resonators rather than the vibrators.

Individual Origins of Speech

584   The infant begins to phonate loudly at birth, but we can hardly call this language. Communication implies consciousness of other personalities, which the new born babe has not. Indeed, we can scarcely credit him with self-expression, because self-consciousness develops only by differentiation between itself and others. Holmes comes much nearer the truth by telling us that the baby instinctively closes the laryngeal valve in order to fixate the chest for muscular activity. He does this in common with the entire animal world. True, he is exercising his whole body.

As soon as the baby begins to struggle, even though the struggle may be limited to waving the arms about and kicking up the feet, he produces vocal sounds. At first, this production of sound is merely a by-product of the struggle. The laryngeal valve closes because the baby is struggling and sound is produced when some of the air imprisoned in the lungs escapes through the closed valve. However, if the valve is closed tightly enough, only unusual pressure on the imprisoned air can force it open. Since the first vocal sound made by a baby is the product of struggle, and since we must use for voice production the same muscular mechanism developed for use during physical struggle, *failing to inhibit struggle behavior when using the valve in the larynx for voice production is the most serious obstacle in the way of efficient phonation.* To overcome this difficulty a person must become critical of his phonatory habits, (Holmes, pp. 13, 14).

585   Voice teachers who use "natural" methods frequently point to the infant as an illustration of correct breathing and urge their pupils to get back to the unspoiled production of the innocents. There is a reason why babes are belly-breathers: their ribs are almost half cartilage, which makes costal breathing impossible. So they inhale by expanding the abdomen and as they exhale their ribs expand from the abdominal pressure. This kind of "see-saw breathing" is normal in infants but pathological in adults. The baby, of course, is lying on his back, which also induces belly-breathing. Some incorrect breathing habits may be the product of inhibitory concepts of good posture, but habits of tight, high-larynx phonation are in a direct line with instinctive voice production, a line that goes clear back to the animals. "Nature"-loving teachers often point to the vocal endurance of the young, not realizing that children, too, become hoarse and actually develop nodules. Has anyone who admires infant phonation made recordings of it? Do his friends enjoy listening to these records as much as they do to cultivated singing? I remember one book on "natural" singing that passed through my hands in which the author directed admiring attention to the voice production of a cow!

Noise versus Tone

586   I mention all this not merely to air one of my favorite "debunkers" (singing is not natural, it is art), but to establish the important point that singing involves two distinct polarities, the use of the vocal mechanism as a musical instrument and its use as a means of verbal communication. The one implies establishing optimum conditions for the production of musical tone, essentially regular and maintained constantly. The other implies the making of a rapid series of symbolical sounds, essentially noisy and in continual flux. Such is the singer's dilemma; he is trying to do two contradictory things at once.

587   Whether or not we call the consonants noise is a matter of definition. Paget[2] argues that they are tone, saying "The conclusion was inevitable that these 'plosive' consonants were not mere noises—they were the effects of the sudden appearance of musical resonances;" (p. 100); but later he admits, "We are, in fact, driven once more to the conclusion. . . that, in recognizing speech sounds, the human ear is not listening to music but to indications, due to resonance, of the position and gestures of the organs of articulation," (p. 125). Here we are dealing with definitions by a phoneticist, not a musician. The sounds of which he speaks may not be noises, but neither are they music. Reading Paget might lead us to think there are no noises in language, but if we turn to another celebrated phoneticist, Scripture, we get the impression that there are no vowels either. In analyzing the wave-forms of speech, he shows that the difference between the vowel in the second syllable of "regard" is only different in degree from the diphthong in the second syllable of "without." He comments:

> A "glide" is, moreover, merely a makeshift to help us out of the difficulties introduced by the erroneous view that speech is made up of a series of independent elements. Not only must we say that every individual sound changes from beginning to end, but we must assert that each one develops out of the preceding sound and into the following one. . . . A comparison of the two cases shows us how little difference there may be in actual speech between what we have been taught to consider a diphthong—or triphthong—and what we believe to be a steady long vowel. A diphthong, in fact, is in many cases simply a long vowel in which the change is considerable, (Scripture, pp. 43, 44).

The Dilemma of the Vocalist

588   In considering articulation we are dealing with sonance, and sonance, as was mentioned at the beginning, is a borderline concept, which to the purist is not a property of musical tone at all. It is a property of the properties! The serious singer often sits down between two stools. He finds himself midway between the comfortably situated entertainer who scorns "classical music," and the ivory-towered instrumentalist who scorns "program music."

589   There are many personalities in show business who are classified as singers, who violate
most of the canons both of good singing and of good music. They violate these canons not only
with impunity, but with great professional success. Any good actor can invade this field profitably, providing he remembers that his gifts are dramatic. As long as he does not try to compete
with proficient vocalists, but concentrates upon that in which he is well qualified—diction and
dramatic projection—he will be well received. This is not entirely because of the weakness of
the American public for personality worship, but because singing overlaps the field of entertainment and to this extent belongs more to the showman than to the musician. Henderson does not
hesitate to say,

> Remind yourself, on the occasions when I will have to stick my finger in your artistic eye,
> that I am writing about singing for money. If the money opportunities for singers were in the
> classical field, I'd be writing about classical songs. But they aren't. The quickest and biggest
> money today—for the trained singer as well as the beginner—is in the effective singing of pop-
> ular songs.
> As a professional singer, you are in the business of furnishing entertainment. Baldly, to get
> money from your customers, the listening public, you must give them what they want. I'll give
> you as artistic a training as the public taste will permit, but when the artistic and the com-
> mercial considerations come in conflict, the commercial will get the call, (Henderson and
> Palmer, p. 5).

I do not mean to imply that all popular singers are poor from the standpoint of healthy voice
production. I am merely describing one aspect of the profession in which any singer finds
himself. To the extent that one feels that his success depends upon the literary or communicative aspects of song, he will be emphasizing articulation—the non-musical element.

590   At the opposite extreme we find a few musicologists who feel that vocalists are not musicians.
These are often the same people who take satisfaction in the fact that most descriptive music is
by second rate composers like Berlioz, and who try to explain that while Beethoven provided a
program for his Pastoral Symphony, he really didn't mean it. They do not understand the attitude of a singer, whose music is essentially programmatic, and to whom there is nothing
repugnant in the idea of wedding words with music. They have no tolerance for romanticism,
and consequently none for songs.

Voices and Instruments in Music History

591   Let us make a few generalizations, historically. In the days of madrigals, voice and instrument were on a par. Compositions were for "Voices or Viols," and when a group gathered for
the social enjoyment of singing rounds and madrigals, those who could not sing, played. Words
were not of too great moment, and they were lost in the counterpoint. As time went on, instruments became more and more capable of virtuoso performance, and voices attempted to keep
pace with them, until in the eighteenth century the words of an aria were only an excuse for
technical display. In the so-called Golden Age of singing the art was in some ways going to
seed.

592   In the nineteenth century vocal composers recognized at last that there were things suitable
to instruments that were unsuitable for the voice, and conversely the distinctive merit of the
voice came to the front. No longer were the same few words repeated senselessly, with occasional syllables prolonged in fioratura until their meaning had been forgotten. At the moment
that the poem became equally important with the music, the Lied was born. Its first great exponent, Schubert, was a man unschooled in counterpoint and with small ability for thematic
development. He was not too successful in the larger forms which depend upon abstract and
intellectual musical concepts for their achievement, but he had the gift for clothing a lyric with

appropriate melody. In this same century, not only *Lieder* but opera flowered. It was the period of dramatic sincerity on the musical stage.

Contemporary Vocal Music

593   Our day has forsaken romanticism, and vocal composition suffers therefrom. In the philosophy of great composers for the voice, music was not an end in itself, but a partner, even a handmaid, of poetry and drama. The spirit carried over into compositions that were purely instrumental. No such spirit seems to motivate the contemporary composer. Today the instrument is king again. Composers feel that nothing can be added to what was done vocally in the nineteenth century and that the future of composition is in absolute music for instruments. They are not even satisfied with the existing instruments but play them in eccentric fashion (like pounding on the piano lid) and strive for synthetic sounds, electronically derived. They regard singers, and the public that wants to hear singers, as a nuisance. One of our greatest contemporary composers, Schoenberg, was asked "if he thought that singers would ever find his music easy to sing." He replied:

> "Why not? They learned to sing Wagner and eventually they learned to sing Strauss. But I have a pet theory that someday in the future the human voice will be supplanted. I think that science will find a way to reproduce exactly the timbre of the human voice by mechanical methods. Then we can have actors on the stage for our operas and not have to worry because the singer with a beautiful voice is a poor musician or vice versa," (Goldberg).

594   Scientists keep working on the project Schoenberg envisioned. Several years ago the RCA Victor Electronic Synthesizer produced a "voice" that sang "Sweet and Low." More recently (1963) Bell Telephone had better success programming a computer to sing "Bicycle Built for Two." The words are recognizable and the "voice" sounds like a mechanical baritone with an absolutely straight tone. Eventual success, if it is deemed worth the effort, will undoubtedly come from analyzing human performance in still more subtle detail, both as to assets and as to liabilities. It seems simpler just to hire a live singer, frail as he is! Automation is less a threat to the arts than to any other profession.

595   Voice is *the* romantic instrument because it is human and expresses personal emotion more directly than any other music. It will be despised to the extent that romanticism is despised. Composers to whom music is primarily a mathematical demonstration ("better on paper than when it is performed") and conductors who resemble nervous metronomes will always be inimical to singers.

596   When a modern composition does include the voice, it is in competition with instruments more than it is supported by them, and it is at a considerable disadvantage in the matter of intonation. The difficulty of singing modern music is not always the vocal line—this may be well written and quite grateful vocally; it is the dissonance that makes it almost impossible. Dissonance seems to be a preoccupation of the present, and this is particularly hard for the voice, because singing in tune depends entirely upon the ear. There is no valve to press down, no key to strike, not even the meagre mechanical reference available to the violinist. Nevertheless, as often as good modern music is written for the voice, singers will master the difficulty of performing it. They may follow reluctantly, but they will gradually accustom their ears to the dissonance. There are composers, like Britten, Barber, Hindemith, Stravinsky, to name a few, who collaborate with vocalists enough to understand their problems and who write brilliant modern vocal music.

597   I hold no brief for the lazy singer who thinks that because he was born with a voice he is not expected to master musicianship. This is not the place to discuss this matter. Our concern

here is the fundamental differences between the voice and other musical instruments. Incidentally, I might mention one tendency of contemporary music that is truly vocal. This is the escape from the tyranny of the bar line. The moderns are interested in rhythmic experiments, and while some of them are unvocal, the general trend away from the monotony of meter toward the rhythm of speech is highly congenial to the voice. A song is not a dance, and one of the problems of the vocal artist is preserving the distinction.

The Acoustical Dilemma

598   A solution for the dilemma of the singer will also be a compromise for the opposing views of Wheatstone-Helmholtz and Willis-Hermann-Scripture. If Helmholtz made any mistake, it was in assuming that the voice functions entirely like a musical instrument. He applied to vowels the same principles which explain the tone color of instruments. Those who dispute this assumption are primarily phoneticists. Scripture, for example, based his studies largely upon the spoken word. He analyzed graphs of the recitations of Joseph Jefferson, and found few vowels of the kind that a singer produces. Instead of diphthongs he found triphthongs, continually merging into consonants, no sound prolonged for enough time to establish musicality. Small wonder he found more inharmonic partials than harmonics. Still today in a beautiful publication for high school students by Denes and Pinson of the Bell Telephone Laboratories, we find the role of the larynx minimized in favor of the role of the articulators.

599   Possibly the confusion could be resolved by saying that in singing, where we want the voice to be a musical instrument, we shape the resonators to be in tune with the fundamental, and so our vowel formants are harmonic, whereas in speech, this need not be the case. As a matter of fact Paget analyzed the vowel [o] as sung throughout a chromatic scale and found that " of the fourteen upper resonances heard, ten were actual harmonics of the larynx, i.e., their frequency of vibration was a numerical multiple of that of the larynx note. In two of the remaining cases, the relation, though not harmonic, was musically a simple one, namely an interval of two octaves and a fourth; in the last remaining cases there was apparently no simple relation between the larynx note and the upper resonance heard," (pp. 48-52). He went on to pioneer some of the ideas to which I have referred in paragraphs 565-571. Of course, to make the voice musical, we must also free the valve to provide more and better partials in the glottal tone. Scripture did not recognize this possibility, and phoneticians generally do not concern themselves with it, though of course speech therapists do.

Poetry and Music

600   There are many languages. Those of words are primarily for communication of literal, concrete ideas. Our most spiritual concepts depend for their expression upon words of physical derivation. The very word "spiritual" actually signifies nothing more than "breath." Our efforts to escape from the concrete to the abstract, from the real to the ideal, lead us into poetry and into the other arts. All these are languages for nobler thoughts. Music is the most abstract. In song, music is added to words, to give them spiritual quality. The combining of two arts need not adulterate them, but causes something greater than either to emerge.

601   The pure, sustained vowel is the musical element of the voice. In our discussion of articulation we shall find that to the extent that our objective is communication at the level of literalism, as in sheer entertainment, consonants will be more important. Enunciation will stay close to that of speech, even colloquialism or dialect. This will be true of popular songs intended for an unmusical audience, for "diction songs," and for comedy. The *buffo* singer, even in grand opera, frequently produces poor tone deliberately, but he never sacrifices a word for the sake of beauty. At the entertainment level vowels serve only the unworthy purpose of display. Virtuosity regarded

as an end in itself depends upon tone production, frequently upon such high notes or in such florid work that good pronunciation suffers.

602   However, as soon as the objective is a higher level of expression, the singer is faced with the problem of preserving the clean vowel. Even the primitive man used phonation for this purpose. It made his gesture audible, *and* it added emotional color to it. To the extent that the singer seeks to lift his audience to abstract, spiritual realms, he must produce more and better tone, and less noise. He must come under the same discipline as the instrumentalist. So as we analyze articulation, it will be in the language of the phoneticist, but with a different objective. Our aim will be to find a diction that is as clear as speech, that gives the illusion of being the same, but is really quite otherwise. To sound "natural" will require studied artifice.

Classification of Speech Sounds

603   The various sounds used in the formation of words are classified from varying points of view. If we classify according to sound, that is acoustically, we find useful such categories as these: *vowels* [a, i, u] etc., *diphthongs* [ɔɪ, aʊ] etc., *semi-vowels* [l, r, m] etc., *consonants* [b, g, k] etc. Each of these groups may be further analyzed. Chapter 5 classified the vowels at length, both acoustically and mechanistically. The consonants fall into two types, *voiced* and *voiceless* or *sonant* and *surd*, to use more technical terms. *Voiced* and *voiceless* are not entirely accurate expressions, because the differentiation does not depend entirely upon phonation. All the consonants can be distinguished in whispering. Whisper the words, "buy pie, tie and dye, fine vine, thy thigh, which witch," and similar combinations, and you will see what I mean. For the sonants the air in the resonators is vibrated continuously (giving what is called *resonance tone*) while for the surds this tone is interrupted and we hear only the noise made by the resistance offered at the lips, teeth, or wherever. To vibrate the air in the resonators we usually phonate, but the mere eddying of breath through a partially closed glottis will also accomplish this. Paget tells us that this rustling of breath is produced partly with the aid of the false vocal cords, that most of the vowels are whispered with the ventricular bands relaxed, but that for the sonants, and for loud whispering in general, they cooperate with the vocal bands, (p. 98).

604   In a highly original attempt to quantify the expressiveness of English, Robson assigns units of *striking power* to the various speech sounds. He assigns low power to the consonants, more to the semi-vowels, and arranges the vowels and diphthongs in order based on their duration in average speech combined with the pitch of their overtones. His estimates of durations are confirmed in a Sonagraphic study at the end of this chapter, Fig. 66. The consonants [b, d, f, h, s, ʃ, t, ð, v, m, z] average .058 seconds per phoneme in speech and .108 sec. p. ph. in song. The semi-vowels [l, m, n, r] average .145 sec. p. ph. in speech and .354 sec. p. ph. in song. The vowels (including the vanishing sounds in the diphthongs) average .280 sec. p. ph. in speech and .797 sec. p. ph. in song. Clearly song has greater striking power than speech, and the difference is largely in the sustaining of vowels.

605   Another classification, at least partially acoustical, recognizes *fundamental tones*, *resonance tones*, *high frequency tones* and *pressure patterns*, (West, et al., pp. 147-151). I disapprove this terminology somewhat because it implies that the vocal cords produce a fundamental but no overtones. The fundamental tone is produced in the glottis itself, determing the pitch of the vowel, diphthong, semi-vowel, or sonant. The resonance tone is produced by the pharynx and mouth (and possibly the nose) and gives a characteristic vowel quality to the sound. This category includes the semi-vowels and also certain sounds produced with the voiceless breath stream: the initial sounds in "whet," "hue," "hot." "In reality, every time a vowel sound is preceded by an [h] sound, that [h] sound is nothing more than the resonance of the succeeding vowel sound produced with the voiceless breath stream," (Holmes, pp. 212-213).

The high frequency tone is produced by friction somewhere in the vocal tract, as in making the consonant [s] or [f]. The pressure pattern is produced by blocking the breath stream momentarily and then releasing it, as in making [p] or [t]. Obviously many sounds combine all of these qualities. While the words of this classification are acoustical, their definitions are mechanistic. Other words of which this is true are: *affricate, aspirate, click, fricative, liquid, nasal, plosive, roll, semi-roll, sibilant, whisper* etc. This brings us to the mechanistic approach.

606   Since we are singers, we are not satisfied with listening, we want to know how to make these sounds. Mechanically, we may classify either according to the parts of the anatomy which are involved, *placement* or *position* categories; or according to the articulatory *movements* (the Paget emphasis), *kinesiologic* categories. The latter vocabulary includes the terms: *continuant, stop* and *glide*. The word *continuant* refers to the passage of the breath through the instrument. either with vibration or without it (voiced or unvoiced) and either with friction or without it (fricative or non-fricative). The implication is that the resonators remain in a relatively fixed position. The continuants include the *nasals*. When a continuant is interrupted, a *stop* is produced. This is the same as a pressure pattern, defined above. Sometimes there is a distinction between a *stop* and a *plosive*. A *stop* is at the end of a word and a *plosive* is at the beginning. In the middle it would be a *stop-plosive*. If the resonators shift position while a continuant is being produced, we have a *glide* which may be a diphthong, or may be the change of timbre heard in moving between a vowel and a semi-vowel, as in the word "are," or between two semi-vowels, as in "earl." This is one of the most difficult problems for singers, and illustrates the fact the kinesiological approach is an unmusical one. We cannot ignore it, but we shall prefer the placement or position approach.

607   Judson and Weaver sum up the situation quite well:

> It is seldom, in the study of phonetics, that any one approach is used exclusively or that the terminology is limited to a single set of terms. It is evident that each approach has its own contribution to make to the study, and the viewpoint of each is necessary to a well-rounded picture. If the terminology seems confusing at times, an understanding of the approaches represented may help to clarify the difficulty. For example, the sound (s) may correctly be referred to as voiceless, lingua-dental, continuant fricative. Of these terms, *voiceless* and *fricative* describe its acoustic qualities, *lingua-dental* refers to the position of the mechanism during its production, and *continuant* to the type of movement involved. In a similar fashion, (b) is described as a bilabial, stop plosive, (p. 175).

The Aspirate

608   There is one consonant that is made in the larynx. It is the *glottal fricative*, [h]. We have already studied it, beginning with paragraph 171. It is graphed in Fig. 21. There can be as many different pronunciations of [h] as there are vowels, because the friction produced in the larynx excites the resonance of the cavities, and their frequencies are sounded faintly. In other words, when a word begins with [h], it means that the vowel is whispered for a moment before it is phonated. Try whispering the words, "at hat," and you will find that the only way to differentiate them is to make a glottal stroke for the initial vowel, or to make more rustling for the [h]. In other words, the initial [h] in speech or song is merely the breathy alternative from beginning a vowel with the *coup de glotte*.

609   Most phoneticists will say that [h] is voiceless and has no voiced analogue. Scripture, however, made recordings which showed that in some cases where the letter was not an initial, phonation continued right through it. He found that his recordings of "aha" varied, those which were more emphatic having an interruption of the vocal tone, and others merely having an in-

crease in breath expenditure. He mentions the fact that certain languages were supposed to include a voiced [h] as a distinct consonant.

610   Judson and Weaver mention what they call an "incidental h" (p. 184), which occurs in the moment after a voiceless consonant before the vowel sound begins. For example, the word "tea" is really [t^hi] and "pay" is really [p^hei]. After the [t] and after the [p], before the vowel is phonated, the passage of breath as the glottis is closing makes an [h]. This has been discussed in Par. 194 and graphed in Fig. 23. Usually the incidental [h] is not notated phonetically unless it has been exaggerated by the speaker. Siebs, the recognized authority on German stage pronunciation, advocates the use of an incidental [h] after [p, t, k]. It is well to imagine an "incidental h" at the end of words with final vowels, to keep them from ending in a grunt. Witherspoon speaks of *nota mentale*, a brief maintaining of the breath support after phonation has ceased, (p. 64).

The Glottal Plosive

611   Another consonant is also made in the larynx, but there is no symbol for it in English, even though we often hear it. The International Phonetic Symbol is [ʔ]. It is produced by closing the glottis firmly and then blasting the vowel through it, making a shock which is sometimes miscalled the "stroke of the glottis." This is the kind of attack I described in paragraph 178. It is graphed in Fig. 20. For vocalizing I much prefer an aspirate attack, to keep the glottis free. However, if we must sing a word that begins with a vowel, we may not give it an initial [h], or we will be singing in British dialect—"Hi say, old chap!"

612   Many singers provide a consonant synthetically by using the *glottal plosive*. They do not sing, "Hi [haɪ] love you," but they sing, "[ʔaɪ] love you." Popular singers do this almost invariably because they think it makes for greater intelligibility, and I am sorry to say that "classical" singers have lately been yielding to this influence. It is considered correct in the pronunciation of German. *Aber* for example, becomes [ʔabɛr]. The sound is also used for the "aspirate H" in French, as in *héros* [ʔero]. To Europeans these effects are perfectly smooth, it is "natural" for them not to hear the stroke. To others there is a distinct interruption of the *legato*. For stage and concert diction, even native Europeans minimize the glottal plosive. It is an unlovely, vocally dangerous sound.

> "In the hard vocal attack the vocal folds approximate tightly prior to sound production so that the glottis must be blown open by the somewhat elevated pressure. Then a slight cracking noise is produced, which is referred to as *Glottisschlag (coup de glotte, spiritus lenis)* and passes over to the vocal sound. . . . The hard attack is often employed in speech. One uses it to express aversion and impatience, in outcries like "A" or "Ach." It should generally be avoided by singers," (Lullies, p. 259).

Note that we have a German authority for the instruction that while the glottal plosive is correct in speech, it is incorrect in song. Note also the term *hard attack*, which is coming into use for *glottal plosive*, or *glottal stroke*. "The amount of air consumption prior to voice production in various vocal attacks decreases in the order of breathy, pressed, soft, and hard attack," (Hülse). In this terminology, *soft* may perhaps be equated with *imaginary h* the term proposed in this book.

613   Of course, when there is a preceding word having a final consonant, that consonant can be used for the transition, by a process similar to *liaison* in French. An "incidental h" before the vowel will separate the words. However, when the preceding word ends with the same vowel as begins the word, as in the words, "the evil," what is one to do? Here a glide solves the problem, and instead of "theʔevil," [ðiʔivɪl] we can sing "theeyeevil," [ðijivɪl]. The y-sound, of course, must be deemphasized. One exception should be mentioned. In the second of "Three Divine

Hymns" by Purcell we have the line, "We sing to Him whose wisdom formed the ear." If the y-sound is used the word "ear" becomes "year," and since it makes good sense it completely misleads the listener. Here the glottal plosive is mandatory, and "the ear" must be sung [ði ʔir]. The final answer to these difficulties is to be found in the mastery of the correct glottal stroke, as Garcia meant it, in which there is no plosive quality, but in which the application of breath pressure is perfectly synchronized with the closing of the vocal cords, and the vowel is initiated cleanly, but not explosively. This is best acquired by using an aspirate which relaxes the valve, and then minimizing it in practice until in performance it becomes imaginary. The singer who has learned this need not sing either, "Harm, harm, ye brave," or "ʔarm, ʔarm, ye brave." The glottal "scrape" or rattle (Par. 195) is another good approach to this problem.

614   The glottal plosive is at its worst when it is substituted for the consonant [t], as is characteristic of the dialects of big cities, Çockney, Brooklynese, etc. They do not say "bottle," they say [bʌʔl]. An amusing song was heard over the air some years ago, about [lɪʔlɪʔli] (Little Italy). This is extreme gutturization, the exact opposite of "singing forward, on the lips."

Labials

615   Those consonants which are made with the lips are called *labials*. If they involve both lips, they are *bilabials*, and if they are made with the lower lip and the upper teeth, *labio-dentals*. The bilabials are the stop-plosives, [p] and [b], and the labio-dentals are the fricatives, [f] and [v]. In each case we have a pair, voiceless and voiced. In German the [b], especially when it is a final, is not voiced as much as in English, that is, it approaches the sound of [p]. According to Siebs the vowel makes a decrescendo but does not stop before [b, d, g] whereas [p, t, k] are preceded by an instant of silence, (p. 78). In addition to the labials I have mentioned we have the nasal labial, [m], and the labial glide [w] to be considered later.

616   The only problem [p, b, f, and v] offer the singer is that of audibility. If they are voiced, there is little difficulty, but [p] and [f] are surds. To them must be applied the most important rule of diction, true for all consonants, but especially for those that are largely noise. It is that they must be exaggerated. They do not carry as well as resonance tones. The fricatives are high frequency tones, and high frequencies require greater energy to produce sufficient amplitude. To move a thing back and forth slowly does not require as much work as to vibrate it rapidly. A given amount of energy, therefore, will cause a low pitch to be heard at a much greater distance than a high pitch. The low formant vowels carry farther than the double formant vowels, and voices heard at a distance seem to have only dark vowels. The consonants disappear first, and then the high formant vowels. If you want your words to be understood at the back of a hall, give great energy to the high frequency sounds, that is, the consonants.

617   The pressure patterns are the most difficult of all, because they involve no tone, not even rustling. They are worst at the end of words. As plosives they initiate a vowel, which gives them carrying quality, but as stops they have almost nothing. There is a tendency among singers to make a stop into a plosive, that is, to add an extra syllable. They sing "hopuh" [hopə] for "hope." I must admit that I do not entirely condemn this practice if it is restricted to the ends of phrases, and if the extra syllable produced is not too loud, is neutral in color, and is very brief. Indeed, I think this is almost necessary for the completion of a phrase, especially with the final [p], and perhaps the [b]. A final [f] can be made as noisy as necessary simply by giving it plenty of breath and offering just enough resistance to make loud friction, but efforts to make a final [p] noisy without phonation are only ludicrous. A final [v] can be made audible with phonation, and this phonation should stop just before the lip leaves the teeth, otherwise the extra syllable will have been made unnecessarily.

618   If a stop consonant comes in the middle of a phrase, it can always be considered a stop-
plosive. If it is followed by an initial vowel, the principle of *liaison* as in French solves the
problem beautifully. The final consonant becomes an initial consonant for the next word, and
both the legato of the phrase and the audibility of the diction are improved. This happens in
speech constantly and should carry into singing as well. When the word following the stop consonant has one of its own, the principle still applies. Just imagine that the initial consonant is
double. Imagine that it is in some foreign language like Russian, and has a long series of sput-
ters before the vowel. It is possible that final [p]s will still be lost, but mid-phrase it will not
matter as much as at the finish of a line, and with the other consonants we are to consider, the
principle of *liaison* will help greatly. Be sure that you do not create extra syllables mid-
phrase!

619   A little thought will convince anyone that perfect legato in a line containing stop-plosives is
an illusion. We have a Gestalt in which the mind interprets the words without analyzing the
fact that every stop has interrupted the flow of tone during the "make" in which pressure builds
up for the "plosion." Several examples of this can be seen in Fig. 66 at the end of this chapter.
Teachers sometimes liken the flow of vowels to a stream and the enunciation of consonants to
leaves which drop into the stream but do not interrupt it. It is an excellent figure of speech and
good for the singer to imagine, but it is not literally true.

Linguals

620   All the rest of the consonants require the aid of the tongue. We shall reserve those which
are nasal and those which involve the velum for a later discussion. This leaves us the *lingua-
dentals*, made with the tongue in contact with the upper teeth, and the *post-dentals*, made with
contact with the ridge behind the teeth. This is called the *alveolar* ridge and so the post-dentals
are also called *lingua-alveolars*.

621   The lingua-dentals are a sonant and surd pair, both represented by the letters, "th." They
are a characteristically English or American sound, not to be found in French, German or
Italian. If a student will remember that those who spoke those languages as children say either
"dis and dat," or "zis and zat," for "this and that," until they have had the most careful training
in English, he will also remember to avoid Americanizing such a word as "Theater, theatre"
when it is in German or French. (I have never heard of a language teacher trying to teach the
English pronunciation of this sound to a German by saying, "Just pronounce it *naturally*.") In
Old English the symbol ð (the crossed d) was used for the voiced "th" and it is now included in
the International Phonetic Alphabet. There was another symbol, þ (the thorn) for the unvoiced
analogue, but since this could easily be confused with [p], the Phonetic Alphabet uses the Greek
Θ (Theta) instead.

622   The lingual alveolars include a pair of plosives, and two pairs of fricatives. The plosives,
[d] and [t], resemble [b] and [p], except that they are made with the tongue against the teeth instead of with the lips. However, there is no problem of the [t] becoming completely silent when
it is a final, because when the tongue releases the pent-up air it eddies past the teeth adding a
fricative sound to that of the explosion. The space between the teeth and the lips, called the
vestibule of the mouth, enhances the whistling thus produced. You can verify this by making
the [t] in the usual way and then making it while retracting your lips with your fingers. The
second sound will not be as loud.

623   If we leave the tongue in its alveolar position, but with only imperfect contact, and cause
breath to pass through the constricted opening, we get the [s] sound, and by adding phonation,
[z]. The friction is almost as much between tongue and teeth as between tongue and alveolar
ridge. The other alveolar fricatives are made with a wider space between the tongue and the

ridge, and with the tongue a little farther back. They are the sound of "g" in "rouge" or "z" in "azure," and the sound of "sh." The former is a sonant, its symbol being [ʒ], and the latter is the corresponding surd, [ʃ]. There is no trouble making these consonants audible, though occasionally in speech one must guard against actually whistling.

624   The German consonant in the word, *ich*, is often confused with "sh" [ʃ]. Its correct pronunciation is with the tongue still farther back than for "sh". The correct position is achieved most easily by whispering the vowel [i]. In other words the consonant is really the surd form of the vowel! It consists of the resonance tones of the vowel without phonation. Try to whisper *ich* and you will get only one sound, except possibly the glottal stroke at the beginning. The way to sing *ich* is to begin with [i] and then stop phonating and add more breath so as to produce a fricative with the tongue in exactly the same position. In pronouncing *ich* one should feel breath against the alveolar ridge, and against the lower lip. Another way to say all this is that the final consonant of the German word *ich* is the same as the initial of the English word "hue," [ç]. The student may pronounce the name, "E. Hugh Smith," and then speak it again, stopping without completing the word, "Hugh." Perhaps I should add the qualifying note that the vowel in "ich" is really [ɪç], but singers generally get better tone by thinking [iç].

625   The *ach* [x] sound is basically the resonance tone of the vowel [a], but in order to produce enough friction to sound it, the tongue and velum are partially approximated, as when one "clears his throat." This sound is much farther back than *ich*, and a clear differentiation must be made. American singers usually find *ach* easy, and try to make *ich* the same way, but if the lingua-velar approximation is attempted when the mouth is as nearly closed as it must be for the [i] vowel, the consonant usually turns out to be [k]. The *"ik liebe dick"* pronunciation is one of the most conspicuous trademarks of poor German diction. *Ich* seems to be easier in speech than in singing, or perhaps it is less desirable in singing because it is more difficult to exaggerate. Anyhow, singers often substitute "sh" [ʃ], which is more audible. Even singers to whom German is native sometimes do this, so it can hardly be considered too bad on the part of Americans. I try to teach my students to pronounce *ich* correctly, and try to do so myself, but whenever we err, we prefer that it be on the side of "sh" [ʃ] rather than [k].

626   When a fricative is preceded by a plosive, the result is called an *affricate*. These are really compound consonants, just as diphthongs are compound vowels. The sonant affricate is found as both initial and final of the word, "judge," which shows two different spellings. "Dg" is really more accurate, since it is the [d] sound plus the sound of "g" as in "rouge." The symbol is [dʒ]. The surd analogue of this sound is found as the beginning and end of the word "church." A better spelling, perhaps, is in the word "itch," because [t] is a part of the sound. The symbol is [tʃ]. The [tʃ] sound is found in the word "righteous." Church singers sometimes are tempted to pronounce the word "ry-te-us," [raɪtiəs] thinking this is better diction. It may be scrupulous, but it is incorrect. Sing, "ry-tchus," [raɪtʃəs]. On the other hand, "beauteous" has three syllables.

Velars

627   There are two *velar plosives*, made by stopping the breath stream by approximation of the back of the tongue and the soft palate. The tongue goes back to meet the velum so that there is a complete closure. If the velum came down to meet the tongue, there would be an opening into the nose. Incidentally, the velum cooperates in the production of all plosives, the labials, [p] and [b], and the linguals, [t] and [d]. If it did not prevent the breath from escaping via the nostrils there would be no implosion, and hence no explosion. Pronounce the word "back," and try to expel breath before you complete the [k] sound by releasing the closure. You will discover that the exit of the breath has been tightly cut off, both orally and nasally. Also you

will discover that there is no consonant sound until you release the closure. All the stop does
is to interrupt the vowel. After the release there is the explosion, which produces both a
brief fricative sound and a brief resonance tone. [p] is the only stop-plosive that makes little
sound, and this proves that the real sound of the plosives is produced by friction and resonance.
[p] has neither of these being too far forward.

628   Of course, [k] is the velar surd, and [g] is the velar sonant. Another sound often classified
as "velar" is "ng" as in "sing." This brings us to consideration of the nasal consonants.

Nasals

629   When the tone is prevented from emerging freely from the mouth, nasality results. This is
accomplished most simply by closing the lips, producing the *labial nasal,* [m]. It can also be
done by pressing the tongue against the alveolar ridge, which gives the *post dental,* or *alveolar
nasal* [n]. The third nasal is "ng" [ŋ], mentioned above, which actually is made with the tongue
against the upper molars, and hence may not be truly velar. In fact, all of these sounds can be
made with the velum arched or with it lowered, or as some people put it, the nasals can be pronounced either in the mouth or in the nose! Of course in neither case does the velum make a
perfect closure so that the resonance of both nose and mouth is in the tone, only the proportions
varying.

630   Pronounce a good buccal [ɑ] and close your lips over it without changing anything else.
You are pronouncing the nasal [m] in your mouth. Your velum may have dropped a little, but the
mouth is still part of the resonance system, and its pitch is high because the opening into it is
fairly large. Pronounce one of the French nasal vowels and close your lips over it. Notice the
difference. You have not entirely eliminated the mouth, but the change in the orifice has changed
its pitch as a resonator. As a matter of fact, it is possible to hum in about as many different
ways as there are vowels. Teachers who use humming as a vocalise usually stipulate that the
hum must be "loose," or in someway describe the kind of quality they consider best. This will
always be the oral or buccal hum, in which the velum is arched. Of course, it cannot arch to the
point of shutting off access to the nose, or the tone will stop because the lips are closed, but the
hum that seems to be "forward," is the one in which the vibrations pass freely into the mouth.
If the tongue bunches, or if the velum sags, the hum becomes throaty and muffled, lacking the
brilliant overtone which the oral cavity should add. Instructions for humming seldom mention
the velum, since this part of the mechanism is not too readily controlled by most people, but they
usually mention relaxing the jaw and "feeling the hum on the lips." All the elements of freedom
of voice production, including lightness of registration are involved. Most of the comments
I have made about the continuant [m] are at least partially applicable to [n] and [ŋ].

631   If one defines a vowel as a sustained glottal vibration, resonated by the cavities above the
larynx, then the sounds we have been discussing certainly must be included. The nasals are all
vocal; they have no voiceless analogues. The only difference is that in the case of the vowels,
the mouth is open, and in the case of the nasal consonants it is not. A considerable amount of
the sound escapes by way of the mouth anyhow, as can be demonstrated by the following experiment: Close your lips and hold your nose. Then phonate by allowing the breath which passes
through the glottis to puff out your cheeks. Of course, there can only be enough for a brief
sound, but it can be fairly loud. Try it again with soft palate lowered and with the breath dis-
tending the nares. Notice how much poorer the tone is. We need the mouth as a resonator.

Semi-Vowels

632   As I have said, the nasal consonants are, except for arbitrary definition, vowels. They are sometimes called *semi-vowels*, a designation which is also applied to [l] and [r]. Henderson has coined the expression *consovowels* (p. 356), under which heading he includes [m, n, ŋ , l, r]. The latter two resemble vowels even more than the nasals, because in pronouncing them there is at least some opening via mouth, as can be proved by singing them while holding the nostrils.

633   The closure, as usual, is lingual. In the case of [l], the breath is allowed to escape around the sides of the tongue. Americans are prone to gutturize the [l] more or less, by making the tongue pressure farther back than necessary, usually against the alveolar ridge. Many Europeans form [l] with the tongue against the teeth, which is much better for singing. For the foreign languages to sound correct, the [l] must be dental, and this practice greatly improves singing in English as well. A fine drill is to pronounce "la, la, la," etc., while keeping the jaw in a low position. The only movement is to raise the front edge of the tongue to the upper teeth and let it flap down. For purposes of discipline, it should fly almost out of the mouth, coming to momentary rest upon the lower lip. This improves articulation and also makes the quality of the vowels better by keeping the tongue out of the throat. Another way to bring the [l] forward is to follow it with one of the dentals, as in "colt" or "cold."

634   In the case of [r], the breath passes over the tongue instead of around it. There are three ways to pronounce this semi-vowel. The Italians keep the tongue forward, with the blade against the alveolar ridge, and cause it to flutter by making it flexible and applying breath. This is called the *rolled r*, or more impressively, the *rolled non-fricative*. It would make considerable noise without phonation, but is always pronounced as a sonant. Any normal person can roll his [r]'s, but if he has not been taught to do so before, should certainly acquire the skill for singing purposes. Italian diction simply is not correct without it, and as in the case of [l], the extreme forward production of it benefits the enunciation of other languages also. The British clip the [r] to what has been called the "one-tap roll." Marshall (p. 8) calls this the "flipped r" and recommends it to Americans.

635   A second pronunciation is the *uvular r* [R], in which the velum is fluttered against the back of the tongue. This is a more difficult skill to master for those of us who did not grow up in France or Germany. If you can do it well, it will give an authentic flavor to your singing in these languages. However, it resembles the *ich* [ç] sound in this respect; it is not too easy to sing, and so even German singers substitute another sound, in this case the Italian rolled [r]. The fluttering sound is much the same, but the rolled [r] carries a little better and does not disrupt good vowel production. We have the authority of Pierre Bernac to the effect that the rolled [r] is used in all serious singing (art songs, opera, etc.) in French and the uvular [R] only in popular singing. So a safe general rule is that the rolled [r] is correct for all foreign language singing, and for most of English.

636   The third pronunciation is, I am sorry to say, characteristically American. It is called the *retroflex r* [ɚ]. The tip of the tongue curls back to make this sound, and there is no "rolling," or fluttering. This is an unpleasant sound and should be avoided as much as possible. Many singers have foresworn it utterly, and either roll all [r]'s or assume the Eastern American Dialect which substitutes for the [ɚ] the neutral vowel [ə] found in the last syllable of "idea." Both the Eastern and the Southern Dialects make this substitution. Ironically, a few people also reverse the substitution and pronounce "idea," [ɑɪdiə] "idear" [ɑɪdiɚ]! However, if you are going to say *"foah"* [foə] instead of "four," [foɚ] you must consistently adopt New Yorker or Southern pronunciations, or it will sound like an affectation. Unfortunately, the character-

istically American pronunciation requires the unpleasant retroflex r [ɚ] in some words and there is no escaping it.

637   In most cases where [r] stands alone among vowels, the Italian roll will be acceptable and should by all means be used in singing. However, one should master the "short roll," or "flipped r." One or two cycles of the flutter are enough. A little practice will keep the [r] forward and also avoid a stilted enunciation. The roll must never be obvious. The great difficulty comes where the [r] is in combination with other consonants. Here the short roll can sometimes be used, if executed with great skill so as to be absolutely minimized, but such words as "Lord," "earth," "world," begin to sound like Scottish Dialect, if there is much rolling of the [r]'s.

638   In 17th century England all [r]s were pronounced, and this usage, like the vowel [æ] (Par. 503), was carried on in the American colonies. The English used a rolled [r] somewhat as in Scotland today, (Kenyon, p. 12). The retroflex [ɚ] is United States usage. The English clipped their [r]s before vowels and dropped them before consonants and pauses. Wise calls this Standard Southern British, or "Stage Speech," (pp. 239-244). Madeline Marshall (p. 9), Judith Raskin, and other authorities on singing in English agree with him, making the [r] silent at the end of words, especially when there is another consonant. I was one of three Midwestern voice teachers (I am from Chicago) who surrounded Miss Marshall at an informal luncheon at the University of Illinois following one of her excellent lectures and plagued her about the silent [r]. Bruce Foote asked whether, " 'Twere best that we were parted," should be pronounced, "Twuh best that we wuh potted." William Miller offered some strong arguments, too. Finally, in order to finish her lunch in peace, Miss Marshall accepted this compromise: if an American singer *thinks* he is making the [r] silent he will reduce it to an acceptable minimum, but force of habit will cause him to sound it enough to meet the requirements of General American English, which the majority uses in the United States. The "silent r" thus becomes a teaching strategem.

639   I can testify that if a foreigner is told to make the [r] silent, he will become unintelligible in English. I have coached singers to whom English was not native and the most important element in their success was practice in making as unpleasant a retroflex [r] as I could persuade them to make. Before the audience they could hardly bring themselves to make the sound and the result was just enough.

640   For American singers I advise singing [ɜ], the vowel in "word," which puts the tongue almost into the position of the retroflex [r]. It is sung like the second part of a diphthong. (Par. 648). Then at the last moment the [ɝ] or [ɚ] is sounded as briefly as possible and if there is an additional consonant it should be reached quickly, making sure that the tongue recovers from the arched position and the blade comes well forward. The sonagrams in Fig. 66 at the end of this chapter illustrate this. The dental consonants [d] and "th" [ð] [Θ] can redeem the word. As you practice the retroflex [ɚ], see how much of the quality you can achieve with a minimum of curling back. You will find yourself tending in the direction of the neutral vowel, as used in the East and South, but a happy medium is possible in which the General American sound is produced with very little stiffening of the tongue.

641   A sluggish tongue sometimes fails to form the [i] or the [r] and [w] is the result. Thus a child who intends to say "real little" [riəl lɪtəl] says "wee wittow" [wi wɪtoʊ] instead. The semi-vowels become *glides*.

Glides

642   We have discussed five continuants which are closely akin to vowels. Three are nasals, and two are semi-vowels, each of which has at least two distinct pronunciations. These differ from

vowels only in the partial or complete mouth closure. To these we must add the *glides*, which differ from vowels only in their transitory nature and their possible fricative components. They are pronounced almost like [u] or [i] but they do not maintain the formation. Instead, they are brief sounds, moving directly into another sound, or emerging from another sound. Because of the fact that they involve considerable constriction in the resonance chambers, resembling the two vowels in which the tongue is brought closest to the palate, there is often a fricative component.

643   There are two pairs of glides, sonant and surd. The pair related to the vowel [u] are found as initials in "wise," and "whiz." The International Phonetic Symbol for the "w" in "wise" is the same, [w]; and its analogue, in "whiz" is [ʍ]. Sometimes it is written [hw]. The pair related to the vowel [i] are found in "you" [j], and "hue" [ç]. The [j], of course, is the same as used in the German word, *ja*. The surds, [ʍ] and [ç] are closely related to [h], in that they amount largely to whispering either [u] or [i] before going into the succeeding vowel. Try to make a whispered distinction between [u] and "who" [ʍu] and you will find that all you can do is introduce friction for the glide by aspirating more violently, or make a glottal stroke for the vowel. Also try the words "east" and "yeast." The sonants consist of speaking the vowel [u] or [i] very briefly and going immediately into the following sound. The surds have more fricative or aspirate noise.

644   For easy reference, perhaps it would be well to recapitulate the International Phonetic Symbols for the consonants.

[h]	hay	[heɪ]	[d]	dye	[daɪ]	[m]	sum	[sʌm]
[ʔ]	*aber*	[ʔabɛr]	[t]	tie	[taɪ]	[n]	sun	[sʌn]
[b]	bay	[beɪ]	[s]	seal	[sil]	[ŋ]	sung	[sʌŋ]
[p]	pay	[peɪ]	[z]	zeal	[zil]	[l]	led	[lɛd]
[v]	vine	[vaɪn]	[ʒ]	azure	[aʒur]	[r]	*caro*	[karo]
[f]	fine	[faɪn]	[ʃ]	sure	[ʃur]	[ɚ]	red	[ɚɛd]
[ð]	thy	[ðaɪ]	[g]	goal	[goəl]	[w]	witch	[wɪtʃ]
[θ]	thigh	[θaɪ]	[k]	coal	[koəl]	[ʍ]	which	[ʍɪtʃ]
						[j]	you	[ju]
						[ç]	hue	[çu]
						[x]	*ach*	[ax]

Diphthongs

645   If we reverse the production of the glide, we have simply a *diphthong,* or double vowel. For example, *ja* consists of a transient [i] sound followed by a prolonged [a]. If we make the sustained [a] first and allow it to glide into a vanishing [ɪ] we have the English pronoun, "I." Americans, especially, chew their vowels. We do not make it a speech habit to pronounce vowels purely, and to sustain them. Pronounce the five so-called vowels, A, E, I, O, and U, and you will find that only E will be produced with the mouth in a constant position. This is only because the jaw is already raised so high for this vowel that it is almost impossible to chew it any more. Even so, one will often hear this letter pronounced, "Eeyuh," [iə]. The jaw simply has to move, so it opens. With U [u] a vanishing sound is almost impossible, so the glide [j] is used to begin it, and we hear "eeOO" [ju]. The other letters, A, I and O, are characteristic diphthongs, in which the true vowel is commenced, and then the jaw closes on it, making either a vanishing [ɪ] or vanishing [ʊ]. There are six recognizable diphthongs used in English, as found in "day," "eye," "owe," "boy," "now," "you." There are also triphthongs, like "earl," "fire," "yea," and "wow."

646   Phoneticians differ as to how to transcribe these words (Coffin, Denes and Pinson, Kantner and West, Wise) reflecting different percepts as they listen, and I suspect different concepts as to what the subject "thinks" as he speaks. A singer need not bother his head over different spellings of the "short" sounds. For example, is "yea" [jeɪ] [jej] or [ɪeɪ]? Or is "wow" [wɑʊ] [wɑw] or [ʊɑʊ]? These questions are more meaningful in speech than in song, since they refer chiefly to the duration of the sounds in speech and duration in singing is a matter of music more than of phonetics. However, it is important to discriminate with reference to the "long" sound. It is argued that in American pronunciation there is no [e] but only [ɛɪ] (Denes and Pinson, Marshall, among others). This may be, but I believe American singers will do well to cultivate the European [e] and think of the diphthong as [eɪ] rather than [ɛɪ].

647   There is discussion as to whether [o] exists at all in English as a monophthong (Wise, p. 108) but I am sure it exists in singing. An example is in Fig. 66, at the end of this chapter. The word "so" is pronounced [soʊ] in speech, but [so] in song.

648   If we include the semi-vowels as possible vanishing sounds, our list of diphthongs is greatly increased. Vowels when followed by [r] take on the qualities of diphthongs, (Holmes, p. 216). I have already mentioned this, (Par. 640). If the retroflex [ɚ] is used, it is one diphthong; if the Eastern or Southern American [ə] is used, it is another even more clearly. The words "are," "air," "ear," "or," "your" are a few examples. In such words as "all," "ail," "eel," "old," "pool" we hear diphthongization produced by the semi-vowel [l]. If the [l] is Italian, produced merely with a flick of the tongue, there is less of it, but if it is an American alveolar or palatal [l], diphthongization is more noticeable and objectionable. We could profitably add another list of words if we accept a final [m, n] or [ŋ] as producing a diphthong.

649   Everyone pronounces the vowel [u] with a preceding glide [ju] in such words as "music," "cure," "cute," "pure," "abuse," "few." Marshall lists these, and adds a useful mnemonic device for remembering the words in which the same practice *should* be followed, but about which there is doubt in many minds. She says that [ju] is used after [d, n, l, s, t] and [θ] which are the consonants in the words "Daniel sitteth," and adds that the rule does *not* apply when [l] is preceded by another consonant, as in "blue," "clue," "flute," "glue," "plume," "slew," (Marshall, pp. 139-141).

650   "Vowel fracture" (Holmes, p. 233) happens all through English because of our lack of nimbleness in forming consonants. We form them sluggishly while the vowels are sounding, and the relatively slow movement produces another vowel on the way. This happens not only before [l, m, n, ŋ, r], as mentioned above, but also before [d, s, t]. The greater the jaw opening necessary for the vowel sound, the more opportunity there is for an intermediate sound to be produced. Some teachers recommend forming the vowels with a high position of the mandible to avoid this, but it seems to me that this sacrifices *all* of the vowels to save *some* of them. Better learn how to make the consonants with livelier movements of the tongue. Chewing of the vowels results from *moving* the jaw, and this can be avoided as much by keeping the jaw down as by keeping it up.

651   In French there is no diphthongization, and in Italian very little. The formation of the vowel is maintained exactly throughout the duration of the syllable. It is true that Italian has a number of words like *miei, suoi,* etc., in which vowels follow one another in rapid succession, but even here, they are to be kept pure and distinct. This is one of the factors that makes Italian a musical language. The consonants are more sudden and brief. The articulation is clean, producing a series of clear tones, rather than a series of sounds in such flux that it is impossible to assert the harmonic structure of any of them. Students often need be reminded that in personal pronouns, such as *io, suo, tuo,* etc., the first syllable must never be slighted. It is [io] not [jo], and [suo] not [swo], (Errolle, p. 13). The first syllable may be brief, but it comes on the beat

and must sound definitely. (Exceptions to this principle in Italian are found in such words as: *"pianto"* [pjanto] where *"i"* becomes a glide, and *"guanto"* [gwanto] where *"u"* becomes a glide, (Errolle, p. 39).

652   In English, the nearer we can approach the Italian standard of vowel production the more musical the words will sound, but immediately we are confronted with the singer's dilemma, because if the language becomes too Italian we cannot expect Americans to understand it. As soon as this happens, the song is lost, and the voice is only competing with wordless musical instruments at a pitiful disadvantage.

653   The popular singer never forgets that he is an entertainer, and that if his words are indistinct, he is failing. Therefore he tries to make his diction as much like spoken American as he can. In the pronunciation of a diphthong his problem is just as difficult as that of the classical singer, because he is required to make two comparatively brief sounds extend over several beats of music. Often he divides the time equally between the "long" sound and the "vanishing" sound. If the "vanishing" sound happens to be a "consovowel," [m, n, ŋ, l] or even [r] he will give the "long" sound about as much time as it would take in rather deliberate speech, and then go into the quasi vowel, humming or crooning it for the balance of the count. Turn on the radio any time, and you will hear such diction as, "I'lllllllll be seeinnnnnnnnnng you." Since rubato is the soul of crooning, popular singers have two other ways of making the diphthong sound "natural." One is to come in so late that it is not necessary to prolong the articulation much more than in speech, and the other is to end the word quickly and wait out the musical time value until whenever the next word is due.

654   Obviously this is carrying rubato to the extent of grand larceny, but within the bounds of good taste, applied with subtlety, it improves the diction of any song. I speak unsympathetically, but not actually with contempt, for I am convinced that most "highbrow" singers have much to learn from popular singers. However, the canons of musicianship make the tricks mentioned above unavailable to the serious singer. If a diphthong is assigned to a held note, the singer must provide a beautiful tone for the indicated number of counts, and he should not change the vowel. Therefore he will sing the "long" vowel for almost the whole time, and go into the "vanishing" vowel, or semi-vowel only at the last moment, almost as if it were no more singable than a stop-plosive. If there are any consonants following the "vanishing" sound, they will all be pronounced along with it, in as rapid succession as possible, without producing an extra syllable. Thus the word, "light," will be sung "lah- (prolonging the [ɑ] for almost the full count)-eet." Both the "l" and the "eet" will be brief. In singing the diphthong [ɑɪ] be sure to sing an unashamed [ɑ] for the sustained part. If you anticipate the second part you will compromise the [ɑ] and get "shallowness" or "whiteness" as in the "bad" vowel [æ]. It is also a good idea to brighten the [ɪ] almost into an [i].

Diphthongs Assigned to More than one Note of Music

655   Diphthongs sometimes give singers trouble when more than one note is given to a single syllable of text. No one would think of trying to sing a consonant like [b, d, f, g, k, s, t, v, z] on the entire value of the last note, but since a glide, semi-vowel, nasal, or "vanishing" part of a diphthong is singable, it often gets such a treatment. This is incorrect. For example, if the word "in" is sung on two sixteenth notes, with [ɪ] on the first and [n] on the second, the second note will drop out of the line, because [n] is so much weaker than [ɪ]. The vowel must be sung on every note assigned to the syllable, especially the last one, and then the final sound (consonant, glide, semi-vowel, or vanishing sound) must be added nimbly before time for the next tone in the music. Incidentally this demands a little rubato, because the final sound or sounds take time. One difference between a pianist and an accompanist is the awareness of

this fact, and a willingness to allow for it. This is another reason why "musicians" are intolerant of singers.

656   A good example of the problem is found in the word "heav'nly." Marshall (p. 55) shows how it must be sung.

Monro, "My Lovely Celia"

Written: Sung:

heav'n - - ly   heav - - - ven - ly

657   An example of diphthongization with the semi-vowel [l] is found in the following:

Handel, "Total Eclipse," (Samson)

My ve-ry soul   in   re-al darkness dwells.

The word "soul" is placed on one note, and the vanishing part, "ool," should be very brief. But the word "real" is given in two notes. In most such cases I should prefer singing the [i] for both notes and pronouncing the [l] quickly. Here, however, I think the tenor must sing [ɑl] on the second note, making a decrescendo on the vowel and raising the tongue quickly for the [l]. By all means do *not* devote the entire second syllable to the [l] sound alone. A moment's thought of the word "reality" will convince you that "real" should not be "reel" in this case.

658   Occasionally a composer will divide a diphthong and give it two different notes. This happens most often with words like "hour," "power" and "flower." I think the syllable "wer" [wɚ] is an unpleasant sound, consisting largely of the retroflex [ɚ], and so I avoid giving it a full count if I can. This means that when "flower" is written for two notes, I usually sing "flah-" [flɑ] for both notes, adding the "wer" [wɚ] as if it were merely a final consonant. The fact that these words are often treated by composers as being of only one syllable seems to justify this practice. However, instances come to mind in which the singer is almost compelled to make two syllables of the words.

Brahms, "Serious Songs," No. 2.

For with their op - press - ors — there — was — pow-er.

In such cases the way out is to accent the first syllable and decrescendo radically, minimizing the [w]. I think that making two syllables of the word "hour" is atrocious, but it illustrates how closely related are the vowel [u] and the glide [w]. No wonder it is called "double-U"!

659   I mention these exceptions merely to remind us that no rules are absolute, and the singer must always use his common sense. One last idea on this subject we owe to Coenraad Bos,

(p. 98-102). When two syllables are on different pitches he advises making the change during the consonant. If the consonant is voiceless it provides opportunity to change pitch cleanly. When it is voiced a portamento will be heard, but if this takes place only on the transitional tone it will be in good taste. The problem of the portamento is present always in the voice, since like the musical saw, it has only one vibrator for all the tones. We must not cease phonation or we will lose the legato, but we must slacken it or the portamento will be too obvious. Making the portamento "on the consonants" is a useful concept.

Unstressed Syllables

660   In the "vanishing" part of the diphthong we have a simple element of speech which becomes a problem for the singer, and equally difficult are the unstressed syllables of speech. I have already anticipated this discussion in writing of the "dull" vowels (Par. 487-492). In speech, the rapidity with which certain syllables are uttered, and the weakness with which they are phonated, result in careless and inefficient resonance. Hence, a vowel which ordinarily would have a characteristic musical quality becomes neutralized into [ʌ]. Often where there are a good many consonants the vowel disappears completely. Thus the word "should" becomes "shd" [ʃd], etc.

661   In singing time values are assigned to these unmusical sounds. What is the performer going to do? The popular singer does much as has just been described. He alters the rhythm to eliminate the sounds. If this fails, he sings them, dull vowels or consovowels, as the case may be. As long as he is understood, he has nothing to worry about. In fact, it is better if he is not too musical. An essential of radio appeal is the listener's identification of himself with the singer. He likes to feel able to join in on the chorus, to imagine that the singer is "one of the boys." If the singer is to show any superiority, it must be in some technical display, like a long note, or a loud note, or a high note—not in artistry, musicianship, or beauty of tone. He may have these attributes but they must be underplayed.

662   The singer who wishes to convey all the words of the poem and at the same time impart the nobility of good tone throughout has a much more difficult problem. He must avoid the dull vowel as much as possible, and refuse entirely to sing consonants, except perhaps to hum a nasal a little more than necessary occasionally. He refuses to do what the phoneticist calls "restressing an unstressed form," (Holmes, pp. 238, 239), that is pronouncing loudly and deliberately a sound that acquired its unpleasant quality through neglect in hurried speech. Instead, he sings the pure "Italian" form of the vowel as nearly as possible and disguises it cleverly to give the illusion of "naturalness." This ability comes only with practice, and is acquired only by those singers who refuse to sacrifice either of the two almost incompatible goals—beauty of tone and unstilted intelligibility. Part of it is in "darkening" the vowels, by shaping the resonators in such a way that the formants are slightly lowered. Part of it is in withdrawing power from the syllables, so that their brilliance is lost, that is, so that the highest partials do not sound as forcibly. This is really "unstressing" the vowel by weakening its intensity instead of shortening its duration. In this way, "open" never becomes "opun," "and" never becomes "und," "willing" never becomes "will'n," "comfort" never becomes "comfrt," or "comfert," unless they appear in dialect songs.

663   In the final "e" in German we have an interesting contradiction. According to Siebs, the final "e" is never accented and always pronounced with the schwa [ə], (p. 29). However, many fine German singers, for example Fischer-Dieskau, refuse to deaden this vowel so much and to American ears they sing [ɛ]. Far be it from me to correct the pronunciation of a first rank artist using his native language, but I find that if American singers imitate this practice they overdo it and *liebe,* for example, comes out [libɛ] or even [libe] when it should

be [libə]. I think native German and Austrian coaches instruct Americans to sing [libɛ] in the hope of avoiding the ugliness of the dull vowel. It would be better if the singer would round his lips a little and "darken" the [ɛ]. Bernac[2] solves the problem of the final "e" in French by admitting that in speech it is [ə], but suggesting that [œ] be substituted in song. This is the lax form of "eu" in French, or ŏ in German, and is closely related to the English [ɜ] as in "word." There must, of course, be no sound of [ɝ], (Par. 479).

664   These same principles apply to the endings "en" and "er" which are neutral in speech, but must be brightened in song, though not too much. I have shown the word "aber" as [abɛr] (Par. 612 and 644) because it is useful for singers to conceive it that way, but it must not get too far from the spoken [abər].

665   A fine discipline for beginning students is to sing a song using only the pure vowels. Thus, "The Lord is my Shepherd," becomes "Ah, Aw, Ee, Ah, Ay, Ah," [aɔiɑeɑ]. It should be sung that way until every vowel comes out clearly, without losing either legato or consistency—two ingredients that make up what is called "line." After this the consonants should be added: "ThAH LAWrd EEz mAH ShAYpAHrd," [ðɑ lɔəd iz mɑ ʃepɑəd]. The song should be sung over and over in this manner, with the consonants sounding distinctly, but not spoiling the "line." Unfortunately, many "classical" singers are satisfied with this. They may even stop short of adding all the consonants. Only the foundation has been laid. The practice must continue until, without loss of vocal excellence, the Ah in "ThAH" has been modified without losing its "focus," the Ee in "EEz" has been toned down without becoming "uz," the vanishing Ee has been added neatly and briefly to the "mAH" without "whitening" the word, the Ay in "ShAY" has become Eh without loss of beauty, and the "pAHrd" has been deemphasized without simply crooning a retroflex [r]. The line will then be, "The Lord is my Shepherd," and it will contain both meaning and music.

Unworthy Texts

666   When a text contains words that will not yield to the method I have just outlined, it is unworthy of song. Usually this is the fault of the composer. It is not that the words are unpronounceable, but the melody to which they must be sung emphasizes their defects. For instance, the word "because" usually has two unstressed syllables, but in that perennial wedding favorite, D'Hardelot demands that the singer restress them with a vengeance. Without going into its merit as poetry, I feel that the setting makes almost impossible anything but a vulgar performance.

667   A common sin of second-rate writers is the use of a text in which a word like "liberty," "eternity," etc., comes at the end of the line. This almost always requires the singer to emphasize the unstressed final syllable, since it is set to the completion of the cadence, on the first beat of the measure, usually on a held note, often on a high pitch. If it happens in French, it does not matter, for in this language the last syllable of liberté is stressed; but in translation it is poor, and in original English composition, unpardonable.

668   Other illustrations could easily be cited, but we hardly need argue the fact that many songs are unworthy, either because of the inferiority of the lyrics, or because of the ineptness of the composer. What should we do with these songs? A purist simply refuses to sing them. He says, "I would rather starve." At the opposite extreme, the commercial singer does not gauge merit by artistic standards, but by the cash register, and if the song is on the Hit Parade, he makes the best of it. The great American Public has spoken, and he obeys. He does not regard himself as a priest of music, with an obligation to lead his followers into better experiences, but he panders to their weaknesses.

669   Most of us find ourselves between the two extremes. We occasionally prostitute our talents, for example, in church, of all places, singing "Because," or some Biblical text set to vulgar music. A singer with no audience is not a singer, and getting a hearing is a matter of individual conscience, and hunger. It is easy to say that such and such a singer has sold his soul, when really we are only annoyed that Satan has never offered us as high a price. All I ask is that when you do sing an inferior piece, you sing it as artistically as you can, and that you do penance for it by singing something worth while at the earliest opportunity. You may not succeed in leading the public into a love of the best, but you can at least have the decency not to love the worst.

670   In a few cases, we actually find an unworthy text set to such fine music that we sing it regardless. Or we find weak spots in good music. For example, the English texts of Handel are occasionally bad, because he was German and at the mercy of inferior librettists. We have already cited a case in paragraph 657. Here again, we make the best of the situation, for different reasons. At the end of this chapter we analyze a passage by Purcell in his native language (Fig. 66), in which he prolongs the word "of." Ours not to reason why, we simply sustain the vowel [ʌ]. However, years of conceiving this vowel as [ɔ] result in creating a "ring" for this vowel at 3000 cps.

Legato and Articulation

671   The quality which differentiates a consonant from a vowel is the noise element. Therefore, in order for consonants to be recognized as such the noise must be exaggerated. This is the essence of making words understood in a large hall. It is true that a sonant carries better because it is voiced, but the fact remains that for it to carry *as a consonant,* the fricative or plosive element must also carry. For this reason, the surds sometimes are better recognized than the sonants, because the noise element in them is more exaggerated. In the case of a surd, the vocal tone is broken and a noise inserted; in the case of a sonant, the noise is superimposed upon the tone, and unless this is done with emphasis it may be lost.

672   A good exercise for improving one's ability to project words is to whisper the lines. This emphasizes the noise element, by eliminating the tone entirely, and makes the student aware of whether or not he is really producing these noises. This may be followed by speaking the lines, and then singing them. Someone should listen from the back of a large hall, and call out whenever a word fails to come through. Let the singer then exaggerate still more whatever consonants are weak. Singing in a poor auditorium, acoustically, is an excellent discipline. A singer should imagine that he is speaking to someone who is deaf.

673   The effect of all this upon legato is clearly detrimental. It is difficult to have good diction and good legato. However, as I have already said (Par. 619), the illusion of perfect legato need not be disturbed by strong diction. In Italian, the consonants are all more brief. If they interrupt the vocal line at all, they do so imperceptibly. We doubtless carry as much of this as possible into the other languages when singing. Scripture[2] tells us:

> In looking over inscriptions of speech it is soon noticed that sounds ordinarily voiceless, such as *t* or *p*, frequently become voiced between vowels. In studying some records by the tenor Caruso I found that he frequently kept his vocal cords vibrating during sounds like *t* and *k*. This was done unconsciously; he was incredulous and indignant when the peculiarity was pointed out to him, yet the general effect of his singing was smoother on account of the peculiarity. I would suggest that it is often not only easier but also pleasanter to voice consonants between vowels. The expression 'aha' with a voiced *h* is the milder and more agreeable word; 'aha' with the unvoiced *h* is an expression with more vigour, aggressiveness, and unpleasantness, (p. 7).

What language Caruso was using is not told us, but we may be sure that his legato was the result of his Italian background. In this quotation the issue is made quite plain: to the extent that we want the singing to be legato, "mild," "agreeable," we minimize the noisy interruptions; to the extent that we want "vigour," "aggressiveness," "unpleasantness" (and I may add, intelligibility) we exaggerate the noises into noticeable interruptions.

674   A French singer thinks of each syllable as beginning with a consonant and ending with a vowel. This produces a fine legato. Marshall wisely applies the same principle to English. Fred Waring uses it in syllabifying choral music. The idea goes back at least to Sieber and his vocalises. Americans have a tendency to let the vowel fade before enunciating the next consonant. To produce greater smoothness such singers need to think of a crescendo in each syllable. It should seem to grow from the preceding syllable into the next. "Line" is an illusion created by consistency of vowel color (Par. 505, 514-520), postponement of diphthongization (Par. 650-654), and a concept of the overall phrase which usually involves a crescendo (perhaps almost imperceptible) to an important word, after which the sound decrescendos.

675   The German and English languages use more noisy consonants than Italian, not only including the *affricates* in which there is a specific symbol for a double consonant, but combining several of the single consonants. In German, sonants approach surds in pronunciation. It is considered good German to break the vowel tone noticeably to produce at least some of the consonants (Siebs, p. 78), and it must also be done in English, if the words are to be clear. The only parallel to be found in Italian is in the double consonant, in which there must be a slight pause between the two.

Relative Merits of the Languages

676   This means that Italian is more singable, more musical. It was the best language for the Golden Age. But for singing in the Romantic sense, a language which emphasizes articulation could well be more beautiful. It is not an accident that vocal music, as such, developed in the *aria*, but that the art of song still awaited the *Lied*, Italian is therefore best for beginners, whose main attention should be upon tone production. For Italian to be lovely requires only that it be correct. There are almost no vocal pitfalls. But for mature artistry the singer should study *Lieder*, Here he will master the difficulties of really great expression. Somewhere between these languages is French, which keeps the Italian legato, with brief consonants and freedom from diphthongization, but which contains many subtleties both of pronunciation and of interpretation. The French literature also requires more use of high *mezza voce;* French singers develop a delicate *voix mixte*.

677   It is a shameful fact that the average American singer who has studied French, German, and Italian, sings them far better than English. We "high-brows" have a combination of snobbery about foreign languages and inferiority complex with reference to our own. This is not the place to discuss reasons and excuses, and therefore I shall only say that English is fully as expressive as Italian, and fully as singable as German. If we would maintain as high standards and work as faithfully to acquire good English diction as we do in the other languages, we who profess musical ideals could do far more for the cause of great singing in our country. In a foreign language we do not realize that we are exaggerating consonants, and so we do it without fear, but in English we are more diffident. Also we have been taught Italian vowels so relentlessly we are ashamed of our own. American audiences have as much right to demand singing in their own language as Italians have to demand Italian, French to demand French, Germans to demand German, Poles to demand Polish, etc. When we recognize that right, and work as hard to serve it as the popular singer does, we shall really be doing justice to the composers we interpret.

678   Each spoken language has its unlovely sounds, or at least sounds adverse to good singing. I have spoken of the final "e" in French and German (Par. 663), the glottal plosive used in both those languages as correct diction and the tendency to use it in English (Par. 611-614). The French [ɛ̃] is unpleasant, (Par. 512). We have also given attention to the Bad Vowel [æ] and the Dull Vowel [ʌ] in English (Par. 487-507) and the American retroflex [ɚ] (Par. 636). Singers must protect their art from the inroads of these pronunciations. Bonci said, "It is a question, and a serious one, whether those who teach singing understand the application of the word to the tone, and the dangers are obvious in languages where nasals and gutterals prevail," (Tetrazzini, p. 63). "All languages affect the tone, unless the tone is first able to carry the weight of the language," (p. 85).

679   Italian can be "shallow" and too much " in the mouth." Errolle tells us that in speech the Italian "a" is [a], but that it should be sung [ɑ], (p. 51). Much the same can be said of French. Husson[3] x-rayed members of the Paris Opera and found that in speech their vowels were comparatively shallow, but that in singing they dropped the jaw and lowered the larynx (Par. 423). Germaine Lubin, great Parisienne dramatic soprano of yesteryear, made this comment on present day French singers: "Our women sing too 'open.' Perhaps it is a little the fault of our language," (de Schauensee, p. 27). I shall never forget the singing of a fine linguist whom I heard on a few occasions. When he sang one song it was flawless in artistry and especially in pronunciation, regardless of what language he chose. But I heard him in a recital that he could barely finish. In the second half he would begin a song in one key and his facile accompanist would have to transpose it down a semi-tone before he had finished. This gentleman made a great point of singing [a] rather than the "incorrect" [ɑ] and the poor production resulting from this fidelity to the spoken pronunciation made us all unhappy.

Essentials of Good Diction

680   The word "diction" refers primarily to the choice of the right word for the idea to be expressed. However, singers have no choice, and they use "diction" to refer to the most effective articulation of the words which have been assigned them. The subject may be viewed from the standpoints of enunciation and pronunciation.

681   Enunciation demands that every syllable be clear and audible. It involves making the consonants noisy enough to be recognized at a distance. This requires generous expenditure of breath, and freedom from too much worry about legato. It is better to sing shorter phrases, making them somewhat *marcato* if necessary, than to sing such a perfect "line" that the words are lost. Incidentally, if the diction is effective, it breaks the legato, so that a skillful technician is able to "steal" a breath almost at any point where there is a voiceless consonant. Some authors say that correct diction uses only the air that is in the mouth, which is restored through the lips as soon as the consonant has been pronounced, without exhausting any of the breath stream that is supplying phonation. This is true for final consonants, but mid-phrase I find that good enunciation uses breath and shortens the possible length of the phrase. I have already affirmed my belief in the somewhat aspirate attack (the imaginary [h]) in place of the glottal stroke in enunciating initial vowels. The same thing occurs with the resumption of phonation after each surd. It helps to blend the noise with the tone, and it is expensive of breath.

682   Pronunciation demands that the sounds be enough like average speech to create the illusion of "naturalness." This means, for example, that while the vowels should be kept as musical as possible they must be modified where necessary in favor of colloquial pronunciation. Whenever there is a spoken line in an opera, the words are easily intelligible; often they are the only understandable moments in the performance. Why does the same person *speak* clearly and *sing* unrecognizably? It must be in the vowels. Part of it is Italianization, but it is fundamentally a

wrong concept of tone production. When an artist speaks, he obeys the instructions of Shakespeare, who knew a thing or two about the theatre.

> Speak the speech, I pray you, as I pronounced it to you, trippingly on the tongue; but if you mouth it, as many of your players do, I had as lief the town-crier spoke my lines, (Hamlet, Act III, Scene 2).

But when the same man sings, he does it like the town-crier, bellowing from the throat. It is excellent discipline to speak a line of a song two or three times as if you were on a stage, and then sing it.

683 It is also true that the requirements of singing necessarily make it different from speech. For example, speech never sustains either a vowel or a pitch for very long. Audiences are attuned to understanding speech, but American highbrow audiences especially need to be educated to recognizing the same words when sung. As long as singers prefer languages the listeners cannot understand, this will be so. As a matter of fact, our popular singers are understood by their audiences very well, and often the singing technic is excellent.

684 The illusion of "naturalness" demands that there must never be so much exaggeration of consonants that they become syllables in themselves. There is a tendency for the consovowels to become separate syllables, either before or after vowels. We have already discouraged this mannerism in final consovowels, under the heading of "vowel fracture," but it can also happen at the beginning of a word if phonation is allowed to begin before the proper articulation and if the semi-vowel or glide is allowed to last too long. "Lover" becomes "Uhlover" [əlʌvər] or "Huhlover" [həlʌvər] and "which," becomes "whooitch" [huɪtʃ]. Where consonants come in succession, they must be closely joined or each one will make a syllable. "Bright" will become "buhright" [bəraɪt] or worse still, "berright" [bɛʀaɪt]. This can even happen when the initial is a surd, "please," becoming "puhlease" [pəliz] simply because the phonation of the semi-vowel began before its articulation.

685 If phonation continues after the completion of a final consonant, an extra syllable is added to the word, as in "lorduh" [lɔrdə] for "Lord." This can be avoided by applying the French principle of *liaison,* that is, by making all final consonants the initial consonants of the next word. If the second word has an initial vowel, this evades the danger of an objectionable *coup de glotte.* If the second word has an initial consonant or consonants, the *liaison* merely compounds them a little more, and by treating them as described above, they pass in rapid enough succession to make only one syllable. None of the consonants in a combination should be allowed to drop out. It is merely a matter of taking time and pronouncing all of them without introducing a vowel. "With thee" must not degenerate into "withee" [wɪði] for instance.

686 Sometimes *liaison* creates a new word, which may be ludicrous. In one of the Kipling texts, "Rolling Down to Rio," set to music by Edward German, we find, "I'd love to roll to Rio, some day before I'm old." A little carelessness makes this "Some day before I mold." One way out of this is to stroke the word "old" with the glottis after sounding the [m], but I prefer a little slackening of the intensity to complete the [m] and a little increase as the vowel [o] is begun, using an imaginary [h] or a sonant [h] as Scripture might call it. One must not allow himself to become too self-conscious about this sort of thing or he will be hearing new and incongruous words everywhere. English is normally full of it, and a punster can ruin the noblest of texts. Even Biblical passages become silly, if not obscene, in superficial minds.

687 At the end of a phrase, if there is a consonant, it should be audible. Even after a long diminuendo, a word deserves completion. Remember that no matter how soft the vowels, the consonants must still be rather loud if they are to be heard. Semi-vowels and nasals can be sung

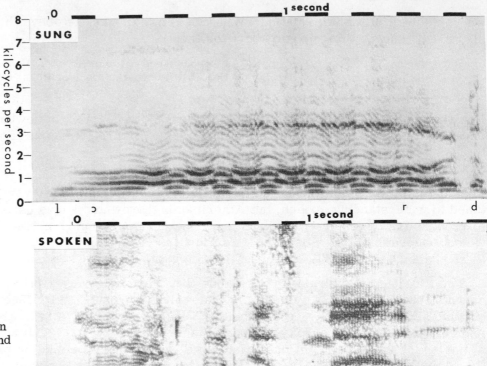

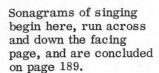

Sonagrams of singing begin here, run across and down the facing page, and are concluded on page 189.

Sonagrams of speaking begin here, run down this page, and are concluded on page 188.

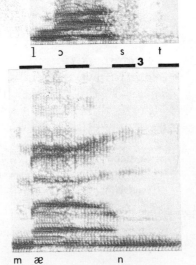

Fig. 66. Song and Speech Compared in Sonagrams

From a study by Vennard and Irwin, *NATS Bulletin*, Dec. 1966. Opening line of *Three Divine Hymns* by Henry Purcell (music in upper right corner facing page) was sung and spoken, and the tapes fed into a Kay-Electric Sonagraph. Time scale across top is in tenths of a second with each second numbered at the end. IPA symbols for the quotation, [lɔrd, ʌʌt ɪz mæn, lɔst mæn, ðæt ðɑu ʃudst bi sou mɑɪndfəl əʌ hɪm?], appear across bottom, each symbol placed at the point where that sound begins. Average duration of phonemes has been discussed in Par. 604.

Speech sounds are constantly changing, forming diphthongs and triphthongs. Their sonagram appears mottled. Song is characterized by "steady states" of sound that look as if they were stroked on smoothly with a wide brush, or perhaps a roller that contains the vibrato pattern. In singing, only the word "mindful" [mɑɪndful] shows continuous change from the [ɑ] through the [ɪ] into the [n]. Otherwise one steadily produced sound changes almost abruptly into the next. This is "line" or legato.

A difference which does not show in these sonagrams is that the sung version is actually ten decibels louder than it appears in comparison with the spoken version. That is, the sonagraph was set appropriately for the sound level of each sample in order to get the best graphic result, and the difference was ten decibels. Had the same setting been used in both, either speech or song would have been distorted by the Sonagraph. Ten decibels is roughly the difference between a violin and a trumpet. This difference exists even though the spoken line is produced as if to be heard by a congregation.

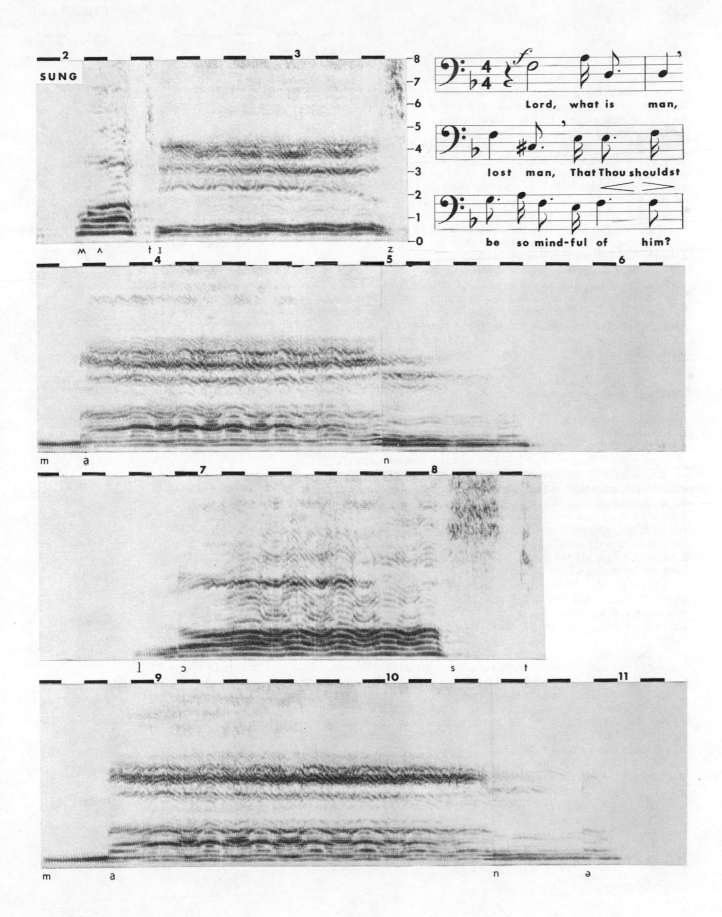

SUNG

Lord, what is man,

lost man, That Thou shouldst

be so mind-ful of him?

Note that the singing voice has better "focus" than the speaking, that is, there are fewer visible formants in each sung vowel, and these are stronger than in the spoken vowel. Anyone can make an approximate scale by marking the edge of a card with the kilocycles from 0 to 8 and placing this scale on the vowel under consideration. In the word "Lord," the vowel [ɔ] shows formants at about 500 cps. and 1000 cps. The second formant is somewhat higher than the average for this vowel. The third formant is located at 2400 cps. in song and a little higher in speech. So far they are much alike. But there are at least 7 formants visible in the spoken [ɔ] extending clear to the top, whereas in the sung [ɔ] there are 6 at most, with negligible sound energy above 3750 cps. In other vowels the difference is still more visible. Compare the spoken pattern with the sung in [æ] in the second "man," [ɑ] in "Thou," [ʊ] in "shouldst," and [i] in "be." In each case the spoken sound energy is "spread" throughout more formants and usually over a greater frequency range.

An example of intentional "spreading" is in the word "lost." This was done technically by forcing what would otherwise be a breathy production, and psychologically by "painting" the word with emotion. The spoken [ɔ] is an almost solid gray mass from top to bottom of the spectrum, except for the vowel formants, which are darker. The sung [ɔ] is also "painted" but in better focus. Compare with the [ɔ] in "Lord."

There are 15 syllables in our text. Visible formants in the main vowel of each syllable (except the word "lost" which is impossible to evaluate) total 89 in speech and 71 in song, an average of 6.34 formants in a spoken vowel and only 5.07 in a sung vowel. The ratio is about 19:15. The number is less significant than the relative strength of the formants. In a good sung tone there will be two or three strong formants which predominate. In speech there is a tendency for several formants to be all the same weight, either all weak or all strong depending upon the overall loudness of the syllable.

This line from Purcell was selected partly because it contains both the Dull Vowel (Par. 487-492) and the Bad Vowel (Par. 500-507) as well as the word "Lord," which presents the problem of the final [r] with another consonant (Par. 636-640). Note that the [r] must be heard, otherwise "Lord, what is man?" becomes "Laud what is man! "

If the singer is scrupulous in stopping phonation while the resonators are still closed, [m] and [n] need have no after-syllables. However this is difficult in emphatic declamation and a final [ə] is recorded in two places in these sonagrams after "man." They may perhaps be called flaws in the diction.

We think of [s] as an unchanging sound, but the sonagram shows vowel formants being whispered under it. As the tongue moves from the [i] position of the preceding word, "be," to the vowel [o] which is to follow the [s] we see the second formant go down from the [i] position (about 3000 cps.) to that of [o] (about 500 cps.). This is marked with an arrow in the second line of this page. Note also that "so" has a diphthong in speech [soʊ], but a monophthong in song [so].

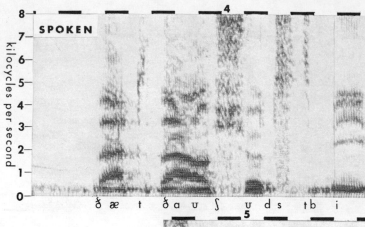

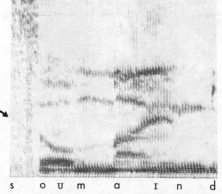

Fig. 66, continued

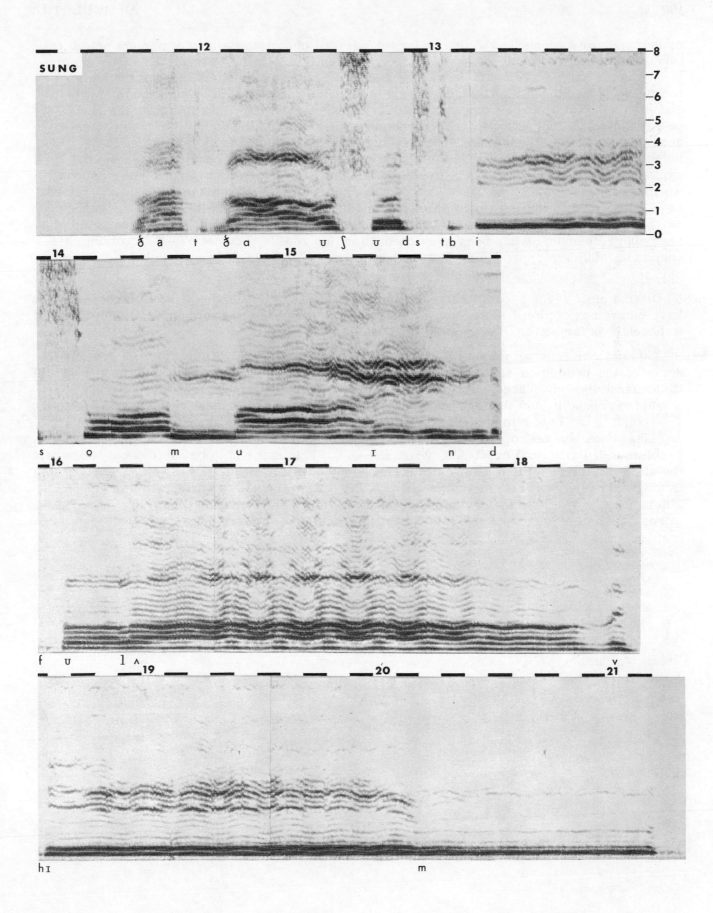

or hummed for a moment, and then released, with the phonation ceasing a moment before the formation is relaxed. Otherwise an extra syllable will be formed. Fricatives should be prolonged in the same way, and if they are voiced, the vocal part must not survive the high frequency. The stop-consonants deserve a little individual attention. The sonants [g], [d], and [b] are bound to make extra syllables at the end of a phrase. I do not think this is too objectionable. If they seem to be too prominent, they can be altered into their voiceless analogues at exactly the moment that they are exploded. That is to say, they should be voiced as they are closing, but in the instant of the stop the phonation will cease, and the explosion should be in the form of the surd. This is largely what the Germans do in such words as *"Lied," "lieb,"* and *"ewig"* which sound to us as if they ended in [t], [p], and "soft k" [ç], (Siebs, p. 73). Those surds which are inside the mouth, [k] and [t], will make enough noise without phonation, by virtue of the resonance of the mouth, but [p] will be inaudible at a very short distance, as has been mentioned. For this reason, I do not object to voicing this sound very delicately, producing just the faintest after-syllable, if it comes at the end of a phrase.

688   Diction must never become a technical display. Like good tailoring it is unobtrusive. "You have marvelous diction," is a fine compliment; but, "I understood every word without giving it a thought," is far better.

689   This chapter ends with a set of sonagrams, the study of which will provide illustration of some of the principles set forth, (Par. 497, 504, 506, 604, 619, 640, 647, 670). The selection is the first line of "Three Divine Hymns" as set to music by Henry Purcell. I sang it and then spoke it, and the tape recordings were processed by James Irwin on a Kay Electric Sonagraph in the Laboratory of Laryngeal Research at the University of California, Los Angeles, Hans von Leden, Director. The passage contains the word "Lord," illustrating the problem of [r] with final consonant, (Par. 636-640). This happens to be another case in which the silent [r] distorts the meaning. Purcell clearly does not mean, "*Laud* what is man!" Man is unlaudable and in great need of the *Lord*. The text also has key words containing [æ] and others with [ʌ, ə]. Note that "man" is pronounced [mæn] in speech, but [man] in song. The words "mindful of" are spoken with schwas, [maɪndfəl əv], but are sung [maɪndful ʌv].

Chapter 8

COORDINATION

690   A knowledge of the various processes involved in singing is like a disjointed skeleton until their interrelation is understood. An organism is greater than the sum of all its parts, and no analytical study discovers the whole truth until it leads to synthesis. Of what use is the valve without the breath pressure? Can one understand the vowels without a knowledge of both vibrator and resonators, and a knowledge of their coordination? What meaning has all this without articulation?

691   A pedagogy can major upon some one essential of voice production, such as breathing, or the developing of the registers, or the shaping of the resonators, or the training of the ear—the mental concept of the tone; and such a pedagogy can succeed if its particular stress is made to imply all the others. Usually such a teacher will say, "I teach breathing; if a pupil breathes correctly it will necessarily release the valve and activate the resonators"; or, "I try to give the student a proper concept of the tone, and the power of the mind over the mechanism is such that the ideal will command the proper support and the correct adjustments"; or will make a similar statement to the effect that some other aspect of production is the touchstone. I agree in each case, as far as the teacher's own pupils are concerned, because each teacher tends to attract those students who will be most benefited by his own method. If after a certain amount of breath-control pedagogy, for example, a student is getting nowhere, he will perhaps go to someone who stresses resonance imagery, and find himself. A versatile teacher tries as many approaches as possible, until he discovers the one that works with each pupil. The important thing is that all the essentials of singing are so interrelated that if a student can be led into a profound knowledge of any one phase of his art, he will learn the others along with it.

692   The one thing that all must achieve is coordination. This is what every teacher works for in his studio. His analytical knowledge of the mechanism is like the sub-basements of a skyscraper; there may never be occasion for it to be displayed, but it is necessary foundation. Studio time should not be spent in academic discussion unless it leads to practical results. The student can learn as much as he likes from books, and can check his knowledge by questioning the teacher, but the main purpose of the lesson time is to practice the coordination of the vocal act. From time to time a teacher may need to bring specific technical details into attention. Most teachers will do this, even though they decry "local effort"; their real hesitation is where they are not sure of themselves. If they are certain that some particular of the pupil's technic is incorrect, they will ask him to correct it. But most of the training is in the coordination of the entire instrument —more than that, the entire personality.

693   The foundation for teaching this is a knowledge of what is being coordinated. There remains a great deal to be discovered by the scientists, but that is no excuse for refusing to learn as much as we can of what is already known. A man may never learn the mechanics of his own car, but if he hires a chauffeur, he has a right to expect him to look under the hood occasionally. It is sometimes said, "You don't have to take your watch apart in order to tell time," and I agree. The singer need not analyze his art in order to sing. But if my watch does not keep good time I take it to someone who can take it apart. To help a singer who does not sing well, a teacher must be able to analyze. Several releases of the National Association of Teachers of Singing, listing the sub-

191

ject matter recommended for the curriculum of a voice teacher, include in addition to musical courses such courses as: Anatomy and Physiology of the Vocal Tract, Physics and Acoustics of Musical Sound, Terminology, etc. Such is the information included in our first six chapters. In this one we shall try to integrate our knowledge, stressing not those technical questions which are still debated by the anatomists, but those general principles which experience tells us are essential to good singing.

Neurology

694   A field which the voice scientists are just beginning to investigate is neurology. The brain is the control of all the individual skills which make up the complex act of singing, and the nerves are the means by which energy is supplied the mechanism at the will of the central control. Forward-looking authors (Gray and Wise, West et al., Denes and Pinson, Judson and Weaver, Van Riper and Irwin) include a chapter on neurology in their writings, and in listing the musculature mention the nerve supply of each muscle. The secret of coordination is somewhere in this realm. Some advocates of the importance of posture intimate that the proper position of the spine promotes healthy nerve supply to the organs of the voice. There can be no doubt that mental buoyancy, confidence, and general well-being are necessary for the most perfect coordination.

695   The nerve supply to the muscles of the body is not "direct," but "alternating current." A more accurate statement would be that nerves cannot activate muscles constantly, but instead provide a series of impulses. As we have seen in several instances, muscular activity always involves antagonism between two sets of muscles. Nerve impulses tend to alternate between the agonists and antagonists, so that one relaxes while the other contracts. This is called *diadochocinesis*. For ordinary efforts this alternating supply of energy results in smooth movements, but not always.

696   We might compare this with the power in an electric motor. Around the revolving part is a series of magnets which exert their pulls successively. Ordinarily the movement of the wheel is smooth and powerful. However, if the motor is placed at a disadvantage, the pull of the magnets becomes jerky. If you will resist the movement of a wheel so energized, allowing it to turn slowly, you will feel the successive tugs against your finger. In delicate performance these irregularities in the power show up unfortunately. For example, the "wow" in a poor recording is due to the fact that although the wire or tape apparently was moving smoothly through the machine, it really was going through in a series of jerks, and the variations in speed made variations in pitch.

697   Ordinarily, the muscles of the body work smoothly. However, if they weary, or if they fail in some other way, they begin to tremble and the movement becomes jerky. If a man will hold his arm out from his side, his hand will be steady until the muscles become tired, and then it will shake. If it is holding a weight, the shakiness will be sooner. If he is ill or "nervous," or intoxicated, it will shake still sooner and more violently. In voice production, small muscles are performing a delicate activity. Their movements result in sound, and the fluctuation in the energy of these muscles makes itself heard in the tone. This is called *vibrato*.

Normal Vibrato

698   Perhaps the greatest scientific authority on the vibrato is Seashore, the same psychologist who developed the famous tests of musical talent known by his name. Seashore supervised extensive research concerning the vibrato by Metfessel, Tiffin, Wagner, Rothschild, Linder, Easley, Hattwick, Hollinshead, Reger, et al., whose findings were published in 1932. Later Seashore summarized and partially revised the original material in a smaller volume, and condensed it still more into one chapter of his book, "Psychology of Music." These studies make it clear that our ears are subject to illusions in this matter and that most of us simply do not hear what

actually happens. I refer you to the original sources and limit myself here to the more established beliefs plus a few personal observations.

699   According to Seashore:[2] "A good vibrato is a pulsation of pitch, usually accompanied with synchronous pulsations of loudness and timbre, of such extent and rate as to give a pleasing flexibility, tenderness, and richness to the tone," (p. 7). The frequency of the vibrato is normally between six and seven times per second. The relation of this to innervation is emphasized by the fact that stammering and other spasmodic movements are at the same frequency. Vibrato is a perfectly normal phenomenon, however, which is the result of the intermittent supply of nerve energy to the mechanism. It may be caused by tremor in any of the muscles involved, breathing muscles, or muscles of the resonators. It can be felt sometimes in the epigastrium, and various authorities have attributed it to the diaphragm. Recently though, two men (Osborn, Wade) working independently came up with fluoroscopic evidence that the diaphragm does not pulsate with the vibrato, but moves steadily upward as the tone is produced. Both of these men, by the way, happen to be flutists and their information about vocal vibrato was incidental to studies of flute vibrato. Sometimes it can be seen in the soft palate or the tongue or even the jaw. The latest electromyographic evidence is that vibrato is in the cricothyroids (Mason and Zemlin) which is not surprising since it is primarily a pitch phenomenon, and the cricothyroids are the main determiners of pitch (Par. 227). Mason and Zemlin also found some diadochocinesis between the cricothyroids and the mylohyoids under certain conditions, though if this leads to a trembling jaw it is usually considered a danger signal.

700   Acoustically, the vocal vibrato is a fluctuation in pitch, intensity, and timbre. The pitch has been shown to vary at least a semi-tone. Recording instruments have measured this definitely in such great voices as Caruso, Chaliapin, Galli-Curci, Gigli, Hackett, Jeritza, Martinelli, Ponselle, Schumann-Heink, Tetrazzini and others, (Metfessel pp. 31, 34). You can prove it yourself by playing at half speed a recording of any good artist. At slow speed the wobble becomes obvious; doubling the speed produces an amusing chatter. The ear ordinarily hears only a mean pitch, which is in tune with the rest of the music. The other pitches one mistakes for timbre, and one is likely to call the presence of vibrato "richness," or "resonance," or even "overtones."

701   If you like disabusing yourself of illusions, you can train your ear to hear the pitch fluctuation. It is largely a matter of concentration. However, I recommend courage in this venture, lest it spoil your enjoyment of vocal music. While acquiring the art of analyzing vibrato, do not lose the ability to listen as most people do. It is particularly dangerous to become self-conscious about your own vibrato, so that you try to alter it consciously and directly. The law of reversed effort is likely to defeat your purpose and make your vibrato more pronounced, even objectionable. When you hear the tremor in your voice, do not be afraid of it. Remember that it is normal.

702   Much of what we seem to hear as variation in intensity is really our ears' interpretation of the pitch variation. However, there is some true intensity vibrato, at least part of the time. It results in fluctuation in timbre, which is not quite so noticeable. Bartholomew shows us four spectra derived from a baritone's singing of the vowel [ɑ] on middle C_4, (p. 22). The first one shows a very strong frequency close to "2800." The second, .050 second later, shows intensity building in the region of the [ɑ] formant (in this case, the fourth partial, C_6 above the treble staff) with the "2800" weakening. The third is a more flute-like spectrum, with a strong second partial, .107 second later than the first spectrum. The fourth is identical with the first spectrum, .160 second later. That is, at intervals of .16 second, the cycle repeats itself exactly. The tone becomes alternately reedy and flute-like, the high ringing partial going on and off like a telephone bell. A glance at almost any sonagram in this book will show the on-and-off nature of certain overtones in the vibrato. Indeed, Helmholtz noticed this back in 1875, and commented,

In powerful male voices singing *forte*, these partial tones sound like a clear tinkling of little bells, accompanying the voice, and are most audible in choruses when the singers shout a little. Every individual male voice at such pitches produces dissonant upper partials. . . . This kind of tinkling is peculiar to human voices; orchestral instruments do not produce it in the same way either so sensibly or so powerfully. I have never heard it from any other musical instrument so clearly as from human voices, (p. 116).

Helmholtz locates the frequency band for these "little bells" at from 2640 to 3168. Notice that he calls them "dissonant" partials. As we have seen, they may even be inharmonic. It requires energy to make the high partials of a tone sound, and only during the moments of high intensity can we expect the "ring" of "2800" to sound.

703   Upon analysis, all this would seem to be unmusical, but as a matter of fact, the ear only finds such a tone more interesting. What I have been describing here is characteristic of the finest production, such as we all enjoy. Indeed, musicians have liked it so much that it is imitated on most of the orchestral instruments. The string players cause the finger to rock back and forth on the string. Actually this produces less pitch fluctuation than in the voice, about one fifth of a tone as opposed to a semi-tone or more. Woodwind players bite their reeds at the desired frequency. Some flutists practice a series of puffs, four to each tick of a metronome set at 100 (which works out to six and two thirds per second) so that when they wish they can impart fluctuating breath pressure to the flute tone. However, as I have mentioned (Par. 699), the modern idea is not to flutter the diaphragm but to cultivate something akin to the vocal vibrato mechanism. The organ, the celeste, the vibra-harp, etc., have mechanical tremulants of one kind or another. All these contrivances make the instruments sound more "human," or "emotional."

Undesirable Vibrato or Tremolo

704   On a violin, *tremolo* is produced by moving the bow up and down in rapid alternations. It is more violent than the vibrato, perhaps more rapid, and creates the impression of excitement. There is variation of intensity, but not of pitch. The piano can be played *tremolando* by striking the same key many times in rapid succession. The term is sometimes borrowed to apply to a fast or violent vocal vibrato. It would be better, perhaps, if it were not used for the voice at all. In an instrument it is good; in the voice it is objectionable. Furthermore, saying "tremolo" instead of "vibrato" implies a mechanistic difference, where the difference is really only in control. It is a distinction of degree, not of kind. One man's vibrato is another man's tremolo. The distinction is largely esthetic. There are those who call any vibrato a "wobble." More about this beginning in Par. 739.

705   When the vibrato becomes irregular, or when it covers too great a range of pitch or intensity, or when its frequency is too slow or too fast, it becomes objectionable. There is no way of controlling this directly. Indirect control by ear sometimes works if the singer can once get the concept in his mental ear; that is, if he can once be lucky enough to get a normal vibrato and remember it. No vocal problem requires more patience. It simply means that the muscular coordination is out of balance, and this can be cured, not by a few tricks, but by gradually learning the correct technic. When the singer is producing as he should, he will have a normal vibrato. If his is abnormal in any way, badgering him about it will only make it worse, since this will make him nervous. He will probably be aware of his problem, but he can still take an optimistic attitude toward it, and the teacher must help.

706   The frequency of the vibrato is a resultant from the normal frequencies of nerve impulses at various levels of coordination.

The rates of discharge for some of the better-known levels are as follows: cerebral cortex level, 8-10 per second; thalamus (emotional) level, 20 per second; medulla oblongata-cerebellum level, 30 per second; cord level, 60 per second. The rate of discharge is always dominated by the highest level which is functioning. Thus, in the normal person the cortical level dominates. Under conditions of disease, injury, or alcoholism, lower centers may gain dominance. For example, an individual with Wilson's disease when holding a teacup will be unable to keep it from vibrating at a rather rapid rate. Again, an elderly individual in speaking may do so with a tremulous voice. Finally, during emotional upsets, the normal rhythm and rate of speech may be completely altered, (Judson and Weaver, pp. 258, 259).

The 8-10 rate may be regarded as a maximum. The 6-7 frequency has been established as the average, but it need not be considered inconsistent with the higher rate, since it has been demonstrated that most artists speed up the vibrato occasionally. Of the singers mentioned in Par. 700, all but Hackett produced numerous examples at rates varying from 8 to 10. My own rate, however, is only 5, as seen in sonagrams in this book and Mason and Zemlin found this same slow rate in their subjects.

707   The pitch extent of the vibrato increases at times to a full tone or more. The ear usually interprets this as greater rapidity, rather than greater extent. Metfessel (p. 62) graphed such a "vibrato crescendo" in the voice of Caruso, near the end of "Favorita," (Victor Record 6005-A). Notice that in the first four seconds (the vertical lines are at one second intervals)

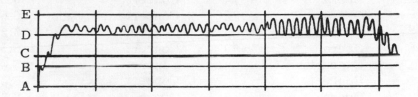

Fig. 67. Vibrato-Crescendo by Caruso

there are 29 vibrati, or a rate of 7.25. This is approximately Caruso's average rate, based upon 988 samplings of his voice by Metfessel, (p. 31). In the last two seconds, there are 15.5 vibrati. The rate has increased to 7.75. At the same time the pitch extent increases from about one third of a tone to at least two thirds. The ear is not likely to hear this at all, but to evaluate the whole thing in terms of increase in rate and intensity. We must remember two things which may explain Caruso's fast vibrato. He was always elated. After all, he was undisputed king of the Met. Also, he forced. It is a matter of medical record that this deprived him of one season at La Scala (Panconcelli-Calzia) and another at the Met. These factors imparted a phenomenal excitement to his voice. Does this argue that we should encourage students to force? It raises an interesting enthical question. Certainly we should try to keep them elated!

708   When the voice is under the control of the highest brain centers the muscular action is steady, and the vibrato is normal, but when the poise of the singer is inadequate, and emotional factors become dominant, the vibrato will be too fast. Attaining the necessary poise is not simply a matter of relaxing momentarily, taking a few deep breaths, smiling, and practicing a little auto-hypnosis. It is all these things applied continuously and courageously over so long a period of time that they have become a way of life. And in addition, the technic of production must be perfected because any unnecessary tension, any forcing, any unbalance of coordination may manifest itself in tremolo.

Technical Control of the Vibrato

709   The technical cause of exaggeration of the vibrato is doubtless overloading. Overtaxing any muscle will induce tremor, and the greater the tax, the more violent the trembling. This is illus-

trated by the fact that opera singers have more rapid vibrati than concert singers, as a rule. It
is not just a matter of opera singers being better, and fast vibrato being related to their superiority, because usually the same singer's rate decreases in concert where he does not have to
compete in volume with a sixty-piece orchestra.

710   In 1929 Easley analyzed the vibrati of five primarily concert and five primarily opera singers, with the following results, (p. 271, 272):

Artist	Type of Singer	Type of Selection	Rate	Extent
Galli-Curci	Opera	Opera	7.4	.46
Caruso	Opera	Opera	7.1	.43
Jeritza	Opera	Opera	6.9	.59
Lashanska	Concert	Concert	6.9	.40
Caruso	Opera	Concert	6.8	.43
Martinelli	Opera	Opera	6.8	.38
Marsh	Concert	Concert	6.7	.43
Martinelli	Opera	Concert	6.6	.30
Galli-Curci	Opera	Concert	6.6	.31
Jeritza	Opera	Concert	6.5	.39
Gigli	Opera	Concert	6.5	.46
Crooks	Concert	Concert	6.4	.36
Baker	Concert	Concert	6.3	.30
Gigli	Opera	Opera	6.3	.48
Dadum	Concert	Concert	6.2	.45

711   Overloading the larynx, either by trying for too much volume or a pitch too high for the register adjustment, may cause the vibrato to bog down and become irregular. These violent jerks in
the voice, unless they become chronic, are no serious problem, since they can be eliminated
merely by relaxing the pressure and removing the overload. If the overloading is habitual, the
jerkiness will be persistent. Here the problem is not so much emotional as technical, though the
two difficulties may easily be interrelated. Proper coordination of breath to laryngeal tension
can be learned directly and consciously by patient application.

712   The descending portamento (see my exercise the "yawn-sigh," Par. 771, 786) is useful to
eliminate vibrato because it relaxes the valve. A few singers will show a bad shake even in
this exercise, but their chances of smoothing it out are better than in another exercise.

713   However, you must not expect the improvement to be sudden. There are many separate skills
involved in good voice technic, and until they all reach a certain level of perfection, they cannot
integrate and the end product is almost as poor as at the beginning of study. There are likely to
be "plateaus of learning," dead levels, which must be traversed patiently and optimistically, without observable progress.

Emotional Control of the Vibrato

714   While the technic is being improved, emotional controls must be developed. Sensitive singers
frequently vary the vibrato while imparting emotional quality to the song. They do this by entering so into the mood of the composition that the intensity of expression involuntarily exaggerates
the vibrato. This is one of the marks of a great artist, whose technical foundation is so correctly
established that he can afford to sing "naturally." Occasional speeding of the vibrato is far from
objectionable. I find that students who have an unpleasantly rapid vibrato correct its qualities
of irregularity and overintensity first. If it is fairly smooth and slows even a little, a slightly ab-

normal rate gives the impression of great vitality and emotion. When the student realizes that the obnoxious qualities have disappeared, his morale is so improved that the rate slackens and the voice becomes peaceful. They are then ready to apply the reverse of the principle I have just described, that is, they are ready to sing restful, sostenuto selections, which will slow down the vibrato still more.

715   A student who is inhibited in dramatic expression, or who is emotionally phlegmatic, may have too slow a vibrato. I have heard some who would allow it to ritard at the end of a phrase. Here emotional stimulation is needed. The singer must be enabled to feel the power of the music and to impart more vibrancy of the voice. It is safe to call attention to absence of vibrato in a singer's voice and to make him conscious of normal fluctuation in well-produced voices. His ear will often induce a vibrato. However, I repeat that it is of no value to make a student self-conscious if he has a tremolo. He will gain no emotional poise if you badger him.

Musical Control of the Vibrato

716   Related to the emotional control of vibrato is the musical control, which consists of establishing the correct tempo of the piece. A good singer sets the tempo in multiples of his vibrato. That is, he tries to have his vibrato "come out even" for each beat, as in the case mentioned above where a flute player practices four vibrato cycles to each tick of the metronome. If, for example, a rapid scale passage is sung at such a tempo that the change of pitch must be at the wrong moment in the cycle, a poor singer finds it almost impossible to keep the notes even, and dotted rhythm results. Stanley[3] offers some interesting ideas in this connection, (Chap. 10, especially pp. 174 and 206-8). However, the speed of the performance is often determined by someone else, the conductor, for example, or one's partner in a duet. In such a case, a good singer unconsciously speeds or slows his vibrato to conform. If he has to sing three notes per second, his vibrato either slows to six per second, in which case he completes two cycles for each note; or it speeds to nine per second, with three cycles for each note. The emotional factors will probably determine whether he will accelerate or ritard. I do not mean to imply that the vibrato will necessarily be audible, but the rhythm of nerve supply is still a factor in the smoothness of the execution.

717   Like most controls of laryngeal function, this is indirect, but it is none the less real and should be cultivated. No exercise in velocity should be allowed to run away with the singer, and certainly an even scale passage must never sound like Dvorak's "Humoresque." Patience is the cure. The scale must be sung slowly and steadily, probably at a tempo in which there will be three or four comfortable nerve impulses for each note. The tone may be somewhat "lifeless" in the practice of keeping it steadily under control, but this will pass. Gradually the tempo can be increased, until the scale is clean and even. When the student is able to sing evenly at any tempo, he will indirectly have brought his vibrato under control.

718   Teachers of singing have always used rapid scales, and they are certainly necessary and beneficial. However, I prefer to use slow and simple scales first, such as the three-tone and five-tone scales, and slow, easy arpeggios, such as the major triad. In always doing rapid work I think there is a great danger of passing through the tones so hurriedly that their quality is not evaluated. I particularly object to fast arpeggios that quickly reach the highest notes of the compass, touching them so briefly that their strained production is not detected. I should like to add the utilitarian suggestion that instead of synthetic exercises for agility it is just as practical to use passages from the composers of the Classical Period. Let the student take them slowly and carefully at first, working for years on them if necessary, but when he has mastered the problem he will have a fine piece of repertoire. The public does not care to hear him do a splendid nine-tone scale, or even a vocalise by Vaccai, Sieber, or Concone, but they would enjoy a fine Bach or Handel aria.

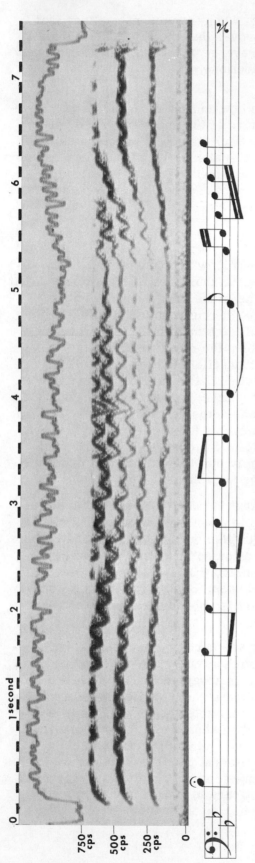

Fig. 68. Vibrato in Scale Passage

Sonagram of the author singing a B flat major scale, by Yasuo Koike at the Institute of Laryngology, Hans von Leden, director. Top line of sonagram is graph of intensity. The two figures on this page cannot be compared with others in this book, because in order to make changes in the pitch of the voice more obvious the time scale (marked at top in tenths of a sec.) is condensed, and the frequency scale (marked in cps. at left) expanded so that only lowest partials appear. Complete scale is seen best in second partial, though the low B₂ flat shows best in fourth partial. Note reduction of vibrato extent with decrescendo on this tone, reverse of vibrato-crescendo in Fig. 67. There are two vibrati for each tone in descending scale, at this singer's normal rate of 5 per sec. Rapid ascending scale, "on the vibrato" (Stanley), is at 6 per sec.

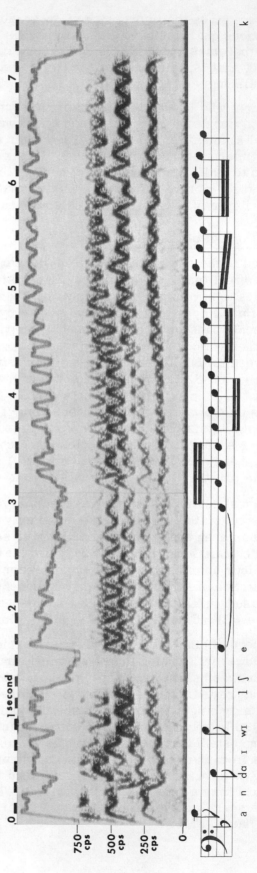

Fig. 69. Vibrato in Baroque Run

Sonagram by Yasuo Koike of the author singing "And I will shake," as these words first are heard in Thus Saith the Lord (Messiah) by Handel. IPA symbols appear across the bottom, each placed as nearly as possible at the point where that sound begins. Since only the lowest frequencies of the sonagram are shown (see comment for Fig. 68) only the lower formants of the vowels are seen, and [ʃ] and [k] show only in the intensity graph, as much weaker sounds than the vowels. Entire run is seen best in second partial. Vibrato-decrescendo appears in C₃ at beginning of word "shake." Normal vibrato rate is 5 per sec, but the run is at 6 per sec. Intensity graph shows marcato on each word and also each 16th note in the run.

719   Fig. 68 is a sonagram of my voice in a slow descending scale followed by a rapid ascending
scale. Notice that in the slow scale the changes of pitch are made at points where the vibrato
cycle will not be disturbed. After four complete cycles on the uppermost tone there are two
cycles for each descending tone. The ascending scale is "on the vibrato" as Stanley put it.
While my normal vibrato rate, 5 per second, is apparent in the sustained tones, the rate for the
ascending scale has been speeded up to 6. Slow passage work is felt to originate in the abdominal
muscles, but the more rapidly one sings the more one feels that the breath pressure is strong
and steady and the articulation of the run is in the glottis itself, an almost involuntary flutter.
Such passages should be learned at slow tempi. At slow speeds each note will sound cleanly and
and the singer should be conscious of attacking each individual pitch in the run. It is sometimes
necessary to delay working for legato and have the singer use an initial [h] for each tone, eventually minimizing it until it is only imaginary. Garcia[2] recognized the value of practicing not only
legato, but also *marcato, portamento, staccato,* and *aspirato,* (p. 20).

720   For an idea of how this works out in a baroque division, see Fig. 69. This is the first word
"shake" in "Thus saith the Lord," (Messiah) by Handel. The sustained tones at the beginning
and the end have a vibrato of 5 per second, while the run itself speeds up to 6. In such passages
I feel that each tone is articulated by a separate impulse from the abdominal muscles. As the
volume increases the intensity display at the top of the sonagram shows a distinct impulse for
each tone in the run. When I produce turns and mordants the rate sometimes reaches 7 per
second, but this is only when the control shifts from the breathing muscles to the larynx.

The Trill

721   The trill is an exaggerated vibrato, initiated voluntarily and maintained under some control
for a specific purpose. Garcia[2] defines it as "a rapid, equal and distinct alternation of two notes
at the distance of a major or minor second, according to the position of the trill in the scales,"
(p. 42). He adds that it is produced "by a very loose and swift oscillation of the larynx." Few
singers today have mastered it, but as it becomes more and more apparent that the public en-
joys florid display more and more singers will give it the practice it requires. It is comparatively easy to make some kind of tremulous imitation, but a really perfect trill is another
matter.

722   In some cases the rate of the vibrato increases for the trill. For example, Richard Conrad
(singing "Care Selve," London Record 5834, "The Age of Bel Canto") has a vibrato of $5\frac{1}{2}$ per
second, but his trill is at 8. In more cases, however, the rate is essentially the same for both.
The exaggeration which causes the ear to hear a trill instead of a single tone is in the pitch extent, and it appears that sometimes, especially when the volume increases, the intensity vibrato
becomes an important factor.

723   In early studies, Metfessel discovered that when musicians were asked to appraise a tone
with a vibrato they reported hearing a "pulsation" of intensity but only one pitch. This pitch
was the mean pitch of the vibrato, which was sounded only in passing; the vibrato actually hovers
around two pitches, one above and one below. Under Metfessel's guidance, Makepeace extended
the listening test, both in number of subjects and in variety of test. He first asked them simply
to tell which of several pitches matched that of a certain electronically produced vibrato that
was mechanically perfect and carefully measured as to pitch. The subjects all chose the
median pitch as being *the* pitch of the vibrato. In the second phase of the test the subjects were
told that the vibrato contained a high and a low and were asked to identify them. They selected
the pitches around which hover the upper and lower loops of the vibrato, (Fig. 71).

724   There are two factors that cause the ear to perceive a difference between the vibrato and the
trill. Both can be seen in the sonagram, Fig. 70, of the famous trill of Galli-Curci at the end of

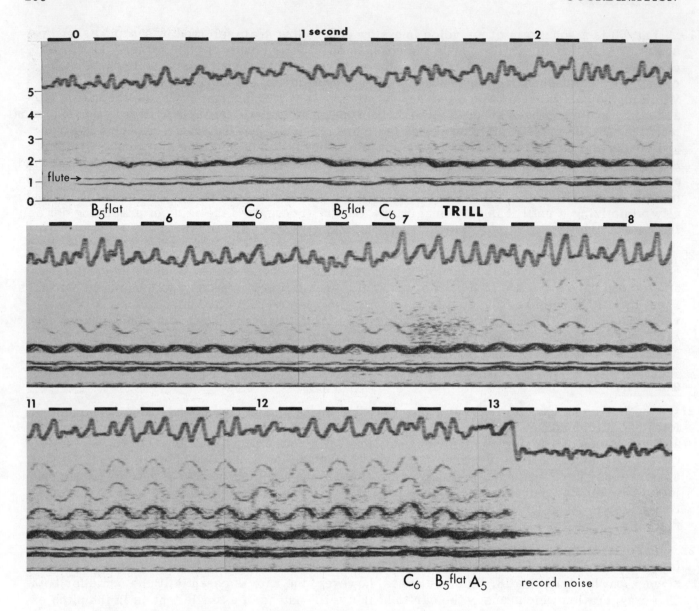

Fig. 70. Trill by Galli-Curci

Sonagram by Yasuo Kioke of trill by Galli-Curci at the end of the Mad Scene (Lucia) by Donizetti, Victor Record 74509. Time scale in tenths of sec. across top. Sonagrams read across both pages. Frequency scale in kilocycles at upper left. Upper line of sonagram is graph of intensity. Note "soft" (imaginary [h]) attack. Full strength of second partial does not show until 0.1 sec. after fundamental begins. Pitch vibrato is best seen in second partial, and in higher partials when they come in. Extent of vibrato on normal tones is about a quarter step above and below perceived pitch, which increases to a minor third or more for the trill. There is a slow trill of B₅ flat and C₆ repeated with acceleration. B₅ flat has 4 vibrati, C₆ has 3, B₅ has 1, C₆ has 2, and then the trill begins. When the trill is really established, a clear pattern has developed in the intensity vibrato, with two peaks for each cycle of pitch vibrato, continuing through the last 10 sec. of the trill. There is one accent for the high pitch and another

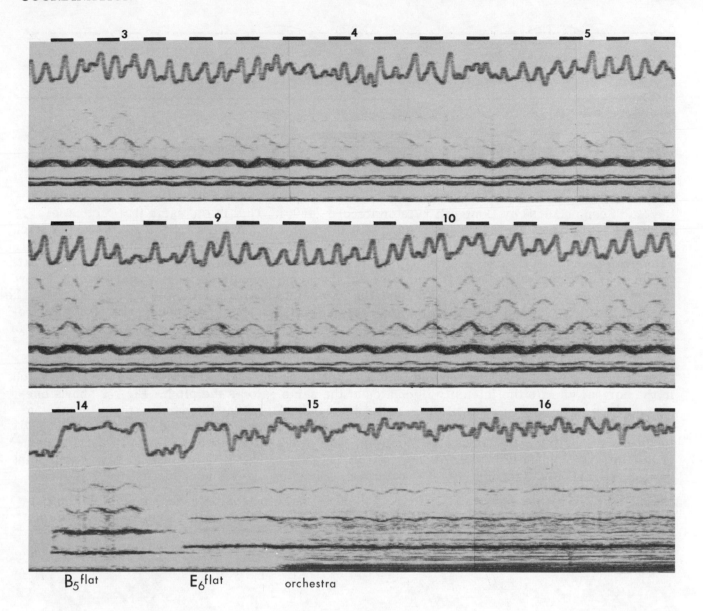

Fig. 70, continued

for the low, thus defining the trill. End of the trill is ornamented with a three tone scale "on
the vibrato" (Stanley), C_6 B_5 flat, A_5. After 0.65 sec. pause, the final cadence, B_5 flat to E_6
flat, is sounded. There is a separation between the two tones, but reverberation in the room
makes the fundamentals seem to overlap. Note that almost all the sound energy of the E_6 flat
is in its fundamental. Intensity vibrato has one main high for each cycle of normal pitch
vibrato, though record noise, orchestra, etc. create confusing irregularities in this curve. The
flute obbligato shows as straight lines between the first two partials of the voice. Note that
during the long trill the flute is in phase with the voice part of the time and out part of the time.
The ear does not perceive any dissonance, proving that the phase relationship between strong
vibrati need not be unmusical as opponents of the use of vibrato argue.

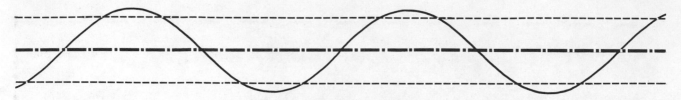

Fig. 71. Schema of Vibrato Perception
Solid line, actual fundamental frequency. Heavy dot-and-dash line, pitch perceived by in-
nocent ears. Fine broken lines, pitches perceived if listener has been conditioned to hear two.
Discussion in Par. 703.

the Mad Scene (Lucia) by Donizetti (Victor Record 74509). This is the same that Metfessel
analyzed years ago. First there is a slow trill in which her normal vibrato can be seen on each
tone. The pitch extent is about a quarter step above and below the perceived pitch. The slow trill
accelerates and then the true shake begins, in which the rate remains Galli-Curci's vibrato rate
(in this case $6\frac{1}{2}$ per second) but the fundamental frequency modulates from a quarter tone below
B_5 flat to a like interval above C_6, causing the listener to hear a whole step trill on B_5 flat. The
great coloratura begins the trill softly and crescendos three times, dropping back to softer production each time in order to make a greater crescendo. From the moment of the first surge of
volume an interesting thing becomes apparent in the intensity vibrato. Two peaks of intensity
vibrato can be counted for each cycle of pitch vibrato. It appears that these impulses call the
attention of the listener to the top and bottom of the pitch fluctuation, rather than the mean pitch.
In the normal vibrato the intensity fluctuates at the same rate as the pitch. Fig. 72 shows one
second each of trills by Callas, Horne, and Sutherland. All are at the same rate as the normal
vibrato, or nearly so. All show the wide pitch extent, between a major and a minor third. The
tendency for the intensity vibrato to double the rate of the pitch vibrato is seen in varying degrees, depending upon the energy being used in the production. It is difficult to say at this point
how significant this discovery is. More analysis including many singers is needed.

725   The traditional way of acquiring a trill, or shake, is an extension of the principles just outlined for all vocal agility. That is, the singer begins with a slow trill, and then speeds it up.

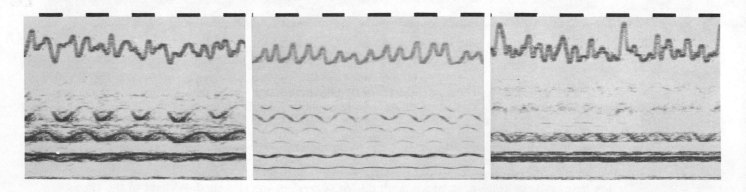

Fig. 72. Trills by Callas, Horne, and Sutherland
Sonagrams by Yasuo Koike, one second each in duration. Extracts from the trill from the
Mad Scene (Lucia) by Donizetti, as sung by, left, Maria Callas (Angel Record 35379), and right,
Joan Sutherland (London Record 5515). Middle, trill on D_5 by Marilyn Horne, sung at the
Institute of Laryngeal Research, Hans von Leden, director. Intensity vibrato at double the rate
of the pitch vibrato similar to the phenomenon in the Galli-Curci trill (Fig. 70) appears in vary-
ing degrees of clarity. Full significance of this finding awaits further investigation.

However, it is impossible to speed up a voluntary action to the frequency expected in a trill. Deliberate action, as the word suggests, is slow. Instrumental trills are produced by alternating contraction in the muscles of two fingers, each of which alone is not moving so fast. Rapid tonguing of a trumpet is thought in syllables like "tu ku" in which the muscles which produce the "t" alternate with those that produce the "k."

726   We may say, then, that when a singer trills, she (today the trill is cultivated largely by women, indeed, mostly sopranos, although our resurgence of interest in Rossini and Donizetti is tempting more men to develop trills) begins with a deliberate alternation of pitch at comparatively slow tempo, and then allows the trill to establish itself, as it were. It is really involuntary. The only controls are those which begin and end it, and a mental concentration which keeps it within such bounds that the audience experiences the auditory illusion that it is on two distinct pitches.

727   A trill which is merely a flutter of intensity without a wide enough variation in pitch is a poor substitute, though one often hears it. In order to induce a good trill, the singer, instead of beginning slowly and gradually speeding up, is more often told to begin at a slow, but definite tempo, and then double it, and redouble, until finally the trill begins. Another exercise consists of sing-

ing several sustained notes with grace notes (half or whole step above) preceding each attack, and then suddenly at the desired moment going into the shake, in which both the upper and lower notes become rapidly alternating grace notes.

728   In a lesson which was being recorded on tape, a soprano student, D. R., sang an F_5 (top of treble staff) with such an excessive vibrato that I told her it was almost a trill. I asked her to exaggerate her already extreme vibrato a bit more while concentrating on F_5 and G_5, which were sounded on the piano. She was asked to sing first a slow trill and then to "throw in the flutter as if giggling or chuckling." The result was a respectable trill, which she said felt like "a very loose note." Miss D. R. was able to produce both a half-step and a whole-step trill, and to differentiate them she said, "I think the top note." She was also asked to inhibit the trill and to sing the exact opposite as nearly as possible. The attempt at a "straight tone" on F_5 produced a normal vibrato.

729   Sonagrams of the three productions are shown in Fig. 73. The three samples were all recorded within a ten-minute period. Note that the rate of the pitch vibrato is the same in all three samples, 6 per second. The extent of the pitch vibrato is greatest for the trill and least for the normal vibrato. The intensity vibrato is much milder in extent for the normal vibrato, though it is difficult to match its rate in any way with the pitch vibrato. It is very rapid, but limited in extent so that the ear does not perceive it. The same rapid fluctuations are hinted in the other intensity vibrato samples, but in the trill one can see two main impulses per pitch vibrato beginning

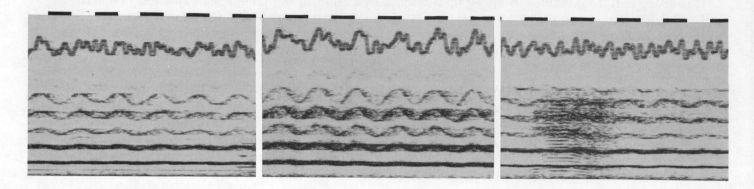

Fig. 73. Varying Extents of Vibrato

Sonagrams by Yasuo Koike, one second each in duration. Left, excessive vibrato or "wobble."
Middle, trill. Right, normal vibrato. All these sonagrams are from a recording of less than
ten minutes from a lesson of a young soprano student. Discussion in Par. 728, 729. What appears to be a blemish in the sonagram on the right is a word of approval from the teacher at
the moment the student achieved a normal vibrato.

to emerge as an audible pattern. The pattern is suggested in the "wobble," but is not as clearly
established.

Tones without Vibrato

730   The opposite extreme from having too fast a vibrato is having none at all. If a tone is well
produced it will have the fluctuation I have described, five to seven times per second, a variation
in pitch, intensity, and timbre. If it is produced with too much effort, or with lack of poise, the
frequency, extent, or both, will be greater. If, on the other hand, it is produced phlegmatically
it may have almost no vibrato. This is just as undesirable.

731   There seems to be a continuum from soft to loud which includes the following productions:
whispering < breathy singing < "spread" singing < yelling, (Par. 494, 495). Whispering is of
course straight, since it consists of resonance tone only. Breathy singing is almost always
straight. Spread singing is likely to be straight, though as it becomes louder, if the singer un-
derstands support, vibrato is likely to come in. If the vibrato is kept out of the fortissimo we
have yelling. Straight tones are not always spread or breathy, but they are likely to be so, and
if a singer is capable of singing either way, the tone always seems to be devitalized and inhibited
in comparison.

732   Some proponents of the straight tone argue that it is more "natural," like a speaking tone.
True, the speaking voice seldom has vibrato, but it is not straight either. It is inflected, that is,
a definite pitch is almost never sustained. In singing, where we must meet musical requirements, the voice modulates above and below the written pitch. Tiffany found that some vowels
are more recognizable when inflected than when not, and Triplett checked this in the singing
voice by preparing a listening test with 100 samples of vowels, 50 with and 50 without vibrato.
Qualified listeners found [i] and [u] to be the most recognizable (confirming Tiffany) but while
[i] was much more clear with vibrato than without, [u] was equally so in both conditions. This
is probably because while even a devitalized production will produce the two low formants of
[u], such production in a straight tone weakens the upper formant of [i] enough to impair the
vowel.

733   Any singer with a vibrato can learn to sing a straight tone if he wishes to do so, say for commercial reasons. The key is to get the straight tone in one's ear and accept the quality that nec-

essarily accompanies it. As long as you are trying to sing with your "best" production and merely inhibit the vibrato you will fail. You must be willing to let the tone spread.

734   Listen to the Bell Telephone recording I mentioned in Par. 594. You may be able to get it from their public relations department. Fill your ear with that mechanically straight tone singing, "Daisy, Daisy, give me your answer true," and imitate it. Or think back to some time you have forgotten when you sang a straight tone, perhaps as a Boy Scout singing at a campfire before vibrato had come into your voice.

735   Popular singers sing straight tones because they imitate each other. They scrupulously avoid imitating "serious" singers, lest it damage their style. A fine young lyric soprano was referred to me by a laryngologist who had treated her throat after she had been singing professionally in a show whose director kept demanding, "Don't sing, yell!"

736   The singer who has no vibrato does not free his larynx enough so that subtleties of tone can sound, and at the same time does not supply enough breath pressure. The tone is likely to be weak. It is almost impossible to sing loudly without vibrato. Stanley[3] points out the fact that vibrato tends to disappear in soft tones, (p. 32). This is not true of voices suffering from too rapid vibrato; from the threshold of audibility their quaver is present. But with ordinary singers, if the pianissimo is produced by allowing the tone to become weak, the vibrato will slow or even cease.

737   The quality of tone without vibrato is usually "dull," or at greater volume, "spread." There is never enough power or buoyancy to make the "2800" overtone sound, unless so much strain is developed that it sounds continuously, which is rare, but equally unpleasant. This on-and-off quality of the highest partials of a tone with good vibrato is what gives it is living, human sound. One explanation of vibrato-less tone might be that the laryngeal adjustment is static, so that there is no exchange of pull between the muscles, no diadochocinesis. The work is being done with such rigidity of the mechanism that such delicacy as the vibrato is impossible.

738   Most people agree that absence of vibrato is deplorable in a solo voice. The cure, as in the case of too much vibrato, is primarily the patient acquiring of better technic. In this case, the emphasis should be upon better breath support, and a more dynamic adjustment of the vocal cords. Some singers have induced vibrato directly in the breathing muscles, by exercises similar to the flute exercise already mentioned. I think, however, that the real difficulty is always to be found in the voice box. Appeals to the emotion through the imagination often help. The student needs to gain freedom, needs to produce tone with more abandon.

Vibrato in Ensembles

739   While there is general agreement that vibrato is essential to a solo voice, there is a strong group of authorities in the choral field who do not want it in the voices of their choirs. Undoubtedly a singer with a noticeable tremolo can ruin the ensemble, but the cure for this is either to correct the single voice or remove it from the choir. To me, "straight" tone can only be acquired at the expense of quality, and I like ringing voices. When I hear the concerts of choirs whose conductors have worked to eliminate all solo quality, I miss this vibrancy. It is true that they blend like one voice, and they make beautiful pianissimos. But this "one" voice is breathy to my ears, and their fortissimos never thrill me. They can do a long decrescendo on the last note of a selection, in which the tone becomes more and more breathy, and one by one the singers become inaudible, while their mouths are still hanging open, until finally the last vibration drifts away. But when there is an assignment for a solo voice in the group, it is usually disappointing, for this weak production is inadequate.

740   Several factors contributed to the vogue of the "straight tone," which I hope is passing. First there was the crystal microphone of the early days of radio. This primitive mike could actually be damaged by a strongly produced tone. Microphone technic in those days consisted of standing well back and turning away whenever you sang a forte. Rosa Raisa always sang with her back to the microphone! Those were the days of the crooner, and fortunes were made by singers who could not be heard in a hall without amplification. Such voices were breathy and straight and the industry preferred them to singers with powerful, vibrant tones. Needless to say, the crystal mike is now obsolete and so is the idea that only weak voices record well.

741   A second factor was the educational philosophy prevalent in the public schools. One idea of "progressive education" was to escape from disciplinarian teaching and drills for the perfection of skills, in favor of the development of the entire personality. In music education, drills in sight reading and anything resembling singing technic gave way to the "musical experience." The objective was to encourage as many students as possible to "make music together," a sociologically desirable end. Therefore the large high school and college chorus came into being and since they couldn't all be good singers, the directors settled for the lowest common denominator, the straight tone.

742   They called it the "a capella tone." A recognized weakness of progressive education was neglect of the gifted child. In vocal music, the gifted singer is the one with vibrato. Various surveys by Metfessel, Tiffin, Kwalwasser, Johnson, and others, show that a vibrato is rare among children, especially boys, and that only about one in five adults has one, (Metfessel, pp. 70-73), and this is usually considered a mark of talent. Such singers, however, stood out in the mass mediocrity which was called the "a capella choir," and either the singer learned to inhibit his vibrato (and incidentally his talent and his personality) or he was asked to leave. I have sympathy for accepting a breathy production from a high school choir because this avoids forcing their voices (See Par. 236). To carry this idea into the young adult university ensemble results in precious singing.

743   A third factor was the knowledge discovered by Seashore and his colleagues, though they certainly warned against the danger. I have mentioned the findings of Metfessel and Makepeace, (Par. 723). Seashore explained that the vibrato is a Gestalt which to the innocent ear gives the illusion of one median pitch, but alas, choir directors had eaten of the fruit of the tree of the knowledge of good and evil, and choral music was locked out of Eden.

744   Choir directors began listening to the two pitches of the vibrato, neither of which is the desired one. Furthermore, in an ensemble one singer's vibrato is going up while another's is going down, and there are different rates of vibrato. So the theory developed that perfect intonation was impossible except with a straight tone. To any good singer this is all a laughable fallacy—witness any operatic chorus in which every member sings like a soloist—but unfortunately many choral conductors are not singers.

745   About a generation ago it was considered essential to ensemble in an orchestra for the violins to play "straight" tone, for exactly the same reasons outlined above. Only in emotional passages and in solos was the performer permitted to move his left hand so as to "vibrate" the tone. Today the major symphonies require vibrato almost continuously, and it does not spoil the "purity" of their tone. Why should it be bad for choirs? Today only barn dance fiddles play "straight" tone. On such programs the same kind of production is appropriate for the vocalists.

746   Today they are moving gradually away from the ideal of no vibrato. The internationally celebrated St. Olaf Choir once gave impetus to the use of the straight tone, but its present conductor, Olaf Christiansen, prefers from his proteges a "stabilized vibrato" in which "the pitch deviation is limited to a reasonable extent," (p. 17).

747   Very little has been done to confirm or deny objectively the opinion that a straight tone is better in tune. Sister Joan Marie asked eight high school girls to sing simple vocalises in the upper, lower, and middle part of their voices, using three different vowels, with and without vibrato. The 72 pairs of recordings were analyzed by Naoaki Yanagihara on the Timcke Melody Writer at the University of California at Los Angeles. In most cases accuracy of intonation was unaffected by presence or absence of vibrato. In seven cases in the upper and middle voice it was found that the tone with vibrato was consistently higher than the straight tone. If the girl sharped with vibrato she was in tune with the straight tone, or if she was in tune with vibrato she was flat with the straight tone. In other words the straight tone is a less energetic production. In the case of one girl this was reversed, in her low voice. When she sang with enough freedom for a vibrato she was in tune, but the effort to inhibit the vibrato caused her to sharp.

748   Lately a few musicological arguments for the straight tone have arisen. It is argued that internal evidence in Renaissance music indicates that a straight tone was used and the paintings and drawings of the period give clues as to the vocal technic. There are many such pictures, and as I look at them I see different mouth openings and various signs of ease or strain—much the same variety as can be observed in any group of contemporary singers. Let us also remember that a painter sometimes paints what he sees literally, but often paints what he wants to see, and who is going to argue that the painters were authorities on singing technic?

749   As for the internal evidence of the music itself, this is a stronger argument. The compass of Renaissance music generally is so limited as to suggest that only one register was used. There are references to popular singing in other registers, but apparently court singers used mostly middle tones. This could mean that they sang rather lightly. There were also many ornaments, and some music historians feel that vibrato was one of these (by some other name, of course). In other words a cultivated singer could alternate straight tones and tones with vibrato at will—a useful skill today, in fact. There is the assertion that the music of Palestrina was to be sung in an echoing stone cathedral, and vibrato plus reverberation would be intolerable. It sounds plausible, especially when one remembers the hooty straight tone of some boy sopranos, but I am still demanding scientific confirmation. I see no reason why reverberation creates any more problem than that of the phase relationship between different vibratos in any choir in any auditorium. The argument has been proposed that the music of Gesualdo has such unusual and dissonant intervals that only with straight tone could it be accurately intoned. Here we go again! I know personally some of the fine young singers who recorded a Gesualdo album a few years ago, and I could tell you the scorn they had for the hoot they were required to use.

750   Hans Lampl has called to my attention two instances where an early musician referred directly to the vibrato, the only such references I know. In *Synlagma Musicum*, written by Praetorious during the years 1615-20, we read, "First of all a singer must have a beautiful, pleasantly vibrating (*zittern- und bebende*) voice, not, however, in the manner to which some singers in schools are accustomed," (Gurlitt, Vol. III, p. 231). Mozart admittedly comes later than the period we have been discussing. By his time singing had become virtuosic and registers were exploited to the full. In Gluck, certainly, we have intimations of power; "Alceste" is for dramatic soprano. (Full power of course waited for Wagner and Verdi. We have discussed the vibrato of Caruso.) But to return to Mozart, who certainly forced no voices, here is what he wrote his father, June 12, 1775: "Meissner, as you know, has a bad habit in that he often intentionally vibrates (*zittert*) his voice. . . and that I cannot tolerate in him. It is indeed truly detestable, it is singing entirely contrary to nature." If we stop at this point we have a musicological argument against the use of vibrato, but read on: "The human voice already vibrates of itself, but in such a degree that it is beautiful, that is the nature of the voice. One makes it also not only on wind instruments, but also on stringed instruments, yes even on the clavier," (Nohl, p. 160).

Apparently the old authorities took much the same view as those of today. A normal vibrato is inherent in a good voice, and excessive vibrato should be avoided.

751   The assumption that vibrato was invented in the 19th century is related to the idea that emotional expression waited till the Romantic period. Both concepts are widely held. They insult the humanity of singers of the past and impair the freedom of singers of the present.

752   Radio and TV ensembles, especially those who do popular music, cultivate a "straight" tone. The loss of vocal quality is more than they can afford. The weakness of tone is overcome by the microphone, but the timbre cannot be improved. Popular soloists often use the same dead type of voice, but when they have a long note they become a little ashamed of it, and many of them acquire the trick of beginning such a note with a devitalized tone and adding a flutter midway in its duration. This may or may not be a really good vibrato, but the effect to my ears is inartistic.

The Hemispheres of Coordination

753   In establishing goals of coordination, the student is likely to be confused by differences of opinion that seem to be incompatible. Even the student's own teacher may appear to contradict himself. One minute he asks for a certain kind of tone, possibly even demonstrating it, and a few minutes later he is asking for the exact opposite, and singing as an example a sound that is radically different. Even if the teacher shows a monotonous consistency in his objectives, the pupil hears that other teachers, equally successful, seem to have contrary standards.

754   Under these circumstances, the pupil can adopt one of two or three creeds. He may decide to worship his own teacher blindly, and to be sure that all who contradict him are heretics or fools, unworthy of respect. This is an extremely common attitude. Many teachers have expected it, and many still do. In fact, without faith in the master and his method the disciple can achieve nothing. The fault of this ideal, however, is that it emphasizes the differences rather than the agreements in the vocal profession. Outsiders have every right to scoff at us on this account.

755   Another creed is really a kind of agnosticism. An advanced student who has worked with several teachers and heard the divergence of their opinions frequently becomes cynical. He has small confidence in any of them. He studies awhile with each, hoping to pick up a few tricks, learn some new repertoire, and most important of all—make a few political contacts. Eventually he will open his own studio and use an impressively superficial pedagogy which consists of quoting—more or less accurately—every celebrity he has known.

756   A third creed, however, recognizes that truth is greater than any of us. Truth is not an angle; it is a sphere. Opposite segments of a sphere appear to be contradictory, but if any one is extended sufficiently it arrives at completeness and includes all the other fragments. Few minds achieve consistency in all their thoughts, but all of us can have the breadth to entertain the concepts of others and make at least some attempt to reconcile them with our own. I think the attitude of a learner should not be so much choosing, or even compromising between opposite polarities, but including both in a well-rounded philosophy. Any sphere can be considered in terms of many overlapping hemispheres. Our world has Northern and Southern, American and Eurasian, Atlantic and Pacific divisions. Time was when these were considered separate but we can no longer afford provincialism. Let us consider some of the antipodes of singing.

The Extremes of Pedagogy—Mechanism and Holism

757   This book has approached vocal problems mechanistically, has made an attempt to analyze the process and to explain it scientifically. I have scouted the "naturalistic" methods of those who prefer not to bother their heads with "scientific" details; but I should make a great mistake if I

were to leave the impression that science has all the answers. The basis of singing is more than this; it is a philosophy. One cannot proceed far enough upon the solid ground of proved fact; one must venture further on the basis of faith. No "fact" is to be trusted upon purely theoretical support; the final reliance must be upon the realities of experience, even though unexplained and mysterious. The pedagogical ideas presented in this book have all been tested in my studio. I do not worship the "Golden Age"; to me it is more gilded than golden; but it is quite possible that the greatest singers who ever lived were those of that period. By our standards, their knowledge was unscientific, but their devotion to empirical guidance achieved marvelous results.

758   Mechanistic pedagogy is applied behavioristic psychology. Behaviorism is a philosophy based upon the famous experiments of Pavlov, who conditioned the salivary reflexes of dogs. This concept assumes that personality is the sum of simple units of behavior called reflexes, and that experience conditions these into various behavior patterns, various habits. The mechanistic voice teacher assumes that singing is a complex skill made up of simple skills, and that when a singer is less than perfect it is because one or more of these skills is deficient. He therefore sets about, first to analyze singing itself, as we have been doing in this book; and second to analyze each of his students to see which skills need development, what new habits must be formed and what old habits need be changed.

759   Behaviorism is still a respected belief. B. F. Skinner is one of the psychologists still analyzing human life—even language and thought—into elementary units. However, there was an immediate reaction to behaviorism which has grown parallel with it. This is Gestalt psychology, which insists that there is much more to personality than reflex and conditioning of reflexes, that when all the details of behavior are assembled there emerges a *form* (which is what the word *Gestalt* means) greater than any or all of the details.

760   This results in the holistic approach, ignoring or seeming to ignore skills or lack of skills, and appealing to the whole personality. Such a pedagog teaches not sing*ing* but sing*ers*. He reiterates that singing is a "total response." I have dealt with these ideas at greater length elsewhere (Vennard[7]) and if ever I attempt a sequel to this book I shall give them still more space. Suffice it to say here that I respect both approaches and feel that they show their weaknesses only when one loses tolerance for the opposite philosophy.

761   I do not think that reliance upon "practical" or holistic methods is incompatible with a continual search for scientific information and application of it wherever possible. The ancients used as much science as was available to them. Huang Ti, editor of the Chinese Canon of Medicine, 2698 B.C., wrote:

> The thorax and abdomen constitute the city wall, the pericardium the palace of the king. The stomach is the granary and the throat and small intestines the post office. Water and grain enter the oesophagus, and air by the trachea. . . . The mouth and lips are the ban for the voice, the tongue the machine, and the uvula the pass. The larynx divides the air. The breath coming from the lungs is supposed to act on the hyoid bone and tongue in speaking, (quoted by Judson and Weaver, p. 351).

Demosthenes, in the fourth century B.C., believed in local effort enough to put stones in his mouth in order to exercise the articulatory mechanism. Galen, in the second century A.D., wrote a treatise on voice, identifying the cartilages of the larynx and distinguishing between intrinsic and extrinsic musculature. Mazzocchi, in seventeenth century Rome, had no recording equipment with which to train the ears of his pupils, so he had them sing against a famous echo outside the Angelica gate. Tosi followed the lead of Caccini in isolating the registers, only instead of using the *voce piena* (full voice), *voce finta* (false voice) terminology, he went anatomical and called them *voce di petto* (chest) and *voce di testa* (head). The dictum of "looseness of the neck" goes back to this period, as well as most of our principles of breathing.

762   Tosi was translated into English by Gailliard and into German by Agricola. Both added footnotes in which they described three registers, much as they are known today (Par. 256-259). Martini, an Italian living in France, wrote of *voix de poitrine, voix du gozier,* and *voix de tête,* and advocated developing smooth transitions between them.

763   In the eighteenth century, Dodart wrote *Memoires sur la cause de la voix* (1703), and Ferrein wrote *De la formation de la voix de l'homme,* (1741), the earliest works that are scientific in the modern sense. Ferrein demonstrated vocal cord vibration for the first time, using excised larynges, a technic that has been perfected by van den Berg.

764   In 1841 Garcia, a superb singer and teacher, invented the laryngoscope and joined the company of the men of science. Ever since then, teachers have been blaming science for what they considered the waning of man's noblest art, and at the same time using as much scientific knowledge as was at their command. For example, Salvatore Marchesi, a pupil of Garcia, wrote that "thousands of undesirable meddlers seized upon the subject and brought about confusion, and, as a consequence, the inevitable decline of the finest of all the fine arts" (p. 2), and then went on to give us a discussion of "position of the mouth," "diaphragmatic breathing," "stroke of the glottis," "sound and noise," "registers," including reference to the hard and soft palate, the sinuses, the turbinated bones, the cartilages, the uvula, the pharynx, etc., not all with accuracy, but certainly without hesitation. He is typical of a whole generation of singers and pedagogs who tried on the one hand to close their minds to science, but at the same time feared it and tried to come to terms with it.

765   The important thing seems to be whether or not the knowledge is accurate and practical. Therefore, are we not obligated to acquire as much information as possible in order that we may test it? Should we refuse to learn a laboratory fact simply because we cannot test it immediately and directly? Perhaps it will provide the basis for our arriving at something else, or at least avoiding some superstitious error.

766   In this respect the teachers of speech are ahead of us. The finest sources of the factual material in this book are either acousticians, anatomists, or speech pedagogs. Singers have been slow to avail themselves of this knowledge. I feel that my own performance, and still more my teaching, has greatly benefited from this study, and therefore I have written down my findings. Only to a small degree are they original. My only excuse for this offering is that in a painstaking search for a textbook on the technic of song, I was unable to find one book that presented all the facts that my reading unearthed, and presented them from the viewpoint of a singer, rather than a physiologist or a phoneticist.

767   True, there is an unexplored region into which we can venture only with theories, but if we are to weave poetic fancies as an aid to singing, why not have as much truth in them as possible? Should the voice teacher emulate a medical doctor or a witch doctor? My answer is, he should emulate the best qualities of both. He should be prepared to correct faults locally, in the light of specific knowledge, but he must at the same time remember that the pupil is a person, and the proper coordination of individual skills depends upon integration of the entire personality. Where science recognizes only enigmas, he can still continue with confidence on the basis of experience, in the language of poetry, appealing to the imagination of the student, with the aid—if you will—of magic.

768   The vocal profession has injured its own dignity by magnifying its differences of opinion, while in reality the body of truth upon which we agree is much greater than one sometimes realizes. Music is a kind of religion with us, and each places a blind faith in his own formulae and creeds, but just as the Church is tending more and more toward unity, so are vocalists, in such organizations as the National Association of Teachers of Singing. With this as background for our thinking, let me recapitulate the principles of this book, and indicate how the controversies may be reconciled.

The Extremes of Phonation—Breathiness and Tightness

769   The coordination of respiration with phonation is epitomized in the attack. It is a problem of balancing tension in the muscles of breathing with tension in the muscles of the larynx. How much should the diaphragm permit the abdominal muscles to build breath pressure, and how much should the thyroarytenoids, by tightening against the cricothyroids and the cricoarytenoids, resist this breath pressure? The answer to this question is not to compromise, to try to find a tone that is midway between breathiness and tightness. This simply results in vascillation between looseness and tenseness. The secret is to flood the tone with as much breath as possible, and to keep from actually making it breathy by offering it as firm a resistance as necessary in the valve.

770   Staccato exercises help to achieve this coordination. Think of the glottis as closing smartly over the breath stream, producing a clear, clean stroke. Make four staccato attacks all on the same pitch, and follow with a sustained tone. If it is done with the same abandon of breath and the same firmness of the glottis as the staccato strokes, it will be full and free. If thinking of the pitch (which is a function of tension) causes the breath to be inhibited and the larynx to tighten, try it without a definite pitch in mind. Make the short tones on any old pitch, and do a descending portamento on the long one. Follow with sustained tones.

771   I ask all my students to do what we call the "yawn-sigh." The exercise is quite informal, and should be done as easily and comfortably as possible. It consists simply of simulating a yawn and exhaling gently and vocally. The emotional atmosphere should be happy, relieved. The mood should be of relaxation, like the feeling at the end of a perfect day, "tired-but-happy." Have the student imagine he is sitting in an easy chair. He has just put on his slippers; he stretches himself and says, "ah-h-h-h-h, what a day!" Students who have the least aptitude for the exercise (that is, whose throats are tightest) will perhaps produce a breathy tone, but the teacher should insist on one that is clear and light. The attack must be with the "imaginary h."

772   In order to get the desired relaxation without breathiness, it will be necessary that head tone or quasi-falsetto be used. The initial pitch should not be a definite one, but it should be one that is comfortably located in the upper part of the range and should then glide down into the chest voice. Tell the student to make his tone child-like, naive, simple, sweet, innocent, happy. Demonstrate! You may have to suggest starting on a higher note. With the less imaginative it will even be necessary to have them use a falsetto tone and let it break as they slur downward, but this should be only a temporary expedient. What is desired is a light, clear, "heady" voice, the heaviness of which can be increased at will as the pitch descends, in other words it is an exercise in dynamic registration, (Par. 267). The yawn-sigh is an exercise for freedom, which also implies dynamic registration. The exercise can be either soft or loud, though it is usually from piano to mezzo forte. If the student has a tendency toward weak, breathy production, call it a "shout" instead of a "sigh" and insist upon more abandon.

773   Do not despise this exercise for its simplicity. I find it most useful. It is easy for any student to understand and perform. The only requirement is that it should not be breathy, but that it should have a clean attack, and should sound with a bell-like quality. It can be done in its simplest form, merely a sigh, at the beginning of vocalization, or as an interpolation at any time that the throat is stiffening—even midway in the rehearsal of a song. It can then be followed with more formal vocalises, say a five-tone descending scale, or repetitions of the difficult phrase of the song, perhaps in different keys, beginning lower and working up to pitch. Any vowel may be used, but the round vowels are the more likely. I prefer to use [ɑ]. The yawn-sigh begins on a relatively high note with an "imaginary [h]." An equally beneficial exercise, especially for breathy voices, is the rattle or "scrape" in attacking low notes. (Par. 195).

The Extremes of Registration—Light and Heavy

774   There should never be a question as to which register to use. The answer is always: Both!
The registration should be coordinated. A great help to this end is the development of what I
have called the "unused register." Stanley, with his gad-fly literary style, must be given credit
for stimulating interest in this aspect of voice culture, but the concept is to be found earlier, even
in the writings of such conservatives as Clippinger:

> There is one place in voice training where the practice of the falsetto has a distinct value. I
> have seen many tenors and baritones who forced the heavy chest voice up until they developed an
> automatic clutch, and could sing the upper tones only with extreme effort. To allow them to con-
> tinue in that way would never solve their problem. In such a condition half voice is impossible.
> It must be one thing or the other, either the thick chest voice or falsetto. The falsetto they can
> produce without effort, and herein lies its value. They become accustomed to hearing their high
> tones without the association of effort, and after a time the real voice appears. The thing which
> prevented the head voice from appearing in the beginning was extreme resistance, and as soon
> as the resistance disappeared the head voice made its appearance. This was accomplished by the
> practice of the very light register known as falsetto. When the head voice appears the use of the
> falsetto may be discontinued, (p, 26).

775   It is not a matter of singing in one register up to a certain point (which has been located on a
different note by almost as many as have written on this subject) and then shifting gears and
continuing the scale in a different register. It is a matter of achieving a dynamic balance in
which the best elements of both registers are functioning. Until the laryngologists provide us
with information which present methods of investigation seem unable to provide, we cannot define
this dynamic adjustment physiologically, but we can describe it in terms of vocal experience, and
we can lead neophytes into this experience.

776   The flooding of the tone with breath discussed in the preceding section will be an essential part
of it. The Bernoulli Effect can loosen static adjustments. A tone that "floats on the breath" has a
kind of fluidity that makes possible variations in color without stopping the production. I find that
some singers discover this release first by abandoning normal production, *voce piena,* and going
into the unused register. For example, men tell me that they experience two kinds of falsetto, one
which is just as tight as their worst chest tone except when they make it weak and perhaps breathy,
and another which often comes as a revelation. One student described this latter as a falsetto "with
a hole blown in the middle of it." The terms, "lip falsetto" and "pharyngeal falsetto" are applied to
these two modes of phonation, but I fail to see their derivation. They are not descriptive, and they
are just as unscientific as chest and head. In my own voice I find a pinched falsetto and another that
seems to take much more breath but which acquires volume and nobility of tone. I have the same
feeling of "blowing the tone open" when I sing my best tones in heavy full voice, and I discover that
when my students apply this technic, learned in falsetto, and carry with it some of the falsetto quality, they no longer have a static chest voice, but a dynamic one. The first time a man sings with
release, it feels like falsetto. I have even been asked, "Is that falsetto?" Both men and women
have had to be reassured about correct production of the upper voice, because to them it seemed
"breathy."

777   In women's voices, especially in light soprano voices, the unused register is at the bottom.
They discover two kinds of chest voice, a tight kind first, which is crude and undesirable, but
later a freer, sweeter kind, produced with more breath. The memory of this tone seems to
impart power and warmth to their true voice, making it really "full." Altos and powerful mezzos, whose heavy voice is well developed, sometimes have to discover falsetto. Coloraturas,
while they are certainly using falsetto, sometimes are using the inhibited kind, and unlock
unexpected power when they learn to "blow it open."

778   Another characteristic of the dynamic mechanism is relaxation of the extrinsic musculature. I prefer to say it this way instead of saying "openness of the throat," because I do not think that the large pharynx is as important as the freedom from esophageal drag. The problem is not as much resonance as it is vibration. When the larynx is moderately low, the intrinsic musculature is free from extrinsic tensions. The "yawn-sigh" tends to lower the voice box; indeed the yawn is the most usable of the reflex methods of lowering it. Adding the sigh results in phonation without strain. The quasi-falsetto attack is all part of the picture.

779   An excellent way to use the exercise is to do it first, careless of pitch, and then to do it on a five-tone descending scale, *sol fa mi re do*. It should be light both in volume and in registration on top, and heavy and loud in the bottom. This is the easiest form of the exercise. As the student becomes more advanced, have him do it and then come back up, using one breath and reversing the dynamics and the registration. This is much more difficult. It is really a variation of the classic Italian *messa di voce*, the one exercise we are sure was practiced by the great singers of centuries ago.

780   The word *messa* may be translated either "mass" or "fund," and doing the exercise is like taking inventory of one's voice. It is the measure of vocal power and control. Performed conscientiously, it comprises the greatest tax that can be laid upon a singer's resources. Do not confuse *messa di voce* with *mezza voce*, "half voice." The beginning and ending of *messa di voce* should be *mezza voce*, but there are good and bad ways of doing this. A breathy or "swallowed" *mezza voce* has no part in the classic vocal discipline.

781   Simply defined, *messa di voce* is the practice of singing a long crescendo followed by a long diminuendo on a single note. The number of notes on which the exercise can be performed, from top to bottom; the length of time to which it can be spun, divided equally between the two phases; the dynamic spread between *pp* and *ff*; the smoothness of laryngeal function in going from quasi-falsetto at the start to full voice and back again; and the purity with which any and all vowel sounds can be maintained—these are the considerations that make the exercise a thorough inventory of the vocal "treasury."

782   It is a trial of breath control. The student must be sure to get a deep breath before attacking the tone, in order that he can prolong the phonation. It is ideal for this purpose, since all the conscious attention to breathing will be upon the inspiratory phase, upon raising the chest high at the start and then expanding in the region of the diaphragm. When the tone starts, attention will shift to dynamics and registration, which is as it should be, lest the student become "breath conscious."

783   It is a drill in proper attack, avoiding either the glottal stroke or the breathy beginning, both of which waste breath. The explosive start ruins the pianissimo and the aspirate is not clear.

784   But most important of all is the practice in transition from one mode of laryngeal vibration to another. This is not just a function of pitch. When one practices the *messa di voce* where the whole exercise is on a single note, one realizes that the "lift of the breath" is not only a phenomenon encountered on specific frequencies in ascending the scale, but that it is related to the dynamics of any pitch within the compass.

785   In doing the *messa di voce* start with as near to a falsetto tone as you can, but have just a little heavy quality in it so that you can crescendo without an audible shift into "chest." There must be an entering wedge. Then as you crescendo, gradually drive in the wedge. There must be no moment when the chest voice is "kicked in," as some writers put it. The addition of deeper and deeper registration must be absolutely smooth. Most singers find this fairly easy in the first phase of the exercise, but have difficulty when they decrescendo. They start with a tone that

is almost pure falsetto and build it into full voice, but when they try to return to the head quality again the voice breaks. They need to learn that the "lift of the breath" is used not only for going from low to high in pitch, but also in going from high to low in volume. It is really going from chest voice to head voice in both cases. To make the shift requires an increase in breath pressure. I find that the variation which consists of doing *messa di voce* on a descending and ascending five-tone scale emphasizes the correlation of registration with both pitch and dynamics.

786   The various ways to use the "yawn-sigh" in a formal vocalise may be summarized in the following notation:

From A to B is the simple vocalise which first follows the informal "yawn-sigh." It may start in a much higher key and be transposed downward by half-steps, depending on the range of the individual student. From A to C is the next stage, and more difficult, involving a *messa di voce* on the scale passage. From A to D is the final, and rather taxing development of the exercise. It is best not to spend too much time and breath on the first part. The last notes, from C to D, carry a pianissimo head tone up to the top of the octave and then a *messa di voce* is done once more in its classic form, on the one tone, before finally making a portamento to the lower tonic and releasing. If a student is unable to do all this in one phrase, he should be given simply from C to D as a vocalise. Later he will do B to D in one breath, and finally the entire exercise.

The Extremes of Resonance—"Focusing" and "Covering"

787   I do not intend to fill space here saying the same things I have already said at length. I am content to remind you that in my opinion, "both 'focus' and 'cover' are approaches to the same ultimate ideal; there is merit in both," (Par. 560). There is much controversy over whether the tone should have "forward placement" or "deep placement." Proponents of the latter usually insist that "placement" is a myth, and prefer to concentrate on ideas like the large throat, but a few actually use expressions like "let every tone go all the way down to the diaphragm," etc. Stanley, who continually derides placement imagery, tells us:

> It is futile to tell the student to open his throat, since such localized control is physiologically impossible. Such direction, however, as: "Go for the throat!" "Form the vowels farther back!" "Hold the throat firm!" "Work with the throat!" "Balance the work done in the production of the tone with firmness of the throat!" "Start the tone with the throat!" "Don't let the throat collapse as you ascend the scale!" "Tense the throat at the moment of attacking the tone!" etc., will, with constant repetition, convey quite a definite meaning, (pp. 128, 129; 4th ed. pp. 68, 69).

I shudder at the meaning these words convey to me, but since this chapter has become my litany of tolerance, I will say that while I dislike the guttural emphasis of the language, nevertheless, I can see value in these concepts.

788   The individualization of word magic in the vocal profession is such that some teachers may say, "I do not teach 'covering' but I certainly believe in forming the vowels in the throat," or "I cannot accept the unscientific concept of 'focus,' but I know 'forward placement' as a fact of my

experience," or the reverse of either of these statements. Is it not likely that if we tried to express our ideas in other phrases, or if we would try to understand the ideas of others, we should discover that the art of song is much the same for all of us? There is real danger that some of us prejudice ourselves against truly beautiful singing, simply because it emerges from another studio, or because we gather that the singer is an exponent of principles with which we theoretically disagree.

789   I am more and more convinced that a tone should have both "focus in front" and "roundness and depth in back"; that "covering" in its best sense achieves this result. that every vowel one sings should be both "pointed and round," "forward and back," "high and deep," "cool and warm," "bright and dark," "gleeful and gloomy." In some songs, the vowel will be more one than the other for purposes of interpretation, but in different songs it might be the opposite.

The Extremes of Articulation—Words and Music

790   A song should be both words and music, not one or the other, nor a compromise at the expense of both. We should make as beautiful tone as possible, and superimpose as audible consonants as possible. The consonants, rather than spoil the vowels, should bring them out.

791   Consonants are used in vocalises with two different objectives. They may be simply a practice in articulation itself, to improve the diction, or they may be used to "place" the vowels, to improve tone production. Exercises of the former variety are to be found in profusion in books on speech. Teachers can easily improvise them, simply by combining the vowels with whatever consonant is poor in the student's enunciation. It may be a series of syllables with the same vowel, or with the whole vowel series: "La, la, la, la, la," or "Lay, lee, loh, loo, lah." Different vowels may be employed in the same exercise, making either words or nonsense syllables. Both vowels and consonants may be varied, as in the well-known series invented by Sieber: "La, be, da, me, ni, po, tu," (Italian pronunciation). These may be repeated *ad libitum*, either on one tone or upon scales and arpeggios. By beginning the series at different points, it is possible to place whatever syllable you like upon the high notes.

792   Rather than practice synthetic drills in diction, I prefer to make exercises of the difficult passages in actual songs. Therefore, the second use of the consonants is more interesting to me. Most teachers have a favorite for this purpose. Lilli Lehmann used the glide (j, as in *ja*); "Yee, yay, yah," so ran her vocalises. Witherspoon tabulates common vocal faults and prescribes combinations of vowels and consonants to be used in their correction, (pp. 97-101). There is probably no consonant that has not been used, each having its own value.

793   The glides, because of their transitional quality, open the vowels and exercise the jaw. The glottal fricative, [h], is used to adjust the vibrator to the breath stream. The velar and nasal consonants discipline the soft palate as do also the plosives, since arching the velum is necessary to the implosion phase. Labials, dentals, and alveolars bring the work "forward." The tongue is exercised by all except the labials and the aspirate. Best are those which bring the tongue to the front and develop flexibility: the dentals, the alveolars, the forward [l] and above all, the rolled [r].

794   There are two principles in the use of consonants to improve tone production. Some consonants tend to put the resonators in the correct position, in which case the vowel should be produced as nearly as possible with the same "placement" as the consonant. This is characteristic of the sounds I have just mentioned: the dentals, the alveolars, the forward [l], the rolled [r], and we may add the labials. Other consonants involve everything that would be undesirable in a vowel, but oddly enough, these are useful also by contrast. In flying out of these positions to form the vowels, the organs of articulation may go into better alignment than from a more neutral po-

sition. It is the principle of reaction from one extreme to the other. Such a sound is the aspirate, which as we have seen, uses a deliberately breathy production to overcome breathiness by the sudden closing of the glottis, making a clear vowel in contrast. The velars, [k] and [g], fall into this category, a wrong position of the soft palate being quickly and radically changed. Much the same has been said of the nasals, but they are somewhat ambiguous, since their real purpose may well be to adjust the pillars properly, the nasality merely being a disposable by-product.

795   The use of any standard consonant has the advantage that the pupil has already learned to pronounce it. However, just as one must understand the vowel triangle in order to use vowels for profitable vocalizing, so one must also know the strength and weaknesses of the different consonants. Some pupils will "swallow" their tones if they use [j] as in *ja*; others will sing nasally if they use [m] or [n]; etc. You must pick the consonant to fit the student.

796   The consonant I prefer is a synthetic. In using it one occasionally feels resemblances to [ð, n] and [j], but it is none of these. It should never have a glottal plosive, so sometimes [h] is used to begin it: [hn]. It is difficult to learn, but it is a direct approach to correct voice production, and to the extent that one has mastered it one has mastered vocalization. I learned this exercise from Theodore Harrison, with whom I studied longer than with any other teacher.

797   For years I thought it was a phoneme found in no modern language, until one day I recognized it as the French *in* or *ain*, [ɛ̃], or more strongly, [æ̃], (Par. 512). It may still be called a synthetic consonant, since in French it is a vowel and would never be used as an initial. I originally called the sound "the hum on the tongue," and used an elaborate vocalizing ritual in teaching it which began by humming with the blade of the tongue loosely between the teeth. Lately this routine has fallen away and my students begin with the sound that I once called "the open hum," actually [æ̃]. We seldom speak of "the hum on the tongue" anymore, and my students simply refer to "that nasty [æ̃] exercise."

798   To explain the merits of this unpleasant sound as a vocalise I need to dichotomize in one more sweeping generalization.

The Extremes of Singing Technic—Freedom and Intensity

799   Under this double heading I risk repeating some of the ideas already set forth, in order to make a summary. It is the paradox of vocalism that a good singer does two opposite things simultaneously. He does not seek a compromise between two contrary pulls; he pulls both ways at once.

800   Necessarily, therefore, a teacher also pulls in two opposite directions and this can be confusing to the student unless there is a clear understanding about it at the outset. About the time that the student has reason to believe he is making the desired sound the teacher begins to ask for the exact opposite, or so it seems until the student learns to keep what he has learned and add something different.

801   It is quite possible to study with a teacher who teaches only freedom. This is likely to be a Gestaltist whose dictum is "Just relax and sing naturally." Such pedagogy does no great harm, and brings out the individuality of the voice. In the rare case of a "natural" (who scarcely needs a teacher) it works admirably. A little relaxed warm-up and away we go learning repertoire with which to win contests. But a singer who is less than perfect naturally is likely to feel after a year or so that something is missing. He then goes to a teacher whose specialty is intensifying voices, very likely a mechanist who knows a trick or two with which to make a big difference in the "maturify," or "professional sound." One such trick I have described as the "depressed larynx," (Par. 378). But let's say there are no radical methods, just an emphasis on "pinging

up the voice." For a few months the singer makes happy progress and then uneasiness returns. His freedom is eluding him.

802   A student can be alternately "loosened up" and "tightened up" until he has wasted too many years, unless he learns somewhere that freedom and intensity are contradictory, but both are possible in maximum degree simultaneously.

803   It is a matter of muscular independence such as is necessary for any delicate skill. In learning to play the piano one exercises to gain finger independence so that, for example, the ring finger can move without moving the little finger. In voice it is similar, but less obvious. In general, the extrinsic laryngeal musculature, the neck muscles which are subject to conscious control, must be relaxed. This is freedom. On the other hand the work must be done somewhere, and this means that the intrinsic musculature, which is largely unconscious, must be activated. This is intensity. We are conscious only of its effects, in the tone and in sensations of "resonance" or "placement," which seem almost magical.

804   The vocalise I use for freedom is the "yawn-sigh" which I have already discussed at length, (Par. 771, 786). Freedom must be established first. I owe this conviction to years of unsuccessful experience working for intensity (which I called "focus" in those days) and also to the reading of "Dynamic Singing" by Louis Bachner. He makes a strong case for the holistic approach and to him freedom is the prime essential, which is achieved by "hookup." This he defines as "the coordination between diaphragmatic action and vocal cord activity during singing" (p. 89), a truly Gestalt concept; neither the breathing mechanism nor the larynx is as important as the coordination between them.

805   No matter how gifted the student, his first lesson with me is always concerned with freedom and dynamic registration only, and the "yawn-sigh" is the vocalise. With students whose production is constricted there may be a month or so of nothing more than this, but the real development of technic comes with the addition of intensity, for which we use the "[æ̃] exercise."

806   Seventeen years ago I described the tone in old-fashioned resonance imagery as "coming up out of the throat, gathering nasal brilliance, and dropping down into the mouth far forward, between the tongue and the teeth." This metaphorical sentence still satisfies me except that I wish I had not mentioned "nasal brilliance," whatever that is! I am still willing to stand behind my more scientific interpretation of the poetry: "The tone, well supported by breath pressure, begins with a light, quasi-falsetto production; the heavier laryngeal function is initiated by adding 'twang,' that is, bringing in '2800'; the whole thing is integrated by concentrating attention on the tip of the tongue. This also has the effect of avoiding stiffness of the tongue."

807   The sound *must* be "forward." It must not be a mere "Humph!" that is back in the throat. If there is more vibration in the root of the tongue than in its tip, the production is wrong. This will happen if the tongue stiffens by pressing behind the upper teeth or upper gums. It is most important that the tongue rest *loosely* in contact with the lower teeth, and probably also the lower lip. The exercise resembles the childhood practice of "playing on a comb." Almost everyone has at some time or another folded a piece of tissue paper over a comb and then played it like a "kazoo." If you will recall your own experience, you will remember that much of the time you were merely humming; there was no response from the "instrument." But every once in awhile the paper would rattle! There would be a violent tingling sensation between paper and lips or tongue, and the toy would give forth a reedy tone. You were really playing it then. This is an illustration of the difference between "focus" in the throat (or back of the tongue) and "focus" in the front.

808   You can see the reason why I prefer this initial to consonants that are readymade, like [m] or [n]. With humming through closed lips, the tone is often "swallowed." "Mee, mee, mee" can can readily become a throaty "mŭ, mŭ, mŭ." Make sure that the tongue is relaxed, and that the tone is really "on the teeth." When the thing is done correctly, if the tongue touches the upper lip there will be an almost unpleasant tingling vibration. Incidentally, the exercise works better if the upper lip is slightly lifted.

809   Most pedagogies utilize some kind of nasality to establish a ring in the voice and to strengthen it. Humming is a good example. There is of course nasality in [æ̃], but I need not reiterate that the idea of "nasal resonance" fails utterly to convince me. (Par. 339). Please note that [æ̃] is not the "honky" nasality that muffles all the partials above 1000 cps. Sonagrams (Figs. 51, 74) show the difference.

810   The real secret is that "twang" is the most aggressive sound we make. It is the "bad vowel" [æ] pinched by nasalization. This demands a firming up of the laryngeal musculature, and herein lies the danger of the vocalise. Pinching and forcing can easily result if the concept of freedom is not established at the start and frequently reaffirmed. The ideal 15-minute vocalizing session is 5 minutes of "yawn-sigh" as outlined above, 5 minutes of carefree scales and arpeggios for range and agility, possibly including the [lu, lu, lu] exercise for head quality described in Par. 548, and 5 minutes of the "[æ̃] exercise." The remainder of the half hour lesson is enough time for working on repertoire (coaching) unless there is a recital or other important appearance in the near future. Indeed I much prefer the arrangement whereby my students learn their repertoire with a coach or on the job and come to me for voice work. We then come near to doubling the above time values and simply devote the last 5 minutes or so to songs for the purpose of applying the vocal principles and solving problems of production which may have arisen in the songs.

811   Whatever the time schedule, the work for intensifying the voice must be controlled. It is the part of the medicine that is healthful or lethal depending on the dosage. The student is working for "ping," or "focus," and not beauty of tone. The sound at this stage of the exercise must still be the somewhat unpleasant, neutral, nasal quality with which the exercise was begun.

812   This is the most difficult part of the discipline to enforce. Many pupils simply reject it. They cannot accommodate themselves to the idea of opening the mouth without singing some lovely vowel. This is especially true of the throaty singer, with considerable native talent, who is well satisfied with his natural production and likes his voice best when he is swallowing it. He is the

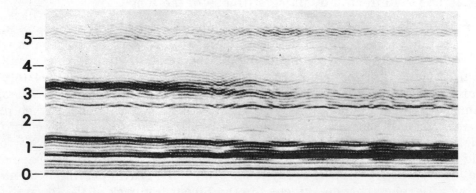

Fig. 74. Sonagram of [æ̃] Exercise
From van den Berg and Vennard, *NATS Bulletin*. Pitch E₃, bass staff. Time, 1.5 sec. Note high partial in the initial [æ̃] sound, dropping to "2800" for [ɑ].

very one who needs this exercise, if you can get his cooperation; but if you cannot, there is no use just going through the motions. Abandon the exercise and try it again some other day.

813   Charles Schulz is a keen observer of human psychology who happens to express his ideas in a cartoon called "Peanuts." I am most grateful to him and to his syndicate, United Features, for permission to reprint the issue in which Lucy is demonstrating the [æ̃] vocalise (Fig. 75). What more perfect evidence could be offered that [æ̃] is the instinctive expression of aggressiveness?

Fig. 75. Instinctive Expression of Aggressiveness
Courtesy of Charles Schulz and United Features Syndicate, Inc.

814   The mood of the "yawn-sigh" is one of contentedness. This creates beauty in the voice. The mood of the [æ̃] exercise is anger. It makes the voice competitive and professional. Singing is one of the most personally competitive of the professions.

815   In the [æ̃] exercise we have a profound psychological principle and we appeal to the whole person. The competitive animal wrinkles up his nose and, baring his teeth for combat, he snarls. The aggressive child does much the same thing. Perhaps, like Lucy, she also sticks out her tongue. It all makes for strength and brilliance in the voice. The nasality is a disposable by-product.

816   Both of these key vocalises, the "yawn-sigh" and the [æ̃] exercise, should be congenial to the holistic teacher because they use the voice as personal emotional expression. They are instinctive phonations, such as have been called "embryonic sounds" in the sense that they are elemental and more cultivated expression grows from them.

817   But these vocalises also have definite mechanistic objectives, the low larynx, the loose jaw, the forward tongue, the exposed edge of the upper teeth, etc. Thus they should appeal to both pedagogical camps, or better still, to those mentors who seek to harmonize the two approaches.

818   The [æ̃] exercise should merge into one gradual progression from a reedy vibration on the tip of the tongue to a clear, clean vowel that retains all the overtones of the initial sound. Continuity is the keynote. Eventually the process can be as brief as the pronunciation of any consonant, but at first it should be practiced deliberately. The vowel which emerges from the [æ̃] should be an Ee [i] at first. This is the most intense vowel. "2800" is a necessary formant, and everyone has learned by trial and error to firm up his laryngeal musculature a bit to achieve this ring in the vowel [i]. The first vocalise after learning the [æ̃] sound satisfactorily is: [æ̃i, æ̃i, æ̃i] intoned on one pitch. I find A_4 flat suitable for most female voices and A_3 flat for male voices. Transpose by step and/or half-steps for variety, but keep near this middle pitch. It is dangerous to use this exercise on high pitches, although some sopranos carry it successfully (with caution) clear to the top.

819   Make the transition from [æ̃] to [i] as gradual and as fluid as possible. The [æ̃] should melt into [i] and it in turn should dissolve into the next [æ̃]. Later use the sequence [æ̃iæ̃eæ̃i], and then [æ̃iæ̃eæ̃ɑ], still intoning on one pitch.

820   Follow the work on a single pitch with:

Low voices should be in a lower key. More elaborate melody patterns may follow, including a complete scale from bottom to top. This, however, is a bit risky, and as I have said, only a few sopranos take it very high. The [æ̃] should not be repreated on every tone, and certainly not on high pitches. The synthetic consonant is used to "focus" the tone and then the move to the next pitch is made without its help, but in order not to lose the "focus," the consonant is repeated on the third step, etc. All exercises involve crutches that will be thrown away when a song is attempted. Therefore the crutches must not be used too continuously, even in the vocalizing.

821   Originally I called this a vocalise for "focus" and I still use this metaphor, but I have come to use the word "intensity" more. Physicists point out to me that this word simply refers to loudness, and chide me for merely exchanging one figure of speech for another. I concede the point (see Par. 16-18) but I come back to the definition of "intensity" as a synonym for "energy."

822   The teacher who works for "focus" is demanding more energetic singing. I admit that I demand more loudness from my singers. They must be able to compete with an orchestra, and this is not done with a breathy tone. When energy is used with freedom the maximum volume can be produced without undue effort. Of course a good pianissimo must also be learned, which requires delicate control of registration, but even here what we think of as a "carrying" pianissimo is by no means weak. I found it to be about 5 decibels louder than a breathy piano tone by tests with several singers in a hall.

Concluding Remarks

823   I believe an eclectic philosophy of voice production is possible to all who have the tolerance to learn from those with whom they seem to disagree. In this spirit I have tried to describe not only the mechanism of voice production, but also those principles which make for the best technic. A knowledge of the mechanism is the foundation of an objective pedagogy, and a mastery of the technic is the prerequisite for artistic expression. A discussion of these advanced phases of singing I must postpone until a later writing.

BIBLIOGRAPHY

BOOKS

Adler, Kurt: The Art of Accompanying and Coaching. Minneapolis, University of Minnesota Press, 1965.

Bachner, Louis: Dynamic Singing. New York, A. A. Wyn, Inc., 1944.

Bairstowe, Edward C. and H. Plunket Greene: Singing Learned from Speech. London, Macmillan & Co., Ltd., 1946.

Bartholomew, Wilmer T.: Acoustics of Music. New York, Prentice-Hall, Inc. 1942.

Behnke, Emil: The Mechanism of the Human Voice. London, J. Curwen & Sons, 1880.

Benharoche, M.: De l'Art Vocal. Pub. by author, Biarritz, 1958.

Bonnier, Pierre: La Voix Professionelle. Paris, Bibliotheque Larousse, 1908.

Bos, Coenraad: The Well-Tempered Accompanist. Bryn Mawr, Pa., Theodore Presser, 1949.

Brodnitz, Friedrich S.: Keep Your Voice Healthy. New York, Harper & Bros., 1953.

Brodnitz[2]: Vocal Rehabilitation. Rochester, Minn., Whiting Press, Inc., 1959.

Brown, William Earl: Vocal Wisdom, Maxims of Giovanni Battista Lamperti. Pub. by author, 1931.

Browne, Lennox, and Emil Behnke: Voice, Song and Speech. New York, G. P. Putnam's Sons, undated, (c. 1890).

Clippinger, D. A.: The Head Voice and Other Problems: Philadelphia, Oliver Ditson Co., 1917.

Coffin, R. Berton (editor): Phonetic Readings of Songs and Arias. Boulder, Colo., Pruett Press, Inc., 1964.

Curry, Robert: The Mechanism of the Human Voice. New York, Longmans, Green & Co., 1940.

de la Madelaine, M. Stephen: Oeuvres Complètes sur Chant, Théorie et Pratique. Paris, Henri Lemoine, 1875.

Denes, Peter B., and Elliot N. Pinson: The Speech Chain, the Physics and Biology of Spoken Language. Baltimore, Maryland, Bell Telephone Laboratories, distributed by Williams & Watkins, 428 East Preston Street, 1963.

DeYoung, Richard: The Singer's Art. Chicago, DePaul U., 1958.

Drew, W. S.: Notes on the Technique of Song-Interpretation. London, Oxford University Press, Humphrey Milford, 1926. (Carl Fischer, sole agents.)

Drew[2]: Singing, the Art and the Craft. London, Oxford University Press, 1937.

Duey, Philip: Bel Canto in its Golden Age. New York, King's Crown Press, 1950.

Errolle, Ralph: Italian Diction for Singers. Boulder, Colo., Pruett Press, 1963.

Fairbanks, Grant: Voice and Articulation Drillbook. New York, Harper & Bros., 1937.

Fields, Victor Alexander: Training the Singing Voice. Morningside Heights, N. Y., King's Crown Press, 1947.

Fillebrown, Thomas: Resonance in Singing and Speaking, New York, Oliver Ditson Co., 1911.

Fletcher, Harvey: Speech and Hearing. New York, Van Nostrand, 1929.

Frisell, Anthony: The Tenor Voice. Boston, Bruce Humphries, 1964.

Fuchs, Viktor: The Art of Singing and Voice Technique. New York, London House & Maxwell, 1964.

Fugère, Lucien and Raoul Duhamel: Nouvelle Méthode Pratique de Chant Français par l'Articulation. Paris, Enoch & Cie, 1929.

Garcia, Manuel: Traité Complet de l'Art du Chant, third edition. Paris, Heugel et Cie, 1911, (first edition, 1847).

Garcia[2]: Hints on Singing, translated by Beata Garcia. New York, Edward Schubarth & Co., 1894.

Greene, Harry Plunket: Interpretation in Song. London, Macmillan and Co., Ltd., and Stainer and Bell, Ltd., 1934.

Greene[2]: (See Edward C. Bairstowe.)

Gurlitt, Willibald (editor): Michael Praetorius, Syntagma Musicum, Facsimile-Nachdruck. Kassel, Bärenreite, 1958.

Helmholtz, Hermann L. F.: On the Sensations of Tone, translated by Alexander J. Ellis. London, Longmans, Green & Co., 1930, (first edition, 1875; now in Dover edition).

Henderson, Charles, with Charles Palmer: How to Sing for Money. New York, Harcourt, Brace and Company, 1940.

Herbert-Caesari, E.: The Voice of the Mind. London, Robert Hale, Ltd., 1951.

Holmes, F. Lincoln D.: A Handbook of Voice and Diction. New York, Appleton-Century-Crofts, 1940.

Husler, Frederick, and Yvonne Rodd-Marling: Singing: The Physical Nature of the Vocal Organ; A Guide to the Unlocking of the Singing Voice. London, Faber and Faber, Ltd., 1965.

Judson, Lyman Spicer, and Andrew Thomas Weaver: Voice Science, New York, F. S. Crofts & Co., 1942.

Kagen, Sergius: On Studying Singing. New York, Rinehart, 1950, (now in Dover edition).

Kantner, Claude Edgar, and Robert William West: Phonetics, an introduction to the principles of phonetic science from the point of view of English speech. New York, Harper, Revised edition 1960.

Kay, Elster: Bel Canto and the Sixth Sense. London, Dennis Dobson, 1963.

Kenyon, John Samuel: American Pronunciation; a textbook of phonetics for students of English. Ann Arbor, Mich., G. Wahr Publishing Co., 1932.

Krone, Max T.: The Chorus and Its Conductor. Chicago, Neil A. Kjos Music Co., 1945.

Laird-Brown, May: Singers' French. London and Toronto, J. M. Dent and Sons, Ltd., 1927.

Lamperti, Francesco: The Art of Singing, translated by J. C. Griffith. New York, G. Schirmer, Inc., Vol. 1587, undated, (reprinted and translated, 1877).

Lamperti, Giovanni Battista: (See William Earl Brown).

Lawson, James Terry: Full-Throated Ease. Toronto, Winnipeg, Vancouver; Western Music Co., Ltd., undated.

Lehmann, Lilli: How to Sing, translated by Richard Aldrich. New York, The Macmillan Co., 1910. This is a translation of *Meine Gesangkunst*. The enlarged edition of 1924 is confusing.

Levin, Nathanial (editor): Voice and Speech Disorders. Springfield, Ill., Charles C. Thomas, 1962.

Luchsinger, Richard, and G. E. Arnold: Lehrbuch der Stimm- und Sprachheilkunde. Wien, Springer-Verlag, 1949.

Lullies, Hans, and O. F. Ranke: Gehör, Stimme, Sprache. Wien, Springer-Verlag, 1953.

Mackenzie, Sir Morell: Hygiene of the Vocal Organs. Belmar, N. J., Edgar S. Werner & Co., ninth edition, 1928 (first edition, c. 1887).

Mackworth-Young, Gerard: What Happens in Singing, a Short Manual of Vocal Mechanics and Technique. London, Newman Neame, 1953.

Mancini, Giambattista: Practical Reflections on the Figurative Art of Singing, translated by Pietro Buzzi. Boston, The Gorham Press, 1912, (first edition, 1777).

Marafioti, P. Mario: Caruso's Method of Voice Production. New York, D. Appleton-Century Co., 1937.

Marchesi, Mathilde: Ten Singing Lessons. New York, Macmillan, 1901.

Marchesi, Salvatore: A Vademecum.

Marshall, Madeline: The Singer's Manual of English Diction. New York, G. Schirmer, 1953.

Miller, Dayton Clarence: The Science of Musical Sounds. New York, The Macmillan Co., 1916.

Miller, Frank E.: Vocal Art-Science. New York, G. Schirmer, Inc., 1917.

Muckey, Floyd S.: The Natural Method of Voice Production. New York, C. Scribners's Sons, 1915.

Myer, Edmund J.: The Voice from a Practical Standpoint. New York, Wm. A. Pond & Co., 1886.

Myer[2]: Vocal Reinforcement. Boston, The Boston Music Co., 1891.

Myer[3]: The Renaissance of the Vocal Art. Boston, The Boston Music Co., 1902.

Myer[4]: The Vocal Instructor. Philadelphia, Theodore Presser Co., 1913.

Nadoleczny, M: Untersuchungen über den Kunstgesang. Berlin, Julius Springer, 1923.

Negus, Victor E.: The Mechanism of the Larynx. London, Wm. Heinemann, Ltd., 1929.

Nohl, Ludwig: Mozarts Briefe, nach den Originalen. Salzburg, Verlag der Manrischen Buchhandlung, 1865.

Paget, Sir Richard: Babel. London, Kegan Paul, Trench & Co., Ltd., 1930.

Paget[2]: Human Speech. New York, Harcourt, Brace & Co., 1930.

Pansera, Charles: L'Art de Chanter. Paris, Editions Littéraires de France, 1945.

Potter, R. K., G. A. Kopp and H. C. Green: Visible Speech. New York, Van Nostrand, 1947.

Proschowsky, Frantz: The Way to Sing. Boston, C. C. Birchard & Co., 1923.

Reid, Cornelius L.: Bel Canto, Principles and Practices. New York, Coleman-Ross Co., Inc., 1950.

Robson, Ernest M.: The Orchestra of the Language. New York and London, Thomas Yoseloff, 1959.

Ross, William E.: Sing High, Sing Low. Bloomington, Ind., pub. by author, 1948.

Ross[2]: Secrets of Singing. Bloomington, Ind., pub. by author, 1959.

Rousselot, P. J.: Principes de Phonetique Expérimentale. Paris, H. Didier, 1924.

Russell, George Oscar: Speech and Voice. New York, Macmillan, 1931.

Russell[2]: The Vowel. Columbus, Ohio, The Ohio State University Press, 1928.

Schaeffer, J. Parsons: The Nose, Paranasal Sinuses, Nasolachrimal Passageways and Olfactory Organ in Man. Philadelphia, J. P. Blakiston's Sons & Co., 1919.

Scripture, E. W.: Researches in Experimental Phonetics: The Study of Speech Curves. Washington, D. C., Carnegie Institution, 1906.

Shakespeare, William: The Art of Singing. Boston, Oliver Ditson Co., 1921, (first edition, 1898).

Shakespeare[2]: Plain Words on Singing, in the Absence of a Master. New York, G. P. Putnam's Sons, undated (c. 1924).

Siebs, Theodor: Deutsche Bühnenaussprache Hochsprache. Köln, A. Ahn, 1930.

Stanley, Douglas: The Science of Voice. New York, Carl Fischer, Inc., 1929.

Stanley[2]: The Voice, Its Production and Reproduction. New York, Pitman Publishing Corp., 1933.

Stanley[3]: Your Voice: Applied Science of Vocal Art. New York, Pitman Publishing Corp., 1945.

Stanley[4]: Your Voice: Applied Science of Vocal Art, third edition. New York, Pitman Publishing Corp., 1957.

Tarneaud, Jean: Traité Pratique de Phonologie et de Phoniatrie, la Voix, la Parole, le Chant. Paris, Libraire Maloine, 1941.

Tarneaud[2]: Le Chant, sa construction, sa destruction. Paris, Libraire Maloine, 1946.

Tarneaud[3]: Pour Obentir une Voix Meilleure. Paris, Libraire Maloine, 1957.

Tetrazzini, Luisa: How to Sing. Philadelphia, Theodore Presser Co., 1923.

Tosi, Pier Francesco: Observations on the Florid Song, or Sentiments on the Ancient and Modern Singers, translated by Mr. Gailliard, London, William Neeves, Bookseller, Ltd., 1926, (first edition, Bologna, 1723).

Van Riper, Charles and John V. Irwin: Voice and Articulation. Englewood Cliffs, N. J., Prentice-Hall, Inc., 1958.

West, Robert, Lou Kennedy and Anna Carr: The Rehabilitation of Speech. New York and London, Harper & Bros., 1937.

Westerman, Kenneth: Emergent Voice. Ann Arbor, pub. by author, 1947.

Wilcox, John C.: The Living Voice. New York, Carl Fischer, 1945.

Wise, Claude Merton: Applied Phonetics. Englewood Cliffs, N. J., Prentice Hall, 1957.

Witherspoon, Herbert: Singing, a Treatise for Teachers and Students. New York, G. Schirmer, Inc., 1925.

Witherspoon[2]: Thirty-Six Lessons in Singing. Chicago, Miessner Institute of Music, 1930.

ARTICLES, ETC.

Bartholomew[2]: The paradox of voice teaching. J. Acoust. Soc. of Am., 11:1940.

Bellusi, G., and A. Viscendaz: Il problema dei registri vocali (I) all'luce della tecnica Roentgen-stratigrafica. Arc. Ital. Otol, 60:1949.

Bernac, Pierre: The French art song. N.A.T.S. Bull., Feb. 1962.

Bernac[2]: Unpublished lecture on singing in French. N.A.T.S. Workshop, Whittier, Calif., 1964.

Brewer, David W., F. Bertram Briess and K. Faaborg-Andersen: Phonation, clinical testing versus electromyography. Ann. O. R. L., 69:1960.

Briess, F. Bertram: (See Brewer, *et al.*)

Brodnitz[3]: Speech after glossectomy. Current Problems in Phoniatrics and Logopedics, 1:1960.

Christiansen, Olaf: Solo and ensemble singing. N.A.T.S. Bull., Feb. 1965.

Cornut, Guy, and Jean-Claude Lafon: Étude acoustique comparative des phonèmes vocaliques de la voix parlée et chantée. Folia Phoniat., 12:1960.

Crandall, I. B.: A dynamical study of the vowel sounds. Bell System Technical J., 60:1924.

Croatto, Lucio, and Caterina Croatto-Martinolli: Physiopathologie du voile du palais. Folia Phoniat., 11:1959.

Delattre, Pierre: The physiological interpretation of sound spectrograms. P.M.L.A., 66:1951.

Delattre,[2] Alvin M. Liberman, Franklin S. Cooper, and Louis G. Gerstwan: An experimental study of the acoustic determinants of vowel color; observations on one- and two-formant vowels synthesized from spectrographic patterns. Word, 8:1952.

Delattre[3]: Vowel color and voice quality. N.A.T.S. Bull., Oct. 1958.

Delattre[4]: La nasalité vocalique en français et en anglais. The French Review 39:1965.

de Schauensee, Max: Lubin revisited. Opera News, Jan. 22, 1966.

Diday, Y. R., and Petrequin: Memoire sur une nouvelle espèce de voix chantée. Gaz. Med. Paris, 8:1840.

Draper, M. H., P. Ladefoged and D. Whitteridge: Respiratory muscles in speech. J. Speech & Hearing Research, 2:1959.

Dupon-Tersen: Physiologie et psychophysiologie de la phonation. La Voix, Cours International de Phonologie et de Phoniatrie, Libraire Maloine, Paris, 1953.

Faaborg-Andersen, Knud: Electromyographic investigation of intrinsic laryngeal muscles in humans. Copenhagen, Acta Physiologica Scandinavica, Vol. 41, sup. 140, 1957.

Faaborg-Andersen,[2] and A. Sonninen: The function of the extrinsic laryngeal muscles at different pitch. Acta Oto-laryng., 51:1959.

Faaborg-Andersen,[3] and William Vennard: Electromyography of extrinsic laryngeal muscles during phonation of different vowels. Annal. Otol. Rhin. & Laryng., 73:1964.

Fletcher, William Wayne: A study of internal laryngeal activity in relation to vocal intensity. Evanston, Ill., unpub. dissertation, Ph.D., Northwestern U., 1950.

Floyd, W. F., V. E. Negus and E. Neil: Observations on the mechanism of phonation. Acta Oto-laryng., 48-1957.

Froeschels, Emil: Hygiene of the voice. Arch. Otolaryng., 38:1943.

Frommhold, W., and G. Hoppe: Tomographische Studien zur Funktion des menschlichen Kehlkopfes, I. Mitteilung: Unterschiede in der Stimmlippenmechanik. Folia Phoniat., 17:1965.

Frommhold,[2] and G. Hoppe: Tomographische Studien zur Funktion des menschlichen Kehlkopfes. Folia Phoniat., 18:1966.

Goerttler, Kurt: Anordnung, Histologie and Histogenese der quergestreiften Muskulatur im menschlichen Stimmbande. Ztschr. Anat., 115:1951.

Goldberg, Albert: The Sounding Board. The Los Angeles Times, Sept. 26, 1948.

Greene, M.C.L.: The cleft palate patient with incomplete palatopharyngeal closure. Folia Phoniat., 7:1955.

Hoppe, G., and W. Frommhold: Tomographische Studien zur Funktion des menschlichen Kehlkopfes, II. Mitteilung: Bewegungen des Zungenbeines. Folia Phoniat., 17:1965.

Howie, J., and Pierre Delattre: An experimental study of the effect of pitch on the intelligibility of vowels. N.A.T.S. Bull., May 1962.

Hülse, Edith: Atemvolumverbrauch bei den vier Stimmeinsätzen. Mschr. Ohrenheilk., 69:1935.

Husson, Raoul: Étude des phenomenes physiologiques et acoustiques fondamentaux de la voix chantée. Folia Phoniat., 3:1950.

Husson,[2] and Albert Djian: Tomographie et phonation. J. Radiologie et d'Electrologie, 33:1952.

Husson,[3]: Special physiology in singing with power. N.A.T.S. Bull., Oct. 1957.

Isshiki, Nobuhiko: Memoirs of research center of voice science. Kyoto, Oto-Rhino-Laryng. Clinic, 52:1959.

Isshiki[2]: Regulatory mechanism of voice intensity variation. J. Speech & Hearing Research, 7:1964.

Isshiki[3]: Vocal intensity and air flow rate. Folia Phoniat., 17:1965.

Katsuki, Yasuji: The function of the phonatory muscles. Jap. J. Physiology, 1:1951.

Ladefoged, P., M. H. Draper and D. Whitteridge: Syllables and stress. Misc. Phonet., 3:1958.

Landeau, Michel, and H. Zuili: Vocal emission and tomograms of the larynx. N.A.T.S. Bull., Feb. 1963.

Liddell, M. H.: Physical characteristics of speech sound. Purdue U. Bull. 16, March, 1924.

Lindsley, Charles Frederick: Psycho-physical determinants of individual differences in voice quality. Los Angeles, unpub. dissertation, Ph.D., University of Southern Calif., 1932.

Lloyd, R. J.: Genesis of vowels. British Assn. Paper, 1896.

Luchsinger[2]: Falsett und Vollton der Kopfstimme (Beitrag zum Registerproblem). Ztschr. Hals- Nasen- u. Ohrenh., 52:1949.

Luchsinger[3]: Schalldruck- und Geschwindigkeitsregistierung der Atemluft beim Singer. Folia Phoniatr., 3:1951.

Makepeace, Ronald Allen: An auditory analysis of the vibrato; a thesis presented to the faculty of psychology, U. of So. Calif., Master of Arts, May 1939, unpublished.

Mason, Robert M., and Willard R. Zemlin: The phenomenon of vocal vibrato. N.A.T.S. Bull., Feb. 1966.

Metfessel, Milton: The vibrato in artistic voices. University of Iowa Studies in the Psychology of Music. Iowa City, Iowa, 1932.

Moore, Paul: The treatment of voice defects following surgery. Connecticut M. J., 19:1955.

Moore[2] and Hans von Leden: Dynamic variations of the vibratory pattern in the normal larynx. Folia Phoniat., 10:No. 4, 1958.

Osborne, Charles: An x-ray view of flute vibrato. Selmer Bandwagon, 8:1960.

Paget[3]: The production of artificial vowel sounds. Proc. Royal Soc. of Arts, 102:1923.

Panconcelli-Calzia, Giulio: Die Stimmatmung, das Neue—das Alte. Nova Acta Leopoldina, 18:1956.

Perkins, W. H., G. Sawyer and P. Harrison: Research on vocal efficiency. N.A.T.S. Bull., Dec. 1958.

Peterson, Gordon E., and Harold L. Barney: Control methods used in the study of the vowels. J. Acoustical Soc. of America. 24:1952.

Pressman, Joel J.: Physiology of the vocal cords in phonation and respiration. Arch. Otolaryng., 35:1942.

Pressman[2]: Sphincters of the larynx. Arch. Otolaryng., 59:1954.

Raskin, Judith: American bel canto. Opera News, Jan.15, 1966.

Ross[3]: Final report of the voice teachers' survey. Research Comm. N.A.T.S., 1947.

Rubin, Henry J.: The falsetto, a high speed cinematographic study. The Laryngoscope, Sep., 1960.

Rubin,[2] Maurice LeCover and William Vennard: Vocal intensity, subglottic pressure, and air flow relationships in singers. In preparation for publication.

Ruth, Wilhelm: The registers of the singing voice. N.A.T.S. Bull., May, 1963.

Ruth[2]: The cause of the individual differences in the sensation of head resonance in singing. N.A.T.S. Bull., Oct., 1966.

Schilling, R.: Der Musculus sternothyreoideus und seine stimmphysiologische Bedeutung. Arch. Sprach- u. Stimmh., 1:1937.

Scripture[2]: The study of English speech sounds by new methods of phonetic investigation. Proceedings of the British Academy, 11:1923.

Sr. Joan Marie Gove, R.S.H.M.: A study to determine the effect of vibrato and straight tone upon the pitch factor of the human voice. Special project in voice pedagogy, School of Music, U. of So. Calif., unpublished, August, 1966.

Smith, Svend: Vocalization and added nasal resonance. Folia Phoniat., 3:1931.

Sokolowsky, R.: Effect of the extrinsic laryngeal muscles in voice production. Arch. Otolaryng., 38:1943.

Sonninen, Aatto A.: The role of the external laryngeal muscles in length-adjustment of the vocal cords in singing. Acta Oto-laryng., sup. 130, 1956.

Tiffany, William R.: Vowel recognition as a function of duration, frequency modulation and phonetic context. J. Speech & Hearing Disorders, 28:1953.

Tiffany[2]: Nonrandom sources of variation in vowel quality. J. Speech & Hearing Research, 2:1959.

Tiffany[3]: Intelligibility of slow-played speech. J. Speech & Hearing Research, 4:1961.

Timcke, R., Hans von Leden and Paul Moore: Laryngeal vibrations: measurements of the glottal wave. Part I, A.M.A. Arch. Otolaryng., 68:July, 1958; Part II, Ibid., 69:April, 1959.

Tokizane, T., K. Kawamata and H. Tokizane: Electromyographic studies on the human respiratory muscles. Jap. J. Physiol., 2:1952.

Triplett, William M.: An investigation of the effects of vibrato and straight-tone productions on the intelligibility of vowels. Special project in voice pedagogy, School of Music, U. of So. Calif., unpublished, August, 1966.

Triplett[2]: An investigation concerning vowel sounds on high pitches. N.A.T.S. Bull., Feb., 1967.

Vallencien, Bernard: Images glottiques des registres vocaux. Communication au 56 Congress Franç. d'Oto-rhino-laryngologie, Paris, Oct., 1958.

van den Berg, Janwillem: Zur Anatomie des menschlichen Musculus vocalis. Ztschr. Anat., 118:1955.

van den Berg[2]: On the role of the laryngeal ventricle in voice production. Folia Phoniat., 7:1955.

van den Berg[3] and J. T. Zantema and P. Doornenbal: On the air resistance and the Bernoulli effect of the human larynx. J. Acous. Soc. America, 29:1957.

van den Berg[4]: On the myoelastic-aerodynamic theory of voice production. N.A.T.S. Bull., May 1958.

van den Berg[5] and T. S. Tan: Données nouvelles sur la fonction laryngée. J. Franç. Oto-laryng., 8:1959.

van den Berg[6] and William Vennard: Toward an objective vocabulary for voice pedagogy. N.A.T.S. Bull., Feb. 1959.

van den Berg[7]: Vocal ligaments versus registers. N.A.T.S. Bull., Feb. 1961.

Vennard, William: More than teaching. Am. Music Teacher, Nov.-Dec. 1953.

Vennard[2]: Pitch difficulties. N.A.T.S. Bull., May 1956.

Vennard[3]: Philosophies of voice pedagogy. Am. Music Teacher, May-June 1958.

Vennard[4]: Registration. Music Journal, Mar. 1959.

Vennard[5]: The Bernoulli effect in singing. N.A.T.S. Bull., Feb. 1961.

Vennard[6] and Nobuhiko Isshiki: Coup de glotte, a misunderstood expression. N.A.T.S. Bull., Feb. 1964.

Vennard[7]: The psychology of the pupil-teacher relationship. Am. Music Teacher, May-June 1964.

Vennard[8]: An experiment to evaluate the importance of nasal resonance in singing. Folia Phoniat., 16:1964.

Vennard,[9] and James W. Irwin: Speech and song compared in sonagrams. N.A.T.S. Bull., Dec., 1966.

von Leden, Hans, Paul Moore and R. Timcke: Laryngeal vibrations: measurements of the glottal wave, Part III. A.M.A. Arch. Otolaryng., 71:Jan. 1960.

Wade, Archie, and Clarence Sawhill: The anatomy of a vibrato. 16 mm. film, 12 min. with sound. Radiology Department, Medical Center, U. of California at Los Angeles, 1960.

Weiss, Deso: Ein Resonanzphänomen der Singstimme. Monatschrift für Ohren. und Laryngo-Rhin. 66:1932.

Weiss[2]: The pubertal change of the human voice. Folia Phoniat., 2:1950.

Whitworth, James R.: A cinefluorographic investigation of the supralaryngeal adjustments in the male voice accompanying the singing of low tones and high tones. Unpublished Ph.D. dissertation, State University of Iowa, August, 1961.

Winckel, Fritz: Die psychoakustische Bewertung des Spektrums, Folia Phoniat., 12:1960.

Wooldridge, Warren B.: The nasal resonance factor in the sustained vowel tone in the singing voice. Doctoral Dissertation Series, University Microfilm, Ann Arbor, Mich., Pub. No. 10, 161, Indiana University, 1954.

Wooldridge[2]: Is there nasal resonance? N.A.T.S. Bull., Oct. 1956.

Wustrow, Fritz: Bau und Funktion des menschlichen M. vocalis. Ztschr. Anat., 116:1952.

Zenker, W., and A. Zenker: Über die Regelung der Stimmlippenspannung durch von aussen eingreifenden Mechanismen. Folia Phoniat., 12:1960.

Zerffi, W.A.C.: Tonsillectomy and its effect on the singing voice. Arch. Otalaryng., 35:1942.

Zerffi[2]: Laryngology and voice production. Annal. Otol. Rhin. & Laryng., 61:1952.

THESAURUS

On the following pages is a compendium which I hope will serve several purposes. First, it takes the place of the usual glossary. Words in common usage are defined with reference to singing. Where two contradictory uses of a word seem to have currency, both are given. Where an expression or a definition seems to belong to a particular author or to have originated with him, his name appears in parentheses. Also included are a great many technical terms often used in books on the voice but not always defined. Finally, the arrangement of the thesaurus makes it a fairly complete summary of the material in the book, although such a dictionary as this cannot hope to be exhaustive and some of the words must be placed arbitrarily.

The index to the thesaurus also includes paragraph references to the body of the text.

GENERAL SCIENCE

| 901 | Miscellaneous Terms |

air: Medium in which humans usually propagate sound waves.

atmosphere: Air

Bernoulli effect: Suction produced by the fact that air in motion has less density or pressure than air that is not in motion.

carbon dioxide: Gas which fills the lungs as a product of metabolism, and which must be expelled.

cone: Figure that tapers uniformly from a circular base to a point.

cylinder: Circular figure of uniform diameter having two circular bases.

diameter: Maximum distance, measured in a straight line, from one side of a circle to the other.

energy: Power to do mechanical work.

fulcrum: Point upon which a lever turns, or upon which it obtains purchase.

gravity: Attractive force by which all bodies tend to move toward the center of the earth.

heat: Form of energy generated by combustion, chemical action, or friction.

hypothesis: Assumption as a basis of reasoning.

kinesiologic: Pertaining to motion.

lens: Object, usually glass, whose shape is such that it focuses rays which pass through it.

lever: Rigid structure turning on a support, or fulcrum, transferring energy from one part to another.

light: Form of energy sensed by the eye.

matter: Substance of which a physical object is made.

molecule: Unit of matter.

momentum: Tendency of matter in motion to continue in same direction.

oxidization: Combining with oxygen.

oxygen: Gas which the blood must absorb from the breath for bodily energy.

physics: Science of matter and energy.

physics of music: Acoustics.

pneumatic: Having to do with mechanical properties of air, or other elastic fluids or gasses.

pressure: Continued application of power.

reflector: A concave object whose shape is such that it focuses rays which reach it.

science: Knowledge gained and verified by exact observation and logical reasoning. Expertness resulting from knowledge.

sphere: Figure whose surface is everywhere equidistant from a certain point, called the center.

suction: Drawing in by creation of partial vacuum.

temperature: Degree of heat.

tension: Act of stretching or straining, or condition of being stretched.

ACOUSTICS

| 902 | Miscellaneous Terms |

acoustics: Science of sound.

compression: Condition in which molecules are closer together than is normal.

compression wave: Part of a sound wave.

concentration: Compression (Marchesi).

coupling: Joining together.

curve: Line which deviates from a straight line according to some mathematical principle. Musical vibrations when projected in time (as on a moving strip) produce curves.

dilation: Rarefaction (Marchesi).

displacement-time curve: Curve such as is made by a musically vibrating body, so called because it shows the displacement of a given point on the vibrator at different times (Judson & Weaver).

elasticity: Property of matter causing molecules to resume normal spacing or causing matter to resume its normal shape.

focus: Point at which rays are made to converge.

oscillate: To move backwards and forwards. Vibrate.

rarefaction: Condition in which molecules are farther apart than is normal.

rarefaction wave: Part of a sound wave.

ray: Straight line between a source of vibration and the point at which the vibration is sensed.

sine curve: Curve of simple harmonic motion.

sinusoid: Sine curve.

sound: Disturbance of the air capable of being heard.

sound wave: One of a series of disturbances of the air consisting of compressions alternated with rarefactions.

supersonics: Science of speeds greater than 1100 feet per second (the speed of sound).

vibrate: To move back and forth. Oscillate.

Continuation of 901

vertical phase difference: Extent to which upper and lower surfaces of vocal folds do not open and close synchronously. In heavy mechanism, lower vibration is slightly ahead of the upper.

volume: Cubic contents of an enclosed space.

water: Common liquid, basis of bodily fluids.

VIBRATION

903	Regular	904	Irregular

903 — Regular

beauty: Harmony of diverse elements which gives extreme pleasure to the esthetic sense. Ant.: ugliness.

concord: Harmony.

cycle: (1) Event that is repeated. (2) Time in which it occurs. (3) Complete vibration, including compression and rarefaction.

double vibration: Complete forward and back movement. Cycle.

dulcet: Sweet; pleasing.

d.v.: Abbreviation for double vibration.

euphony: Pleasant sound.

harmony: Pleasing agreement of musical sounds.

Hz.: Cycle; double vibration. Abbreviation used in Germany in honor of a great physicist, Hertz.

melody: Pleasing and rhythmical series of tones.

music: Expression of beauty in melody, harmony, dynamics, and timbre.

musical tone: Tone.

pendular: Oscillating regularly.

pendulum: Swinging or oscillating body whose frequency remains constant.

phase. Particular point or moment in a cycle. Vibrations whose moments of compression or rarefaction coincide are said to be "in phase."

pleasing: Gratifying to the senses.

regular: Constant; cyclical; even; harmonic; isochronous; musical; oscillatory; pendular; periodic; recurrent; rhythmic; steady; vibratory.

resounding: Prolonged; far-reaching in sound.

simple harmonic motion: Simple regular vibration, such as the motion of a tuning fork.

singing: Producing musical tone, especially with the voice.

tone: Regular series of sound saves. Ant.: noise.

tune: Melody.

vowel: Speech sound that is a tone.

wave-length: Distance between beginning of one vibration cycle and the beginning of the next.

904 — Irregular

blare: Loud, brazen sound.

cacaphony: Unpleasant sound.

caterwaul: To utter a discordant cry like a cat.

clamor: Noisy confusion of voices.

clang: Metallic noise.

clatter: Rattling noise; racket.

consonant: Speech sound that is chiefly noise.

crash: Loud noise as of breaking.

din: Continuous distressing noise.

fracas: Noisy brawl.

harsh: Rough or grating to the senses.

hubbub, hullaballoo: Confused noise.

inharmonic partial: Overtone whose frequency is not an exact multiple of the fundamental.

irregular: Erratic; inharmonic; jerky; nonperiodic; spasmodic; uncertain; uneven; unsystematic; variable.

noise: Irregular series of sound waves. Ant.: tone.

pandemonium: Devilish noisiness.

racket: Loud, confused sounds. Clatter.

rustle: Succession of frictional noises.

susurrus: Gentle rustle.

ugliness: Opposite of beauty.

unmusical: Opposite of musical.

uproar: Violent noise, disturbance.

vociferation: Noisy exclamation.

PROPERTIES OF TONE

905	Pitch	906	Duration

compass: Extent of a given series of pitches, either in a voice or a register of the voice. Range.

consonant interval: Relation between two pitches, the ratio of whose frequencies is such an easy fraction that the ear hears the notes as "sounding together."

dissonant interval: Relation between two pitches, the ratio of whose frequencies is such a difficult fraction that the ear hears the notes as "sounding separately."

enharmonic: One of two or three notes that are written differently but played the same on a tempered keyboard.

flat: (n) A symbol for lower pitch; (v) to lower pitch.

frequency: Rate of recurrence of a vibration.

glissando: Playing all possible pitches between the first and last sounded, as when the finger is slid over a sounding string.

high note or tone: Note or tone having high frequency.

International Concert Pitch: Standard whereby A_4 on the treble staff is tuned to 440 cycles per second.

interval: Difference between two pitches, expressed in scale degrees.

intonation: Reproduction in performance of the pitches indicated.

low note or tone: Note or tone having low frequency.

Middle C, C_4: Note centrally placed in pitch notation, having a frequency of 261.6 cycles per second, International Concert Pitch.

note: Strictly, a symbol for the pitch and duration of a tone; loosely, a synonym for "tone."

octave: Interval between two pitches whose frequencies are in the ratio of 2 to 1.

pitch: Subjective aspect of frequency.

portamento: Gliding through all the pitches between the first and last sounded. Vocal glissando; slur.

range: Compass.

scale: Series of pitches in order of frequency.

scoop: Slang for an upward slur, applied to careless attacks below the pitch which must be tuned up.

sharp: (n) Symbol for higher pitch; (v) to raise pitch.

slur: Portamento.

tempered scale: Scale in which the pitches are slightly altered to facilitate modulation.

tessitura: Pitch region in which most of the notes of a given role lie. That part of a singer's compass in which he sings with most ease and beauty.

threshold of audibility (pitch): Lowest frequency recognized by the ear as a tone (15 or 16 vibrations per second).

ultrasonics: Science of vibrations of frequency too great for hearing.

906 Duration

beat: Unit of duration.

cadence: (1) Rhythmic beat, as in marching. (2) Succession of tones producing more or less satisfactory close.

duration: Continuance in time.

held note: Note prolonged beyond its assigned duration.

long note: Note with considerable duration.

meter: Characteristic rhythm, for music or poetry.

metronome: Clock-like instrument for marking meter.

rest: (1) Cessation of tone for a definite time period. (2) Symbol for the cessation.

rhythm: The systematic grouping of notes according to their duration.

rubato: Lit.: robbing. Changing time values for artistic effect.

tempo: Speed at which music is performed.

tenuto: Held note; long note.

time: (1) Indefinite measurable duration. (2) Characteristic rhythm. Meter.

907	Intensity

amplitude: Spatial correlative of intensity.

bel: Unit of loudness. If a sound is 10 times as great as another, it is said to be "1 bel higher." If it is 100 times as great, it is "2 bels higher."

crescendo: Increase in volume.

damping, dampening: Stopping or decreasing the amplitude of a vibration by pressure on the vibrator. Term is applied to the appearance of the ends of the vocal cords in rapid vibration.

decibel: One tenth of a bel. Examples:
- 0 db. Threshold of hearing.
- 20 db. Leaves rustling in light breeze.
- 40 db. One typewriter in small room.
- 50 db. Animated conversation.
- 70 db. Range of symphony orchestra.
- 85 db. Riveter, heard from street.
- 95 db. Niagara Falls.
- 100 db. Subway train or station.
- 120 db. Airplane, close at hand.
- 130 db. Loudness at this level is painful.

decrescendo: Reduction in volume.

dynamics: That part of musical expression which has to do with intensity or loudness.

half-voice: Voice that is weak in intensity and often light in registration.

intensity: Energy of a sound wave.

loudness: Subjective aspect of intensity.

mezza voce: Lit.: half-voice.

power: Energy; intensity.

soft: Having low intensity. Ant.: loud.

stentorian: Loud-voiced.

threshold of audibility (intensity): The weakest sound that can be heard (0 decibels).

volume: Loudness.

weak: Soft.

908	Timbre	909	Sonance

acoustic spectrum: Spectrum.

Chord of Nature: Harmonic series.

clang-tint: Translation given by Ellis to the expression *klang-farbe* by Helmholtz.

color: Tone color; timbre.

component plot: Graph similar to a spectrum, but showing inharmonic partials (Scripture). See harmonic plot.

consistency: Uniformity of timbre throughout production.

dissonant partial: Overtone that is dissonant with the fundamental but is not inharmonic.

fundamental: Lowest in the series of partials.

harmonic: Harmonic partial.

harmonic partial: Any of the simple components of complex tone, the frequencies of the upper components being exact multiples of that of the lowest fundamental and overtones.

harmonic plot: Harmonic spectrum. (Term used by Scripture when all the partials are exact multiples of the fundamental frequency.)

harmonic series: Series beginning with the first harmonic partial (fundamental) and continuing without omission.

harmonic spectrum: Chart of the partials of a tone, showing their relative intensities.

inharmonic partial: Partial whose frequency is not an exact multiple of that of the fundamental.

klang-farbe: Tone color; timbre.

overtone: Partial higher than the fundamental.

partial: Component of tone.

pure tone: Tone having no overtones; simple tone.

quality: Timbre. Marchesi differentiated "quality" from "timbre."

simple tone: A tone having no overtones. Pure tone.

spectrum: Harmonic spectrum; harmonic plot; component plot.

timbre: Subjective aspect of the harmonic structure of musical tone. Quality; tone-color.

tone-color: Timbre.

Continuation of 909

tremulant: Mechanical device to produce instrumental tremolo.

tropidatio: Obsolete word for vibrato.

trill, *trillo:* Rapid alternation between two notes, step or half step apart.

vibrancy: Having vibration.

vibrato: Regular fluctuation in pitch, timbre, and/ or intensity.

vibrato crescendo: Exaggeration of the vibrato, toward the end of a sustained tone (Metfessel).

"vitality": Quality of tone due to vibrato.

vox humana: Lit.: human voice. Organ stop representing the voice, always played with tremulant.

wave: Abnormally slow vibrato.

wobble: Excessive vibrato.

---

agitation: (1) Shaking irregularly. (2) Emotion producing shaking in the voice.

"alive": Having good vibrato.

amplitude modulation: Regular fluctuation in loudness. Intensity vibrato.

barn dance fiddle: Violin played without vibrato.

barn dance voice: Twangy voice, usually pinched and "straight."

beat: Regular augmentation of intensity at moments when two tones are in phase.

crispiato: Obsolete word for vibrato.

"dead": Lacking vibrato; "flat"; "straight."

decay: Manner in which a sustained tone ends, following its steady state. May be gradual, rapid, or abrupt. See growth, steady state.

deviation: Departure from perfect regularity or uniformity of production of tone. See envelope, sonance.

envelope: Pattern of deviation of a tone. Includes growth, steady state, vibrato, decay. Sonance.

"flat": Lacking vibrato; "dead."

fluctuation: More or less regular variation, as of waves.

flutter: Rapid beating, as of wings.

frequency modulation: Regular fluctuation in pitch. Pitch vibrato.

growth: Development of a tone from its beginning to its steady state. May be gradual, rapid, or sudden. See steady state, decay.

"intensity": Acoustical term often misapplied to vibrato.

intensity vibrato: Regular fluctuation in loudness. amplitude modulation.

melism: Factors of sonance in the voice aimed at listener reaction, as urging, questioning, calming, irritating (Moses).

ondeggiamento: Obsolete word for vibrato.

quaver, quiver: Involuntary shake.

"resonance": Term misapplied to vibrato.

reverberatio: Obsolete word for vibrato.

shake: Agitation; vibration. Specifically a trill.

"shimmer": Tremulous light, applied figuratively to vibrato.

sonance: The pattern of change in timbre, pitch, intensity, or admixture of noise in a given tone (Seashore).

steady state: Condition of a sustained tone after its initial growth. May be with or without vibrato. See growth, decay.

"straight": Lacking vibrato; "flat"; "dead."

"tenderness": Quality of vocal tone, attributed to vibrato.

tremble: To shake involuntarily, as with cold or fear.

tremolando: Played with tremolo.

tremolo: In instrumental music, the repetition of a tone in rapid succession. The term has been applied to any vocal vibrato that is undesirable.

tremor: Quiver.

910	Actuator	911	Vibrator

Examples:

    piano: Action, plus arms of player.

    violin: Bow, plus arm of player.

    oboe: Respiratory system of player.

    trumpet: Respiratory system of player.

    voice: Respiratory system of player.

Definitions:

action: System of levers including the keys and the hammers of a piano.

actuator: Source of energy of a musical instrument.

bow. Rod with stretched horsehair used to actuate the violin.

generator: Actuator (Marchesi).

motor: Actuator.

respiratory system: Organs of breathing.

Examples:

    piano: Strings.

    violin: Strings.

    oboe: Reeds.

    trumpet: Lips of player.

    voice: Vocal bands.

Definitions:

embouchure: Adjustment of the lips of a wind player.

natural frequency: Frequency at which a body will vibrate if it is allowed to vibrate freely.

play harmonics: To cause a string to sound at the frequency of one of its overtones instead of its fundamental.

reed: Thin strip of reed, wood, or metal, forming the vibrator of a wind instrument.

segment: To vibrate as two or more parts instead of as a whole.

string: Strand of gut or metal forming the vibrator of piano, violin, or kindred instrument.

vibrator: That part of an instrument which turns the energy into oscillation.

vocal bands: Muscles of the larynx which vibrate to produce phonation.

913

bagpipe: Wind instrument actuated by a bag under the player's arm.

bell: Hollow metallic percussion instrument.

brasses, brass instruments: Those wind instruments whose vibrators are the lips of the player, like the trumpet, horn.

celeste: Small keyboard instrument with steel plates suspended over wooden resonators.

clarinet: Soprano member of the single reed instrument family.

clarino, (clarini, p.): Shrill trumpet, now obsolete. Also, overblown clarinet register.

English horn: Double reed instrument pitched a fifth below the oboe.

flute: Wind instrument consisting of a pipe with holes which are covered by the fingers.

French horn: Wind instrument descended from the hunting horn. Only such instrument in which valves are played by left hand. Right hand is used as a mute in the bell.

horn: French horn.

instrument (musical): Machine for producing musical tone.

912   Resonator

Examples:
    piano: Sounding board.
    violin: Sound box.
    oboe: Column of air.
    trumpet: Column of air.
    voice: Air in the throat, mouth, etc.

Definitions:

bell: Part of a wind instrument through which the tone finally emerges.

cavity: Hollow space with definite boundaries.

chalumeau: Those tones of the clarinet which can be produced without overblowing.

overblow: To cause a pipe to sound at the frequency of one of its overtones instead of its fundamental.

pipe: Tube in a musical instrument, of such length that the air contained will vibrate at a desired frequency.

resonator: Secondary vibrato; specifically, that part of an instrument which reinforces the primary vibration.

sound box: Wooden framework of a violin.

sounding board: Large, hard surface, usually wood, which is forced to resonate a vibration, usually of strings.

wolf tone: Tone produced by sympathetic resonance in a poor violin.

MUSICAL INSTRUMENTS

---

kazoo: Toy instrument in which humming excites sympathetic resonance in paper diaphragm.

marimba: Percussion instrument whose vibrators are bars of rosewood, and whose resonators are metal tubes underneath.

musical instrument: Machine for producing musical tone.

mute: Object placed in the bell of a wind instrument to alter the tone.

oboe: Soprano member of the double reed instrument family.

oboe d'amore: Double reed instrument pitched a third below the oboe.

organ: Elaborate keyboard wind instrument with mechanical actuator and many pipes.

percussions, percussion instruments: Those instruments which are sounded by being struck.

piano: Large keyboard instrument with strings.

reeds, reed instruments: Those wind instruments whose vibrators are reeds, like the clarinet, oboe.

saxophone: Brass instrument with a reed vibrator.

siren: Scientific instrument producing tone by generating a regular series of puffs of air.

strings, stringed instruments: Those instruments whose vibrators are strings, like the violin, piano.

trombone: Brass instrument that changes pitch by means of a slide instead of valves.

trumpet: Soprano member of the brass choir in the orchestra.

tuning fork: Scientific instrument having two arms which vibrate at a constant frequency, giving forth a tone.

vibra-harp: Percussion instrument similar to a marimba, but having metal vibrators and electrically rotated valves in the resonators which produce vibrato.

viol: Almost obsolete form of the violin.

violin: Soprano member of the string section of the orchestra.

winds, wind instruments: Those instruments which are actuated by breath.

woodwinds: Reeds.

xylophone: Percussion instrument family, of which the marimba is typical.

| 914 | Miscellaneous Terms | 915 | Harmonic Theory |

aria: Song, especially an operatic solo.

arpeggio: Notes of a chord played or sung in succession.

bravura: Display of elaborate, brilliant execution.

buffo: Musical clown.

choir, chorus: Vocal ensemble.

classical music: Specifically, music of the 18th Century. Generally, music which requires a certain amount of cultivation to be appreciated. Ant.: popular music.

commercial music: Music primarily for making money.

concert: Musical performance before an audience.

counterpoint: Combining two or more melodies.

descriptive music: Program music in which the "program" is quite literal.

diction song: Song, usually fast, in which words are of primary importance.

embellishment: Ornament.

ensemble: Group for concerted music making.

fioriture: Embellishments to ornament the music.

flautati: Uniformly continued series of small swelled sounds, multiplied as much as possible (Garcia).

florid: Ornamented, embellished, virtuosic.

Golden Age of Singing: Phrase chiefly derogatory to present-day singing, applied to almost any past age, but usually to the 18th Century.

grace note: Short note played or sung an instant before a note of longer time value.

imitative music: Lowest form of program music, in which the music reproduces sounds of nature.

legato: Quality of being smooth and connected.

Lied, (Lieder, pl.): Song, especially German song.

"line": An essential of musical artistry, implying legato and consistency of timbre.

lyric: Poem especially suited to music.

madrigal: Contrapuntal vocal form which flowered in the 16th Century.

marcato: Each note accented.

marking the part: Rehearsing a vocal assignment without using full voice.

mordant: Rapid ornament, on the beat, consisting of the written note followed by the note below and the written note sounded again.

musicology: Musical scholarship. Knowledge about music, as opposed to experience of music itself or skills of music making.

opera: Large musical work in which drama and music are combined and soloists both sing and act.

ornament: Notes not in the score, added to enhance the music. Originally improvised, later indicated by conventional symbols. Embellishment.

patter song: Song with many rapid words.

poetry: Expression of beauty in figurative words, usually rhythmical.

Fourier, Jean Baptiste Joseph: French mathematician who in "Théorie analytique de la chaleur," (Paris, 1822), set forth a formula for analyzing timbres in terms of harmonics.

harmonic theory: Theory that resonators merely augment harmonics which already have been produced by the vibrator. Ant.: puff theory.

Helmholtz, Hermann L. F.: German physicist who supported the view of Wheatstone in a book, "On the Sensations of Tone," (1885). The harmonic theory is sometimes called the Helmholtz, or the Wheatstone-Helmholtz Theory.

Miller, Dayton Clarence: American physicist who as late as 1926 aligned himself definitely with Wheatstone and Helmholtz. Since his time most authorities are inclined to minimize the differences between the theories, and to consider both necessary to a full understanding of resonance.

overtone theory: Harmonic theory.

relative pitch theory: Theory that the strong partial or partials of a tone will always be in the same relation to the fundamental. This is largely true of instrumental tone. Ant.: fixed pitch theory.

Wheatstone, Sir Charles: British physicist who in 1837 commented upon the work of Willis, adding the idea that the resonator probably augmented one of the partials of the vibrator tone. This was the germ of a theory that was the opposite of that of Willis.

Continuation of 914

popular music: Music produced especially for and accepted by the masses; commercial music. Ant.: classical music.

prima donna: Lit.: first lady. Soprano soloist, especially the lead in an opera.

program music: Music which expresses something outside of itself, such as poetry. See descriptive music, imitative music.

romanticism: Movement in the arts, especially in the 19th Century, away from intellectualism toward the emotional and the ideal.

song: Musical composition for the voice.

tessitura: That portion of a singer's range in which production is easiest and most beautiful. Pitch region in which most of the notes of a given part lie. If this is high, the role is said to have a "high tessitura."

text: Words, as of a song.

thematic development: Elaboration and combination of musical materials.

turn: Ornament, usually rapid, consisting of the note above, the written note, and the note below, returning to the written note on the beat.

| 916 | Puff Theory | 917 | Miscellaneous Terms |

cavity tone theory: Theory that vowel quality is determined by the pitch of the cavity through which the glottal tone passes. Originated by Willis in 1830. Formant theory; fixed pitch theory.

Dodart: French scientist whose book "Mémoires sur la cause de la voix (1741), first enunciated the puff theory, and stated that pitch is dependent upon tension in the vocal bands.

fixed pitch theory: Theory that the strong partial or partials of a tone will be determined by a fixed formant, and will be in the same frequency band, regardless of the pitch of the fundamental. This is largely true of vowel production. Ant.: relative pitch theory.

formant theory: Fixed pitch theory; cavity tone theory.

Hermann: German mathematician who in 1890 offered a formula for interpreting a Fourier analysis in terms of inharmonic rather than harmonic partials. This went back to the original idea of Willis.

puff theory: Theory that the vibrator of the voice emits puffs which only determine the pitch of the tone and excite the resonators, which add their own frequencies, harmonic or inharmonic. Ant.: harmonic theory.

Scripture, E. W.: British physicist who in 1906 strongly supported the Willis-Hermann theory, preferring the puff theory to that of Wheatstone and Helmholtz. He considered the vowel formants to be inharmonic.

Willis, Wilfred: British physicist who in 1830 advanced the idea that reeds of various pitches would speak the same vowel if sounded through the same pipe, implying that the vowel timbre was dependent upon the frequency of the resonator and independent of the fundamental.

coupling: Joining vibrator and resonator, which may be "loose" or "tight."

eddies: Circling currents in gas or liquid, caused by motion past a point of resistence at sufficient speed to cause turbulence.

forced resonance, vibration: Exciting a second vibrator by means of a direct physical connection with the first.

formant: Cavity (or cavities) in the resonance system that tends to produce a particular frequency among the overtones; the frequency band itself.

free resonance, vibration: Sympathetic resonance.

Helmholtz resonator: Turnip-shaped brass resonator to fit the ear.

impedance: Ratio of the pressure to the volume displacement at a given surface in a sound-transmitting medium. Roughly analogous to electrical resistence.

laminar: Smooth-flowing. Ant.: turbulent.

loosely coupled: Expression applied to vibrator and resonator that are in sympathy.

low-pass filter: Trap for high frequency vibrations which will not dampen low frequencies.

megaphone: Cone-shaped resonator, used for amplifying tone non-selectively.

node: Boundary at which a pipe or string segments in complex vibration.

non-selective resonator: Resonator which builds tones regardless of their frequencies; a megaphone.

primary vibrator: That part of a musical instrument to which power is applied, and which converts steady power into oscillation.

resonance: Reinforcement of sound by synchronous vibration.

secondary vibrator: That part of a musical instrument which vibrates synchronously with the primary vibrator. Resonator.

sympathetic resonance, vibration: Exciting a second vibrator having no connection with the first except the air.

sympathy: Relationship between two vibrators having the same natural frequency.

tightly coupled: Expression applied to vibrator and resonator that is forced to vibrate with it.

turbulent: Flowing at a rate producing audible agitation.

vortex theory: Theory that eddies are produced in the larynx, sending corkscrew currents of air throughout the resonators.

whirling currents: Eddies. Phrase used to translate *Wirbeln* in Lilli Lehmann, "How to Sing."

Wirbeln: Eddies. German word in Lilli Lehmann, *Meine Gesangkunst*, translated "whirling currents," and giving rise to vortex theory.

PHYSIOLOGY

918   Miscellaneous Terms

adenoid: Organ like a tonsil in the naso-pharynx.

anti-gravity muscles: Postural muscles.

antrum: Cavity of the body.

aorta: Great artery from the left ventricle of the heart.

aponeurosis: Tendon in the form of a broad sheet.

biceps: Muscle in upper arm which flexes the arm.

blood: Fluid that circulates in the heart, arteries, and veins.

bolus: Mass of food passing through the alimentary canal.

bone: Part of the rigid framework of the body.

buttocks: Gluteal prominences. Rump.

cartilage: A firm elastic tissue, forming part of the framework of the body, but not as rigid as bone. Gristle.

chondrification: Formation of cartilage.

circular muscle: Muscle whose fibres are circular, forming an elastic tube.

deglutition: Swallowing.

dilate: To enlarge; to expand.

esophagus: Passage through which food and drink pass into the stomach.

facet: Small smooth area on a bone or cartilage.

fixate: To render immovable

flesh: Softer tissues of the body.

fossa, (fossae, pl.): A shallow depression or cavity. There are two nasal fossae.

gluteus: Muscle connecting leg to pelvis, forming the buttock.

gristle: Cartilage.

gullet: Specifically, the esophagus; more loosely, the throat.

gulp: To take a large draught or swallow.

heart: Muscular pump that circulates the blood.

heel of the hand: That part of the palm which is nearest the wrist.

humerus: Bone of the upper arm.

levator: Muscle which elevates an organ or structure.

ligament: Band of tough tissue joining two bones or cartilages.

membrane: Thin, pliable tissue serving as a cover, connection, or lining.

mucous membrane: Lining of cavities which open to the exterior. Such a lining secretes mucous.

muscle: Organ which by contraction produces bodily movement.

myoelastic: Having to do with the elasticity of muscles.

myoelastic-aerodynamic theory: Theory that vocal fold vibration is determined by muscular tension and breath pressure. (See neuro-chronaxic.)

orifice: Aperture or opening.

osseous: Bony.

ossify: To become bony.

ostium, (ostia, pl.): Opening or passageway.

palpation: Touching or feeling.

patent: Open or distended.

peristalsis: Successive contractions of circular muscles causing the bolus to pass through the body.

polydactilism: Condition of having more than five digits on one hand.

postural muscles: Those muscles which maintain the position of the body. Anti-gravity muscles.

posture: Position of the body.

process: Projection of bone or cartilage.

raphe: Joint between two similar structures.

sphincter: Muscle or group of muscles which serves to close an orifice upon contraction.

stomach: Digestive pouch just below the diaphragm, into which the esophagus empties.

subscapularis: One of the muscles connecting the upper arm with the shoulderblade.

swallow: To pass food from the mouth and throat into the esophagus.

synovial joint: Joint enclosed in a membranous capsule containing lubricating fluid.

tendon: Band of tough tissue joining a muscle with a bone or cartilage.

teres: One of the muscles connecting the upper arm with the shoulderblade.

tonicity, tone, tonus: Amount of contraction in a muscle; elasticity of living parts.

tonsil: One of two oval organs situated between the faucial pillars.

triceps: Muscle in upper arm which straightens the arm.

vallecula: Furrow, such as is between the tongue and the epiglottis.

valve: Device for controlling the flow of liquids or gasses. In the body, a membranous or muscular fold or folds.

vena cava: Great vein entering the right auricle of the heart.

viscus, (viscera, pl.): Internal organ, especially in the abdomen.

vomit: To expel food from the stomach via the esophagus.

Continuation of 919

pseudovoice: Voice produced without phonation; e.g.: esophageal voice.

short-windedness: Weakness of running out of breath too soon.

spastic dysphonia: *Aphonia paralytica.*

struma: Goiter.

strumectomy: Removal of thyroid gland.

submucosal hemmorrhage: Discharge of blood under the mucous membrane of the vocal cord.

trachoma of the vocal folds: Nodes; nodules.

919	Pathology	920	Anatomical Orientation

adjuvent: Substance added to a prescription to assist the action of the base. "Drugs can be used as adjuvents in vocal rehabilitation," Brodnitz.

anhelation: Difficulty with breathing. Panting.

aphony: Inability to phonate.

aphony clericorum: Clergyman's sore throat.

aphony hysterica: Loss of speech due to hysteria.

aphony paralytica: Loss of speech due to paralysis or disease of laryngeal nerves.

chorditis tuberosa: Nodes, nodules.

cleft palate: Congenital fissure of hard and/or soft palate. Makes all vowels sound like nasals, spoils stop plosives by making implosion phase inadequate.

contact ulcer: Open lesion produced by friction between arytenoid cartilages. Common among men who abuse their voices. Rare among women.

corditis: Inflammation of vocal cord.

dyspnoea: Difficulty in breathing.

esophageal voice: Voice produced by swallowed air expelled from the esophagus, cultivated after laryngectomy.

gasp: To breathe violently.

goiter, goitre: Morbid swelling of thyroid glands. Struma.

granuloma: Grain-like prominence, usually found where a sore has healed. There are sometimes postanesthetic granulomas on vocal cords.

harelip: Congenital cleft in upper lip. Usually associated with cleft palate. Interferes with articulation. Chiloschisis.

hoarseness: Pathologically harsh voice.

hyperfunction: Overuse of phonatory mechanism, or use with more than optimal tension. Leads to hypofunction. (Froeschels)

hypofunction: Underactivity of phonatory mechanism, resulting from prolonged hyperfunction (Froeschels). Myasthenia, phonasthenia.

laryngectomy: Excision of the larynx.

laryngitis: Inflammation of the larynx.

myasthenia: Weakness of laryngeal function through prolonged abuse (Jackson). Hypofunction, phonasthenia.

node, nodule: Knot or tumor produced by friction between vocal ligaments. Common among women who abuse their voices. Rare among basses or baritones.

oedema: Swelling due to influx of fluids in muscle tissues.

papilloma: Tumor of the skin or of the mucous membrane, usually covered by a layer of thickened epidermis or epithelium; e.g.: a wart, corn, condyloma, etc.

phonasthenia: Myasthenia, hypofunction (Flatau).

polyp: Growth on the mucous membrane of the vocal cord. May be on upper or lower surface, difficult to discover in the latter case. Differs from nodule in not being on the edge of the cord.

abduct: To move away from the axis of the body. Muscles that open the glottis are abductors. Ant.: adduct.

adduct: To move toward the axis of the body. Muscles that close the glottis are adductors. Ant.: abduct.

anterior: In front; nearer the head; ventral. Ant.: posterior.

approximate: To come close together.

arise: A muscle is said to arise from that part of the framework which is comparatively fixed, and to be inserted in that part which the muscle moves.

articulate: To join together. Applied to parts of the bodily framework, or to speech sounds.

attachment: Connection of a muscle to a bone or cartilage.

bilateral, bilaterally: On both sides.

caudal: Toward the tail; posterior. Ant.: cephalic.

cephalic: Toward the head; anterior; superior; cranial. Ant.: caudal.

dorsal: In back; posterior. Ant.: ventral.

inferior: Lower, or below. Ant.: superior.

insertion: That part of the bodily framework to which a muscle is attached at the opposite end from its origin. See "arise."

ipsilateral: On the same side.

lateral: At the side.

longitudinal: Running lengthwise.

lumen: Cross-section area of the interior of a tubular structure.

medial: In the middle; median; central; mesal. Ant.: lateral or external.

occlude: To shut off.

origin: That part of the bodily framework from which a muscle arises.

posterior: In back; dorsal. Ant.: ventral.

pretracheal: In front of the trachea. The pretracheal muscles are sternothyroid, sternohyoid, omohyoid.

rostral: Toward the head. Ant.: caudal.

sagittal: Plane dividing the body into right and left portions.

somatic: Relating to the body or body wall. Ant.: visceral.

subglottal: Below the glottis.

superior: Higher or above. Ant.: inferior.

supraglottal: Above the glottis.

transverse: Lying across the axis of the body, at right angles to sagittal.

unilateral, unilaterally: On one side.

ventral: Relating to the belly. Ant.: dorsal.

visceral: Within the body. Ant.: somatic.

PHYSIOLOGY OF BREATHING

| 921 | General Anatomy | 922 | Rib Breathing |

abdominal ribs: False ribs; floating ribs.

alveolar cells: Small cavities; for example, the smallest air cavities in the lungs. Their total capacity is about 360 cc.

armpit: Cavity under the arm.

articular process: Projection from a vertebra articulating with a similar process on another vertebra.

backbone: Vertebral column; spine.

belly: Abdomen.

bifurcation: Division into two branches, like the division of the trachea into the bronchi.

breast bone: Bone to which the ribs join in front; the sternum.

bronchotracheal tree: System of tubing made up of the trachea and its branches.

bronchus, (bronchi, pl.): One of two branches into which the trachea subdivides on its way to the lungs.

cage: The ribs.

cervical vertebra: One of the seven vertebrae in the neck.

chest: Upper part of the trunk; the thorax.

clavicle: Bone extending between the shoulder and the breast bone; the collar bone.

coccyx: Four rudimentary vertebrae fused in one below the sacrum. Tail bone.

collarbone: Clavicle.

costa, (costae, pl.): Rib.

dorsal vertebra: One of the twelve vertebrae to which ribs attach. Thoracic vertebra.

false ribs: Five ribs below the true ribs. The false ribs do not attach directly to the sternum, though the three upper ones attach to the lowest (7th) true rib.

floating ribs: Two lowest ribs (11th and 12th). The floating ribs attach to the spine at the back, but to no part of the skeleton in front.

ilium (ilii, pl.): Wide upper portion of the side of the pelvis. Haunch bone.

ischium: Lower back part of the pelvis.

lobe: One of two or more roundish parts separated by a fissure. (In this book, one of the two divisions of the lungs.)

lumbar vertebra: One of the five vertebrae below the ribs, above the pelvis.

lung: Each of two breathing organs in the thorax.

manubrium of the sternum: Upper part of the sternum, to which the first two ribs attach.

pelvis: Bony structure of the lower trunk.

phrenic nerve: Nerve controlling the diaphragm.

rib: One of twelve bones on each side of the body that form a bony protection for the contents of the thorax.

sacrum: Spade-shaped bone in the middle of the pelvis, below the lumbar vertebrae.

scapula: One of two flat bones in the back of the shoulders. Shoulder-blade.

auxiliary breathing: Rib breathing (Witherspoon).

bellows action: Mechanical action similar to rib breathing.

"breath of activity": Rib breathing (Witherspoon).

costal breathing: Rib breathing.

erector spinae: Large group of muscles in the middle of the back, primarily postural but capable of assisting in pulling ribs downward. Sacrospinalis.

external intercostals: One of three groups of muscles between the ribs. They pull the ribs upward.

iliocostalis: Subgroup of muscles in the outer parts of erector spinae. Pulls ribs toward ilium.

intercostalis intimi: Thin layer of intercostal muscles with fibres parallel with main internal intercostals. Covers layer of nerves and blood vessels.

intercostals: Three sets of muscles between the ribs. Interni and intimi are expiratory. Externi are inspiratory.

internal intercostals: One of three sets of muscles between the ribs. They pull the ribs downward.

lateral breathing: Costal or rib breathing. (Term used by Marchesi, who deplored both this and clavicular breathing.)

levatores costarum: Small muscles from backbone to ribs, raising them.

longissimus dorsi: Subgroup of muscles in the middle of erector spinae. Can be expiratory.

rib breathing: Breathing by moving the ribs; costal breathing.

sacrospinalis: Erector spinae.

scalenus: Muscles in the neck that help elevate upper ribs.

serratus posterior superior: Muscles attaching to the spine and pulling upward upon the ribs.

subcostals: Small muscles inside the ribcage near the spine, each pulling a rib toward a lower rib.

transversus thoracis, triangularis sterni: Muscles attaching to the inside of the sternum and pulling down upon the second to sixth ribs.

triangularis sterni: Transversus thoracis.

Continuation of 921

shoulder-blade: Scapula.

shoulder girdle: Bones of the shoulder. Clavicles and scapulae considered as a unit.

spine: Vertebral column; backbone.

spinous process: Bony projection in middle of a vertebra at the back.

sternum: Bone to which the ribs join in front; the breastbone.

thoracic vertebrae: One of twelve vertebrae to which the ribs attach. Dorsal vertebra.

thorax: Upper part of the trunk; the chest.

trachea: Cartilaginous tube through which air passes in and out of the lungs; the windpipe.

transverse process: One of two sideward projections from a vertebra.

Continued, bottom of page 241

PHYSIOLOGY OF BREATHING

923	Belly Breathing	924	Shoulder Breathing

abdominal breathing: Diaphragmatic-abdominal breathing. Sometimes applied to a somewhat unsightly habit of allowing the belly to protrude unnecessarily.

ascending oblique muscles: Internal oblique muscles.

belly breathing: Breathing by descent of the diaphragm and contraction of the abdominal muscles, in alternation.

"belt" muscles: Abdominal muscles which move inwardly when one coughs, which are antagonistic to the diaphragm (Holmes).

"breath of life": Diaphragmatic breathing Witherspoon).

"breathing muscle": Epigastrium (Greene). More correctly, the whole belly breathing musculature.

central tendon: Large flat tendon in the middle of the diaphragm.

deep breathing: Belly breathing.

descending oblique muscles: External oblique muscles.

diaphragm: Large dome-shaped muscle that provides a floor for the thorax.

diaphragmatic breathing, diaphragmatic-abdominal breathing: Belly breathing.

epigastrium: Upper part of the abdominal wall, over the stomach. Erroneously called the "diaphragm."

external oblique muscles: Obliquus abdominis externus, or descending oblique muscles.

flanks: Transverse and oblique abdominal muscles (Husler and Rodd-Marling include the lower intercostals also, and emphasize the importance of breathing with these muscles.)

internal oblique muscles: Oblique abdominis internus, or ascending oblique muscles.

linea alba: Ligamentous separation between the two rectus abdominis muscles. Runs vertically in the middle of the abdomen.

midriff: Epigastrium. Confusing synonym for diaphragm.

obliquus abdominis: Muscles forming the sides of the belly. They include obliquus internus and obliquus externus abdominis, also called internal or ascending oblique and external or descending oblique.

piston action: Mechanical action similar to diaphragmatic action.

quadratus lumborum: Muscles from the ilii to the lowest ribs, holding them down to provide anchorage for the diaphragm.

rectus abdominis: Muscles forming the front part of the belly. The fibres run up and down.

serratus posterior inferior: Postural muscles in the lower back which may assist quadratus lumborum.

transversus abdominis: Deep abdominal muscle cooperating with the other abdominal muscles in exhalation. Its fibres run from side to side behind the oblique abdominals.

"breath of exhaustion": Clavicular breathing (Witherspoon).

chest breathing: Shoulder breathing.

clavicular breathing: Shoulder breathing.

cucullarius: Trapezius muscle.

deltoideus: Shoulder muscle.

heaving: Shoulder breathing.

high chest breathing: Shoulder breathing.

latissimus dorsi: One of two large flat muscles arising from an aponeurosis in the lower back and inserted in the armpits to the shoulders. They attach also to some of the lower ribs, pulling them upward. Shakespeare felt that latissimus dorsi and serratus magnus were useful in back breathing, and they may aid in steadying exhalation.

levator scapulae: One of the muscles attaching to the cervical vertebrae and pulling up on the scapulae.

pancostal breathing: Breathing for singing while holding in the abdominals strongly, on the theory that this would maintain a high central tendon, causing the diaphragm to raise the ribs; chest breathing.

pectoralis: One of two sets of breast muscles, arising at the shoulder and attached to the sternum, clavicle, and some of the ribs. They help in chest breathing.

rhomboideus: One of the muscles under trapezius, joining the scapulae to the spine. They retract the scapulae.

serratus anterior, serratus magnus: Muscles attaching to the scapulae and exerting a pull upon eight or nine of the upper ribs. They are buried under the broader back muscles, but may be felt under the arms. They assist in forced inhalation, especially when the shoulders are drawn up.

shoulder breathing: Inhaling by fixing the shoulders and pulling up the ribs by means of muscles which normally move the shoulders. Provides no control over exhalation. Chest or clavicular breathing.

sternocleidomastoid: Muscle extending from behind the ear down to the breastbone.

subclavius: Muscle joining the clavicle and the first rib. Helps in shoulder breathing.

trapezius: Large, flat, triangular muscle joining the scapula and clavicle to the spine, and running up to the back of the skull. Lifts the clavicle and retracts the scapula, thus participating in shoulder breathing. Cucullarius.

Continuation of 921

true ribs: Seven uppermost ribs, which attach to the sternum.

vertebra, (vertebrae, pl.): One of the twenty-four bones which form the spine. There are seven cervical vertebrae in the neck, twelve dorsal vertebrae to which ribs attach, five lumbar vertebrae below the cage.

windpipe: Trachea.

PHYSIOLOGY OF BREATHING

aerodynamic: Having to do with air in motion, and its mechanical effects.

apnoe: Condition of holding the breath.

back breathing: Breathing technic in which attention is centered upon expansion in the back.

blowing: Supplying air as in sounding a wind instrument.

breath control: Smooth maintenance of breath pressure over extended periods of time.

breath flow: Volume of breath expenditure.

breath management: Efficient use of respiration for singing or playing a wind instrument.

breathing: Process of taking in breath and expelling it again.

complemental breath: Air which may be inhaled in addition to tidal breath, by effort. About 1600 cc. or 3 pints.

cough: To expel air from the lungs spasmodically and/or noisily.

dead space: Capacity of the trachea, bronchi, etc., so called because oxygen can be absorbed only from that air which is in the alveoli. About 140 cc. of the 500 cc. tidal air.

exhalation, expiration: Expelling breath.

flow rate: Number of cubic centimeters of breath expelled per second.

forced breathing: Breathing in which effort is made to inhale and exhale as much air as possible each time. Ant.: tidal breathing.

gesture of inhalation: Bodily position reached after deep inspiration.

"holding the breath": Psychological breath control expedient (Stanley).

hookup: Coordination between breathing mechanism and larynx (Bachner).

inhalation; inspiration: Taking in breath.

mental note: *Nota mentale*

minimal air: Small amount of air still remaining in the lungs after they have been collapsed.

nota mentale: Imaginary note sustained for an instant beyond the note actually sung, a psychological device for maintaining breath support throughout the tone.

panting: Taking of rapid short breaths.

phrasing: Division of a piece of music into small units for some artistic or technical purpose; especially, into units which can be sung on breath.

pulmonary: Relating to the lungs.

reserve breath: That part of the unforced lung capacity which is not used in tidal breathing; the total of supplemental, residual, and minimal imprisoned air. About 2600 cc. or 5 pints.

residual breath: Air remaining in the lungs after forced exhalation, which cannot be voluntarily expired, but which escapes when the lungs are collapsed. About 1000 cc. or 2 pints.

respiration: Breathing.

"sitting on the breath": Maintaining breath pressure without collapsing the thorax.

stationary air: That part of the lung capacity which is not emptied in breathing. In forced breathing, stationary air is same as residual breath; in tidal breathing stationary air is same as reserve breath.

supplemental breath: Air which may be exhaled in addition to tidal expiration, by effort. About 1600 cc. or 3 pints.

tidal breath: Air which is inhaled and exhaled in quiet breathing. About 500 cc. or 1 pint.

vital capacity: Maximum breath which can be exhaled after forced inhalation; the total of complemental, tidal, and supplemental breath. About 3700 cc. or 7 to 8 pints.

PHYSIOLOGY OF THE LARYNX

| 926 | Framework |

Adam's Apple: Protuberance of the thyroid cartilage.

ala of the thyroid, (alae, pl.): Wing of the thyroid.

apex of the arytenoid: Head of the arytenoid.

arytenoid cartilage: One of two cartilaginous levers at the posterior ends of the vocal cords, attached to the cricoid cartilage.

conus elasticus: Tough membrane on the under side of the vocal folds. Includes vocal and cricothyroid ligaments. Cricovocal membrane.

corniculate cartilage: C. of Santorini.

cornu of the thyroid, (cornua, pl.): One of four horn-like projections at the back of the thyroid.

cricoid cartilage: Base of the larynx.

cricoid plate: Large, flat surface at the back of the cricoid.

cricothyroid ligament: Thickening of the conus elasticus between cricoid and thyroid cartilages at the front. Middle cricothyroid ligament.

cricovocal membrane: Conus elasticus.

cuneiform cartilage: C. of Wrisberg.

epiglottis: Leaf-shaped cartilage forming a lid for the larynx.

glottal process: Vocal process.

greater horn of the hyoid: One side of the hyoid bone, projecting to the back.

head of the arytenoid: Upward projection of the arytenoid cartilage.

horn of the thyroid: Cornu of the thyroid.

hyoid bone: U-shaped bone in the root of the tongue, from which the thyroid cartilage is suspended.

inferior cornu or horn of the thyroid: One of two downward projecting horns of the thyroid.

lesser horn of the hyoid: One of two small upward projections at the front of the hyoid bone.

ligamentous glottis: Part of the glottis which is bounded by the vocal ligaments. Muscular glottis.

lower horn: Inferior cornu.

middle cricothyroid ligament: Ligament joining the cricoid and thyroid, situated between the pars recta of the cricothyroid muscles, providing origin for part of the thyroarytenoids.

muscular process: Sideward projection of the arytenoid cartilage, to which various muscles attach.

notch of the thyroid: Space at the top and front, where the wings of the thyroid do not join.

oblique ridge: Ridge on the outside of the wing of the thyroid, to which various muscles attach.

pyriform sinus: Space between the collar of the larynx and the wing of the thyroid.

Santorini, cartilage of: Small hornlike cartilage, flexibly attached to the head of the arytenoid and connecting it with the mouth of the esophagus.

superior cornu or horn of thyroid: One of two upward projecting horns of the thyroid.

thyrohyoid ligament: Strong ligament between body of the hyoid and notch of thyroid.

thyroid cartilage: Largest cartilage of the larynx.

tongue bone: Hyoid bone.

triticeal cartilage: Tiny vestigial cartilage found between each superior horn of the thyroid and the ends of the hyoid bone.

upper horn: Superior cornu.

vocal ligament: Thickened edge of the conus elasticus forming the edge of the vocal fold.

vocal process: Forward projection of the arytenoid cartilage which merges with the vocal cord. Glottal process.

wing of the thyroid: Half of the thyroid cartilage.

Wrisberg, cartilage of: Stiffening cartilage found in each aryepiglottic fold.

PHYSIOLOGY OF THE LARYNX

aditus laryngis: Upper opening of the larynx.

anticus: Cricothyroid muscle.

aryepiglottic, arytenoepiglottideus: One of two muscles extending from the arytenoids to the sides of the epiglottis, and containing the cartilages of Wrisberg. They are the sides of the collar of the larynx.

arytenoepiglottideus, arytenoepiglottic fold: Aryepiglottic fold.

arytenoid muscles: Transverse arytenoid and oblique arytenoid muscles, and possibly the cricoarytenoids also.

arytenovocalis: Aryvocalis muscle.

aryvocalis: Certain fibres of the thyroarytenoid.

cartilaginous glottis: Part of the glottis which is bounded by the arytenoids.

ceratocricoid: Fascicle from the posterior cricoarytenoid which helps to make the bond between the cricoid and the lower horn of the thyroid.

closers: Interarytenoid muscles (Husler and Rodd-Marling).

collar of the larynx: Muscular ring formed by the aryepiglottic folds, with the epiglottis, the cartilages of Wrisberg, and the arytenoids. Vestibule of the larynx.

cricoarytenoid: One of four muscles which rotate the arytenoids upon the cricoid.

cricothyroid: One of four muscles attaching to the front of the cricoid cartilage and pulling down on the thyroid. There are two pars recta, with vertical fibres pulling directly; and two pars obliqua at the sides, with diagonal fibres which not only pull the thyroid down, but also pull it forward. Anticus.

depressor epiglotticus: Thyroepiglottic muscle.

external oblique fascicle: Part of the false cord (Curry).

external thyroarytenoid: Part of the thyroarytenoid which parallels the internal thyroarytenoid, lying between it and the thyroid cartilage. It can contract independently. Thyromuscularis.

false vocal cord: Ventricular band.

fasciculus, (fasciculi, pl.): Bundle of fibres; fascicle.

fold: Muscle or part of a muscle.

glottal bands, folds, lips, shelves, wedges: Lower folds of thyroarytenoids.

glottis: Space between the vocal cords.

glottis respiratorio: Space between the vocal lips in ordinary breathing.

horizontal fascicle: Internal thyroarytenoid (Curry). Vocalis.

inferior fold: Lower part of thyroarytenoid. True cord.

inner oblique fascicle: Part of the true cord (Curry).

interarytenoids: Transverse and oblique arytenoids. Closers.

internal thyroarytenoid: The edge of the lower fold of the thyroarytenoids, forming the muscular rim of the glottis. It can contract independently. Vocalis. Horizontal fascicle. Thyrovocalis.

intrinsic musculature of the larynx: Muscles which have both origin and insertion in the larynx.

larynx, (larynges, pl.): Organ of phonation.

lateral cricoarytenoid: Muscle arising from the upper edge of the cricoid at the side near the back, and pulling forward upon the muscular process of one of the arytenoids. There is a pair of these muscles.

middle oblique fascicle: Part of the thyroarytenoid (Curry).

muscular glottis: Ligamentous glottis.

oblique arytenoid muscle: One of two muscles that arise at the base of one arytenoid and are inserted in the head of the other.

openers: Posterior cricoarytenoid muscles (Husler and Rodd-Marling).

pars obliqua: Lit.: diagonal part. See cricothyroid.

pars recta: Lit.: upright part. See cricothyroid.

plica vocalis: Vocal fold.

posterior cricoarytenoid: Muscle arising from the cricoid plate and pulling back upon the muscular process of one of the arytenoids. There is a pair of these muscles. Posticus.

posticus: Posterior cricoarytenoid muscle.

rima glottidis: Glottis.

ring-shield muscles: Cricothyroid muscles (Marchesi).

shield-pyramid muscles: Thyroarytenoid muscles (Marchesi).

sinus of the larynx: Ventricle.

stretchers: Cricothyroid muscles (Husler and Rodd-Marling).

superior fold: Upper part of thyroarytenoid. False cord.

superior oblique fascicle: Part of the false cord (Curry).

tensors: Vocalis muscles (Husler and Rodd-Marling).

thyroarytenoid muscle: One of two complex muscles arising below the notch of the thyroid and inserted one in each arytenoid. The origin of this muscle is not only the thyroid cartilage but also the middle cricothyroid ligament.

thyroepiglottic: Fibres of thyroarytenoid that enter the aryepiglottic fold and reach the epiglottis.

thyromuscularis: External thyroarytenoid muscle.

thyrovocalis: Internal thyroarytenoid, vocalis m.

transverse arytenoid: Single muscle extending horizontally between the two arytenoids, under the oblique arytenoid muscles.

transverse fascicle: Part of the false cord (Curry).

true cords: Vocal cords.

ventricle of Morgagni: Pocket between the false and true cord on each side of the larynx.

928   Extrinsic Muscles

biventor: Digastric muscle.

cricopharyngeus: Those fibres of the inferior constrictor of the pharynx which attach to the
cricoid cartilage.

diaphragm of the mouth: Mylohyoid muscles; the
floor of the mouth.

digastric: Muscle with two bellies united by a central
tendon which is attached to the hyoid bone. One
belly arises from the point of the jaw, and the
other from the base of the skull near the ear.
There is one diagastric on each side and they pull
the hyoid up and forward or back depending upon
which belly contracts more. Biventor.

elastic scaffolding: Extrinsic laryngeal muscles
(Husler and Rodd-Marling, who also use: suspensory mechanism, and inspanning).

external laryngeal musculature: Extrinsic muscles,
plus the cricothyroids.

extrinsic musculature of the larynx: Muscles which
attach to the larynx, but which have origin elsewhere. Muscles that pull the larynx up or down.

geniohyoid: One of two muscles attaching to the
mandible at the front and pulling the hyoid bone
forward.

hyothyroid: Thyrohyoid muscle.

infrahyoid muscles: Infralaryngeal muscles.

infralaryngeal muscles: Muscles which pull the
larynx downward. They help to groove the tongue.

inspanning: Extrinsic laryngeal muscles (Husler and
Rodd-Marling).

mylohyoid: Paired muscle attaching to the inside
edge of the mandible, the hyoid bone, and a raphe
in the center, forming the floor of the mouth, pulling the hyoid and the tongue up and forward.

neck muscles: Loosely, extrinsic laryngeal muscles.

nucal muscles: Muscles of the back of the neck.

omohyoid: Muscle with two bellies united by a central tendon which is attached to the clavicle and
first rib. One belly arises from the scapula, and
the other from the hyoid bone. There is one omohyoid on each side and they pull the hyoid down
and back.

sternohyoid: One of two muscles arising at the top
of the sternum and pulling down upon the hyoid
bone.

sternothyroid: One of two muscles arising at the top
of the sternum and pulling down upon the thyroid
cartilage.

stylohyoid: A muscle attached to each styloid process and pulling the hyoid bone upward and
backward.

stylopharyngeus: A muscle in the wall of the throat,
from the styloid process to the thyroid cartilage.

suprahyoid muscles: Supralaryngeal muscles.

supralaryngeal muscles: Muscles which pull the
larynx upward.

suspensory mechanism: Extrinsic laryngeal muscles (Husler and Rodd-Marling).

thyrohyoid: Muscle joining each wing of the thyroid
to a side of the hyoid bone, pulling them together.

thyropharyngeus: Those fibres of the inferior constrictor of the pharynx which attach to the wings
of the thyroid, drawing them together and thus
stretching the vocal bands.

tongue muscles: Muscles which pull the larynx
forward and upward.

upper diaphragm: Diaphragm of the mouth;
mylohyoid.

Continuation of 927

ventricular band: Upper fold of the thyroarytenoid
muscle. The false vocal cord.

ventricularis: Fibres of thyroarytenoid which form
part of the wall of the ventricle and perhaps the
false cord, and which reach the epiglottis.

vestibule of the larynx: Collar of the larynx.

vocal cords, bands, folds, lips, shelves, wedges:
Lower part of thyroarytenoid. True cords.

vocalis: Internal thyroarytenoid.

voice box: Larynx.

PHONATION

929 Miscellaneous Terms	930 Free Valve
activity-passivity of vocalis: Registration factor in laryngeal function.	dynamic: Adjustment of the larynx which can be altered considerably, changing the quality without breaking the tone.

activity-passivity of vocalis: Registration factor
in laryngeal function.
bleat: Sound like that of a goat, probably made by
maintaining tension in the larger intrinsic muscles of the larynx, but alternately relaxing and
contracting the posterior cricoarytenoids (Negus).
"break": Sudden shift in registration. "Crack."
bridge: Register transition.
changing note: Note above which the voice is one
color and below which it is different.
chuckle: Low, rattling laugh.
cluck: Guttural click, like the sound of a hen.
"crack": Sudden shift or "break" in registration.
diphonia, diplophonia: The simultaneous production
of two vocal tones, one by the true and one by the
false cords.
dynamic adjustment, balance, etc.: Adjustment of
the larynx which can be altered considerably,
changing the quality without breaking the tone.
Ant.: static adjustment.
efficiency: Producing with minimum expenditure of
energy for maximum effect and esthetic gratifi-
cation (Van Wye, Perkins). Factor of laryngeal
function governed by interarytenoids and lateral
cricoarytenoids (Vennard).
embryonic sound: Instinctive sound.
fry, glottal or vocal: Term used by speech and
phonetics authorities for "rattle" or "scrape" of
the glottis.
giggle: Convulsive laugh, largely falsetto. Titter.
glottid: Sound produced by the glottis.
"hookup": Proper coordination of muscles of breathing and muscles of phonation (Bachner).
hum: Vocal sound made with closed lips.
hypothetical approach to registration: Theory of two
extreme laryngeal adjustments, coordinated.
idealistic approach to registration: Assumption that
registration may be ignored and a healthy voice
will have no register problems.
inflection: Irregular modulations of the pitch of the
speaking voice.
laugh: A series of spasmodic aspirated sounds
expressing mirth.
"lift" note: Note upon which "lift of the breath" is
needed. Changing note.
"lift of the breath": Feeling of suddenly increasing
breath pressure to smooth the transition to a
higher register (Witherspoon).
longitudinal tension: Stretch placed upon the vocal
folds by the cricothyroids, etc. The pitch factor
in laryngeal function.
medial compression: Action of lateral cricoarytenoids in causing the vocal processes to press together in each cycle of vibration. An efficiency
factor.
opening quotient: Ratio of the time the glottis is open
to the length of the whole vibratory cycle (Moore,
Timcke, von Leden). In heavy mechanism o. q. is
small; that is, the glottis remains closed for a

dynamic: Adjustment of the larynx which can be
altered considerably, changing the quality without breaking the tone.
"floating": Free; well-supported.
"flowing": Smoothly produced; free.
free: Produced without extrinsic muscular tension.
"golden": Poetic adjective often applied to a well-
produced voice.
liberated: Free; released.
normal production: Technic usually used by good
singers.
pouring tone: Producing tone freely and fully.
released: Free; liberated.
ringing: Ant.: "veiled"; breathy (Garcia).
roar: Loud, free tone.
"soaring": Free; well-supported.
supported: Having adequate breath pressure.
vibrant: Having good vibrato.

Continuation of 929
considerable portion of the cycle and then opens
more or less abruptly. In light mechanism o. q.
is large; that is, the glottis closes only briefly.
passaggio: Register transition.
phonation: Producing vocal sound.
ponticello, il: Lit.: The little bridge. Register
transition.
pop of the glottis: Delicate, voiceless explosion of
breath in the larynx.
production: Generation of tone, with emphasis on
vocal and esthetic values; distinguished from pronunciation, which stresses literal communication.
rattle: Rapid series of glottal pops. "Scrape of the
glottis." Vocal or glottal fry.
realistic approach to registration: Recognition of
the presence of registers in most normal voices.
register: Adjustment of the larynx which produces
tones of a particular quality, for particular demands of range, dynamics, etc.
registration: Control of the laryngeal mechanism
in the production of different qualities of tone.
"scrape of the glottis": Voiceless rattle of escaping
breath in the larynx (Bratt).
static adjustment, balance, etc.: Adjustment of the
larynx from which it is impossible to readjust
without breaking the tone. Ant.: dynamic
adjustment.
un trou dans la voix: Lit.: a hole in the voice.
Place in the range where the voice is weak because of indecision as to registration (Marchesi).
unused register: Laryngeal adjustment which a given
singer has neglected to develop. In men it is
usually falsetto, and in women, "chest."
ventriloquism: Phonation with little or no facial indication, giving the illusion that the voice is coming from another source.
voice: Phonation plus resonance.
yodeling: Singing characterized by obvious shifts
in registration.

PHONATION

931	Tense Valve	932	Lax Valve

"bad" vowel: Vowel [æ] as in "bad," "act," "at," especially with tight production.

barbaric: Uncultured; savage.

barn dance voice: "Twangy" voice, usually pinched, and "straight."

Buggs Bunny: Animated cartoon character whose speech is "twangy" and "tight."

"clear timbre": Timbre produced with a high larynx and lowered velum. *Timbre clair;* "open timbre" (Garcia). Ant.: "closed timbre."

constricted: Tight.

depressed larynx: Adjustment produced by dropping the jaw and pressing it against the larynx.

driven: Forced.

dynamomagnetic irradiation: Raising of pitch, caused by the fact that certain vowels tense the tongue and this is communicated to the larynx (Taylor).

forced: Produced with too much effort for the adjustment.

harsh: Raucous; driven through a tight valve.

"held": Tight; stiff.

high larynx: Adjustment produced by dropping the jaw only a minimum and allowing the larynx to rise. "Shallow" tone.

interference: Usually, tightness.

metallic: Having high, perhaps inharmonic, partials in too great proportion.

"neck-tie tenor": Tenor whose tone is tight, driven.

"open" tone, timbre: Tense tone, too high for the laryngeal adjustment. "Clear timbre."

piercing: Shrill; tight; painful to the ear.

pinched tone: Constricted laryngeal valve (Holmes).

raucous: Rough sounding; harsh.

"reaching for the tone": Extending the head and jaw upward and forward while allowing the larynx to rise with the pitch.

screech: Shrill, high-pitched animal cry; squeal.

squeal: Shrill, high-pitched animal cry; screech.

strained: Forced.

strident: Loud and harsh; shrill.

tense, tight throat; tense larynx: Constricted laryngeal valve (Holmes).

"throaty": (1) Tight, pinched (Witherspoon, Stanley). (2) "Swallowed," "dark."

tight: Produced with too much tension, often with high larynx and constricted pharynx. Ant.: breathy.

timbre clair: "Clear timbre" (Garcia). Ant.: *timbre sombre.*

yell: Loud cry, produced with a tight valve.

yelp: Shrill bark of a dog.

aspirate: Breathy.

breathy: Characterized by unvocalized breath escaping during phonation. Aspirate. Ant.: tense, tight.

"buzzy": Nasal, with breathiness.

"diffused": Breathy; "fuzzy."

"dummy boy" quality: Voice used by Mortimer Snerd.

flaccid: Produced with too relaxed a valve. Flabby; breathy.

"fuzzy": Breathy; "diffused."

lax: Loose; flaccid.

loose: Produced with too relaxed a valve. Breathy.

Mortimer Snerd: Radio character whose speech is breathy and swallowed.

mutational chink: Triangular opening between the arytenoids during phonation, causing breathiness characteristic of immature voices.

"veiled": Breathy (Garcia).

"velvety": Soft and "diffused," usually somewhat nasal.

weak: Poorly supported; lacking intensity.

whisper: Completely breathy sound.

wild air: Waste air in a breathy tone.

"windy": Breathy.

933	Attack

aspirate: Attack in which breath flow precedes closure of the glottis, producing the phoneme [h] .

attacco della voce: Vocal attack. (Used by Marchesi as synonymous with "stroke of the glottis.")

attack: Beginning of a musical tone.

breathy: Aspirate.

coup de glotte: "Stroke of the glottis."

glottal click, shock: "Stroke of the glottis." (2)

glottal plosive: Attack in which the glottis closes firmly before breath pressure is applied.

glottal stroke: "Stroke of the glottis."

hard attack: Glottal plosive.

imaginary aspirate, imaginary [h]: Beginning a tone by allowing the closing of the glottis to be completed by the Bernoulli effect of breath flow without allowing an aspirate to be heard.

instantaneous attack: Simultaneous attack.

pressed attack: Attack that is not breathy and yet is not as crisp as the "soft" attack (Hülse).

shock of the glottis: "Stroke of the glottis." (2)

simultaneous attack: Perfect synchronization of closure of the glottis and application of breath pressure; instantaneous attack. Best achieved by use of imaginary [h].

soft attack: Imaginary [h].

spiritus lenis: Glottal plosive (Hülse).

"stroke of the glottis": (1) Attack in which breath pressure and glottal closure synchronize. (2) Attack in which breath blasts through a tight glottis.

| 934 | Heavy | 935 | Coordinated |

"body": Heavy registration with low formant resonance.

chest register, voice: Adjustment producing heavy tones, suitable for forte singing and for the lower part of the compass. "Body."

coarse: Crude. Applied especially to the heavy feminine mechanism when it is not well developed and is a static adjustment.

cricothyroid voice, register: Term inaccurately applied to heavy mechanism, (Stanley).

crude: Uncultivated; coarse. Usually applied to static chest register.

heavy mechanism: Laryngeal adjustment in which vocal bands are thick. Chest voice; full voice (Wilcox).

long reed voice: Chest voice (Mackenzie).

low register: Series of tones produced with an adjustment making possible the lower range. Ant.: high register.

low voice press: A method of getting extremely low notes in the bass voice.

lower process: Low register (Weer). Ant.: Upper process.

masculine voice: Heavy register, especially in women's voices.

natural voice: Term applied to a man's speaking voice to distinguish from falsetto.

"open": Produced with heavy registration without vowel modification, on too high a pitch. Ant.: "covered."

"rich": Containing many partials.

speaking voice: Register in which one speaks, usually heavy.

thick register: Heavy mechanism (Behnke).

voce di petto: Lit.: Chest voice (Tosi).

yell: Loud cry, produced with a tight valve, usually motivated by anger. Compare: scream; shout.

cackle tone: Witch voice (Frisell); voce finta (Reid).

combination tone: Coordinated or mixed tone (Ruff).

coordinated registration: Adjustment having some qualities of both light and heavy registration.

"covered": (1) Produced with comparatively light registration. (2) Pronounced "darkly."

"covered" register: Expression used by Marchesi as synonymous with voix mixte, voce coperta, gedecktes Register. He applied it to the adjustment for the upper part of the male voice, which he called "middle register," distinguishing it from falsetto.

dynamic: Adjustment of the larynx which can be altered considerably, changing the quality without breaking the tone. Ant.: static adjustment.

full-throated: With free valve and large pharynx.

full voice: Coordinated registration; voce piena.

Gaumenton: "Palatal register."

gedecktes Register: "Covered register" (Marchesi).

"groove of Oo": Covered register.

head voice: Intermediate adjustment, especially in the male voice, easily confused with falsetto, but continuous with full voice (Clippinger).

medium voice: Middle voice of a woman (Garcia, who originally called this register falsetto).

mezzo-falso: Middle falsetto (Frisell).

middle falsetto: Intermediate adjustment between chest and falsetto (Frisell). Cackle tone; mezzo-falso; voce finta; witch voice.

middle register, midvoice: Register between chest and falsetto, combining the best properties of both.

mixed registration: Adjustment having some qualities of both light and heavy registration. (Stanley uses this expression only for such adjustments when the production is bad, as opposed to "coordination," which is good.)

"palatal" register: Misnomer involving resonance factors as well as registration, applied to the middle register.

pharyngeal falsetto: Strong falsetto from which the head voice will emerge. Secret of the development of the tenor voice (Ross, who distinguishes it from oral falsetto).

shout: Loud, free cry. Compare: scream, yell.

thin register: Midvoice in women (Behnke, who applied the same term to a man's falsetto.)

voce coperta: "covered register" (Marchesi).

voce finta: Lit.: False or feigned voice. Originally synonym for falsetto. Used by Reid for a special voice overlapping chest and falsetto, by means of which coordination may emerge. See middle falsetto, pharyngeal falsetto.

voce piena: Lit.: Full voice (Caccini).

witch voice: Development of the falsetto from which the middle falsetto or mezzo-falso emerges (Frisell).

REGISTRATION

936	Light

arytenoid voice, register: Term inaccurately applied to light mechanism (Stanley).

child-like: Like the unchanged effeminate voice.

coo: Sweet low-pitched sound like that of a dove.

crooning: Style of singing which is light in registration and intensity and depends upon a microphone.

effeminate voice: Falsetto, especially in men's voices.

falsetto: Lightest register, originally applied only to men's voices, but now also applied to women's.

flute-like: Having a few low partials only.

head register, tone, voice: Adjustment producing light, flute-like tones, suitable for soft singing, and for the upper part of the compass. The term originally applied to what is now recognized as the woman's light mechanism.

high register: A series of tones produced with an adjustment making possible the upper range. Ant.: low register.

light mechanism: Laryngeal adjustment in which vocal bands are thin. Falsetto; "head" voice (Wilcox).

"lip falsetto": Tense, inhibited falsetto, often produced with high larynx.

naive: Child-like.

oral falsetto: Falsetto which will not develop into mixed registration, as opposed to pharyngeal falsetto (Ross).

pharyngeal falsetto: Well-supported falsetto, resonated by an open throat. See "lip falsetto."

pure falsetto: True falsetto.

scream: Loud, high-pitched, falsetto cry, usually motivated by fear. Compare: shout; yell.

short reed voice: Falsetto (Mackenzie).

shriek: Scream.

simple: Flute-like; sweet.

small register: Highest female falsetto (Behnke). Whistle register.

sob: Falsetto break, expressive of grief.

sweet: Containing few partials, chiefly low ones, and free from inharmonic partials. Flute-like.

small register: Head voice in women (Behnke).

"tear" in the voice: Hint of falsetto as if the voice were breaking. Not to be confused with a stage sob.

thin register: Falsetto in men (Behnke, who applied the same term to a woman's midvoice.)

true falsetto: The extreme light mechanism, as distinguished from "falsetto" meaning light registration in general. Pure falsetto.

upper process: Light mechanism (Weer). Ant.: lower process.

upper register: High register. Ant.: low register.

voce di testa: Lit.: head voice (Tosi).

voce finta: Lit.: feigned or false voice (Caccini).

voce mista: Lit.: mixed voice.

voix mixte: Lit.: mixed voice. Term usually applied to masculine tones having a large proportion of falsetto.

whine: Prolonged nasal or twangy sound, usually light in production, on a descending portamento, expressing pain or disappointment.

whistle register: Highest female falsetto. Small register.

NOTE: The assignment of several of these definitions is necessarily arbitrary because of ambiguous usage. See definitions of "head voice," "pharyngeal falsetto," and "voce finta" in both Par. 935 and Par. 936. Present knowledge of registration is inadequate to resolve differences of usage in this field. See Par. 234-271.

PHYSIOLOGY OF RESONANCE

buccopharyngeus: Part of the superior constrictor which joins the buccinator at the pterygomandibular raphe.

ceratopharyngeus: Part of the middle constrictor which attaches to the greater horn of the hyoid.

chondropharyngeus: Part of the middle constrictor which attaches to the lesser horn of the hyoid.

constrictor of the pharynx: One of three pairs of muscles, superior, middle, and inferior, which form the walls of the pharynx.

cricopharyngeus: Part of the inferior constrictor which attaches to the cricoid.

deep pharynx: Throat resonator with low larynx.

gaping: Yawning.

gargling: Rinsing the throat with a liquid, agitated by air from the trachea.

glossopharyngeus: That part of the superior constrictor which attaches to floor of the mouth.

hiation: Yawning.

inferior pharyngeal constrictor: Lowermost of three constrictors of the pharynx. A pair extending from the posterior median raphe to the thyroid and cricoid cartilages.

keratopharyngeus: Ceratopharyngeus.

large pharynx: Open throat.

laryngopharyngeus: Inferior constrictor.

laryngo-pharynx: Lower part of the pharynx above the larynx and below the oro-pharynx.

low larynx: Larynx drawn down by contraction of infrahyoid muscles with relaxation of the suprahyoids.

lower constrictor: Inferior constrictor.

middle pharyngeal constrictor: Midmost of three constrictors of the pharynx. A pair extending from the posterior median raphe to the hyoid bone and stylohyoid ligament.

mylopharyngeus: Part of the superior constrictor which attaches to the lower jaw or mandible.

open throat: Condition agreed upon by most voice teachers as desirable for resonance. Large pharynx.

oro-pharynx: Middle part of the pharynx, behind the mouth, below the naso-pharynx, above the laryngo-pharynx.

oscitance; oscitation; oscitancy: Yawning.

pandiculation: Stretching arms and legs, etc., while yawning, before or after sleep.

Passavant's cushion, ridge: Ridge in the posterior pharyngeal wall formed when the superior constrictor tenses to meet the arching of the velum, closing off the nasopharynx.

pharyngeal membrane: Membrane lining the pharynx.

pharyngeal raphe: Posterior median raphe.

pharynx: Resonator above the larynx and behind the mouth, consisting of laryngo-, oro-, and naso-pharynges. Throat.

posterior median raphe: Place at the back where the constrictors of the pharynx join, a ligamentous vertical seam for the throat muscles.

pterygomandibular raphe: Ligament extending from the mandible to the skull on each side, providing a seam between the buccinators and the superior pharyngeal constrictor.

pterygopharyngcus: Part of the superior constrictor which attaches to the upper jaw.

salpingopharyngeus: Muscle arising from each Eustachian tube and joining the posterior pillar of the fauces. The two together raise the upper part of the pharynx and narrow the fauces.

stylohyoid ligament: Ligament paralleling the stylohyoid muscle, joining the hyoid bone and the styloid process, providing origin for part of the middle constrictor of the pharynx.

stylolaryngeus: Fibres of stylopharyngeus which reach the thyroid.

stylopharyngeus: Muscle extending from each styloid process into the pharynx between the superior and middle constrictors, some fibres reaching the thyroid. It raises the larynx and distends the pharynx.

superior pharyngeal constrictor: Uppermost of three constrictors of the pharynx. A pair extending from the posterior median raphe to the hard palate, pterygomandibular raphe, the side of the jaws and tongue.

throat: Pharynx.

thyropharyngeus: Part of the inferior constrictor which attaches to the thyroid.

upper constrictor: Superior constrictor.

yawn: Opening the mouth and throat wide, usually beginning with deep inspiration. Usually an expression of weariness or boredom. Gaping; hiation; oscitancy; oscitance; oscitation.

PHYSIOLOGY OF RESONANCE

938   Mouth

alveolar ridge: Ridge behind the upper teeth.

bucca (buccae, pl.): Cheek.

buccal cavity: Mouth.

buccinator: Broad muscle attaching to both jaws, the pterygomandibular raphe, and orbicularis oris. The cheek muscle.

bucco pharyngeal resonator: Mouth and throat acting as one resonator.

caninus: Muscle that raises the corner of the mouth. Levator anguli oris; triangularis labii superioris.

caput angulare: Muscle attaching to the maxilla and pulling upward on the nostril and upper lip. Levator labii superioris alaeque nasi.

caput infraorbitale: Muscle attaching to the inside edge of the eye socket, pulling up on the upper lip. Levator labii superioris.

caput latum of triangularis: Part of triangularis which pulls the corner of the mouth down and to the side.

caput zygomaticum: Muscle attaching to the front of the zygomatic arch, pulling up the corner of the upper lip. Zygomaticus minor.

cavity lengthening: Increasing the front-to-back dimension of the mouth (Delattre). Involves lip rounding and tongue backing.

cheek: Side of the face.

cheek muscle: Buccinator.

chewing: Mastication.

depressor anguli oris: Triangularis; triangularis labii inferioris.

depressor labii inferioris: Quadratus menti; quadratus labii inferioris.

external pterygoid: Muscle under the zygomatic arch which joins the ramus of the mandible with the maxilla, causing the lower jaw to drop. Lateral pterygoid.

frowning muscles: Muscles which pull down the lips. Quadratus menti; triangularis; mentalis.

internal pterygoid: Muscle inside the mandible which pulls it upward and forward toward the maxilla. Medial pterygoid.

labia oris: Lips.

lateral pterygoid: External pterygoid.

latissimus colli: Platysma.

levator anguli oris: Caninus; triangularis labii superioris.

levator labii inferioris: Mentalis.

levator labii superior: Caput infraorbitale of quadratus labii superioris.

levator labii superioris alaeque nasi: Caput angulare of quadratus labii superioris.

levator menti: Mentalis; levator labii inferioris.

lip: One of two muscular folds forming the external opening of the mouth.

lip rounding: Pursing or trumpeting the lips. One of two means of cavity lengthening (Delattre).

macrostomia: Mouth larger than normal.

masseter: Muscle which attaches to the zygomatic arch on each side and the angle of the mandible, pulling up the jaw bone.

mastication: Grinding food with the teeth, aided by the tongue.

medial pterygoid: Internal pterygoid.

mentalis: Muscle attached to the mandible which wrinkles the skin of the chin, and protrudes the lower lip. Levator menti; levator labii inferioris.

mouth: Cavity bounded by the lips, cheeks, tongue, and palate. Oral, buccal cavity.

oral cavity: Mouth.

orbicularis oris: Circular muscle forming the sphincter of the mouth; the muscle of the lips, closing them, or by tightening more, pursing them.

platysma: Broad, thin muscle which covers the lower jaw, the neck, and the shoulders. Platysma myoides; latissimus colli; tetragonus; subcutaneous colli.

pterygoideus externus: External pterygoid.

pterygoideus internus: Internal pterygoid.

pursed lips: Lips drawn up, puckered.

quadratus labii inferioris: Muscle on each side of the mouth, between triangulairs and mentalis, pulling down orbicularis oris. Depressor labii inferioris; quadratus menti.

quadratus labii superioris: Name applied to three sneering muscles: caput angulare, caput infraorbitale, caput zygomaticum.

quadratus menti: Quadratus labii inferioris, depressor labii inferioris.

risorius: Muscle attaching to the fibrous covering of the masseter, pulling out the corner of the mouth and bulging the cheek.

smiling muscles: Muscles that produce a smile: risorius; zygomaticus; caninus.

sneering muscles: Quadratus labii superioris.

sphincter oris: Orbicularis oris.

subcutaneous colli: Platysma.

temporalis, temporal: Muscle which attaches to the temple and to the coronoid process, pulling up the jaw bone.

tetragonus: Platysma.

tongue backing: Moving the tongue toward the throat. One of two means of cavity lengthening (Delattre).

triangularis: Muscle that pulls down the corner of the mouth. It has two parts: caput latum, caput longum. Depressor anguli oris; triangularis labii inferioris.

triangularis labii superioris: Caninus; levator anguli oris.

trumpeted lips: Lips distended to form a bell.

vestibule of the mouth: Space between lips and teeth.

zygomaticus major: Larger muscle just back of zygomaticus minor, pulling the corner of the mouth in the same manner.

zygomaticus minor: Caput zygomaticum of quadratus labii superioris.

PHYSIOLOGY OF RESONANCE

939	Tongue	940	Nose and Velum

basioglossus: Part of hyoglossus which arises from the body of the hyoid.

blade of the tongue: Front part of the tongue, when it is flat.

ceratoglossus: Part of hyoglossus which arises from the greater horn of the hyoid.

chondroglossus: Part of hyoglossus which arises from the lesser horn of the hyoid.

dorsum: Upper surface of the tongue.

furrowed tongue: Grooved tongue; troughed tongue.

genioglossus: Muscle whose fibres radiate from the chin, some attaching to the hyoid bone, some to the side of the pharynx, and others curving into the tongue throughout its length. Helps to groove the tongue, also moves it in various directions.

genio-hyo-glossus: Genioglossus and hyoglossus as a unit (Stanley).

glossoepiglottic folds: Muscles attaching the tongue to the epiglottis.

grooved tongue: Tongue with a central depression from back to front. Furrowed, troughed tongue.

hyoglossus: One of two sets muscles from the hyoid bone to the sides of the tongue, which depress the sides and retract the tongue.

inferior lingualis or lingual: Longitudinalis inferior.

lingua: Tongue.

longitudinalis inferior: Pair of muscles forming the under sides of the tongue, with fibres running lengthwise. They pull the tip of the tongue down, shorten the tongue, make it convex. Inferior lingualis.

longitudinalis superior: Pair of muscles forming a middle layer of the tongue with fibres running from side to side. They shorten it, widen and thicken it, or cooperating with genioglossus, make it groove.

root of the tongue: Back part of the tongue.

styloglossus: Muscle running from each styloid process into the sides of the tongue. They raise the back of the tongue, help to groove the tongue.

superficial lingual: Superior lingualis; longitudinalis superior.

superior lingualis: Superficial lingual, longitudinalis superior.

tongue: Organ occupying the bottom of the mouth, and attached to the mandible, the hyoid bone, the pharynx, and the soft palate. It is composed of several muscles and can assume many shapes, useful for mastication and articulation.

transversus linguae; transverse lingualis: Pair of muscles forming a middle layer of the tongue just above longitudinalis superior. They elongate, narrow, and thicken the tongue.

troughed tongue: Furrowed tongue; grooved tongue.

verticalis linguae; vertical lingualis: Muscles forming the upper layer of the tongue. They widen and flatten the front part of the tongue, help to groove the tongue.

azygos uvulae: Muscle which forms the uvula.

circumflexus palati: Tensor veli palatini.

constrictor isthmi faucium: Palatoglossus.

faucial arch: One of two arches formed by the pillars of the fauces.

faucial pillars: Pillars of the fauces.

glossopalatine arch: Arch of the anterior pillars.

glossopalatinus: Palatoglossus.

isthmus faucium: Opening between mouth and pharynx.

levator palati: Levator veli palatini.

levator veli palatini: Muscles which arch the soft palate. Levator palati, staphylinus internus, petrostaphylinus, petrosalpingostaphylinus.

musculus uvulae: Muscle which forms the uvula. Azygos uvulae, staphylinus medius.

nares: Nostrils or nasal passages.

nasal port: Opening between naso- and oropharynx, closed by action of velum and Passavant's ridge.

nasality: Quality produced by using the nose as a resonator.

naso-pharynx: Upper part of the pharynx, above the oro-pharynx, behind the nose.

nose: Organ of smelling, filtering the breath.

nostril: Fleshy outer opening of each nasal fossa.

palatoglossus: One of two muscles extending from the soft palate to the side of the tongue, partly continuous with lingualis transversus. Lifts back of tongue, helps to groove it if mid-part does not rise, narrows fauces, may lower velum. Glossopalatinus, constrictor isthmi faucium, anterior pillar of the fauces.

palatopharyngeus: One of two muscles extending from the soft palate into the pharyngeal wall, joining the salpingopharyngeus, reaching the thyroid. Some fibres may join the aryepiglottic folds. Raises the larynx or lowers the velum and narrows the fauces. Pharyngopalatinus.

palatosalpingeus: Tensor veli palatini.

palatum molle: Soft palate.

petrosalpingostaphylinus: Levator veli palatini.

petrostaphylinus: Levator veli palatini.

pharyngopalatine arch: The arch of the posterior pillars.

pharyngopalatinus: Palatopharyngeus.

pillar of the fauces: One of four muscles extending the velum into the sides of the throat. The palatoglossus and palatopharyngeus muscles.

soft palate: Muscular and tendonous extension of the roof of the mouth. Its lower edge is the velum. In the center is the uvula, and at each side, extending into the sides of the throat, are the pillars of the fauces.

sphenosalpingostaphylinus: Tensor veli palatini.

staphylinus externus: Tensor veli palatini.

staphylinus internus: Levator veli palatini.

staphylinus medius: Muscle which forms the uvula.

941   Framework

angle of the mandible: Corner of the jaw, where it turns up into the ramus.

bicuspid: One of the four teeth in each jaw between the canines and the molars. Premolar.

brain pan: Part of the skull which contains the brain.

canine: One of the two "dog teeth" in each jaw, next to the incisors.

capitulum: Condyle.

cheekbone: Malar bone.

condyle: A knob on each side of the mandible, which articulates with a socket in the skull.

coronoid process: A point at the top of the ramus of the mandible in front of the condyle, to which the temporalis muscle attaches.

cranium: Skull, specifically the bones which enclose the brain.

ethmoidal sinus: One of two sinuses between the eyes, at the root of the nose.

Eustachian tube: Small canal from the inner ear to the nasopharynx.

external pterygoid plate: The outer of two jagged projections from the skull, on each side, back of the upper teeth. Lateral pterygoid plate.

frontal sinus: One of two sinuses in the forehead.

gums; gingivae; Tissue covering the alveolar processes at the necks of the teeth.

hammular process: A bony hook at the back end of the internal pterygoid plate. The tendon of tensor palati goes around this hook.

hard palate: Roof of the mouth, distinct from soft palate.

incisor: One of the four front teeth in each jaw.

infundibulum: Funnel-shaped passage from nose to the frontal or the ethmoid sinus.

internal pterygoid plate: The inner of two jagged projections from the skull, on each side, back of the upper teeth. Medial pterigoid plate.

jaw; jawbone: One of two bones which hold the teeth. Usually applied in the singular only to lower jaw, or mandible.

lateral pterygoid plate: External pterygoid plate.

malar bone: Cheek bone.

mandible: Lower jaw.

mastoid process: Knob on the base of the skull just under and back of the ear.

maxilla: Upper jaw.

maxillary sinus: Sinus above the upper teeth on each side.

medial pterygoid plate: Internal pterygoid plate.

molar: One of the rearmost teeth, six in each jaw.

nasopharynx sinus: One of two sinuses behind the sphenoid sinuses.

occiput: Bone in the lower back part of the skull.

orbit: Eye socket.

palate; palatum: Roof of the mouth, called "hard palate" to distinguish between it and the soft palate.

paranasal sinus: One of the sinuses which are near the nose. This includes all those sinuses sometimes counted as vocal resonators. There are five pair: ethmoid, frontal, maxillary, nasopharynx, sphenoid. All have tiny openings into the nasal cavities.

pharyngeal tubercle: Projection on the under side of the skull in the middle just in front of the backbone, from which the pharyngeal raphe hangs.

premolar: One of the four teeth in each jaw between the canines and the molars. Bicuspid.

pterygoid plates: External and internal pterigoid plates.

pterygomandibular raphe: ligament extending from the internal pterygoid plate, near the hammular process, to the mandible. It forms a connection between buccinator and the superior constrictor of the pharynx.

ramus of the mandible: Part of the lower jaw that comes up near the ear.

roof of the mouth: Hard palate; palatum.

septum: Bony partition between the nasal fossae.

sinus: Small cavity within a bone or other tissue. The ones sometimes thought to be resonators are the paranasal sinuses.

skull: Bony framework of the head.

sphenoidal sinus: One of two sinuses at the back of the nasal cavities.

styloid process: Long, sharp projection of bone from the base of the skull on either side of the first vertebra, between it and the mastoid process.

symphysis of the mandible: Union of the two halves of the mandible, in the front of the jaw.

tooth, (teeth, pl.): One of 32 hard processes in the ridges of the jaws, used for biting, chewing, etc. There are 4 incisors, 2 canines, 4 premolars or bicuspids, 6 molars in each jaw.

turbinate: One of 3 scroll-like fins of spongy bone in each nasal fossa.

uraniscus: Palate.

zygomatic arch: Bony arch from the cheek, or malar bone to a part of the skull farther back.

Continuation of 940

tensor veli palatini: Muscles which tense the soft palate and open the Eustachian tube in swallowing. Circumflexus palati, palatosalpingeus, sphenosalpingostaphylinus, staphylinus externus.

uvula: Bit of muscle hanging in the center of the velum which seems to serve no purpose except to set off the gag reflex. It retracts when the velum tenses.

velum: Soft palate, especially the lower edge.

RESONANCE IMAGERY

942	Mouth	943	Nose

"bad" vowel: Vowel [æ] as in "bad," "act," "at."

bell-like: Clear; full; ringing; mouthy.

"bright": Having high partials. Ant.: "dark."

"brilliance": Presence of high partials. "Sparkle"; "glow."

carrying power: Elements of timbre which make the voice heard better, probably high partials.

clear: Unmuffled and free from breathiness.

"cone-shaped": "Pear-shaped."

"cool": Lacking warmth.

"core": Ring of the voice, "2800"; twang.

dans la masque: Lit.: in the mask (de Reszke). Having "forward placement."

"edge": Ringing high partials; "2800"; "focus"; "ping."

flat: Shallow.

"focused": Clear; ringing; "forward"; Ant.: "diffused"; "back"; "swallowed."

"forward": Having the resonance of the mouth. Ant.: "back."

"front" vowels: Vowels for which the tongue is forward.

gay: Happy; ringing; brilliant.

"gleeful": A tone that sounds gay because of high partials. Ant.: "gloomy."

"head" resonance: Misnomer applied to light registration with high formant resonance.

"high": "Placed above the throat." Ant.: "Deep."

high formant: Higher of the two frequencies characterizing vowels. Applied to the "front" vowels.

high larynx: Adjustment producing "shallow" tone.

"mask brilliance": "Forward placement."

"metallic": Having high, perhaps inharmonic, partials in too great proportion.

mettle: "Brilliance"; "edge"; ring.

mouthy: Characterized by oral resonance.

"open": Having a large bucco-pharyngeal resonator and comparatively heavy registration. Ant.: "covered"; muffled.

"open timbre": Timbre clair; "clear timbre" (Garcia).

oral quality, vowel: Quality associated with "forward placement." Used with unsympathetic connotation by Holmes.

oral-staccato voice: Voice that is placed too far forward, and in speech is pitched too high (Holmes).

"pear-shaped": Figure of speech usually applied to Ah [ɑ], suggesting that it should begin with "focus in front" but fill the entire throat.

"ping": Slang expression for ringing high partials. "Focus"; "edge."

"pointed": "Focused."

"pointed" vowels: Ee [i], Ay [e], etc.

"projected": "Focused."

reedy: Having strong high partials, and some nasality.

ring: Quality produced by high partials, perhaps inharmonic, "2800."

---

barn dance voice: Twangy voice, usually nasal, pinched, and "straight."

Buggs Bunny: Animated cartoon character whose speech is twangy and "tight."

"buzzy": Nasal, with breathiness.

cleft palate: Pathological palate which causes all phonation to be nasal.

"honky": Like the snort of a pig or the cry of a duck or a goose. Nasal.

hypernasal: Having too much nasal resonance.

hyponasal: Having no nasal resonance.

nasal: Having nasal resonance, produced by lowering the velum.

nasal vowels: Four French vowels not found in English, produced by lowering the velum while phonating.

nosey: Nasal.

reedy: Nasal, with twang. Having strong high partials.

rhinolalia aperta: Hypofunction of soft palate. Hypernasality. "Honk."

rhinolalia clausa: Hyponasality. "Twang."

snarl: Angry sound, with twang and perhaps nasality.

sniff: To inhale or exhale forcibly through the nostrils.

"stem of the pear": "Focus" of the vowel. Twang. See "pear-shaped."

twangy: Like the sound of a plucked string. To be distinguished from "honky" or nasal, with which it is often associated. "2800."

"velvety": Soft and diffused, usually somewhat nasal.

whine: Prolonged nasal sound, usually light in production, on a descending portamento, expressing pain or disappointment.

Continuation of 942

"salty": Adjective sometimes applied to the tone of an oboe.

screech: High-pitched animal cry.

"shallow": A tone made with the jaw too high. Lacking in low partials; white; toothy.

"sheen": "glistening" quality; "brilliance."

shrill: Sharp; high-pitched; piercing.

smiley: Toothy; "shallow"; "white."

"sparkle": "Brilliance."

"steel": "Brilliance"; ring; "edge."

strident: Loud and harsh; shrill.

"thin": "Shallow"; weak.

timbre clair: "Clear," or "open timbre" (Garcia).

toothy: Having the resonance produced by exposing teeth. Smiley; "shallow"; "white."

"2800": Approximate frequency of the overtone which gives ring or "edge" to the voice.

voce sgangherata: Lit.; Ungainly; immoderate. "White" voice; voix blanche (Marchesi).

voix blanche: Lit.: white voice. Shallow production which may have light, quasi-falsetto registration.

"white": Lacking strength in low partials. Voix blanche; shallow.

944   Throat

"back": Having the resonance of the throat. Ant.: "forward."

"back" vowels: Vowels for which the tongue is back.

"body" resonance: "Chest" resonance.

booming voice: A voice related to the throaty or guttural voice. In speech it is pitched too low and spoken too loudly (Holmes).

"bottled up": "Swallowed."

"chest" resonance: Misnomer applied to heavy registration with low formant resonance.

choked: Muffled by tongue backing.

"closed" timbre: *Timbre sombre;* "dark timbre" (Garcia). Ant.: "open timbre."

"clutch": Pressure on the larynx by jaw and tongue. Depressed larynx production. Choked.

"covered": (1) Pronounced "darkly." (2) Produced with comparatively light registration. Ant.: "Open."

"dark": Depressing because of lack of high partials. "Gray"; "muddy."

"dark brown": Depressing because of lack of high partials. "Swallowed."

"dark" timbre: The timbre produced with a low larynx and an arched velum. *Timbre sombre;* "closed timbre" (Garcia).

"deep": Formed in the pharynx. Ant.: "high"; "forward."

depressed larynx: Adjustment produced by dropping the jaw and pressing it against the larynx. "Clutch"; "hyoid tone;" "tonsillar tone."

"diffused": "Dull"; breathy. Ant.: "focused."

"dull" vowel: Vowel Uh, as in "the" [ə], "cut" [ʌ].

"dummy boy" quality: Voice used by Mortimer Snerd.

full-throated: Produced in a large pharynx with a free valve.

"gargled": Produced with a stiffly activated throat. "Swallowed"; "tonsilar"; "hyoid."

"gloomy": Depressing because of lack of high partials. Ant.: gleeful.

"gray": "Dull"; "muddy."

groan: Mournful sound even deeper than a moan.

grunt: Short guttural sound.

gutturize: To enunciate in the throat.

"held": Stiff; "throaty."

"hollow": "Swallowed" and/or "spread."

"hooty": *Tono frontale;* "spread."

"hyoid" tone: Tone produced with stiffness in the root of the tongue; "tonsilar" tone.

low formant: Lower of the two frequencies characterizing vowels.

mellow: Having strength in the low partials. "Rich"; "sweet"; "full"; "pure."

moan: Low mournful murmur.

Mortimer Snerd: Radio character whose speech is breathy and "swallowed."

"mournful": "Gloomy"; "sad."

"muddy": Lacking high partials, and perhaps containing inharmonic partials. "Dull."

muffled: Lacking power and brilliance because of obstruction by tongue or velum.

neutral vowel: "Dull" vowel.

"opulence": "Richness."

pectoral voice: Booming voice (Holmes).

pharyngeal voice: "Dark," throaty voice.

rigidity: Stiffness of the resonators. (Considered desirable by Stanley.)

"round": Applied to those vowels in which the lips are rounded and the pharynx is large.

"sad": Unhappy sounding because of lack of high partials. "Mournful"; "gloomy."

"soft": Mellow; "sweet."

"sombre": "Gloomy"; "dark."

"spread": Containing inharmonic partials. Out of tune. A "dull" vowel sung loudly. "Hooty"; *tono frontale.*

stiffness: Rigidity of the resonators, producing "metallic" quality.

"swallowed": "Placed too deeply." Lacking high partials. Muffled.

"throaty": (1) Characterized by too much pharyngeal resonance. "Swallowed"; "dark." (2) Tight (Stanley, Witherspoon).

timbre sombre: "Dark" or "closed timbre" (Garcia). Ant.: *timbre clair.*

tono frontale: Lit.: forehead tone. "Spread"; "hollow."

"tonsilar" tone: Tone produced with stiffness in the region of the tonsils (Graveure). "Hyoid" tone.

umlaut: One of the German vowels formed by rounding the lips and arching the tongue, thus producing a sound partaking of the quality of two other vowels at once, ö and ü. Also the two dots which are the symbol of the process.

"warm": Having low partials. Ant.: "cool."

yawny: Characterized by pharyngeal resonance, and perhaps muscular tension, resulting from a yawn.

Continuation of 945

umlaut: German sounds ä, ö and ü. Also the two dots placed above the letters.

unstressed syllable, vowel: Short syllable, vowel. "Vanishing."

"vanishing" sound, vowel: Second part of a diphthong or the first part of a glide. Unstressed; short.

vowel: Continuant consisting of a single musical tone.

vowel triangle: Chart showing the relationship of the vowel sounds.

PHONETICS

| 945 | General Terms | 946 | Acoustical Terms |

ach-laut: The sound of "ch" after "a" in German, and its symbol [x] (Siebs).

allophone: One of various possible productions of a given phoneme.

American r: Retroflex [r]. (Marshall).

analogue: Sound which is closely related to another different sound. For example: [p] and [b] are analogues.

consonant: Speech sound, chiefly noise, used with vowels to form sound patterns having symbolical meaning.

consovowel: Nasal or semi-vowel (Henderson).

crossed d: Symbol for the lingua-dental sonant [ð].

deep vowel: Vowel produced with a low larynx. Oh [o] or Oo [u], (Rousselot).

final: Last speech sound in a word.

ich-laut: The sound of "ch" after "i" in German, and its symbol [ç] (Siebs).

initial: First speech sound in a word.

International Phonetic Alphabet: Symbols agreed upon in 1938 by the International Phonetic Association, to represent the various speech sounds, so that words that sound alike can all be resolved to one spelling, and different pronunciations of the same word can have different spellings. Vowels are tabulated in par. 482; consonants in par. 644.

Italian [r]: Rolled [r].

Latin vowels: Ee [i], Ay [e], Ah [ɑ], Oh [o], Oo [u]. Pure vowels; long vowels.

long vowels: Vowels which are usually accented or prolonged in speech. Pure, Latin vowels.

phoneme: A speech sound serving a given phonetic or linguistic use. If two sounds cannot be interchanged without changing the meaning of a word, they are phonemes. Allophones are interchangeable.

phonetics: Study of speech sounds.

phonogram: Written symbol of a single sound.

pointed vowels: Ee [i] and Ay [e] , etc.

pure vowels: Ee [i], Ay [e], Ah [ɑ], Oh [o], Oo [u].

restressing unstressed form: Pronouncing deliberately a sound that acquired its unpleasant quality in hurried speech (Holmes).

round vowels: Oh [o] and Oo [u], etc.

schwa vowel: Vowel in above, below, constitute, [ə]. "Dull" vowel (Judson and Weaver).

sharp vowel: Vowel produced with a high larynx. Ay [e] or Ee [i], (Rousselot).

short vowels: Forms taken by the long vowels when they are brief and unaccented. Unstressed; "vanishing."

stress: Emphasis or accent.

striking power: Expressive force of speech sounds quantified in terms of loudness and duration in average speech as well as height of upper formant (Robson).

thorn: Old English symbol for the lingua-dental surd "þ."

Continued, bottom of page 255.

aphthong: Letter which is not sounded in the pronunciation of a word. Mute.

click: Short, dull sound.

clustered formant vowels: Vowels having the first two formants near together in frequency.

diphthong: Continuant consisting of two vowels in succession.

diphthongization: Making two vowel sounds in succession; allowing a vowel to change.

double formant vowels: Vowels having two distinct characteristic overtones.

fundamental tone: Tone produced by the glottis itself (West, Kennedy, and Carr).

glide: Continuant resembling a diphthong except that the first vowel sound is brief.

high formant vowels: Vowels having relatively high second formants.

high frequency tone: Consonant produced by the friction of breath passing through some constricted passage. Fricative. (West, Kennedy, and Carr.)

incidental [h]: Aspirate which follows a surd before the phonation of the succeeding vowel.

liquid: Smoothly flowing, like double "l" in French.

low formant vowels: Vowels having relatively low second formants.

mute: Aphthong.

pressure pattern: Consonant produced by confining the breath and then releasing it suddenly. Plosive. (West, Kennedy, and Carr.)

resonance tone: Tone produced by vibrating the air in the resonators. (West, Kennedy, and Carr.)

semi-vowel: Continuant differing from a vowel in that the mouth is partially or completely closed.

separated formant vowels: Vowels having the first two formants far apart in frequency.

sibilant: Consonant made by hissing, [s].

single formant vowels: Vowels whose first two formants are so close in frequency that a single formant at the average of the two frequencies will be heard as the same vowel.

soft attack: Imaginary [h].

sonant: Voiced sound. Ant.: surd.

surd: Voiceless sound. Ant.: sonant.

triphthong: Continuant consisting of three vowel sounds.

voiced consonant: Consonant in which there is phonation. Sonant.

voiceless consonant: Consonant having no phonation. Surd.

vowel fracture: Diphthongization, especially when undesirable.

vowel glide: Transitory sound between two vowels. Diphthong.

PHONETICS

947	Mechanistic Terms

affricate: Combination of plosive and fricative. [dʒ] "judge," [tʃ] "church."

aspirate: Speech sound characterized by breathiness; the consonant [h].

break: Explosion.

continuant: Speech sound which can be prolonged as long as breath lasts. It may be voiced or voiceless, fricative or unobstructed.

continuant fricative: Continuant which encounteres some obstruction which produces friction sound. It may be voiced or voiceless.

explosion: Third phase in the production of a stop-plosive, when the air is released. Break.

flipped [r]: Briefly rolled [r] (Marshall).

fricative: Continuant fricative.

imaginary [h], imaginary aspirate: Initiation of a vowel by Bernoulli effect. Ant.: Glottal plosive.

implosion: First phase in the production of a stop-plosive, when the air is dammed up. Make.

incidental [h]: Flow of air, with possible sound, after a voiceless plosive before the following speech sound.

inverted [r]: Retroflex [r].

lax vowel: Vowel in which the mylohyoid is relaxed. [ɪ] is the lax analogue of [i].

make: Implosion.

one-tap roll: Semi-roll; short roll; flipped [r].

plosion: Second phase in the production of a stop-plosive, when air pressure is increased. Stop.

plosive: Stop-plosive, especially when used before a vowel.

retroflex [r]: [ɚ], "produced by curling the tip of the tongue back over the body of the tongue" (Holmes).

roll: Fluttering of the tongue in [r].

rolled non-fricative, rolled [r]: [r] made by fluttering the tongue. Italian [r].

semi-roll: Briefly rolled [r].

short roll: Semi-roll.

stop: Stop-plosive, especially when used after a vowel. Plosion.

stop-plosive: Consonant characterized by three phases: implosion, or make; plosion, or stop; explosion, or break. If it comes before a vowel it is called a plosive, after a vowel, a stop.

tense vowel: Vowel in which the mylohyoid is tense. [i] is the tense analogue of [ɪ].

948	Anatomical Terms	949	Articulation

alveolar: Consonant made with the tongue against the ridge behind the upper teeth. Post-dental.

bilabial: Consonant formed with both lips.

dental: Pertaining to the teeth. Consonant formed with the aid of the teeth.

French nasal: Vowel which sounds through the nose because of the lowered velum.

glottal fricative: Consonant [h].

glottal plosive: Speech sound produced by suddenly exploding air through the glottis.

labial: Consonant formed by the lips.

labio-dental: Consonant formed by contact of the upper teeth and lower lip.

lingua-alveolar: Consonant made with the tongue against the alveolar ridge. Post-dental.

lingua-dental: Consonant produced with the tongue against the teeth.

lingual: Consonant formed by the tongue.

nasal consonant: Voiced continuant that is directed through the nose by obstruction of the oral resonator.

nasal vowel: French nasal.

post-dental: Consonant produced with the tongue back of the teeth. Lingua-alveolar.

uvular [r]: Velar [r].

velar plosive: Consonant made by suddenly releasing breath between tongue and velum.

velar [r]: [r] made by fluttering the velum. Uvular [r].

articulation: Joining speech sounds. Enunciation.

communication: Exchange of ideas.

dialect: Modification of a language characteristic of a locality.

diction: In singing, enunciation and pronunciation.

echolalia, echophrasia: Reiteration, more or less automatically, of words or phrases.

elision: Omission of a speech sound, as in " 'tis" for "it is." (Not to be confused with *liaison*.)

enunciation: Utterance of speech sounds. Articulation.

lalling: Continuous repetition of a single sound, as in infants or idiots.

language: Expression of thought by words.

liaison: Lit.: linking. Carrying over a final consonant to form a syllable with the initial vowel of a following word, as in, *C'est un petit homme.*

linking: *Liaison.*

onomatopoea: Words imitating natural sounds.

perflation: Lit.: blowing through. Whispering (Paget).

pronunciation: Correct utterance according to linguistic rules.

sign language: Expression of thought by gestures.

speech: Expression of thought by vocal and articulatory sounds.

whisper: Speech sound made by glottal friction without phonation.

whistle: Sound of air forced through a narrow aperture, such as pursed lips, or across an edge, such as teeth.

NEUROLOGY

PSYCHOLOGY

| 950 | Miscellaneous Terms | 951 | Miscellaneous Terms |

agonist: Muscle which is resisted by the antagonist.

antagonist: Muscle which resists the tension of another, called the agonist.

Broca's area: Part of the cerebrum in which are concentrated most of the nerves of speech.

central control: The highest level of control; volitional control.

cerebellum: The mid-portion of the brain, between the cerebrum and the medulla oblongata.

cerebral cortex: Outer gray matter of the cerebrum, the highest level of the brain.

cerebrum: Largest part of the human brain. In man it is larger in proportion than in the animals.

chronaxy: Minimum time required for excitation of a nerve cell by constant electric current of twice the threshold voltage.

clonic: Characterized by alternate contractions and relaxations of the muscles; said of spasms as in epilepsy. (Negus applies the word to the neuro-chronaxic theory.) Ant.: tonic.

diadochocinesis: (Greek *diadochos*, working in turn; *kinesis*, movement.) The alternate contraction and relaxation of the opposing muscles in muscular antagonism.

exteroceptive: Activated by stimuli impinging on the organism from without, as in touch, smell, sight, etc. See interoceptive, proprioceptive.

fibrillation: Quivering or tremor of muscle fibres. Common in certain pathological conditions of the heart. (Husson uses the word to describe vocal fold vibration without current of air.)

fore-brain: Cerebrum and lesser parts.

innervation: Supply of nerve energy.

interoceptive: Activated by stimuli arising in the viscera, as stimuli to the mucous membrane. See exteroceptive, proprioceptive.

kinesthetic sense: Sense by which movement of muscles is perceived. Proprioception. "Sixth sense."

medulla oblongata: The hind portion of the brain, an enlargement of the top of the spinal cord.

mid-brain: Cerebellum.

muscular antagonism: Physiological principle that no muscle works alone, but is steadied by the opposition of other muscles.

nerve: Fibre or fibres which convey impulses between the brain and parts of the body.

nervous: Excitable; easily agitated.

neuro-chronaxic: Having to do with the chronaxy of a nerve. Sp. the theory that the frequency of vocal fold vibration is determined by the chronaxy of the recurrent nerve, and not by breath pressure or muscular tension (Husson). See myoelastic-aerodynamic theory.

neurology: Science of nerves and nerve energy.

olfaction: Sense of smell.

phrenic nerve: Nerve controlling the diaphragm.

pons: Part of the brain connecting the cerebrum, cerebellum, and medulla oblongata.

proprioceptive: Activated by stimuli produced within the organism by movement or tension in its own

acuity: Sharpness, or distinctness with which one is able to hear.

aggressiveness: Unprovoked self-assertion, or attack.

androgynous mosaic: The composite of masculine and feminine characteristics in an adult (Moses).

auto-suggestion, -hypnosis: Insinuation of a belief into one's own mind by constant repetition.

behaviorism: That school of psychology which lays emphasis upon reflexes and their conditioning, and sees little more in human personality than the sum of all these units of behavior. Mechanistic teaching is applied behavioristic psychology.

cognition: Mental process of knowing; consciousness. Compare: emotion, volition.

conception: Making judgements about percepts, and imagining future behavior. What the singer thinks he is doing. Compare: sensation, perception.

conditioned reflex: A unit of behavior which by long association is now triggered by a stimulus different from that which originally or naturally caused the behavior. Roughly, a habit.

conscious control: Voluntary control with cognition, awareness.

coordination: Harmonious, orderly combination of functions towards the operation of a complex skill.

"ear": The whole auditory complex which consciously or unconsciously monitors phonation.

Continuation of 950

tissues, as in muscle sense. Kinesthesia. See exteroceptive, interoceptive.

recurrent nerve: Branch of the vagus nerve which supplies all the laryngeal muscles except the cricothyroid.

solar plexus: Nerve complex at the pit of the stomach.

spinal cord: Large bundle of nerves extending from the brain down the spinal column, from which nerves branch to parts of the body.

superior laryngeal nerve: Branch of the vagus nerve which supplies the cricothyroid. It also carries intero- and proprioceptive fibres.

synergy: Muscle action which does not produce motion but which provides anchorage for action of other muscles. See muscular antagonism.

tetanic: Characterized by rapid muscular spasms.

tetanus: State of prolonged contraction which a muscle assumes under rapidly repeated stimuli.

thalamus: Part of the fore-brain. It is a higher level than the mid-brain, but not as high as the cerebrum, which comprises the greater part of the fore-brain.

tonic: Relating to tension. In medicine, muscular tension that is continuous, unrelaxing; said of spasms as in tetanus. (Negus applies the word to the classic theory of phonation, the myoelastic-aerodynamic). Ant.: Clonic.

vagus nerve: Tenth cranial nerve. The superior and recurrent laryngeal nerves are branches.

PSYCHOLOGY   PEDAGOGY

| Continuation of 951 | 952   Miscellaneous Terms |

emotion: Mental feeling of passion. Compare: cognition, volition.

gag-reflex: Reflex whereby stimulating the uvula or velum induces vomiting.

Gestalt: Lit.: form, shape, image. A total effect consisting of a fusion which cannot be perceived by observing the details separately. "The whole is greater than the sum of all its parts."

Gestalt psychology: A reaction from behaviorism laying emphasis upon the total response and more complex levels than that of the reflexes. Inspirational or "psychological" teaching is applied Gestalt psychology. See mechanistic pedagogy.

gesture: Expression of thought by bodily movement.

habit: Behaviour pattern learned by repetition.

illusion: Sensuous perception involving false belief or conception.

indirect control: Control of subconscious function by means of some conscious activity.

instinct: Unlearned behavior tendency or drive.

instinctive: Unlearned.

involuntary: Not subject to conscious control.

law of reversed effort: Principle whereby direct conscious effort to control subconscious processes fails, whereas cessation of effort will succeed.

muscular independence: Ability to use a limited group of muscles without unnecessary movement of others.

natural: Normal; uncultivated; unaffected.

negative suggestion: Insinuation of failure by use of negative phraseology.

ontogeny: History of the evolution or development of the individual. See phylogeny.

perception: Taking knowledge of external objects. Implies a judgement upon a sensation but not at the level of conception or cognition. What the audience thinks they hear. See sensation, conception.

phylogeny: History of the evolution of a species or group. Tribal history. See ontogeny.

psychology: Science of the mind and of behavior.

reflex: Unlearned behavior pattern.

relaxation: Freedom from tension or rigidity.

sensation: The process of receiving stimuli which underlies perception.

skill: Practical knowledge; ability; dexterity.

stagefright: Discomfort because of the presence of an audience.

subconscious: Unconscious.

sublimation: Redirection of natural mechanisms to higher functions.

superimposed function: Use of bodily organs for a purpose in addition to their primary function.

total response: A complex act, like singing, which must be contemplated as a whole. A Gestalt.

unconscious: Below the level of awareness or cognition.

vegetative: Pertaining to mere physical living.

volition: Mental act of willing or resolving. Compare: cognition, emotion.

aspirato: Beginning each sound with [h], as in some staccato vocalises.

bel canto: Lit.: beautiful singing.

consonant pedagogy: Use of consonants to induce desired voice production.

creative hearing: Empathetic hearing (Moses).

empathetic hearing: Faculty of duplicating intuitively in one's own throat the adjustment used by the singer. Creative hearing (Moses); functional listening (Vrbanich); sympathetic hearing.

empirical pedagogy: Teaching based upon experience rather than scientific research.

exercise: Work for the sake of attaining proficiency.

figurative language: Imagery.

functional listening: Empathetic hearing (Vrbanich).

holistic pedagogy: Teaching addressed to the whole personality, seeking to elicit a total response.

"hum-on-the-tongue": Vocalise for developing "ping."

imagery: Figures of speech to express concepts which are difficult to understand literally.

inspirational pedagogy: Teaching that avoids analysis and mechanistic details, seeking to build confidence and the right mental concept. Holistic pedagogy.

manipulation: Holding the vocal mechanism in correct adjustment by hand.

mechanistic pedagogy: Method of teaching which majors upon the mechanical details of technic.

messa di voce: Classic Italian exercise consisting of a prolonged crescendo and decrescendo on a sustained tone.

metaphor: Figure of speech in which a comparison is implied.

nasty [æ] exercise: More recent designation for the old "hum-on-the-tongue." Vocalise for developing intensity, "focus," or "ping."

phonetic pedagogy: Use of existing speech habits to build vocal technic. Includes vowel and consonant pedagogy. Sing as you speak.

"placement": Figure of speech describing the illusion that tones of differing timbre are in different parts of the body.

practice: Exercise for the purpose of attaining proficiency.

progressive education: Philosophy of John Dewey that true learning only takes place when there is a goal that inspires the entire personality. Learning through singing.

simile: Figure of speech in which a comparison is expressed.

skill: Practical efficiency acquired by exercise.

staccato: Each note separate, detached by a brief silence.

sympathetic hearing: Creative hearing.

technic: Practical details of artistic expression.

vocalization: Exercise of the voice.

"yawn-sigh": Vocalise for relaxation, consisting of a portamento from quasi-falsetto tone to a lower tone in full voice.

RESEARCH

artifact: Effect produced by the nature of the scientific instrument which could be mistaken as something produced by the subject under study.

cineradiography: Taking motion pictures from a fluoroscopic screen.

Delta-F Generator: Refinement of the stroboscope invented by Jw. van den Berg, which receives impulses from a microphone and either flashes a light at the same frequency or creates a controllable difference between the frequency of the light and that of the sound. As the pitch changes the difference remains the same, giving the illusion that the vibration remains in the same very slow motion. A hand control makes it possible to stop the motion, move it forward, or move it backward, at will.

electrode, myographic: One of two contacts made with the muscles studied in electromyography. Such electrodes work best when they are needles, but if the muscle is near the skin, a flat plate held by adhesive tape is satisfactory and for obvious reasons, often preferable.

electromyograph: Device which amplifies the electrical energy generated by a muscle and registers it either on a sensitized strip of paper, or over a microphone as a sound resembling static. It is necessary to place two electrodes, one for the muscle studied and another on a neutral part of the body to complete the circuit.

excised larynx: Larynx removed from the body. It can be made to phonate artificially and much has been learned about voice in this way (van den Berg).

Fastax camera: Movie camera developed by Bell Telephone. It has a revolving prism assembly instead of a shutter, so that the images are focussed on the film without stopping it for each frame, thus making it possible to take up to 8000 frames per second. Ultra slow motion studies are thus possible.

fluoroscope: Glass screen which is coated with a substance that shines when struck by x-ray. Subject stands between an x-ray tube and the screen, and the denser structures of his anatomy (as well as metal he may have in his teeth!) cast shadows on the otherwise illuminated screen.

guttural mirror: Essential part of the laryngoscope.

harmonic analyzer: Machine designed to compute the number of partials in a given tone, with their relative intensities.

intensity display, sonagraphic: Graph which can be produced at the top of a sonagram in which the height of the line registers the total intensity of the sound at each moment in the 2.4 seconds.

laminography: Tomography.

laryngo-periskop: Device combining a guttural mirror with others in such a way that the observer can see his own glottis. Invented by Russell.

laryngoscope: Device invented by Garcia for looking into the larynx, consisting of a mirror on a slender handle and a means of reflecting light into the throat.

melody writer: Electronic device that receives the voice and transcribes its fundamental frequency on a moving strip of paper. Invented by R. Timcke. Difficult to use with singing voice because a strong overtone will cause the line to jump from the fundamental.

microphone: Instrument that transforms sound into electrical impulses.

oscilloscope: Electronic device the main element of which is a cathode ray tube like a TV screen, upon which any vibration fed into the machine appears as a curve, its components corresponding to those of the vibration.

palatogram: Drawing indicating the area of the palate contacted by the tongue in the production of a given sound.

palatography: Making and study of palotograms.

pattern playback: Device invented by Franklin S. Cooper reversing the principle of spectrography. Spectrograms with the formants in arbitrary locations are made by hand and light reflected from them is transformed into sound, producing synthetic vowels.

planography: Tomography.

pneumograph: Device for recording respiratory movements.

pneumotackograph: Device for measuring breath flow. The subject phonates into a mask so that all his breath passes through a fine screen. The imperceptible resistence of the screen can nevertheless be measured by sensitive strain gauges and registered on a moving strip of paper in a manner which indicates both rate and volume of breath expenditure.

radiography: Photographs taken by means of x-rays. These are essentially shadow patterns, and more dense structures obscure the less dense.

rhinoscopy: Examination of the nasal cavities.

section, sonagraphic: Graph produced by a special process of the Sonagraph, in which the relative intensities of all the components of the tone at a given moment shows more accurately than they can be estimated in the normal sonagraph.

Sonagraph: A particular type of spectrograph. A sheet of sensitized paper revolving on a drum is marked by an electric stylus in accordance with live or taped sound fed into the sonagraph. Distance from left to right represents time, usually 2.4 sec., and vertical distance represents frequency, usually from 0 to 8000 kilocycles. Blackness of the marks indicate intensity. See intensity display, section.

954	Miscellaneous Terms

alto: Contralto.

baritone: Average male voice, higher than bass and lower than tenor.

bass, *basso*: Lowest of the male voices.

bass-baritone: *Basso-cantante*.

basse-contre: *Contra-basso*.

basse taille: Baritone with bass quality.

basso-cantante: Lit.: singing bass. A bass that is not as heavy as a *basso profundo* but more flexible, and can sing as high as F_4 above middle C.

basso guisto: *Basso cantante*.

basso profundo: Lit.: deep bass. Lowest and heaviest of the bass voices. Can sing at least as low as D_2 below bass staff, with full tone.

Continuation of 953

spectrograph: Electronic device to produce spectrograms, graphic records of the harmonic components of a sound. Examples: sonagrams, voiceprints.

spirometer: Device which measures vital capacity.

stethoscope: Instrument for listening to bodily sounds.

Strobocon: Stroboscope developed by Conn laboratories, for measuring small pitch differences and for tuning musical instruments.

stroboscope: Optical instrument for "stopping the motion" of rapidly moving objects. See Delta-F Generator.

synthesizer, electronic: Device for combining vibrations to produce new sounds and to simulate the sounds of existing instruments and even voices. RCA Victor has an elaborate one.

tomogram: Special x-ray in which both the plate and the x-ray tube rotate during the exposure, so that nothing appears in the finished picture except that part which is at the axis of rotation. Even this part is not in perfect focus, but it has the advantage that denser objects which might obscure it have dropped out.

visible speech: Sonagram. Also the title of a manual on the use of the Sonagraph (Potter, Kopp, and Green).

voiceprint: New development in spectography which is claimed to be more accurately readable in detail than a sonagram. Its developer, Lawrence G. Kersta, believes that voiceprints are as accurate as fingerprints in legal identification.

x-ray: Means of photographing through bodies that are opaque to ordinary light.

x-ray image intensifier: Refinement of the fluoroscope whereby a very weak x-ray image, otherwise invisible, is amplified electronically and appears on the equivalent of a TV screen. This eliminates the danger of x-ray burns and makes possible long enough exposure for more extended cineradiography.

castrato: Male singer emasculated in boyhood so as to retain his contralto or soprano voice (18th century or earlier).

changing voice: Voice at puberty.

coloratura soprano: Highest of the female voices, with considerable range above high C_6. Uses more falsetto than the other female voices.

contra-basso: *Basso profundo*.

contraltino: Contra-tenor.

contralto: Lowest of the female voices. Can sing F_3 below middle C with full tone. Range includes all of the treble staff.

contra-tenor: Male voice that is largely falsetto, singing in the same frequency range as a contralto.

dramatic soprano: Soprano whose voice is powerful enough for dramatic roles. Sings up to high C_6 with full voice.

dramatic tenor: Tenor whose voice is powerful enough for dramatic roles. *Tenore robusto; heldentenor.*

haute-contre: Contra-tenor.

heldentenor: Lit.: heroic tenor. Tenor suitable for Wagnerian roles. *Tenore robusto;* dramatic tenor.

heroic tenor: Dramatic tenor, *Heldentenor.*

high baritone: Operatic baritone.

lyric soprano: Soprano with a light, flexible voice, but not as high as coloratura soprano.

lyric tenor: Tenor whose voice is lighter and more flexible than *tenore robusto.*

lyrico-spinto: Lit.: singing-thrust. A lighter voice that is capable of rising to moments of dramatic intensity. (Usually applied to soprano or tenor voices.)

male alto: Contra-tenor.

mezzo: Mezzo-soprano.

mezzo-contralto: Lit.: half-contralto. Mezzo-soprano, with the implication that it is slightly lower and heavier, but not actually contralto.

mezzo-soprano: Lit.: half-soprano. Average female voice, higher than contralto and lower than soprano.

mutation: Change of voice at puberty.

operatic baritone: High baritone voice, of sufficient power for opera. Can sing at least as high as G_4 above middle C.

soprano: Highest of the female voices.

soprano acuto: Lit.: high soprano.

soprano assoluto: A soprano who can meet the requirements of all the soprano classifications.

soprano drammatico: Dramatic soprano.

soprano guisto: Dramatic soprano.

soprano sopracuto: Highest possible soprano.

spinto: Lit.: thrust or pushed. See lyrico-spinto.

tenor: Highest of the male voices, except the contra-tenor.

tenore-contraltino: Contra-tenor.

tenore robusto: Lit.: strong tenor. A tenor with a big voice. *Heldentenor;* dramatic tenor.

tenore serio: Dramatic tenor.

INDEX

Numbers following words refer to paragraphs in the text. Where the subject is discussed for more than one paragraph, only the first number appears. Numbers higher than 900 locate the word in the thesaurus. Numbers following the abbreviation "Fig." refer to illustrations.

265

INDEX

oxygen, 111, 146, 157, 901